The Writer's Way

The Writer's Way

NINTH EDITION

JACK RAWLINS
California State University Chico

STEPHEN METZGER
California State University Chico

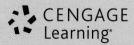

CENGAGE
Learning·

Australia · Brazil · Mexico · Singapore · United Kingdom · United States

CENGAGE
Learning®

The Writer's Way,
Ninth Edition
Jack Rawlins and Stephen Metzger

Product Director: Monica Eckman

Product Manager: Margaret Leslie

Content Developers: Megan Garvey and Sarah Turner

Product Assistant: Cailin Barrett-Bressack

Media Developer: Janine Tangney

Senior Marketing Manager: Lydia LeStar

Art and Cover Direction, Production Management, and Composition: PreMediaGlobal

Manufacturing Planner: Betsy Donaghey

Rights Acquisitions Specialist: Ann Hoffman

Cover Image: © Katie Edwards/Getty Images

For product information and technology assistance, contact us at **Cengage Learning Customer & Sales Support, 1-800-354-9706.**

For permission to use material from this text or product, submit all requests online at **www.cengage.com/permissions.** Further permissions questions can be e-mailed to **permissionrequest@cengage.com.**

Library of Congress Control Number: 2013946113

ISBN-13: 978-1-285-43854-2

ISBN-10: 1-285-43854-X

Cengage Learning
200 First Stamford Place, 4th Floor
Stamford, CT 06902
USA

Cengage Learning is a leading provider of customized learning solutions with office locations around the globe, including Singapore, the United Kingdom, Australia, Mexico, Brazil, and Japan. Locate your local office at **www.cengage.com/global.**

Cengage Learning products are represented in Canada by Nelson Education, Ltd.

To learn more about Cengage Learning Solutions, visit **www.cengage.com**.

Purchase any of our products at your local college store or at our preferred online store **www.cengagebrain.com.**

Printed in the United States of America
2 3 4 5 6 7 17 16 15 14

Brief Contents

Contents

Preface

One of the key principles of *The Writer's Way* when it was first published in the early 1990s was that effective writing rarely results without lots of revision. Practicing what it preaches, the book has now been revised eight times, five times by Professor Jack Rawlins and three times by me. And like an essay, it just keeps getting better, not only as we've learned more about how students learn but also as we've responded to dozens of professional reviewers and scores of students who've provided observations and suggestions for improvement. Additionally, we've responded to changing classroom environments and technologies—early editions noted that some students would actually compose their essays on computers, and the last edition suggested the possibilities of online research! Naturally, the current edition assumes that students will be doing most of their research online, although I still discuss how to access materials from a real "brick-and-mortar" library, hoping that some of you might still appreciate their many, often unexpected, rewards.

This revision reflects current composition pedagogy that emphasizes "inquiry" and focuses more on research and academic writing than did previous editions. That's not to say it downplays narrative—far from it. In fact, the part of the book about personal writing is still key, although the ninth edition points out the often blurry lines between genres of writing, suggesting that an effective piece of writing often incorporates several different forms.

I've also added new essays—both by students and by professionals—and deleted others, some of which were dated, some of which, reviewers and students had told me, weren't very useful. I'm excited to be including a hilarious essay by Dave Barry as well as very moving essays about writing by three of my favorite writers: Annie Dillard, Anne Lamott, and Dave Eggers. The book concludes with one of the best essays ever written about writing, a classic by a master: "Politics and the English Language," by George Orwell.

Another significant structural change: previous editions included discussions of audience, thesis, purpose, style, tone, and organization in Part 3: "Revising and Editing." But good writers—and the book— argue that writers need to think about those things very early, that you set out to write with your audience and purpose in mind. To that end, I've moved audience, thesis, purpose, tone, style, and organization to Part 2: "Planning and Drafting," while at the same acknowledging that writers should continue to consider— and feel free to adjust—those things in the revising stage.

Finally, previous editions indicated that there are many different types of informative writing, and many different places where it appears ("in service manuals, cookbooks, technical and scientific reports, encyclopedias, textbooks, travel guides, and 90 percent of every newspaper or magazine"). But the chapter really discussed in depth only "how-to" essays. In the ninth edition, along with the corresponding section in "A Collection of Good Writing," I've added other examples of informative writing, including profiles, along with a discussion of how to write effective ones yourself.

TEACHING YOURSELF

That said, the spirit of *The Writer's Way* remains, as do its two core principles: (1) good writing begins when you know your audience and write for the right reasons and (2) knowing your audience and having good reasons to write will teach you everything you need to know about technique. A writer constantly makes choices: Should I do *this*, or *that*? Should I do it *this* way, or *that* way? Real writers don't answer such questions by asking themselves, "What's the rule?" or "What do good essays do?" Instead, they ask, "Who's my reader?"; "What am I trying to accomplish here?"; "Will this help me accomplish that?"; and, "Is there another way of doing it that will accomplish it better?" In short, the real writer asks, "What *works*?" not "What's the rule?" The goal of *The Writer's Way* is to train you in this new way of thinking.

And while the book makes every attempt to "teach" you how to write better, it does so mostly by providing models and encouraging lots of practice (and revision), grounded in the philosophy that really we teach ourselves. As Timothy Gallwey writes in *The Inner Game of Tennis:* "Fortunately, most children learn how to walk before they can be told how to by their parents."

HOW THE BOOK IS LAID OUT

This book is divided into seven parts. The Prologue is a two-part introduction to the art of going to college. The first part is a list of things good students do in order to get good grades. The second part is an instruction manual on how to study. You'll want to have the Prologue down cold before you walk through the classroom door, or as soon thereafter as possible.

Part 1 is an introduction to the attitude toward learning to write that lies behind the rest of the book. This part of the book also offers an overview of writing in school, including responding to different kinds of assignments—even in-class, timed-writing prompts. I encourage you to read it before doing anything else.

Parts 2 and 3 are a step-by-step walk-through of the writing process: from first thoughts through brainstorming, drafting, rethinking, organizing, peer editing, stylistic polishing, and cosmetic editing. Part 2 covers all the messy, creative steps from first thoughts through the first draft. Part 3 is about ways to take that draft and revise it into something better. It would be lovely if you could know everything in Parts 2 and 3 before you wrote an essay, but you won't be able to wait, so you will probably find yourself writing essays while reading one chapter after another, and in fact you can read them in almost any order.

Part 4 introduces you to three main essay genres: personal writing, writing to inform, and argument. For each genre, there is a corresponding collection of sample essays in Part 6, "A Collection of Good Writing." You'll want to read those samples along with the chapter.

Part 5 further explores writing for college courses, with an emphasis on research. Here you'll learn how to approach traditional academic writing assignments and how to perform basic scholastic writing skills: documentation, paraphrasing, and quotation, as well as drawing conclusions and presenting findings. Part 5 also provides guidelines for determining the credibility of your sources, as well as exercises on effective paraphrasing. If your writing course gives assignments that use these forms and techniques, you'll want to read these chapters, but even if it doesn't, these chapters will help you with other college courses that involve writing. There are sample academic essays in "A Collection of Good Writing," and two complete research papers appear at the end of Chapter 18.

Part 6 is the fun part. It's a collection of essays written by students in both Professor Rawlins's and my classes, as well several essays by professionals and four published essays about writing. You'll want to read them, because they're wonderful, and because the easiest way to learn to write better is to read some great writing and fall in love with it. Then the most natural thing in the world is to go out and try to do something like the writing you love.

KEEP ON WRITING IN THE REAL WORLD

While *The Writer's Way* is in fact a textbook, intended to be used in the classroom, it's very much based on the concept that there is actually very little difference between writing in school and writing in the "real world." Again, it's all about audience and purpose. Once you're clear on what you want to say and to whom you want to say it, everything else (length, level of formality, use of sources) falls into place.

In fact, although I have been teaching writing for over twenty-five years, at the same time I have been working as a freelance writer—I've written hundreds of articles for skiing, travel, health-and-fitness magazines, newspapers, and other publications, as well as travel books—and I have made every attempt to bring what I've learned about "real" writing not only to my classes but to *The Writer's Way* as well. Peer review, for example, is not just an academic exercise, students passing papers around and writing "I liked it" on them. Rather, peer review is about caring enough about what you're trying to say to show a reader a draft and ask specific questions about what's working and what isn't. So the chapter on peer review in *The Writer's Way* tries to duplicate the process I go through when I ask a friend to give me feedback (which I rarely do before about the fourth or fifth draft), and I always acknowledge my gratitude for the feedback. And while that might take the form of a beer at a local pub if it's a friend, or dinner out if it's my wife, I suggest that in students' cases that might involve offering to reciprocate or to take your reader out for pizza to thank her.

In the end, the emphasis on writing for real reasons in the real world will help prepare you for writing you'll be doing once you graduate, with everything from resumes and letters of application to interoffice memos, internal reports, and employee evaluations.

OTHER UNIQUE FEATURES

The Writer's Way has several other features that set it apart from traditional composition textbooks.

The Prologue addresses questions you need answers to before you can begin any school work: What do good students do that poor students don't do? What does it mean to "study" a chapter in a book? How can I tell if I'm "learning" anything? What do good readers do beyond looking at the words and trying to remember them?

The Writer's Way contains more than *fifty complete essays*—about half sprinkled throughout the chapters to illustrate principles, and half collected at the end of the book in "A Collection of Good Writing" (Part 6). More than forty of these essays are written by students, so you can see that your peers can and do write wonderful essays, and you can as well.

Most of the chapters end with *Writer's Workshop* sections. These workshops are similar to the lab sections of a science course: first you watch a hands-on demonstration of one of the concepts presented in the chapter; then you dig in and get your own hands dirty.

Almost all the chapters end with *exercises*. These obey the spirit of the book and the Writer's Workshop sections by avoiding drills and mechanical activities whenever possible and focusing on whole-language activities, in which you are asked to work with entire blocks of text. As often as possible, the text being worked with is your own, since anything you learn about someone else's writing is far less powerful than what you learn about your own.

Several additional topics that often are not found in composition textbooks are covered in this book. There are chapters on critical thinking, peer editing (including explicit instruction on how to do it well), titling, and how to make a too-short essay longer. The chapter on first-drafting examines writer's block, explores where it comes from, and offers a list of strategies for overcoming it.

ACKNOWLEDGMENTS

First of all, of course, I'd like to thank Professor Jack Rawlins, whose original vision (and language) still informs and defines *The Writer's Way* and who trusted me to carry on the book's legacy. I hope that you continue to approve of the work I've done on it, Sir. I'm also grateful to the reviewers who provided keen observations about the book as well as concrete suggestions for revision: Peter Donahue, Wenatchee Valley College at Omak; Michael McClelland, Wittenberg University; Jim McKeown, McLennan Community College; Deborah Montuori, Shippensburg University; and David Roloff, the University of Wisconsin–Stevens Point. I'd especially like to thank Professor Roloff, for sending along essays by two of his students (both of which are included). And: Thanks to Assistant/Development editor Sarah Turner at Cengage Learning for her suggestions and insights, and also for the freedom she allowed me to pursue my own instincts and ideas, some admittedly unconventional for a college writing textbook.

Also, special thanks to all the students in my writing classes at California State University Chico and Butte College who have used the book in class over the last eight years and provided invaluable feedback, especially those who submitted essays to be included, whether or not they found their way to publication.

And, once again, love and thanks to three of the best and most beautiful writers I know: Liz, Hannah, and Gina. You're awesome!

The Writer's Way

Prologue

How to Succeed in School

HOW TO GET A GOOD GRADE

Here are three lists of suggestions to help you succeed in your classes. The items on the first list are time tested, though a surprising percentage of students still resist them. The second list is less obvious, although familiar to the best students. The third is in response to the prevalence of cell phones and other technology on campus and in the classroom.

"We hold these truths to be self-evident":

1. Go to class every day.
2. Be on time for class—even better, get there five minutes early.
3. Study the course syllabus.
4. Do all the assigned reading, by the time it's due—even better, do each reading assignment twice.
5. Hand in all assignments on time.
6. Take part in class discussion.
7. Take notes during class.
8. Write at least two drafts of every paper.
9. Print your drafts and proofread from hard copy.
10. Follow directions carefully and precisely.
11. Stay awake—no snoozing!

Less self-evident truths:

12. Sit near the front of the classroom, or where the instructor can see you clearly.
13. Become an expert on the course grading system.
14. Come to each class session with a question about the material.
15. Visit the instructor during office hours.
16. Study for tests over as long a period as possible.
17. Take notes, recording your thoughts and reactions as you're doing the course reading—not after.
18. Write in your textbooks—highlight, underline, jot marginal notes.
19. After all assigned readings and all class sessions, write answers to these questions:
    What was the point? What am I supposed to learn from it?
    Why does it matter?
20. Before each class session, remind yourself where the class left off last time.

21. Reflect on assignments on and off, all the time, from the moment they're assigned until they're due.
22. Study by *talking* with classmates, in addition to reading or note taking.
23. Be respectful to your instructor and classmates.
24. Address your instructor appropriately, always erring on the side of being too formal: "Professor Brown" or "Dr. Brown," even if you're not sure he has completed his doctorate. It's far better to have him say, "Please, you can call me Matt" than for him to think you don't respect his PhD or know that he has one.
25. Do not begin closing notebooks and stashing your books away in your backpack before class is over. I guarantee there is little that is more annoying to your instructor.

Smart phones, laptops, tablets, and iPods:

26. If you must bring your phone to class, turn it off, or at least set it on the vibrate mode. Do the same when you visit your instructor's office.
27. Don't check your phone for messages in class, even sneakily. The instructor can see you. Do the same when you visit your instructor's office.
28. If you bring a laptop or a tablet to class, use it for taking notes on course material or for researching topics of discussion—no emailing, no games, no Facebooking.
29. If you do use your laptop in class for taking notes and doing research, do not ignore your instructor. She should still be the primary focus of your attention.
30. Do not sit in class listening to your iPod when your instructor is talking. Do you realize how offensive that is and what the message is that you're sending?
31. If your cell phone does happen to go off in class, shut it off immediately, without checking to see who's called. Apologize profusely, to your instructor and classmates, then again to your instructor after class, and, ideally, in a separate email later. And then never, ever let it happen again.
32. If your cell phone does happen to go off in class, and it's not obvious that it's yours, look around, as though attempting to discern the identity of its owner, and scowl, making sure your instructor sees that you are as appalled and disgusted by this shameless display of disrespect as he is. And then never, ever let it happen again.

A final note: Look, your instructors are human, too. We know that you've got a life—that you've got kids (or parents) to take care of, employers demanding your attention, obligations other than our courses. We get that emergencies come up. The bottom line is, Be respectful. If your son is sick at home and you absolutely have to be on alert for a text message from his babysitter or the doctor, just let your instructor know ahead of time what's going on ("I'm sorry, but my son's sick at home and I really have to keep my phone on during class today …"). Most reasonable instructors will find a way to make that work for you.

HOW TO (RE)LEARN IN SCHOOL: A GUIDE TO STUDYING

The basic school experience is this: you hear a lecture, read a chapter of a book, or do an exercise in class, and the instructor says, "Go learn that." If you're like most students, despite having been in school for umpteen thousand years, you don't have a very clear notion of how to go about it. To help, here's an introduction to the art of studying. The first ten principles are about the attitude you bring to the task, and the next six are about what you actually do.

1. You Learn by Reflecting

You begin by having an experience—you read, see, hear, or do something—and then you think about it. No reflecting means no learning. No one can reflect for you, which means no instructor can hand you the understanding or the insight or force you to have it. Learning goes on inside you, and it takes place in the quiet moment after the activity (or, less often, during the activity). You ride your mountain bike over a rocky spot; you fall; you stop and ask, "What went wrong?" You read a book; you stop and ask, "What did that mean? What are the consequences of accepting it as true?"

School rarely gives us time to reflect. It's always rushing on to the next activity. So the most difficult and most necessary part of learning is to *make time for reflection.*

Don't fall for the trap of performing actions that substitute for reflecting and calling them learning. For instance, taking notes in class, making up flash cards, or outlining assigned readings all *look* like learning, but if you aren't reflecting while you do those things, they're just more pointless motion.

2. Learning Equals Changing

Experiencing and reflecting are merely the first two in a series of five steps to learning: (1) you experience something; (2) you reflect on the experience; (3) you arrive at an insight ("Now I see what I did wrong!"); (4) you resolve to be different ("Next time I'll take water before I go into the desert"); and (5) you implement the change—you do it differently next time. Going through just some of the steps and stopping short of number 5 equals learning nothing. If you want to assess how much you've learned at the end of a lecture, book, or class, ask yourself, "How different am I from when I started?"

3. All Learning Is Self-Teaching

The five-step program goes on in your head, where no one but you can get at it. An instructor or textbook can encourage, guide, inspire, or bribe, but that's all in **support** of the teaching; it isn't the teaching itself. And self-teaching can't fail, if you stick with it. Let's assume you act, reflect, and come to an erroneous conclusion. You act on that conclusion and reflect on the outcome. You conclude that your first resolution was misguided. So you conclude that you should try something else. Then all you have to do is continue running the five-step program until by trial and error you've figured things out.

4. Learning in School Is Relearning

Learning when you're eight or ten years old is easy because you're writing on a blank slate. But by the time a person gets to age sixteen or so, her worldview is complete and any teaching is reprogramming. You "know" what writing an essay is like, and you have to unlearn what you know and replace it with a new model.

Relearning is harder than learning. Breaking an entrenched habit is much harder than picking up a new one. I started taking piano lessons in my early forties, after "teaching" myself and playing for about ten years. At my first lesson, I sat down at my instructor's gorgeous Steinway grand and played what I thought was a pretty decent rendition of the Beatles' "Let It Be." My teacher shook her head. "You're not paying attention to your fingering, are you?" she asked. I wasn't. "I think the best thing for you to do," she continued, "is to start over." She went to a cabinet and pulled out a first-time beginner's book. "I want you to take this home and do the exercises on pages one to five." I was heartbroken, but I also figured it would be easy to relearn, since I thought I could already play pretty well.

Well, it might have been if I hadn't already learned the "wrong" way. But you know what? I stuck with it, and with time it did get easier, and now not only does she compliment me on my fingering, but the songs sound *much* better as well.

5. Relearning Is Uncomfortable

Change is momentarily destabilizing. You feel like your feet aren't firmly on the ground. And they aren't: change is like stepping off a ledge into the dark. You can't be sure where the new path will take you, and it only makes sense to feel uneasy. Instructors or classrooms or textbooks lessen the discomfort but can't make it disappear. When I was first trying to learn correct piano fingering, I got extremely frustrated. I was afraid that I wouldn't be able to "relearn" and that I'd fail. I even got angry. "Why do I have to do it like this?" I thought. "I already play pretty well." But once I got past the discomfort—and the anger—everything started to fall into place, and the change was remarkable. That's because the discomfort is in proportion to the potential for change. There needs to be some risk, at least some potential for failure. Remember that the more comfortable you are, the less likely you are to learn anything that matters.

You must learn this lesson well, because if you don't, every time you get close to important learning, you'll feel discomfort, assume something is wrong, and run away.

6. Relearning Feels Wrong

The old way feels "right" because it's familiar. We are so committed to the familiar that people will let their lives be ruined by alcohol or spousal abuse simply because that's what they're used to. You have to accept that period when the new way feels wrong, wait out the discomfort and uncertainty, and allow yourself time to become familiar with the new way.

7. You Have to Want to Be Different

Relearning means becoming a different person, and you have to be willing to let the old person die so the new can be born.

The ego defines change in one of two ways. In the first, change is defined as a condemnation of the self: "I need to change because there's something wrong with the old me." The ego's only healthy response to that is to fight off the learning to avoid adopting the toxic message that comes with it. That's why dieting because you're fat and feel disgusting doesn't work. In the second way, change is defined as growth: "I want to change because I see a way to become a more enriched, more complete person." Now the ego can embrace the learning.

8. Learning Can't Be Scheduled

You can't know when insight will come or how to make it come. So don't schedule a time to study—"I'm going to have insights about my composition assignment between 6:00 p.m. and 7:00 p.m. tonight." Instead, *reflect all the time*—muse on the assignment or the course material constantly, with a part of your brain, while you go through your day. But no reflective day dreaming in class.

Reflecting all the time sounds like work, but it isn't. Your mind works all the time whether you want it to or not, as we discover when something is worrying us. Any yogi will tell you that it takes years of practice to learn to turn the mind *off*, even for a minute or two. And it's physiologically impossible for your brain to get tired, which is why you can study or write all day, go to bed, and find your mind still racing while your body cries out for rest. With practice, keeping a part of your mind on a task becomes effortless—you just tell your brain to call you when something pops into it (like the chime that says, "You've got mail"), and it does.

9. Learn by Joining the Club

For every skill or body of knowledge, there is a club of people who practice or study it. Sometimes the club is a physical group of people with a clubhouse and dues—the Garden Club, the Chess Club, the Amnesty International Club, the Gay-Straight Alliance. Just as often, the club is virtual—the club of writers or the club of fans of Stephen Colbert. In either case, you must join up. You can join literally, by paying dues and attending meetings, or you can sign up mentally, by calling yourself a writer and acting like one.

This act of joining is very powerful. Notice the difference between "I'm taking piano lessons" and "I'm a pianist"—wow! Joining means you stop defining yourself as a "student" and start defining yourself as a doer. All doers are learners—Martin Scorsese is still learning about movies.

A member of a club flaunts membership—by wearing the uniform, talking the talk, reading the magazines devoted to the discipline, hanging with other members, talking shop, sharing work with colleagues, going to meetings. Writers' "clubs" tend to be more private and personal, but they still exist. Members pass around favorite essays they've come across and discuss new authors they've discovered. They also share drafts of their own work.

10. Learn by Imitating

Learning is done by imitating the mentors, the older and wiser members of the club, and mentors are all around you. Every time you read a CD review in *Rolling Stone,* the op-ed page of the newspaper, or good writing on a Web site, there's a potential mentor at work—and lots for you to learn.

So much for the learning attitude. Now let's talk nuts and bolts. Let's say you just read a chapter or heard a lecture and are setting out to "learn it." What does that actually mean?

11. Learning Means Understanding

If I know that $E = mc^2$, I know nothing unless I understand what that means. Let's divide understanding into three rounds. Round 1 consists of five basic questions about the experience you just had:

a. *What just happened?* (What did I/we do?) Answers sound like "We practiced outlining essays." Don't think this question is somehow beneath you or irrelevant. Frequently, when students are asked what happened in their last class meetings, they can't say. It's important to know—and remember—what your instructor decided to spend class time doing.

b. *What was the purpose?* (Why did I/we do it?) Answers sound like "We did it to understand how essay titles work." In school, "Why?" can be a threatening question because it's so powerful, which is why you need to ask it.

c. *What did it say?* (What was the content?) This question works only with texts (books, lectures, movies). What you're seeking is a *paraphrase,* a brief rewording of the content in your own words. *Don't react yet.* Reacting is a way of skipping over this step.

d. *What was the point?* What did it mean? What was the message? What lesson was I supposed to learn from it? Never do anything that's pointless, and never do anything until you're clear on what the point is. In school, the instructor typically has a point in mind. Know what his intended lesson is, but feel free to draw as many lessons of your own as possible.

Because "point" is scary, people often want to substitute purpose. When I ask my students to explain the point of a previous exercise to me, they typically give me verbs: "The point was *to learn* how to outline." A verb is a purpose; a point must be *a sentence:* "The *point* was, you should outline your essays."

e. *How can I use this?* Learning something is meaningless unless you can do something with it. How can you use the things you learn in school? However tricky a question that may be, you must answer it.

Round 1 is the groundwork for understanding. Round 2 is about bringing order to the material. If you're learning material that has no structural logic, such as the alphabet, you have to pound it into your brain via jingles, mnemonic gimmicks, or massive repetition. But that won't work with college lessons (chapters in a book or class lectures) because just one of them consists of literally thousands of parts: sentences, points, examples, explanations, statistics, formulas. No one is smart enough to make up a jingle for all that. But there are tricks you can learn to make it easier to understand and retain that material. Read on.

12. Reduce the Material to Something You Can See at a Glance

In other words, make a *summary*. If you wrote a paraphrase for a basic question, you may already have done this. *The Writer's Way* offers you two concrete ways to write a summary on paper, the outline and the abstract (Chapter 7).

How small is small enough? Psychologists have an answer: seven items. Seven is the number of items a typical human mind can hold at one time (a phone number, for example—without the area code). So shoot for a summary that's seven average-length sentences or fewer. The magic number seven never changes, so don't make the summary longer—regardless of the length of the essay. A summary of an essay is as long as the summary of a book.

13. See the Pattern

The pattern, also known as the design, structure, organization, governing principle, logic, paradigm, system, map, model, template, outline, or algorithm, is the idea that arranges the pieces, explains why they're all there and arranged just so, and lets us see the whole pattern at a glance.

Since most of us can hold only seven things in our brains at once, the only way we can master material larger than seven sentences is to see the structure—the organizing principle that makes a book, for instance, be *one* thing, consisting of a certain number of chapters, thousands of paragraphs, and tens of thousands of sentences.

Everything that makes sense has a pattern. If I ask you to remember the following:

123456789

it's easy, because you see the pattern and therefore have to remember only one thing. If I ask you to remember this sequence of numbers:

112358132134

it's brutal slogging beyond seven numbers or so, until you see the pattern: each number is the sum of the previous two numbers (what mathematicians call a Fibonacci series). Now there's only one thing to remember, and it's easy. And notice how size doesn't affect learning difficulty—if I add numbers to either series, the series doesn't get harder to learn as long as its generating principle remains the same.

Often the pattern is spelled out for you. Books have tables of contents; meetings have agendas; theme parks have maps; car manuals have wiring diagrams; houses have blueprints. When the pattern isn't handed to you, you have to figure it out.

14. Connect the New to the Old

When you learn something new, it needs a place to attach itself on the network of knowledge in your head, like a mollusk that settles on the hull of an ocean liner. The more links you can find between new knowledge and old, the more you'll understand and the better you'll remember. If I ask you to remember a random number, that would take some mental work; but if I ask you to remember your age, which is also a number, you can remember it effortlessly.

The links are for you to invent, and you can construct a personal connection to anything. When I talk about learning by imitating your instructor, connect it to your mental map by imagining yourself imitating horrid Mr. Roarer in fifth grade.

15. Consider the Implications

To understand something is to be aware of its logical consequences: "If X is true, then Y must be true." All ideas have implications. A lesson will lay down a principle, such as "Read for the bigger issues first"; you make it real by deducing the logical consequences: "If you're having trouble reading a text, read faster, not slower." Understanding isn't about whether you like an idea or think it's true; it's about whether you can live with its consequences. In the 1950s, America committed itself to the idea that African Americans should have social and legal rights equal to those of whites. We've spent the last fifty-plus years working out the implications of that decision, and we haven't finished yet. Einstein said "$E = mc^2$," and most of the scientific and technological advances of the last century have resulted from exploring the practical applications of that simple equation. We'll talk about ideas and their consequences in detail in Chapter 14.

16. Test Your Learning by Talking

When the learning process is over, how do you know it worked? That's easy: *say* what you've learned to someone. Tell the material to a classmate, partner, or friend. With knowledge, the proof of ownership isn't being able to write it or think it. Writing is too passive—it's too easy to transcribe without comprehension. And thinking is so insubstantial that we can always tell ourselves we think well. The proof of learning is being able to teach it. This is why generations of instructors have said, "The person who's really learning a lot in the classroom is the instructor."

Part One

Introduction to Writing

Chapter 1

Learning to Write

WE ALL WRITE, ALL THE TIME

One day when my younger daughter was sixteen, I walked by her bathroom door, and she was brushing her teeth and texting at the same time. Honestly. Apparently, she had something important to say and someone she felt needed to hear it (right then?). And while I harbor no fantasies that the language she was using was "correct," I can guarantee that it was perfectly suited to her reader and purpose. And that's all good writing is.

Every time you email someone, write a note in a birthday card, jot down a recipe or directions to your house, every time you text or tweet, or leave a note on the refrigerator reminding your roommate that you're out of half-and-half, you're writing. In this book, I hope to convince you that what you've come to think of as "real" writing—writing for classes and writing that you read in journals, magazines, and newspapers—is really not that different. If it has a purpose and knows and addresses its audience, even if it does its work fairly matter-of-factly and without flair and flourish, chances are it's good writing. Naturally, some writers are more "creative" than others—some writers bring more flair and flourish to their work—and some writers can work with less effort and more quickly than others. Truth be told, some writers are naturally "better" than others. Just like some people take to music or sports more naturally than others. But I'm convinced that everyone can learn to write: (1) well enough to be effective, convincing, and compelling; and (2) well enough to enjoy it.

WHAT IS AN "ESSAY"?

When a mid-nineteenth-century California gold miner had a nugget or some dust whose value he wanted to determine, he went to the assayer's office. The assayer would examine, analyze, and test it to identify its metallurgical content. "Assay" and "essay" have the same root, and in fact have been used nearly synonymously in the past: "He essayed to cross the river by canoe" only means "He tried to cross the river by canoe." The sixteenth-century French writer Michel de Montaigne, generally considered the founding father of the modern essay, defined "essay" as an *attempt* at self-analysis.

So don't think of an essay as an answer. Think of it as an examination, an analysis, a test, an attempt. You've got an idea; you put it out there to see what others think of its value. I'll talk a lot more about this later, but a good way to get in trouble writing an essay is to think you have to have the last word. Far better to use your essay to invite conversation and dialogue, even disagreement.

More practically, essays take many forms, but are most commonly seen as opinion pieces, features, and columns in newspapers and magazines, from an endorsement of a proposition or candidate to a rant about how a particular third baseman is overpaid. I have many favorite essayists, but among them are Chuck Klosterman and Charles P. Pierce who write for *Esquire* magazine, Rick Reilly for *Sports Illustrated,* Dave Barry for the *Miami Herald*, and Cynthia Tucker, a Pulitzer Prize–winning, widely syndicated journalist. I've included pieces by Barry and Tucker in *The Writer's Way* (Barry on p. 282 and Tucker on p. 274). I also love Annie Dillard and Anne Lamott—examples of their work are in "A Collection of Good Writing" in Part 6.

In school, essays, as opposed to academic papers (see below), tend to be more observation based than source based, although citations and references almost always enrich any writing. School essays range from first-person narratives ("Write about something significant that happened to you"—more on that later) to end-of-semester "essay tests," in which students are asked to advance a thesis or a claim about something that was covered in the course; sometimes the students are encouraged to personalize the material and by so doing engage in the self-analysis to which Montaigne referred. Sometimes students are asked to evaluate their own performance in a course—and sometimes the course itself. Again, you've got purpose, you've got audience. Go ahead, essay to write one.

WHAT IS AN ACADEMIC "PAPER"?

Two things tend to distinguish academic papers from essays, although there's plenty of overlapping—many essays incorporate the "ingredients" of academic papers and vice versa:

1. Academic papers are generally more source based than observation based. That is, the writer starts with a question or claim and researches it as thoroughly as possible, assembling sources that answer that question or support that claim.
2. Ideally, academic papers bring something new to the table. While that can't always be the case—you might, for example, be asked to write a paper about what led up to the collapse of the Soviet Union—oftentimes you're asked to find a new angle on a topic or a new way in.

This is especially true of theses and dissertations, where it is your responsibility to look at what's already been said, perhaps about Hamlet's relationship with his father or the sustainability practices on your campus, and find something new to say. Think about it: if someone else has already said it, why wouldn't you just send your reader to where it's published? A student once submitted to me an "informative" paper on how to make Betty Crocker fudge brownies. In his conclusion, he wrote: "Betty Crocker fudge brownie mix is available at your local grocery store." My reply? "So is the recipe. F."

Naturally, it can be daunting to try to come up with something new to say about a topic, and it can be tricky. We'll talk more about it later, but for now, remember that much of it is about the angle you take and audience for whom you choose to write. That is, while much has been written about the value of growing your own organic produce, it's likely that no one has researched the topic for the purpose of establishing a garden on your campus or in the quad area outside your dorm. Or the student could have recommended the perfect music to listen to while making those brownies.

Students also often think that since an academic paper is so source based, it will be nothing but quotation after quotation, with citations after every sentence. Again, more on this later, but remember that you're assembling and organizing your sources in such a way as to answer your initial question or support your original claim, and while a successful academic paper does feature many quotations and citations, you as the writer are what provides the glue that holds it all together—glue that comes in the form of your own observations and interpretations and in the form of transitions ("Baker agrees with Smith, pointing out that ...").

Lots more about all of this in Part 5 of *The Writer's Way*.

LEARNING TO WRITE WELL

In the rest of this book, we'll talk about what to do at the moment you're writing. But here in the beginning, let's think about what you do *in your life* to learn to write well. Here's a lifelong approach to writing, one that makes good writers.

Learn Like a Child

As far as we know, the way a baby teaches itself to talk is an excellent way to learn language skills. Generally, people learn to speak effortlessly, happily, and voluminously in seven years or so, starting from nothing.

Here's what we know about how children learn to talk:

1. It takes a long time—years. Learning to write also takes time. There is no trick or device or weekend workshop that will hand good writing to you.
2. Children practice constantly—not fifteen minutes a day, not an hour a day, but all the time, as an ongoing part of living. In the same way, writing must be a part of your daily life—you can't just write once a week or when an assignment is due.

3. Children work hard, but the work doesn't hurt, and it doesn't leave them exhausted, resentful, or hostile to talking. Writing also takes work to learn, but the work shouldn't hurt.

4. Children need constant exposure to models. They must be surrounded by adult speech, and the more they hear, the easier it is to learn. There's no alternative to listening: if children don't hear English, they can't learn to speak English. Thus you need constant exposure to examples of good writing. The more you've read, the easier it is to learn to write. There's no alternative to reading: if you haven't read essays, you can't write an essay.

5. Children want speech desperately. You don't have to make them talk, and bribing them doesn't help much. They want to learn for two reasons. First, language is powerful: if you can talk, you can get things you want. When my younger daughter, Gina, was learning to talk, she had a terrible speech impediment, due to chronic ear infections—she was repeating what she was hearing, but it sounded like she was talking underwater. We literally couldn't understand her. Finally, when she was three, a doctor recommended that she have tubes inserted in her ears. Voilà! She could hear ... and talk, clearly. And, naturally, this empowered her: she was now understood when she asked for things—Cheerios, quesadillas, hot dogs, all her favorite foods—and so the chances of her getting them were greatly increased.

    Second, language is a primal joy, like music. Babies babble long before they know sounds can "mean" things, just because it's fun. It's also fun to listen to. Think of Dr. Seuss. Reading—especially listening out loud—about the Cat in the Hat or Horton makes me smile every time. Likewise, although I'm no real fan of rap—especially in its violent and sexist forms—I nonetheless absolutely love some of the clever rhymes I hear good rappers come up with. So you have to want to write, and the only effective reasons to write are to get something you want and to have some fun and perhaps even provide an opportunity for your reader to have some fun as well.

6. The whole world expects children to learn. Not talking is a sign of a disability or severe psychological trauma. A child is treated as a talker from before she utters her first word, not as a person learning to someday talk. So the world must expect you to write and treat writing as an expected, normal human activity. You must call yourself a writer, not a person trying to learn how to write. (See "Learn by Joining the Club," in the Prologue.)

    It's easy to try too hard or care in the wrong way. If we tell a child to try hard and to watch his speech carefully, he won't speak better; he'll become tongue-tied. *If you try too hard, you probably won't write better and you may give yourself writer's block. The more you write in fear or write to avoid error, the worse you'll write.*

7. Nobody tells children how to do it; children teach themselves. *You'll teach yourself to write. Teachers can encourage, but they can't explain how to do it.*

8. Children practice all aspects of talking at once, holistically. They never break language into pieces or steps. No child ever said, "First I'll master nouns, then move on to verbs; first I'll learn declarative sentences, then work on interrogatives." Instead, the child starts out trying to say the whole messages that matter to him the most. *Don't break writing into pieces or "work up to" writing with drills or mechanical exercises. If you want to learn to write essays, write whole essays.*

9. And finally, children never stop learning about the spoken word— even after they're no longer children. *Every time you discover a new slang term or hear a clever rhyme in a rap song, or learn a new word in a class or on the job, you're improving your ability to use English and increasing your understanding (and for many of us, our appreciation) of it. So allow for new words, and new ways of using old words, in your writing. It's fun. I promise.*

The Four Basics

To learn to do anything well, you need at least four things: exposure to models, motivation, practice, and feedback. Take golf, for example. If you want to learn to play well, you need to watch good golfers, you need to want to get better, you need to practice, and you need someone to tell you what's working and what isn't and to offer tips and suggestions. Same with language— Vietnamese or formal essay English. You need exposure, motivation, practice, and feedback, and it needs to be the right kind.

Exposure. Exposure, all by itself, will teach you most of what you need to write. Children learn to talk by listening, not by talking. If you went to live in England for a year, you'd come back speaking with a British accent and using British vocabulary without consciously practicing, doing drills, or being corrected.

We make language the way we see it made. We have no other choice. That's why we should expose ourselves to models that are written the way we want to write. And being exposed to one thing doesn't teach us to do another, so we must expose ourselves to exactly what we want to write. A lifetime of reading cartoons won't teach us how to write formal essays. If you want to write essays, read essays.

Exposure works faster than you'd imagine. It takes only a Western movie or two to catch on to how Western movies "go." If you read six or seven Dave Barry essays in a row, afterward you should be able to write a Barry-esque essay.

Ordinary reading will work, but a special kind of reading works better: *reading for the craft.* If someone loved to watch dance and went to a ballet, how much would she learn about dance by watching? A little. But if a practicing dancer went to the ballet, how much would she learn? A lot. The difference is in the way the two people watch. The first watches like an audience. The second watches like an apprentice.

To write, you must read the way the dancer watches dance and the director watches movies: for the craft, not merely to experience the *effect* of the art, but to see how the effect is wrought. The masses see a movie like *The Big Lebowski* and laugh; the artist sees *The Big Lebowski* and, while laughing, studies how the director makes us laugh. How do essays end? Most people have seen it done hundreds of times but haven't noticed how. To learn, as you go on with your reading life, notice with a small part of your mind how each writer you read solves the problem of ending. After a while, you still might not be able to *say* how endings go, but you'll *know,* and when you write, you'll be more likely to do it like that.

You need a second kind of exposure as well: besides exposure to the finished product, you need exposure to the writing process. If you were in a band and wanted to learn how to record an MP3 file, you'd need to do more than just listen to finished songs. You'd have to go into a recording studio and watch an engineer working with the different tracks, adjusting volume levels, and listening closely to playbacks. Writing is the only complex skill we're asked to master without spending a lot of time seeing someone else do it.

This second kind of exposure is hard to get. When was the last time you watched a skilled writer rewrite a draft? For most of us, the answer is "Never." Where can you go to get such exposure? To a writer's colony. There's probably one meeting in your composition classroom.

Motivation.   To write well, you have to want to write well. How obvious. If someone hates tennis and plays only when he's forced to play, he probably won't play well. Yet in our world we usually accept hating to write and try to work around it: of course, you hate to write—doesn't everyone?—but we'll force you to write with grades or convince you to care by telling you no one will hire you if you can't write. That doesn't work. If you can't find real reasons to write, you won't write well. Period.

Luckily, those reasons aren't hard to find. All humans love writing, the way we love music, dancing, or talking. All children are dying to write, and they scribble long before they can make letters. We even love the supposedly unrewarding parts of writing, like spelling—as you know if you've ever done crossword puzzles or jumbles, or played Hangman or Scrabble or any of the many word-game apps such as Words With Friends. We love puns, word games, tongue twisters, the latest slang phrase, rhymes, and secret codes like Pig Latin.

Even the people who "hate English" in school write secret notes to each other in class the minute the teacher's back is turned and rush off to read the latest X-Men comic book or see a movie or listen to a rap album, all of which are forms of literature and are made out of "English." And what about jokes? Every time you laugh at a joke, you're enjoying English. For example, this old chestnut: "Last night I picked up a woman hitchhiking. She told me she was a magician. I didn't believe her, but she touched my knee and I turned into a motel." That's funny! And it's funny because of what's happening in it with the English language. (For the record, and for any language geeks like me out there, what's happening in the joke is that it's playing with the spelling— yes the *spelling*!—of "into." If it were two words—"in to"—instead of one, it would mean something very different. But of course the joke is spoken, not written, so "into" is the same whether it's spelled as one word or two.)

But something gets in the way of all that natural love of language, because most people, by the time they're grown up, say they don't like to write. And when they try to motivate themselves, things get worse. They try harder and hate writing more. People usually write poorly not because they don't care enough, but because they care too much. Most people who "hate to write" care so much that they dare not do it—the chance of failure and pain is too high. Example: You're at a party and find out the person you're talking to is an English major or, even worse, an English teacher or professor. Suddenly you fear that the way you use English "matters." Does that make you speak better, or worse?

We let fear of criticism and failure kill a lot of things we once loved. We all love to dance and sing as children, but when we grow up, we learn to raise our standards, critique our dancing and singing sternly, and think about how we sound or look to others. As a result, we decide we "don't like" dancing and singing, and never do it where anyone can watch. But it's not the dancing and singing we don't like; it's the value system we've learned to impose on it.

So what can you do? First, relax. Write the way you used to paint or play with clay. Pablo Picasso said, "Every child is an artist. The problem is how to remain an artist once he grows up." (Of course, you'll have to polish the writing before you submit it to your instructor or an editor.)

Second, use writing to accomplish something you passionately want to do. A former student of mine—a nice guy and a good but not great writer— got in a minor scrape with the law a few years ago and had to write a letter to the judge explaining his actions and what he had learned from the experience—that is, from getting arrested. The letter would determine in part the severity of his punishment. He brought a draft by my office, and you know what? That was the best piece of writing he'd ever done—because it mattered to him. He had purpose, and he had an audience (much more on that later).

Practice.   Of course, you have to write to learn how to write, and the more you write, the better. But practice is vastly overrated as a teaching device. Children will never learn to speak French, however much they "practice," if they never hear it spoken, and doing something over and over again won't make you remember it if you don't care.

Additionally, you need to believe in yourself as you're practicing. If you're practicing free throws and you're standing there at the line saying to yourself, "This one won't go in," guess what? It won't—or at least it's not as likely to. On the other hand, tell yourself that "This one's goin' in! Nothin' but net," and you greatly increase your odds. Same idea if you're standing in skis or on a snowboard at the top of a run. Tell yourself you're going to fall, and you probably will. Tell yourself it's a piece of cake, and you greatly increase the chances of making it to the bottom not only without falling but in pretty darn good form as well. Oh, and don't forget how great you can really sing ... in the shower or all alone in your car!

Feedback.   When you're learning, you try something and see what happens. You hit the tennis ball and watch where it lands. Where it lands tells you if the shot worked or not. That's feedback. Writing has no built-in feedback system. You write the essay and hand it in, and it's like playing tennis in the dark: you hit the ball, it flies off into the blackness, and you learn nothing. You need to know where the ball went. You need readers who will tell you: Were they convinced? Was the explanation clear? Did the opening paragraph capture their interest? Did they like the writer's voice? Were the jokes funny?

Feedback can go horribly wrong, however, and maim the user. If you ask someone who "hates to write" where she learned to hate it, she'll probably say, "My Xth-grade teacher ripped every paper I wrote to shreds, covered every page in red ink, and I've been afraid to write ever since." We know the damage it does, yet against all evidence people remain convinced that mechanical error marking is the single most necessary element in a successful writing program. Many students demand that I mark their writing up, like patients who demand that the dentist's drill hurt so they know they're getting their money's worth.

Here are four reasons that error marking won't teach you much about writing. First, it equates good writing with error-free writing, yet we all know that a piece of writing with no "mistakes" is not necessarily effective. In fact, to underscore this point, I've assigned students (usually the first assignment of a semester) to write a paper that would get an F but that contains absolutely no mechanics errors (spelling, punctuation, etc.). Second, because error marking works best on minor mechanical features (e.g., spelling, noun-pronoun agreement) and worst on big issues (e.g., thesis, structure, intention, tone), it implies that minor mechanical features are the most important aspects of writing. Third, it overloads the writer: the essay comes back a blur of red, and the writer doesn't know where to begin. Fourth, it speaks to the "what" and not the "how": it labels what's wrong but doesn't tell you why or how to prevent it. It's as if a snowboard instructor watched you come down the mountain and said, "You fell, there and there." You know that. You want to know what to do to *avoid* falling.

So what kind of feedback helps? Chapter 10 is all about that, and writers will tell you that feedback helps when it is offered as suggestions (instead of orders) given to help accomplish what the writer wants to do (instead of to correct errors or follow rules or do what the instructor wants). Ideally, the writer says to the reader, "I'm trying to do *this;* how could I accomplish that better?" And the reader says, "Maybe if you did a little of *that* it would work better."

The Purpose of a Composition Class

A composition class can help with all four basics. It can't give you the thousands of hours of reading you need, but it can **expose** you to a world of great writing you might never encounter otherwise. And it can help you practice reading for the craft, so the reading you do for the rest of your life will be writer's training. A writing class can also **motivate** you, by helping you find real reasons to write, by introducing you to the great writers who inspire you and make you say, "Hey, I wish I could do that!" And it can help by giving you a real audience of classmates who will react enthusiastically and thoughtfully to your work—and by surrounding you with working writers who are excited by language and reading and writing and who will quicken your excitement for these things.

A writing course will also give you plenty of time to **practice**. It may be the one time in your life when you can treat writing the way it should be treated, as an ever-present, integral part of your thinking, reading, and conversing.

Finally, **feedback** may be the greatest thing a writing course has to offer. A writer's most precious possession is a thoughtful colleague willing to read her writing carefully and offer considered advice. In life, you're lucky to find two; in a writing class, you should be surrounded by them. Think of it: a group of twenty-five people whose job it is for four months to help you learn to write better.

How Can I Write Well Right Now?

What if you have an essay due this Friday? We can use the principles of exposure, motivation, and feedback to find a way to write well today.

Since you need exposure, write in a language you already know—your speaking language, or close to it. Most writing situations allow for—and most readers appreciate—a less formal language than you might expect. In fact, you'd be surprised how many student writers get in trouble by trying too hard to "sound like writers" and use big words just for the sake of using big words. *Use big words when they're the right words, not to impress your reader.*

Since you need motivation, write something you want to write; say something that matters to you; write to people you want to talk to. *Write something you'd want to read.* Naturally, some assignments allow you more freedom in this area than do others, but keep in mind that most instructors also *want* you to write about something that interests you. Try to take the assignment in a direction that will make the material important to you. And remember, from "How to Succeed in School," that your instructor will probably be very happy to talk with you about how to approach the assignment. After all, she'll be reading your paper in the end.

Since you need feedback, find a classmate—a fellow member of the club of writers—and two days before the essay is due spend an hour kicking a rough draft around. Ask your classmate what he thinks in response to what you said. Ask him how the essay could be made to work better. Pay him back by doing the same for his rough draft or take him out for pizza.

Sometimes you have to do only the first of these three. Here's a writer who learned to write well overnight by using the language she spoke. Her first draft began like this:

> The use of phonics as we discussed after reading Weller's book is like start-ing at the end of learning to read in which no meaning or insight is given to the context of the concept of reading.

In conference, she described, in plain English, what she meant. When she realized that it was okay to write like that, she went home and tried again. Her next essay (on how to teach spelling) began.

> Spelling should be taught as a subject separate from reading. Good read-ing skills do not mean good spelling skills. Spelling is learned by writing.

Beautiful!

Now here's another writer who learned to write well overnight by writing in a form she knew well. Her first essay began like this:

> As a teacher of young children the act of censoring literature is an impor-tant task. This prevents bad material from entering the classroom. On the other hand, who has the right to judge what is considered "bad mate-rial"? However, our society has a set of basic human values and it is neces-sary to protect these morals through the act of censorship in regards to textbooks and other various forms of reading material.

That's in trouble. Her second essay was a narrative, and she wrote like this:

> Finally, the moment had arrived. Summer was over and the first day of school was just three days away. Jennifer was so eager and anxious to go to school. She got up bright and early, put on her favorite jeans, her new T-shirt, and her new blue tennis shoes. Her mom and dad were still asleep, so she made her own lunch and left a note telling them she went to school early because she did not want to be late for her first day. With her lunch pail in one hand, and her Pee-Chee folder in the other, she set out for her little journey to the bus stop alone ... and three days too soon.

BELIEVE IN YOURSELF

When I was a sophomore in college, I took a beginning creative writing class from Dr. Clark Brown, a highly regarded author. In addition to having published countless essays and short stories, he had actually published a novel, which I had finished by about the third week of class. I was in awe—taking a writing class from a real novelist!

By midsemester we had submitted several pieces of work, and he had returned mine with mildly encouraging comments. After class one day, I gathered up the courage to take his book, *The Disciple,* up to the lectern at which he was standing and ask him to sign it, which he did, graciously, before handing it back.

As I walked down the hall afterward, I opened the book to the page he had signed, and there it was, scrawled beneath the title but clear as day: "Steve, Be a writer." I was ecstatic. The novelist had recognized the student's talent. It fueled the fire. From then on, I could hardly keep from writing. I wrote, and wrote, and wrote. It was largely why I became a professional writer. For more than twenty years, I kept that book on a prominent shelf in our living room and brought it down from time to time to show friends. "See, Clark Brown told me I should be a writer, way back then."

Except for one minor problem: a couple of years ago, I took the book down and looked again at the inscription, looked hard and closely, from every angle. Oh no! It didn't say "Be a writer" at all. It said, "Best wishes."

I was crushed. Brown hadn't been inscribing the book in response to any talent he had seen in me. It was just a generic inscription. But you know what, because I *thought* it said "Be a writer" and because I *thought* Brown had written it to encourage me to continue writing, I did. And frankly, that little misreading—at an impressionable age and time in my life—played a huge role in how I saw and defined myself. In fact, had I not had an image in my head of myself as a writer, I'd most likely be pounding nails this very moment instead of sitting at a computer keyboard talking to you about how to become a better writer.

WRITER'S WORKSHOP

Some of the chapters in this book end with Writer's Workshop sections like this one. If you would like a word on how they work and how you might read them, see the Preface.

Students Talk About Learning to Write

Every term I ask my students to examine their past for the events that shaped their attitudes toward writing, then turn the responses into conclusions: What works, what doesn't? What experiences make for strong, happy writers and what make for frightened, weak ones? Here are some typical responses:

In elementary school, I was very proud of all forms of my writing, including my speeches, especially with so much support I received. I would spend countless hours on my writing and practice my speeches for my family again and again, taking advice from my mother on being enthusiastic and varying my hand gestures and facial expressions. She would also act as my guide through essay writing as well, helping me improve my papers as a whole and focusing on more than just syntax errors.

However, I will never forget a remark one of my fellow classmates in my tenth grade English class made to me after I made one of my speeches on which I had worked so hard. All he had to say was, "You look so fake up there." This is all it took for me to second-guess everything I did from then on. Ever since then, I have hated speaking in public, and even writing essays, in fear of sounding "fake" to the readers and listeners. My main focus has been on not smiling the entire time and not sounding too sophisticated. I would only let my mom correct grammatical errors in my essays to ensure my writings would sound exactly how I intended them in the first place. Otherwise I felt it would not be what first came to my mind, and therefore not "me." It may sound ridiculous, but anyone could compare my first and final drafts and see that the only corrections I truly made were ones that spell check had searched out and fixed for me.

I have been extremely lazy and dread every time I have to write an essay. But even as recently as a few days ago, during my first week as a sophomore in college, my views on writing changed yet again. I realized that you should not fear the idea of writing an essay; you have to want to do it. That is what makes a good essay, not the grammar, not the length, but truly expressing yourself and not always worrying about impressing everyone. Many times this takes more than one draft. The best way to communicate to someone is not necessarily the first phrasing that you may think of. You have to constantly be thinking about ways to improve, and look forward to writing your thoughts down on paper. So for the first time in a long time, I am going to take on a new perspective for writing, a more optimistic one, for fun.

(KATRINA NELSON)

My love for capturing my imagination in ink was encouraged from a very early age beginning, perhaps, in my toddler years. My parents used to keep my room stocked with picture books. My sister and I would spend hours flipping through them, making up the story line. When we were old enough, we wrote our own books. I remember one of my sister's about a zebra called Lacey. (I told her that was a dumb name. She cried.)

My development as a writer can be accredited largely to *The Hawk's Eye*. This annual publication of poetry, short stories, and drawings submitted by my home town's primary and middle school students, accepted and printed my submissions as early as my second grade year. *The Hawk's Eye* was reason for me to write; it gave me an audience and motivation to improve, and most importantly it gave my writing value.

The opportunity and experience of being published (in a loose sense of the term) was great, but it was nothing compared to the experience of *being* a publisher. In sixth grade I was in Pam Giuliano's class. Ms. Giuliano was queen of all things literature in the middle school and the woman responsible for the birth and life of *The Hawk's Eye*. Sixth grade offered me the chance to be a part of the team that critiqued, chose, and then compiled all the submitted works to be published in the small literary magazine. *The Hawk's Eye* placed value on unstructured creativity throughout my grade school years. Not only was I able to exercise imaginative writing, but I was also exposed to other students' writing, and challenged to think about what was good writing.

(LAURA KATE JAMES)

Before my second year of high school, my teachers, peers and parents encouraged me to write. I remember in the sixth grade, my class had a writing assignment in which we were supposed to write a thirty-page story, and most people chose to write with few words, in the format of a children's book. My story was a solid thirty pages of text, not including the illustrations. By freshman year of high school, I had started a few books out of boredom, and had gotten past the one-hundred-page mark in one of them. However, sophomore year stopped me cold when it came to writing.

In the first place, my sophomore teacher was mainly into theater and drama. What he was doing teaching English, I have no idea. As a director of our school plays, he had to pick his favorite actors all the time to play lead roles, and this policy carried over into his English class. I found myself unable to get above a C in his class on written assignments—not because my papers were particularly "average." My friend, one of the aforementioned favorites, had papers that seemed about the same quality as mine and she consistently received As. We believed he took the score from the first essay and just carried it over without reading and seeing how much we had improved, especially since he wrote few comments on our essays besides those concerning spelling. I found myself frustrated with that class and infuriated time and time again with the teacher; worse yet, I found myself growing to believe that I was truly a bad writer. If anything, that class lowered my writing ability, something I am as of yet trying to recover from. That year, I stopped writing my stories, even though I still believe their plots and characters had merit. Those books are still sitting, dead, on my laptop.

My junior and senior year I spent with another English teacher, who was much more helpful in showing me how to organize formal essays and much more encouraging. After those two years, I got back into the habit of jotting down story ideas and maybe expanding on them later; I even wrote a short screenplay as my senior project, something I got full credit on. Although I write more often, I do not have the love of writing that I once possessed. Sadly, after that one bad year, I will spend a lifetime trying to regain that passion.

(DANIELE SMITH)

Throughout junior high school, my papers always came back to me with a large A up on the top. However, my first high school paper had so many red marks on it that I thought a pen had exploded on my paper. I rewrote that paper three times; I am proud to say that I finally ended up with a B+ for my effort. Since then my papers have had a kind of hit-and-miss effect. I either just do average or I hit a home run. Topics that were inspiring or gave me a cause to fight for always brought about my best work.

I may never have a book that is on the *New York Times* bestseller list, or make millions writing for a famous magazine, but writing is a passion of mine. Truth be told, one could even say that it is all I have ever known.

(NICOLE BENBOW)

I had always loved writing when I was in school; I considered English to be my best class. During my sophomore year of high school that changed. Whenever I would write an essay it would return to me with the text barely legible. My teacher would mark up my entire essay with a series of "whys," "hows," and "explains." It seemed that however detailed I thought the paper was, it wasn't detailed enough for her.

After receiving a few less than desirable grades on my essays, I came up with a new plan. I decided that I would write the essay early, have her edit it and then I would revise it. I thought that surely with this new plan I would be able to revise the paper to her specifications and receive the grade I believed I had deserved all along, an A. Suffice it say, my plan failed.

My revised essay came back with just as many pencil marks as before, if not more. For the rest of the year I was completely shut off to writing. I didn't know what my teacher wanted and I was so focused on trying to please her that it wasn't fun anymore. I felt that I didn't grow as a writer that year because I was so preoccupied with what my teacher wanted that I didn't really focus on my writing.

(ASHLEY YATES)

At the age of ten I was turned on to writing by my fourth grade teacher. Early in the year, she assigned us the task of writing a paper using animals. One stipulation was that each student had to incorporate a myth into his/her paper. I chose to write "How Turtles Got Their Shells." I wove my story around a turtle named Shelly. Original, I know. The tale told of how defenseless turtles were constantly plagued with birds that would peck at their backs. Alas, the dutiful Shelly took it upon himself to go in search of protection. As the tale unfolded, our hero accidentally had cement poured onto his back, which the birds couldn't penetrate.

I had an enjoyable time writing my paper, but I was even more thrilled at what happened after I turned it in. The teacher announced to the class that out of all the papers, one was exceptionally good. She then proceeded to read that paper aloud. My anxiety grew when the story commenced and I realized she was reading about a turtle named Shelly. When she was done, she told the class that the author was Tommy Parker, as my face turned a color of crimson that Crayola "ain't got nothin' on."

Ever since that day, thanks to Shelly and a nurturing elementary teacher, I have counted writing as one of the joys in life.

(TOM PARKER)

By the time I entered junior high, I had learned that "school writing" was far different than the creative story writing I enjoyed doing with my spare time. Bland essay assignments on wars and presidents eventually led me to dread the sight of pen and paper. When I stepped into my eighth grade English class, my entire view changed. With her personal passion and enthusiasm, my teacher restored a love for writing within me that had dimmed over time. I learned in that small classroom that with imagination and interest, a writer can make any type of work exciting.

There is no strict pathway I followed to become the writer I am today. Many essays, journals, experiences, and teachers played a part in shaping me, no matter how subtly. In all honesty, a writer cannot be a writer unless they enjoy their work, and the drive and inspiration that dwells within me truly created my writing skills.

(KATIE BROWN)

Obviously, many people are feeling a lot of pain about their writing. And the people in these histories are the system's *successes*, those who thrived and went to college, most of them intending to become teachers! But there's comfort to be taken here, too. All of us writers are having the same experiences, reacting the same way, thriving on the same things, and being curdled by the same things. We're all in this together, and we agree on what helps and what doesn't. For instance, being read to a lot by your parents helps; being forced to push your personal message into cookie-cutter patterns like five-paragraph essay paradigms doesn't. Critical feedback in the form of conversation with a mentor making suggestions about alternatives helps; critical feedback in the form of red-pen corrections doesn't. All we have to do is do the things that help and avoid the things that don't.

So what should you do to become a healthy writer? First, tell your own story. Get clear on what assumptions about writing you now own and where you got them. Second, using the histories in this section and your own experience, make a list of things that work and things that hurt. Third, reject the poisonous messages you've been fed. Finally, create for yourself a writing environment that nourishes you as a writer.

Now It's Your Turn.   In this chapter you've been listening to a conversation about how people learn to write. It's time to join the conversation.

Step 1: Make your own contribution to the collection of tales in Writer's Workshop. Write a two-page narrative detailing everything you've done or had done to you that has helped form your writing or your view of yourself as a writer. Remember to go back to the beginning—most people's attitudes toward reading and writing are formed long before they get to school. And think about what isn't in your life as well as what is—sometimes what's lacking is profoundly educational, like never seeing your parents reading for pleasure.

Step 2: Make a list of experiences that promote writing and a list of experiences that obstruct it. For instance, you might have "Mom puts sample of my writing on the fridge" in the plus list.

Step 3: As a class, pool your anecdotes and your lists, until you have answered this question: what would a person do if she were setting out to create for herself the writer's perfect upbringing and environment?

EXERCISES

1. Write a two-page essay exploring how well your writing career up to now has provided you with each of the Four Basics. Discuss how you could improve the amount and type of each you're getting now.

2. For each of the nine principles in "Learn Like a Child," write a paragraph discussing how well your writing program up to this point in your life has followed that principle. List changes you could make to follow it better.

3. Write an essay discussing the kinds of feedback your writing has received throughout your life. Begin with your earliest memories of writing, and continue through recent school experiences. Rate each kind of feedback for effectiveness: Did it help, or did it hurt? How much healthy feedback have you received in school?

Chapter 2

What Makes Writing Effective?

I t'd be impossible to list, describe, or quantify all the ingredients of an effective piece of writing, for the same reasons that it's impossible to list, describe, or quantify all the ingredients of a Beethoven concerto, a great Beatles song, or even a well-played soccer game: the finished products equal more than the sum of their parts. That said, there is one thing that all effective writing has, and it's easy to learn to use it in your own work.

THE SENSE OF AUDIENCE

The key that separates good writing from bad is a sense of *audience*. Writers who write for the wrong reasons think of writing as a mechanical act with certain "good" surface features, and when they write, they try to make an essay that includes them: correct spelling, an outlineable structure, a thesis statement, a large vocabulary, esoteric sources, and so on. That approach produces essays like Dr. Frankenstein's early experiments: however meticulously you sew the bits and pieces together, it's never going to get up off the operating table and walk. The alternative, the only approach to writing that works, is to set out to do *something to the reader*.

You can do anything to your reader you want—move her to tears, annoy him, convince her to vote for your candidate, convince him you're right, teach her how to make jambalaya, or make him feel what growing up with your big brother was like. And you know you've succeeded when you get what you set out to get: she cries, he feels annoyed, she votes your way, he thinks you're right, she learns how to make jambalaya, or he knows what growing up with your big brother was like.

You already know all this. And (here is the really wonderful thing) you already know how to do it, too. All children begin their writing careers by writing the messages they think will pack the biggest wallop for their readers: "I love you." "I am Ericka." "Come to my party." But somewhere along the line we forget we know it.

Once you get the secret of good writing firmly in your mind, you think in a different way about writers' decisions. Instead of saying, "What's the rule?" when a question arises, you say, "What works? What does my reader want? What will be most effective here?" For instance, let's say you're writing your way through an essay and you approach the conclusion. You have a decision to make: should you summarize the essay in the final paragraph? With the old attitude, you recall someone telling you that in an essay you should "tell them what you're going to tell them, tell them, then tell them what you told them." So you summarize. With the new attitude, ask yourself, "Does my reader want or need a summary? Will a summary conclusion be effective?" For many essays the answer to both questions is no. Readers can remember what they've read and usually don't need to be told again. In other words, summary conclusions often *don't work*.

Having a Reader in Your Head

As you write, imagine a first-time reader reading it and guess how she'll respond. The more you hear the reader's responses, the better you can decide how to react to and respond to them, so the better you'll write.

When you think about hearing the writer's responses in your head, think literally. If you're writing a recipe for novice cooks and you write, "Then add a tablespoon of oregano," you should hear your reader responding, "What's oregano? Where can I get some? What if I used *two* tablespoons?" If you write, "All recent U.S. presidents in this century have been owned by the oil companies," you should hear the reader responding, "How do you know? Can you prove it? That sounds awfully wild to me. Are you putting me on?" and so on. If you write, "Cleaning up our environment is a humongous task," you had better realize that some readers will respond, "This person talks like a kid," or "This guy doesn't speak my language."

You can never be sure how your reader is responding, because people are unpredictable and different readers have different values and knowledge. If you write, "Gun control violates the right to bear arms guaranteed by the Constitution," you'll evoke a firestorm of reactions:

Right on!

Just another gun nut.

Not that old cliché!

What does the Constitution say?

Is that what the Constitution really means?

So we can't control guns at all?

Can't we change the Constitution?

What's "the Constitution"? That old sailing ship?

You can't speak to all these voices, and you don't have to—as long as you're imagining your reader responding *in any way at all*, you're being a writer.

Nor does this mean you have to do what the reader wants. You may want to frustrate him, make him mad, trick him—but you have to know he's feeling frustrated, angered, or tricked, and you must be doing it to him for a reason. And the reader doesn't need to be *pleased* all the time; she just needs to be able to look back, when the reading is over, at what was done to her and see the reason for it—she says, "I see now why the writer refused to tell me what was going on until the end—he had his reasons."

This does *not* mean that writing is good only if it causes a reaction in the reader. Any and all writing causes readers to react—lousy writing often causes readers to react with confusion, frustration, boredom, or anger, for instance. The true principle is, Writing is good if it causes the reaction *the author set out to cause* in the reader, and then *works with* that reaction—hears it, reacts to it, addresses it, honors it.

Giving the Readers What They Need

Good writers give readers everything they need to read them well. Good readers are busy doing lots of jobs; it's your job to assist them. For example,

They're summarizing, so you must give them an essay that's summarizable.

They're trying to put what they're reading to personal use—"What good is this to me?"—so you must give them something they can use.

They're trying to understand how you got to your conclusion, so you must include the evidence and reasoning that took you there.

They're trying to understand, so you have to explain.

They're trying to connect with you, so you have to be human on the page.

They're trying to connect to something else, so you have to show how your topic fits into a bigger picture.

The clearer you are on what a reader's jobs are, the more you can help him do them and the better you'll write.

Seeing Writing as Performance

Good writing knows it's a performance. Good writers are hams on the page. They feel the presence of the audience the way a stage actor does. The only difference is that the writer's audience must be imagined. People who read aloud well are usually good writers, and a simple way to write well is to *write something you'd love to read out loud*.

A great example of that principle at work is Megan Sprowls' essay, "The Do's and Don'ts of Getting Over That Summer-Between-High-School-and-College Fling ..." on p. 342. Check it out. See how it's like a performance. In fact, while it works wonderfully on the page, it worked even better when she read it out loud to the class the day she turned it in. We were in stitches laughing so hard.

Let's look at a piece of the real stuff and see what it's got. Here's a professional essay. What does it have that bad essays don't have?

SOMETHING HAPPENED A LONG TIME AGO

JON CARROLL

As near as I can figure, today is the 30th anniversary of the death of Jeanne Steager. She was riding in a car on a stretch of Route 17 near Scotts Valley. The road was slick with rain. There was no median barrier back then, just a double yellow line. A truck crossed over and hit her car. The only virtue that anybody could find in her death was that it was immediate. She was, as near as I can figure, 25 years old.

Jeanne Steager was a graduate student in anthropology at the University of California, a colleague of my then-wife. I did not know her all that well; my impressions of her today are all blended into one long dinner party at her house, with graduate student spaghetti and graduate student conversation. She had a husband named Peter, who later became one of my closest friends; she had smooth olive skin and deep brown eyes. She wanted to go to Europe; I remember that. First her doctorate; then the trip to Greece. She had it all planned.

I was at the time commuting from Berkeley to a job at the San Jose Mercury News. I worked in the promotion department for a large, blustery man named Mr. Stern. He used to leave early and hide under the stairs to see if anyone tried to sneak out before 5. It was like working for your vice principal.

He was kind of a cartoon boss, really; he would have been amusing in a slapstick sort of way if my noncartoon salary had not paid the rent on my noncartoon house.

I wrote radio advertisements for the Mercury News that were read at the halftimes of San Jose State football games. I ran a kind of Keno-like circulation promotion game; I had to check thousands of entries a week to see if the numbers matched the ones I had previously drawn.

As I did, I repeated a sentence that had stuck in my head from some political science class. I thought it was from Marx: "Man shall be saved from repetitive labor." Maybe Marx did say it; silly man.

So then Jeanne Steager died of multiple head wounds, died instantly within sight of a gigantic plaster Santa Claus two days after Christmas. She was the first person I actually knew who died.

And what I could remember about her was her plans. What I could remember about her was the neat rows she had set down for her life, the lines on the graph paper that stretched in pleasing geometry well into the future.

I doubt that she was thinking, when she turned her head and saw the truck coming, "Well, there goes that trip to Greece." But I thought that, later. I thought that the overlooked corollary to "it's never too late" is "it's never too early."

The day after Jeanne Steager died, I went into Mr. Stern's office and quit my job. I was out of there in an hour; I was back home for lunch. It's never too early. Plans are just guesses.

I suppose I am bringing tidings of subversive cheer; I suppose I am suggesting that you consider a change. Quit your job if you hate it. Go on. I know these are hard times, and people fall off the edge, but God is passing out brain tumors too, and you might as well take the plunge. The plunge is all we've got.

When you're young you think that life stretches out indefinitely and you can take this crap for another decade. And the lesson of Jeanne Steager is, No, you bloody well can't. Life is of varying lengths, and actuarial tables are only averages, and sometimes you gotta close your eyes and jump. Even if it's scary; especially if it's scary. Easy for me to say now; I have my dream job. I have my dream job because I quit that other job; that's a fact.

Transcendence happens at precisely the same rate as that other stuff. As Wendell Berry says: Practice resurrection.

Used with permission of SAN FRANCISCO CHRONICLE from Carroll, Jon.
"Something Happened A Long Time Ago," December 27, 1995.

Jon Carroll is a columnist for the *San Francisco Chronicle*.

WHAT GOOD WRITING ISN'T

If good writing results from knowing your readers and giving them what they need, let's list the things that a good essay *doesn't* need:

A large vocabulary. We know all or almost all of Carroll's words.

Complex sentences. In fact, look at the sentence *fragments*!

A brand-new idea. Carroll isn't saying anything that hasn't been said before. In fact, the essay's thesis, or main point, is a big fat cliché, isn't it? "Seize the day," "Carpe diem," etc. But he's brought something new to it—more on that later.

An argument that's absolutely and exclusively true. The essay has a nice thesis, but the opposite—that you need to live cautiously—is just as true.

The last word on its topic. The essay doesn't end discussion of how to live our lives meaningfully and completely; it just adds a little something to it.

Profound thinking. The ideas in the essay aren't subtle or brainy.

Extensive research or expertise. Carroll's only outside reference is the line from Wendell Berry, the poet.

Extraordinary experience. Lots of people have had experiences like Carroll's; it's not at all extraordinary or unusual.

Since Carroll's essay doesn't have these things, they can't be what makes good writing good, and you don't need to have them either.

There are things Carroll's essay does have that make it *better* but that won't make the essay good by themselves: transition between ideas, overall organization, thesis, examples, details, conclusion, unambiguous language. They're not the heart of writing, the way reaching home is the heart of baseball—they won't make your writing good unless you have the "other thing" too.

There are also things the essay *must* have but for which it gets no credit at all: spelling, punctuation, appropriate usage, and the other mechanical aspects of writing. You'd never say to a friend, "Oh, I read the most wonderful article in the paper yesterday. Such comma placement! And every word spelled just right!" Or: "He's such good driver! He never runs stop signs." These things don't make you "good"—only legal.

One more thing about the Jon Carroll essay: The first time I read it, I clipped it out of the newspaper planning to use it in my writing classes as an example of an effective argument essay. A couple of months later I was reading it to my students when I had the strangest feeling—I realized I was reading it as much to myself as to them. I finished, took a breath, let the students go early, and walked downtown to our local travel agency and put four tickets to Maui on my credit card and gave them to my family for a Valentine's Day gift. I later wrote to Jon Carroll and told him the story. Great, he said, send me a postcard, which, of course, I did. We've been in off-and-on contact ever since. True story. And an example of the impact a simple essay can have on its reader. Even one with sentence fragments in it.

PROOF THAT IT WORKS

If good writing is all about having a reader firmly in mind, we should be able to take writers who are trying to "make essays" and tell them to write to real people instead, and their writing should get better instantly. And it works. Here's a passage from an essay on hypnotism, written by someone with no sense of humans reading him:

> For some types of material, learning while in an actual state of hypnosis is best, while for other types of material, it is better to study in a waking state with post-hypnotic suggestions providing the improvement. Rote memorization is best done in a hypnotic state, but material of a technical nature which requires integration into one's present knowledge of the subject area should be done in the waking state. The reason that technical material can't be effectively learned while under hypnosis is because the subconscious mind lacks the ability for critical and inductive reasoning. Only the conscious mind has this ability. However, post-hypnotic suggestions can help to improve the learning of technical material.

The writer was asked to rewrite it as if he were talking to real people, and he produced this lovely stuff:

> If you're trying to learn a foreign language, memorize a definition or a speech, or anything that requires rote memorization, then it is best to do it in an actual hypnotic state. However, technical material is another

matter. You can memorize the material easily enough, but all you can do with it is repeat it, just like a parrot. With post-hypnotic suggestions, you can improve your ability to concentrate, retain, and recall the technical material.

We should also be able to find good writing that "breaks the rules" when breaking the rules does what the writer wants to do to the reader. Here's an example of a rule-breaking essay by my former student Laura Kate James (you'll find more of Laura Kate's work on pp. 25, 351, 352, and 382):

SCHOOL IS COOL

LAURA KATE JAMES

Student Essay

So you've found the school. You've found *the* school. And surprise, surprise, you've been accepted. Congratulations—I should be so lucky. The headaches are behind you now. No more essays, applications, scholarships. Your fate has been decided. Take your foot off the gas, recline your seat, fold your hands behind your head. Time for that long overdue air-jam tribute to Tom Petty's "Free Falling"—cruise control. You're bound for glory, a genius, a prodigy. The future is bright, my friend. Put on your shades.

You're awake, staring up at a dark ceiling, the last night in your own bed. Scenes from *Animal House* and *Legally Blonde* playing over and over in your head. You envision friends, family, ex's, enemies huddled in dark corners whispering your name softly between fistfuls of Fiddle Faddle, tortured by your absence. You imagine your weekends immediately being booked with dinner-movie-coffee-date plans by handsome young males, job offers pouring in, ceremonies held, awards dedicated, benches—no, libraries—built in your name. Your clothes and books and CDs and eight pairs of high heels you'll never wear but don't want to leave with your little sister (the thief) all packed in big black garbage bags and prune boxes, piled up in the corner, waiting.

At last. The Day has come. You are a College Student. You've finally entered the world, the real world, the over-romanticized, over-glamorized collegiate world. You begin to uncover truths John Belushi never let on. You have to go to class. Reading is still a big part of your life. Learning? What? Direction, goals, a major, all have to be decided. Now. And you thought high school was hard. You find that such a large concentration of teens and twenty-somethings all trying to *find themselves* can be exhausting. Everyone is dyeing their hair and piercing their nose and getting tattoos, and they all wear Diesel jeans and spend their money at Urban Outfitters. They complain about rent and roommates and talk about their parents (either they love them, or they hate them and hope they die). And everyone plays guitar and everyone is *really into music*. They all pledge their allegiance to Bob Marley and Fallout Boy and Zeppelin and walk around wearing their Dark Side of the Moon T-shirts, headphones in their ears. And everyone is smoking and drinking or drunk, or they don't and they won't and never will (either/or, black and white, pick a side dammit). They use words like *exoneration*—always in the wrong context—everyone does it and it's the worst. And they all talk about politics and exchange rates and diplomacy and *oh our corrupt government* (they all hate the government). And everyone's heart is broken or breaking, they're falling all over love, in and out and all over it. Love and adore, or hate and abhor. No in between. Abandon all but the extremes. Supposed to make you more interesting, I guess, unique maybe. You'll see that it's really just the same kind of kids grouped in the same place learning the same things living the same kind of life saying the same stuff fighting the same battles with the same opinions and trying to be different in the same ways. It's annoying and tiresome, but the price you have to pay for that degree (not to mention thousands and thousands and *thousands* of dollars).

Try not to add to this hopeless demographic. Yes, yes, I believe education is vital, knowledge is power, learning is loving, school is cool, all that kind of crap, but if you can find a way around this insane sameness and still get the dream job—which, let's face it, you probably won't get even if you *do* go to college— attack. Pursue the alternative path, ferocious and foaming at the mouth. Get a library card or something.

—Permission provided by Steve Metzger.

Here are some of the essay-making rules Laura Kate breaks:

Avoid redundancy.

Combine short sentences to avoid choppiness.

Avoid long paragraphs.

Avoid sentence fragments. (She's got one-*word* sentences!)

Reveal topic, thesis, and purpose in the opener.

Don't start sentences with "And."

Laura Kate breaks the rules because breaking the rules "works." She breaks rules to create a tone and style that show her frustration with college (and her peers). The rest of this book will offer you scads of rules for good writing. They're good rules, and your writing will usually get better if you follow them. But trying to write well by building an essay around them doesn't work as well as asking, "What works?" And there is no answer to that question until you know what you're trying to *do* with your writing.

How to Feel About Rules

My students often take this "don't follow rules" stuff too far, so let's clear a few things up.

There are two extreme attitudes about rules. The first says, "I am a student; I must obey." The second says, "Hey, writing is creative— I'm above rules." The first reduces you to marionette status; the second suggests that you're not thinking about your reader.

Writing consists of two principal stages: the creative stage (composing) and the corrective stage (editing and polishing). Your attitude toward rules should be different for each. In the creative stage (from first thoughts through brainstorming, freewriting, drafting, and revising), follow these principles:

Do what works.

Something "works" if it gets you the results you want.

Break a rule when breaking a rule gets you the results you want.

Break a rule when you have a good reason for breaking a rule.

When you break a rule, know you're breaking it.

Follow rules unless there's a good reason not to.

If you're not sure what to do, try following the rule—it might help.

In the corrective/editing stage (spelling, grammar, formatting, following the boss's instructions), think another way. Here, follow rules slavishly. It makes no sense to say, "I am an *artiste*—I am above indenting paragraphs or spelling 'accommodate' correctly." If you don't see why, the next time you play baseball, try telling the umpire you'd like four strikes, please, instead of three. See where that gets you. On the other hand, during batting practice (the creative stage), you should have been taking lots of swings and trying new stuff.

EXERCISES

1. Here are the title and opening lines of an essay. Cover them with a piece of paper and pull the paper down slowly to reveal one line at a time. (If you read the whole text at once, this game doesn't work.) After exposing each line, write down one or two responses you have to the line— questions you want to ask, feelings you want to express, desires you want met. When you've gone through the text, look it over and write a half page about how successfully the author predicted and dealt with your responses—was he hearing you?

STREETS OF SORROW

(DAVID RAKOFF, CONDÉ NAST TRAVELER, NOVEMBER 2006)

Superman has taken the morning off. Although appearing among us in mufti, he is immediately identifiable by his square jaw and the comma of dark hair upon his forehead. He greets with an affable hello the other Hollywood Boulevard regulars who have gathered, along with a small crowd of tourists, outside the classical facade of the former Masonic Temple, now the TV studio where Jimmy Kimmel does his evening talk show. The USC Trojan Marching Band, or at least a skeleton crew thereof, goes through its paces, a casually synchronized, loose-limbed routine in which its members instrumentally exhort us to do a little dance, make a little love, and above all, get down tonight. Superman bops his head, enjoying his moments of freedom. In a while he will have to put on his blue tights and red Speedo and go to work, posing for pictures with the tourists in front of

Grauman's Chinese Theatre. Maybe he'll stop on the way at the Coffee Bean & Tea Leaf, at the corner of Hollywood and Orange. Batman and the Cat in the Hat go there sometimes.

---

2. Do the same exercise with the title and first six or seven sentences of a piece of your own. Don't forget the half-page discussion at the end.

3. Do Exercise 2 using a classmate as audience. Reveal your essay opening one sentence at a time and have him write his reactions down after each. Then look at the dialogue and write a half-page essay that assesses how successfully you predicted his responses.

4. Take one of the following essay first sentences and discuss what kinds of reactions the author should expect and why he might want those reactions and use them to his advantage.

   a. Once upon a time, a little boy loved a stuffed animal whose name was Old Rabbit.

   (TOM JUNOD, WRITING ABOUT MR. ROGERS, ESQUIRE, NOVEMBER 1998)

   b. I recently read the opinion column in the campus newspaper.

   c. This country has a rich tradition of producing fads that make a great portion of the populace look ridiculous.

   (SAN FRANCISCO CHRONICLE, AUGUST 16, 2006, P. E1)

5. Write a thesis statement for one of your essays. Write three different likely responses readers might have to it.

6. Write an essay you'd love to read out loud to the class. Then read it out loud to them with as much drama and "performance" as you can manage.

7. Find an essay, in a newspaper or magazine, that "breaks the rules" in a way you like. Write a short (a page or so) essay discussing what rules are being broken and why, and explain why the rule breaking works, or doesn't, if you don't think it does. Bring it to class, and share it with your classmates. Find out what they think about the rule breaking and what they think of the essay. Did they respond like you did?

Chapter 3

Writing in School:
An Introduction

NOT AS DIFFERENT AS YOU MIGHT THINK

It's easy to think that much of what we've discussed so far about writing has nothing whatsoever to do with writing in schools. Not so fast. While there are big and important differences, the basic ideas still hold true: your writing still needs to have a purpose, and you need to know, as specifically as possible, who your readers are.

Purpose

Often in academic writing, your purpose is simply to show your instructor that you understand the course material. In that case, your task is pretty straightforward. Keep in mind, however, that what really pleases most instructors is that their students not only understand the material but can also take the ideas from it outside the classroom. For example, let's say you're writing a paper for an American Studies class that asks you to discuss the connections between the 1954 *Brown v. Board of Education* Supreme Court decision and the career of Elvis Presley (not as crazy an assignment as you might think). You could discuss how Elvis crossed racial barriers and combined traditionally white and black music in a way that wouldn't have been possible before 1954. That's probably what your teacher's looking for. But if you went beyond that and discussed, for example, how Eminem did the same thing fifty years later, you would be showing not only that you understand the course material but that you can also make connections to it *outside the classroom door*. You'd be surprised how happy that will most likely make your teacher. (Of course, if you're not sure whether such a tactic would be appropriate, ask your instructor.)

In other types of courses, instructors are also looking for particular things, ideally explained in the assignment itself (see How to Read Writing Assignments, p. 37). A first-year writing course, for example, might emphasize research, and the instructor would most likely be looking at the legitimacy and range of your sources, the degree to which you gracefully integrate them into your own text, the degree to which the material is correctly documented (usually MLA, in this case), and the way in which you draw insightful and meaningful conclusions from the sources. Now, while that might sound like a lot, it's actually fairly straightforward, with lots of models, advice, and instruction available—in addition to that which you most likely have already discussed in class. For example, when making sure that your work is correctly documented, it's very easy to look at a handbook or Web site that tells you *exactly* how to do it.

Similarly, in some courses the purpose is to demonstrate in your paper that you learned something from and drew some conclusions from actually doing the writing—a noble purpose. Again, this isn't that difficult, since you're the one who did the work: it should be easy to show what you've learned.

But note how all of this is intimately linked to knowing who your reader is.

Audience

In order to write well in school, you need to understand your audience. Naturally, "the teacher" or "the professor" is your primary reader/evaluator, and in some cases he knows more about your subject than you ever will. For example, if you're writing a paper for a history class and your professor asks you to discuss the causes of the Civil War, she's looking for something very specific—most likely the very causes covered in her lectures and/or her assigned reading. So, of course, you give her that. Keep in mind, however, that she might be reading as many as a hundred responses to that same question, so imagine how most of the other ninety-nine students will respond and try to do something a little different. When I took American history in college, we were to discuss in our final papers some of the results of Manifest Destiny. I wrote a fairly conventional essay in which I discussed what I thought my instructor wanted to hear, including how the settlers basically committed genocide on indigenous peoples as they moved west. When I looked at the paper and realized how generic it was, I wadded it up and round-filed it. Then I started over, writing about a trip I took to Arizona with my parents when I was a child and about some moccasins I bought as a souvenir and finding, when I got home, "Made in Japan" stamped on their soles. My point was the same, but my approach was different. She loved it, and she read it to the class as an example of what she thought was an excellent response to the assignment. Not only did she give me an A, but when I'd see her on campus subsequent semesters she'd never fail to tell me how much she liked the paper.

Caution: Obviously, not all teachers/professors appreciate an original approach and some may in fact be put off by it, so you need to have a sense of whether that will work, which brings us right back, of course, to knowing your audience.

In other academic classes, such as first-year writing courses, professors often tell students that their audiences are their peers. Or they get more specific: fellow first-year students or even their classmates. The professor might go so far as to include as part of the assignment that the student choose her own audience. In that case, you're in great shape. You can choose to write for overweight, red-meat-eating, first-year male students at your university. Then, while your instructor is indeed the reader in terms of who will be evaluating your paper, she will consider the audience you have identified and assess your work based in large part on the degree to which it works for *that audience.*

A Word About Level of Formality

Students often come to college thinking that all academic writing is highly formal and that they need to use as many big words and to make their sentences as long and complex as they can. I've had students tell me that they learned in high school never to start sentences with "And," or never to use "I." And I think that's just crazy. We'll look more closely at this in Chapters 5 and 6 but keep in mind that the first answer to almost all questions about writing is "It depends." Should you use first person? It depends. Can you begin a sentence with "And"? It depends. If, for example, the assignment asks you to examine several Web sites and discuss the degree to which they're appropriate for college-level research, then it might be fine to say, "I found one Web site that seems particularly relevant...." I recently read a long, very thorough research paper that discussed how the closing down of a large lumber mill pretty much destroyed the economy of the nearby town. Turns out the student had grown up in the town, and in her introduction and conclusion she talked about the differences she saw before and after the mill closed down. She could have done that without using first person, but her first-person observations made the paper both more readable and more credible.

Note: Don't confuse suggestions for deleting "In my opinion" or "I believe" with cautions against using first person altogether. In those cases, the first person isn't necessarily inappropriate; it's just needless. If you're arguing that the Coen brothers' films are overrated, you don't need to say, "In my opinion ..." That *is* your opinion. So the suggestion to lose that phrase is probably a suggestion to tighten your writing rather than to make it more formal.

Often when students try to write in a voice that's too formal, they lose control. They'll use a thesaurus to find a "bigger" word and it won't be quite right. A couple of general rules: (1) Use a big word when it's the right word, not just *because* it's a big word. On the other hand, there might be certain terms that you're expected to use to show you understand the course material. (2) If you do use a thesaurus, make sure you look up the meaning of the word in the dictionary to ensure you know exactly what it means.

Finally, remember that formality takes a number of different, well, forms. For example, while the voice in your paper might be fairly informal (first person, breezy tone, etc.), you can still use a formal (prescribed) documentation format. The student's paper about the closing of the mill was rather informal in voice but was documented perfectly, with dozens of in-text citations and a works-cited page that listed nearly twenty sources. However, some writing situations call for both: a formal voice, in which first person is inappropriate, *and* formal documentation. Ask your instructor if you're not sure.

A BRIEF REVIEW

Sorry, but I just want to go over some stuff, to remind you of the similarities between writing in the real world and writing in school.

1. You Need Exposure to Learn How to Write

Chapter 1 says you can't write something until you've been exposed to lots of models and seen "how it goes." How much academic writing have you read? Unless you're a professor, the answer is probably none. So ask your instructor for sample essays to use as patterns, or ask her to recommend a journal or two in the field whose articles you can browse through in the library.

2. You Need Motivation

However hard it may be to find motivation when you're overworked, out of time, and writing on a topic you aren't fond of in a course you're being forced to take, you still need it. And fear or a need for a grade won't work well. How you learn to care is largely up to you, but here are two hints. Everything in the world is intellectually interesting to a thoughtful mind, and the true performer gets up for every performance, however small or cold the audience may be.

3. You Need Time to Prewrite and Revise

Writing is supposed to be a multistage process allowing you to think, reflect, rethink, and revise repeatedly. School will rarely give you the time. *The single most difficult thing about writing in school is the lack of revising time.* There is no way to create extra hours in the day, so all you can do is learn to use the little time you have well:

> *Start thinking about the assignment from the moment it's assigned.* Even if you have only an evening to *write* it, you can *mull it over* for days with a part of your mind and jot down thoughts while doing work for other courses.

Plan to do at least two drafts. Nobody's first draft is all that good.

Write a one- or two-sentence summary of your paper after your first draft. If you can do this, and it makes sense, your paper probably does, too. This will take five minutes and pay big dividends.

Devote thirty minutes or an hour to peer feedback with a respected reader. Once you've drafted, another mind will take you further faster than yours will.

Don't try to save time by not proofreading. One grisly typo can shatter your reader's confidence in you. And remember, proofread from hard copy, not from your computer. You'll see things on the paper that you won't on your screen.

Thesis in Academic Writing

In most school writing, thesis is absolutely key.

Making a thesis is no easy task, but it helps to turn to three old friends: (1) start thinking about the assignment from the moment it's assigned; (2) don't press for thesis too early—if you're going to arrive at an insight about *Hamlet,* it should happen near the end of your thinking process, not the beginning; and (3) ask yourself a question (What drives Hamlet mad? What is the effect of increased numbers of Hispanic voters on recent presidential elections?). A question helps you stay focused on the idea that you're seeking *an answer.* The answer will be a thesis.

In Chapter 5, I'll talk more about thesis, particularly how they frequently incorporate, or imply, a "should." The following are some examples:

You should become vegan.

College students should take a semester to study abroad.

Those interested in preserving our downtown should boycott big-box stores.

The "should," however, often has little place in academic writing. If your thesis is "Hamlet had good reasons for going mad" or "The North was no less racist than the South during the Civil War," and there's nothing your reader "should do" about it, that's OK.

Audience in Academic Writing

Your audience in school is unlike any you'll encounter in the outside world, but you do have one, and the game is the same: understand how the reader thinks so you can predict his reactions and control them, in order to get what you want. In school you have a readership of one, one whose worldview is unknown and probably wildly different from yours, so predicting his responses becomes a Herculean task. But you have one advantage over the nonschool writer: the reader is standing right in front of you. So *ask him:*

What does he want? What format does he like? Does he want you to include a paraphrase of the reading assignment? Can the assignment be done as a list, or does it have to be in paragraphs?

And you can make some intelligent guesses. If you try to imagine how a teacher thinks, you can put together a list of things that are likely to please him and get the grade you're after. Grading papers is a chore, so if you make grading yours painless and rewarding, your teacher will love you. Thus you should do the following nine things:

1. *Answer the question,* if one was asked. State the answer boldly, so it's easy to see, and put it up front.
2. *Follow directions slavishly.* Every teacher has something specific in mind when he gives an assignment. Doing something else, no matter how well you do it, misses the point.
3. *Waste not a word.* Make sure the first sentence jumps right to the heart of the matter.
4. *Have a strong thesis,* and show the reader where it is.
5. *Highlight structure,* so the reader sees easily what's going on. If the assignment has asked you to do three things, consider using headings to show the grader where you're doing each one.
6. *Follow format.* Make the essay visually easy to read and to grade by having dark, clear print, a conventional font, and neat corrections, and by including all pertinent information—your full name, the course's full identification, and the date.
7. *Use a colon title* (Chapter 9) to let the reader know at the outset which assignment this is and that you have a point.
8. *Be interesting.* Boredom is the paper grader's biggest enemy. Your mission, should you choose to accept it, is to rouse the grader from her slumber and make her glad she read your essay. Be funny, daring, provocative, dramatic, and lively—if appropriate.
9. *Use a clear structure.* Both because the grader wants to read your work fast and because time is short, you may want to fit your essay into one of two standard cookie-cutter structures:

Thesis and Defense

a. State your thesis.
b. Explain, defend, support, gather evidence.
c. Discuss implications of your discovery.

Problem—Solution

a. Ask a question or state a problem.
b. Gather evidence and reason your way toward an answer.
c. Arrive at an answer or solution.

Purpose in Academic Writing

You have several purposes. The first to come to mind is getting a good grade. To accomplish this, follow Rules 1–9 above. Next, since your instructor usually has a very specific purpose in mind for every assignment, be sure you know exactly what it is and make it yours. If you're in any doubt, ask. Finally, school has a short list of general educational goals you can assume are yours unless the instructor tells you they aren't:

Show you did the reading and understood it through class discussions and written work. This is the skill at the heart of most college assignments.

Use the course tools. The course has been teaching you a set of skills, a methodology, a philosophy, and a body of knowledge; put them to use. If you've spent the last weeks working with feminist theory, use feminist theory in your paper. If the course has been practicing statistical analysis, use statistical analysis in your paper.

Talk the talk. In the Guide to Studying, we talked about the importance of joining the club. Write to demonstrate your membership in the club of scholars. The primary badge of membership is talking the talk—using the language of the course adopted by every course and each discipline. Literary criticism talks, for instance, about symbols, subtexts, archetypes, genres, and deconstruction. At first, using a dialect that isn't your own feels like faking, but mimicry is key to learning, and using the new words is the only way to ever make them your own. Also, you need the jargon—it helps you say things easily and concisely. To talk about literature without words like "symbol" and "archetype" is like talking about cars without being able to say "brakes" or "transmission." If the jargon doesn't facilitate your message making, you probably aren't using the course tools.

Note: This isn't contradictory to what we discussed earlier about not using big words just for the sake of using big words. In fact, this is using big words precisely *because* they're the right words. They're the words of the discipline, the language of the field of study in which you are working.

Perform a research-based analytical task. Academic writing seeks to teach you to gather data and to think critically. So *don't* design essays where your feelings, opinions, or personal experience are the sole source: "I love my old rickety car"; "Nobody I know cares about popular music anymore"; "I'll never forget my rafting trip through the Grand Canyon"; "There are no good men out there."

You can certainly use personal issues as a starting place, but redefine the task as an academic one. "My father's alcoholism tormented me when I was young" becomes "According to experts, what common psychological problems do children of alcoholic parents face?" "I think parents should stay home and take care of their small children instead of shipping them off to daycare" becomes "According to authorities in the field, how do children raised by stay-at-home parents and children raised primarily in daycare environments compare in terms of later mental health and success?" "I hate this short story—it's confusing" becomes "Why does the narrator in this story choose not to tell its events in chronological order?" Here are more such refocusings:

Personal Essay	Academic Essay
Infant circumcision is sexist.	Routine infant circumcision is brutal, has no demonstrable medical or health benefit, and should be discontinued.
Rape is a horrifying affront to women.	What are the accepted psychological theories on why people rape? What cultural factors produce a rape-prone society?
Nobody reads anymore.	How has technology changed teenagers' reading habits?

You'll know you have an academic task when you ask yourself, "How do I know my thesis is valid?" and the answer is *not* simply "Because that's how I feel" or "Because that's what I believe" but

because that's what the experts say.

because the evidence and the research say so.

because that's the logical conclusion to be drawn from the facts.

even, because that's what I've *witnessed.*

Use citations. Citations are those little asides in which you tell the reader where you got a quote, opinion, or piece of information (more on this in Part 5). If you are having that dialogue with other writers, you'll have to tell your reader every time you use someone else's words or ideas by adding a citation. The more citations you have, generally, the more academic the writing.

Students can get cynical about citations, and nearly everyone has ponied up a faked bibliography to make an essay look more researched than it is. But if you think about it, whenever you write on an issue of interest to a discipline, your writing is making a contribution to an ongoing conversation. So wouldn't you want to hear what other contributors have been saying on the matter?

Avoid plagiarism. Plagiarism is using a writer's work without attribution and thus implying it's yours. You're plagiarizing if you use another's words, thoughts, sequence of ideas, or anything else of value, without telling the reader where you found it. Since in the academy one's scholarship is the most valuable possession one has, and since academic writing requires constant use of other people's work, the danger of plagiarism is sky-high and the punishment Draconian: in any university with integrity, the penalty for plagiarism is expulsion.

The Internet has made plagiarism epidemic for lots of reasons: the information on the Internet is being given away and doesn't seem to belong to anyone; an author's name is often hard to find; it lacks the "weight" of publishing—no editing, printing, binding, or bookstore shelving—so you don't feel you owe it anything; there's no visible place of origin; traditional citation format doesn't work. For more on avoiding plagiarism—and on documenting and paraphrasing properly and legally—see Chapter 17.

Academic Writing as Performance

Even in school—in the most academic of writing—it's possible to write to real people who are interested and involved in what we're saying, who need our help or want to be touched, entertained, or amused—for most of us, that's the payoff in writing. Yet often in school, all that seems to have little place. One way to come back to that is to imagine that you're writing a paper to read to your classmates—or all geology majors, or all freshmen—at the end of the semester, maybe in a large lecture hall. Maybe it will win first place in your program's academic-writing contest, and there's a reception. You will be called to the lectern to share it with the crowd, who will appreciate your wit and enjoy being entertained. Imagine that.

There's another solution. I once had a student whose writing was playful and personal and delightful to read. I told him, "I love this stuff, but you know you can't write like this for other professors." He said, "Odd that you say that. I've been writing like this for years, and every instructor has liked it but told me that all the other professors wouldn't. I still haven't met the instructor who doesn't like my work, so I just keep doing it." If you try writing to your professor as if he were a real person reading you for pleasure, there's a good chance that he'll be grateful. (Again: Not sure what you can get away with? Talk to your instructor. Run a draft by her.)

HOW TO READ WRITING ASSIGNMENTS

You'll find a huge range of types of writing assignments in school. In some, you'll have lots of freedom to choose your topics, purposes, and audiences. In others, you will be more confined by the demands of your instructor and the nature of the assignment itself. In a basic-writing or first-year composition course, your instructor might ask you to write a simple narrative (about a significant event from your past, for example) or to respond to a brief quotation (for example, "Don't let your schooling interfere with your education"—Mark Twain). This assignment would probably come very early in the semester, and most likely the instructor would be using it to "diagnose" your writing: to look at how well you use specific supporting details, to determine your ability to acknowledge your reader, to measure your command of mechanics and convention. Some students like these kinds of prompts, because they're so open ended; others hate them for the same reason.

At the other extreme—and probably later in your academic career—you will run across assignments that ask you to do very specific things, usually incorporating lots of research (compare Frederick Douglass's and John Brown's views on abolition, or choose a major American corporation and discuss that company's environmental record for the purposes of potential "green" investors). Again, some students love these kinds of assignments, while others hate them. Either way, though, and for all kinds of assignments, there are certain things to keep in mind.

Following the Advice of Woody Allen

One of my favorite lines from the great American philosopher Woody Allen is from his film *Love and Death:* "Eighty percent of success is showing up." In fact, I use this in my classes all the time, by way of explaining how to read an assignment. I tell students that if they "show up," that is, simply do all that the assignment asks of them, they are almost guaranteed to do at least moderately well. If the assignment asks that they include at least three citations, then, by God, include at least three citations. If the assignment asks for MLA documentation format, then use MLA documentation format. If the assignment asks them to attach an abstract, then attach an abstract.

Obvious? Perhaps. But I'm always amazed at the number of students who fail an assignment simply because they didn't "show up" or follow the instructions. So that's the first rule: *read the instructions carefully, and do everything they ask you to do.* I recommend taking a highlighter to an assignment and highlighting everything that's required—and not just the due date. Then, before you hand it in, make sure you've done everything you highlighted. Chances are good you'll have completed Allen's "Eighty percent of success."

Instructions You're Likely to See on an Assignment— Highlight Them

Due date: Obvious, but hugely important.

Length: Some assignments ask for a specific number of pages, others for parameters (eight to ten pages). Give the instructor what she asks for. However, keep in mind that page requirements are *usually* provided to help you choose an appropriate topic and to suggest the degree to which your instructor expects you to explore that topic. Some instructors will ask for a ten-page paper and expect exactly that. Most are more interested in what you have to say than in whether you can meet a precise page requirement.

Format: MLA? APA? Cover page? Letter of transmittal? Abstract? Some instructors specify margin width, type size, even font. That stuff's easy. Do it as assigned. (For more on documentation format, see Chapter 17.)

Audience: Often instructors suggest an audience for your papers (your classmates, the local community, etc.). Make sure you know whom the

instructor expects you to write for. Sometimes instructors ask you to identify your audience yourself, perhaps in a simple sentence at the top of
page 1. Do so.

Required sources/citations: Some assignments will specify a certain number
of required citations, and sometimes there are requirements in addition to
the *number* required. Does the assignment specify at least two nonelec-
tronic sources? Real books? A personal interview? Do what it asks.

References to course material: Oftentimes instructors will ask that you
try to tie in material from the course. Example: You're taking a film
class and you've been assigned to choose a recent U.S. film to discuss.
Earlier in the semester, the instructor showed *Casablanca* to the class,
which he introduced with a lecture and then followed up by leading a
lively class discussion. Try to bring to your paper relevant material
from the lecture, the film, even the class discussion. It will show him
that you have internalized material on which he is basing his course.
Note: This suggests the importance of taking notes, sometimes even
when doing so might not seem immediately useful.

Asking Questions

Instructors generally do the best job they can to make their assignments as
clear as possible. That doesn't necessarily mean those assignments are going
to make perfect sense to everyone. In fact, chances are pretty good that at
least some of the class will have questions. If you're among them, instead
of guessing what your instructor meant—instead of feeling your way in the
dark and taking a chance on not "showing up"—meet with her. Tell her
you're not sure what she meant by something and that you'd like
clarification.

Important note: Don't accuse the teacher of being unclear, even if he is.
Turn it around: "Now it's probably just me, but I'm not really sure what
you meant by this passage about including only academic journals. Are online
journals acceptable?"

It's also good to approach your instructor if you have an idea for a
response to the assignment that might be "risky," or outside the assignment's
parameters. Let's say your instructor has asked you to research and write
about a woman who has had an impact on U.S. culture and has provided
examples such as Susan B. Anthony, Betty Ford, and Maya Angelou. But
you have an idea: you think that Tina Fey or Beyonce has also had a large
impact on U.S. culture. Would she be an acceptable topic for the paper?
Maybe or maybe not, but you can easily find out by asking your instructor.
She'll say either, "No, I want you to write about someone in politics," or,
"Yes! That's a *brilliant* idea. I can't wait to see your paper." But ask whether
your idea is appropriate *before* you do the work and turn it in. Otherwise,
you might not even be "showing up."

IN-CLASS AND TIMED WRITING

This kind of writing is not as common in schools as it was in the past, for good reason: most instructors realize that a good piece of writing comes about as a result of thinking, researching, assembling sources, revising, and so forth—all the things we've been talking about. That said, there are two reasons instructors might have students do timed writing or give an in-class essay exam: (1) A writing instructor (or composition program or English department) might simply want to see that you have a decent command of mechanics—spelling, subject-verb agreement, sentence boundaries, and the like—to include when assessing your work for your final grade, knowing that you most likely had help editing your take-home work (as we all do!). (2) The instructor of a "content" course (French, Art History, Introduction to Psychology, etc.) might want to make sure that you've learned the concepts of the course and have internalized them enough to discuss them without using other sources.

In a Writing Course

1. Allow yourself some time to mull over your approach before you begin writing, since you probably won't have time to go back and do major rewriting or restructuring. Jot down some notes, ideas, details, and possible support.
2. Make sure your thesis or main claim is clear and straightforward.
3. Use concrete and specific support. If it's a narrative or personal essay ("Write about a teacher who had an impact on you"), use lots of interesting and specific details (see Chapter 12).
4. Have an imaginary reader in your head.
5. Allow plenty of time to proofread, and do so carefully, assuming you'll find some mistakes. If you have time, read your essay backward, sentence by sentence, so that you don't get caught up in the "flow" of what you've written.
6. Know what types of mistakes you habitually make ("there" for "their," for example, or run-on sentences), and pay special attention to those areas.
7. Write as neatly as you can, and make corrections unobtrusive. Best just to cross out a misspelled word and write it correctly above.
8. If, as you're proofreading, you think of something that you'd like to add—perhaps another example—insert an asterisk where it should go, and then put another asterisk several lines below the end of the essay, and add your example. A fair-minded reader should follow your instructions, understanding the nature of the situation.

In a Content Course

1. Study for the essay by going over the course concepts. Use note cards. Make sure you're clear on definitions.

2. Practice using the course concepts in contexts other than that which your instructor or textbook has provided. If you've been talking about French impressionist painters, research a painting or painter from the period *not* covered in a lecture or the book. Show your instructor that you've made connections outside the parameters of the course.

3. Keep in mind how many essays your instructor will be reading in response to the prompt—and how many she's probably read in the past. Imagine your essay buried in a pile. Surprise her.

4. See points 5 through 8 under "In a Writing Course", p. 40.

Part Two

Planning and Drafting

Chapter 4

Choosing Topics and Getting Started

The next eight chapters guide you through a series of steps called the writing process: prewriting, drafting, organizing, polishing, editing, and submitting. The step-by-step approach can be helpful because it reminds you that you don't have to do everything at once. But there's a danger to steps: they suggest that the writing process is a lot neater and more regimented than it really is.

Most writers don't do one step, then the other; instead, they do them all, all the time. The mind's a messy place, and it's happiest when multitasking: it will leap from note taking to paragraph writing to outlining to rewriting. When you're writing page 7, it will be rewriting page 5 and thinking up great lines for page 10 or another essay. You must let your brain go about its messy business. *Take what comes, whenever it comes.* When I write, I constantly insert into parentheses stuff that I don't have time to think about right then. It might be a note to find a better word, later; it might be a reminder to keep that part of the essay in mind when I write the conclusion. It might be a note to myself to remember to return someone's phone call, or to prune the hedge out back. Naturally, all that parenthetical stuff comes out later.

WHERE DO GOOD ESSAYS COME FROM?

Some people have no trouble finding things to write about. For others, it's the hardest part of writing. Sometimes, we don't have as much choice as we'd like to because of the assignment and the parameters we're forced to work within.

In a sense, we know we all have lots to say because we all talk effortlessly and endlessly with our friends. So "having nothing to write about" can mean only *that we define writing in some unhealthy way* that gives us writer's block. So we can solve the problem by *redefining writing to be more like talking to our friends*.

First, we know that writing isn't about having a rare moment of inspiration or a unique experience, because we know we don't talk to our friends only when we've had a stroke of genius or have just gotten back from Nepal. We talk all the time, about everything. And writers write about everything. Writing essays is like being funny. A comic isn't a person who happens to have funny things happen to him; he's a person who sees humor in whatever happens. Similarly, an essayist lives a life like yours; she just sees the potential essay in what she experiences. Here's the essayist John Gregory Dunne explaining how it works:

> My house was burgled twice and the two resulting pieces netted me a lot more than the burglars got. I can recall one columnist who eked three columns out of his house burning down: one on the fire, a second on the unsung dignity of fire fighting, and a third on his insurance adjuster and a long view on the charred artifacts of a lifetime. So avid for material is your average columnist that once, when my daughter caught my wife and me *flagrante delicto,* I seriously wondered if there was a column in it. (As it turned out, only a column mention.)

Once you catch on to the trick, you'll have more essay topics than time to explore them.

Second, the difference between talking to friends and writing is not one of *content* but of *audience*. It's not that you have nothing to say; it's that you have nothing to say that *you think your imaginary essay audience wants to hear*. You're trying to write to instructors, bosses, or other authority figures, and you're telling yourself they want to read only something that's never been said before and is brilliant. But most writers don't write to those audiences. Granted, sometimes circumstances force you to write only to your instructor, and you will probably someday find yourself writing a memo to an employer. On the other hand, most writing is for the author's peers or novices (people like themselves or people who know less than they do), and they only ask themselves to say something their peers will find touching, interesting, or useful. Once you think this way, you realize that everything you know or have experienced is of use to someone, because people who haven't experienced it can profit from your knowledge and people who have will appreciate knowing they're not alone:

> If you've ever been anywhere, you can tell people who haven't been there what it's like.

If you've ever done anything, you can show how to do it to people who don't know.

If you've ever read a book, seen a movie, or eaten in a restaurant, you can review it and tell potential customers whether it's worth the money.

If you've ever suffered, you can assume others are suffering the same way, and you can assure them what they're going through is normal.

If anything ever happened to you that was funny, touching, or infuriating, you can describe it, ideally getting at what was universally human about the experience.

You don't even have to be smart, because humans are happy to hear you talk about your ignorance, confusion, and doubt. In fact, not only do you not need to be exceptionally smart, but look at it this way: how do you respond to someone who talks as though he has all the answers, that he's got everything, or at least the topic at hand, all figured out? Personally, I immediately get skeptical, turned off by arrogance. I much prefer to be around people who have questions, who are puzzled, and who are self-effacing. Writing's like that too. You're much more likely to win over your reader if you demonstrate a sense that you're trying to figure it out. Obviously, your reader will feel ripped off if she gets to the end of your essay and isn't rewarded in some way; your thesis can't be "I don't have a clue." However, if you ask some interesting questions, or even suggest looking at something in a new way, you're way more likely to be successful than if you "preach." For example, wonderful essay topics—for the appropriate audiences—would be how bewildering it is to be a freshman on campus, how hilariously confusing it was the time you tried to set up the Bluetooth in your car stereo by following the instructions in the owner's manual, or how you're of two minds about getting married.

To convince yourself that most good writing springs from minds and lives like yours, consider these topics of student essays:

I went home for vacation and had to listen to my father tell me one more time how he disapproves of my life.

Mornings with my two-year-old are a joyous, comical circus.

I wonder if this semester I'll finally get organized and actually get something out of school.

Why are men genetically unable to clean bathrooms, pick up their underwear from the floor, or find the milk in the refrigerator?

The last time I got panhandled I said no. I felt guilty, but I'm not sure I should have.

My mother never listens.

I may have finally found a car mechanic I can trust.

There's nothing new or dazzling there, but they all made good essays. And for a final bit of evidence, here's a splendid essay about the most trivial of subjects:

THE EGG AND I REVISITED

KRIS TACHMIER

Student Essay

Kids can be finicky eaters. My own three-year-old son will put up determined resistance if he sees one Brussels sprout on his plate. One hour after dinner that singular Brussels sprout will still be on his plate, undisturbed. Similarly, my seventeen-month-old daughter cringes at the sight of a carrot and immediately clamps her jaws shut, making passage into her mouth by a fork laden with the vegetable impossible. But I really have no right to single out my children when their own mother is the classic persnicketist: I cannot and will not eat eggs.

Ever since I can remember, I have hated eggs. I'm not really certain why—maybe it's their texture, or maybe it's the notion that they're really hen ova, or maybe it's the idea that eggs can assume so many disguises. A Brussels sprout will always remain a Brussels sprout; a carrot remains a carrot; but an egg will scramble, fry, poach, coddle, benedict, and devil in the twinkling of an eye. I simply cannot trust eggs.

For a while, my childhood breakfasts included some sort of egg concoction, but the minute my mother stepped out of the kitchen I would sneak over to the sink, tilt my plate upside down, and watch the shimmering yellow creation slip down into the darkened cavity of the drain. This bit of cunning was a great success until one fateful morning. I must have left a few damning fragments of eggy evidence. I was interrogated by my mother: how long, how often, how come? The next morning a glorious bowl of Cheerios was awaiting me. The egg and I were finally separated.

In the years following, my mother learned to keep eggs out of my path, but all her efforts were not enough. During lunch at high school I would invariably sit next to someone who would pull a hardboiled egg out of his sack (together with one of those miniature salt shakers) and sit there happily sprinkling and munching on it. Too bad he never stopped long enough to notice me turning green on his left … I might have spoiled his appetite. And there was always some inconsiderate friend who ordered egg salad sandwiches at restaurants. The mixture would always be thick and runny, and globs of it were forever dripping out of all sides of the sandwich.

With marriage, I realized that my attitude toward eggs was a little ridiculous. I decided to give the egg a second chance. I can remember the event clearly: the morning sun was shining, the smell of fresh-perked coffee filled the kitchen, and there, flattened out in submission on my plate, was one fried egg, barely distinguishable for all the salt and pepper I had poured over it. I resolutely picked up my fork, stabbed a section of the egg, thrust it into my mouth, gulped it down, felt it rumbling its way toward my stomach, and blanched as I realized it was rocketing out of my mouth. So much for a second crack at the egg.

Today I still keep my mouth empty of eggs, but my refrigerator is full of them. For the last year or so I've been raising chickens. Every day I march out to the coop and gather a half-dozen freshly laid eggs. As soon as I have several dozen I call up friends to check if they want any eggs free of cost. I think the operation a stroke of genius: I have cleverly combined charity with penitence.

—Permission provided by Steve Metzger

Assuming you hate at least one kind of food, I'll rest my case. Now let's look at some practical ways to encourage those potential essays to make themselves known to us.

FOUR PRINCIPLES FOR GETTING GOOD IDEAS

Here are some things to keep in mind that will greatly increase the chances of your finding good ideas to explore in essays:

1. Don't begin with a topic.
2. Think all the time.
3. Go from little, concrete things to big, abstract ones.
4. Connect.

Since getting ideas and learning are similar processes, many of these are revisitings of principles in the Guide to Studying. We'll talk about each in turn.

1. Don't Begin with a Topic

A topic is the thing you're writing about, the subject: human trafficking, performance-enhancing drugs, your first date, how to apply a tourniquet. Anything that fits in the following blank is a topic: "This essay is about ___." If a topic could start an essay, we could open the dictionary and point.

Good seeds for essays come in other forms:

Questions: "Is there any real difference between the Republicans and the Democrats anymore?" "Will recycling my glass and plastic really make any difference?" "Is there a realistic future for electric automobiles?"

Problems: "I'm always behind in my work." "Violent crimes against women are on the increase."

Intentions: "I want to tell people about what's really going on in this class." "I want to let people know about alternatives to the corporate coffee chains."

Theses: "You should patronize locally owned coffee shops instead of corporate-owned ones." "Old people are the victims of silent injustice in our culture."

Feelings: "I was furious when the instructor suddenly announced there would be a term paper no one knew about due in three weeks." "I was surprised to see my father crying."

2. Think All the Time

We talked about this earlier. If you have a sense of humor, you know that the surest way to prevent yourself from being funny is to have someone demand that you be funny *now*. Instead, mull over ideas for essays—and essays in progress—all the time as you go through your days. Honestly, I've come up with some of my best ideas for essays while riding my bicycle through the park, trout fishing, listening to music, watching movies, and reading my favorite magazines.

Reacting.   One popular, poisonous metaphor for thinking is the lightbulb clicking on over our head—the notion that ideas spring from within us, caused by nothing. To become good thinkers, we have to replace that metaphor with another: think of thoughts as billiard balls on a pool table, idle until other balls—external stimuli—slam into them and set them in motion. Seeds for essays are *re*-actions—we have them in response to prompts. Many of us have learned to separate input and output modes: we are either putting information into our brains or asking our brains to put out thoughts, but we don't do the two jobs at the same time. But when things are going in is the best time to try to get things out. Children do this naturally; try reading a book to a three-year-old, and listen to her react to everything she hears or sees, or take her to a movie and watch her struggle not to talk back to the screen.

I recently overheard an odd conversation in the hallway outside my office. A young woman of eighteen or nineteen was talking on her cell phone, and I was hardly paying attention. But then I heard her say, in a bit more urgent voice than she had been using, "We've got to get her to stop doing meth." I was astonished. College students talking about meth with firsthand experience? I was suddenly forced to reconsider what I thought were the life experiences my students were bringing to college. I had thought these "kids" led pretty sheltered lives, but here was evidence to the contrary. And a perfect essay topic: not all college students are as naïve as they might seem to be.

And there are lots of ways to explore such an essay. It could be written as the personal story of a college instructor's epiphany, learning his world was not what he thought it was. It could be written as an argument, with either students or instructors as its audience: get to know your classmates/students; they might need more help navigating their personal lives than you think. Or it could be written as an informative piece about the prevalence of drugs on campus, in which case it would require a significant amount of research.

Are you a reactor? Answer the following questions:

Do you find yourself silently talking back to the newspaper when you read it?

Do you write in the margins of books you read?

Are at least 25 percent of the notes you take during course lectures your own thoughts, questions, doubts, and reactions?

As you meet up with life's outrages, do you find yourself complaining to imaginary audiences in your head?

After you see a movie that you really like, are you eager to tell people about it and encourage them to see it?

When you listen to a speaker or a teacher, do you find yourself itching to get to the question-and-answer period?

If you said no to these questions, you're going to have to practice your reacting skills.

Content Prompts. Reading can move you to write if it makes you want to say something back. Many years ago, *Harper's* magazine published an essay by Jerry Jesness called "Why Johnny Can't Fail" (September 1999), in which Jesness, a career teacher, slammed the public school system for what he called "the floating standard," by which all students are allowed to pass and standards are simply lowered when students can't meet them. One of Professor Rawlins's students was bothered by the piece and was moved to respond:

LONG LIVE THE FLOATING STANDARD

NANCY GUINTA

Student Essay

He's a beautiful child, kind-hearted, personable. He loves people and they love him. Last winter he worked at a ski resort in the mountains, and they loved him for his enthusiasm and his energy. He even won the Employee of the Month award. His dream was to be allowed to run the snow plow. He's now working his way through the local community college while toying with several dreams: being a professional snowboarder and being a brewmaster are just two.

High school was difficult for him. Science and chemistry lured him, math tormented him, English often baffled him. He was triumphant at high school graduation, and it never would have happened if a host of sympathetic teachers hadn't given him the extra credit assignments and art projects that allowed him to pass. I thank them—those teachers with the floating standards. Without them, my son would be without a diploma, unable to go on to college, branded a failure ... and who would have gained?

Kids the schools fail—what happens to them? Homeless people, criminals, welfare recipients, drunks—people who have been rejected by society, and who take it out on themselves and us for the rest of their lives. If we let them pass, we just prolong the time they have to find themselves and choose to become productive and not live off you and me. And how much does it really matter if they don't do the science experiment very well or their insight into *To Kill a Mockingbird* isn't sufficiently deep? Failing them just makes sure they're cut off from the real lessons of school: how to be a member of the team, how to work with other people, how to communicate, how to love learning. My son is a perfect example. The essays may have had a lot of spelling errors, but he came through the system looking at life and saying, "I can do this."

Anyway, floating standards don't end at the high school's parking lot. They're in every college, every company, on every job site. In any university you can find classes where the assignments are few and the grading is easy. Yet every study shows that going to college benefits those who go. The system is always set up to let those who can't perform slide by. By letting them slide, we let them learn.

Eventually, each individual decides what standards to set for himself in this life. I hope my son sets high ones for himself. He seems to be doing that. And I believe he is doing that largely because the System kept telling him "You're still one of us" until the maturity had time to kick in.

—Permission provided by Steve Metzger

Models.   You can use your reading to inspire you to explore new techniques. You read the piece and say, "Wow! I like the way she did that. I'd never have thought to do it that way. Maybe I could do something sort of like it." That's called *modeling*. People who are learning to do things do it all the time. You watch a good dancer, tennis player, or guitarist, and then you try to do it like that. Naturally, in time, you'll develop your own moves, serve, or licks, but when you're learning, it's a good idea to try to do it like people who do it well. You can use any technical feature as a model: the structure, the opener, the tone, the use of dialogue or narrative, the use of the ellipsis or the dash—anything you never tried before. Here's an inspiring model, a description by the poet E.E. Cummings of his father:

My father ... was a New Hampshire man, 6 foot 2, a crack shot & a famous fly fisherman & a first-rate sailor (his sloop was named The Actress) & a woodsman who could find his way through forests primeval without a compass & a canoeist who'd still-paddle you up to a deer without ruffling the surface of a pond & an ornithologist & taxidermist & (when he gave up hunting) an expert photographer (the best I've ever seen) & an actor who portrayed Julius Caesar in Sanders Theatre & a painter (both in oils & watercolors) & a better carpenter than any professional & an architect who designed his own houses before building them & (when he liked) a plumber who just for the fun of it installed all his own waterworks & (while at Harvard) a teacher with small use for professors ... & my father had the first telephone in Cambridge & (long before any Model T Ford) he piloted an Orient Buckboard with Friction Drive produced by the Waltham watch company & ... my father's voice was so magnificent that he was called on to impersonate God speaking from Beacon Hill (he was heard all over the common) & my father gave me Plato's metaphor of the cave with my mother's milk.

Here are two essays that students were inspired by E.E. Cummings' model to write:

Dave's porch has everything you ever wanted in a porch and more & it is located right next to the freshman dorms & you sit there in the sunshine & you can meet tons of people and most of those people are girls & they like to drink beer & we are always drinking beer on the porch & that way we can meet girls & we like the porch because it has a big chair on it and it's comfortable and the porch is made of redwood and Dave and Phil built it (with Dave's dad's wood) & it's sturdy & it's small but it's fine & you get to see all the people drive by & I can't think of where I'd rather be than on Dave's porch.

(JEFF OCHS)

My ex-boyfriend was a baby-faced, wavy-haired blonde with blue eyes that could be warm as a smile while his thoughts would be as cold as ice scraping against raw metal and he could charm anyone like an alligator and you couldn't get away because he would find you and follow you silently and he would watch and find out every move you made and he would just wait and wait until you made a wrong move and then he would pounce with words like claws and he was a better liar than anyone I ever knew and he would look at you with those alligator eyes and you would freeze like a deer caught in headlights because he knew you were scared and he wanted you to be scared because he let you know that he would hurt you if you ever crossed him because he collected guns and throwing stars that he would throw, embedding them deep into wood, and he would always carry two knives on his belt, one visible and one hidden, and you knew they were there and he knew that you knew and that's what he wanted and he would manipulate anyone like a chess piece (not that he ever learned to play chess, it was a sissy game) and he would do whatever he could to whoever he could to get what he wanted with that alligator smile that was like someone walking over your grave and he wants to be a politician.

(KATHLEEN SIEMONT)

Responding to Visuals.   Many writers get inspiration from what they see. In fact, while a picture may indeed be worth a thousand words, sometimes a picture can *inspire* millions. Consider how much has been written in response to the flag raising on Iwo Jima or the Twin Towers collapsing on 9/11, for example. I was recently inspired to write a short essay about one of the most powerful visual images I've ever come across: at the Lincoln Memorial in Washington, D.C., several years ago, I watched a young African-American father bend down on one knee beside his small son, point up to the words on the wall, and read out loud to him the "Emancipation Proclamation," just yards from where, forty years earlier, Martin Luther King Jr., had given his "I Have a Dream Speech."

Similarly, a poet might respond to a sunset or a rainstorm—or like William Wordsworth to a field of daffodils and Walt Whitman to a battlefield. Woody Guthrie, John Lennon, Bruce Springsteen, and Bono—among countless others—have written songs in response to visual images. And in fact, it's some writers' jobs: the art critic, for example, has to look at a photograph, painting, or sculpture and respond with written words—and indeed, it's common in art history classes for students to be assigned to write papers in response to artwork.

Technical writers, too, frequently must look at graphs and charts and drawings and put those data into words. And then sometimes it works the other way around: they convert text into visual images. Either way, in technical writing, and often in long research projects in school, images and text complement each other to make the material more accessible to the reader. (I'll talk about this more in Chapter 18.)

As a student writer, you can use what you see to inspire you to write. Certainly you've been moved by images: Why did you choose the screen saver you're currently using? Why use that particular photo for your Facebook profile? Obviously, those images mean something to you. Can you convey that in a meaningful way to a reader? Can you use the image as a springboard into an essay? Perhaps the photo on your parents' wall of you and the first fish you ever caught could inspire an essay about your decision to go into the field of wildlife management. Perhaps the photo of the cows crowded into the corral and awaiting slaughter could jump-start an essay about the reasons to be a vegan.

3. Go From Little, Concrete Things to Big, Abstract Ones

The best thinking follows a predictable course: from little, concrete bits of experience to large, abstract implications. You see an ad on TV, start thinking about it, and it leads you to speculations on American consumerism, media manipulation, and the marketing of women's bodies. Or you see a parent disciplining a child in a grocery-store aisle just for being alive, and it makes you think, "Why are people without training or talent allowed to do this all-important job called child raising?" or "Parents need time off too."

Many of the essays in this book model this progress from a minor personal experience to a big issue. In "Why I Never Cared for the Civil War" ("A Collection of Good Writing"), Shawni Allred studied a muddy pool of water in the fifth grade and used the experience to discuss what's wrong with traditional classroom teaching styles. In "Given the Chance" (Chapter 14) Melissa Schatz met Stacey, and her experience with Stacey led her to question the entire state drug rehabilitation program.

4. Connect

We talked about connecting before (Prologue). A lot of thinking begins by noticing that two things are related. Here's an example. One day when I was a freshman at a community college in California, I was driving to an afternoon class. It was pouring rain, and I was on the freeway in an old

Volkswagen Beetle, the windshield wipers working feebly to try to keep the windshield clear of sheets of water.

It so happened that I hated the class I was going to; in fact, I didn't like most of my classes and wasn't even very happy about being in college. I didn't have a major, didn't have direction. Everything seemed too complicated, too difficult. I wished I were back in high school, where little mattered except my friends and just showing up for class. Life was so much simpler then.

As I drove through the rain, I found myself glancing into the rear-view mirror, out of which I could see perfectly clearly. When I looked ahead into the storm, I could hardly see. I looked through the mirror again and out the back window. Perfectly clear. So clear, in fact, that I was drawn to keep looking out the back window instead of out the front.

Suddenly, I felt the bump, bump, bump of the lane dividers. I had accidentally almost swerved into the next lane! I quickly corrected, and told myself to keep looking ahead.

That's when it hit me: "Keep looking ahead." Of course, it was easier to look behind me, but that's not what I needed to see. I needed to look in front of me, even if that were more difficult, not as clear. If I kept looking behind me—wishing I were still in high school—I would surely drive right off the road.

I didn't go to class that afternoon. Instead, I went to see an academic adviser to talk about my future, and I ended up filling out the application to a four-year college. It would be difficult, I knew, and sometimes not as clear, but at least now I was looking forward, not behind me.

It's hard to say how those kinds of connections are made, and sometimes you make them when you try to, when you think about making them. But, strangely, sometimes you just make them. They seem to come out of nowhere. All the more reason to be thinking about—or at least be open to—new ideas and ways of seeing your world.

Naturally, the more *un*-like two things are and the less obvious the connection, the more fresh and stimulating is the connection when you make it. This is the Head Principle. Howard Head was an aeronautical engineer who went skiing for the first time in 1947. Apparently no one had ever connected aircraft technology and skiing before. Frustrated with his wooden skis, Mr. Head suspected that he could make a better ski if he simply made it with the principles and materials used in making airplane wings. He invented the Head ski, the first metal, laminate ski, revolutionized the ski industry (as many of you know, the Head company now makes snowboards, as well), and made millions of dollars. He then did the same thing with tennis, inventing the Prince racket. Apparently aircraft engineers didn't play tennis either.

The Head Principle says you can't predict what will connect with what. So you can't tell yourself what information to seek. You can only amass experience and information voraciously and stir it all up together. If I'd been trying to think about how driving through the rain was symbolic, or trying to think of something that reflected where my life was heading, I might never have made the connection, but because I was open to the possibility of connection—to the fact that unexpected things can relate to one another—it happened. If you're writing about Charles Dickens and you read only about Charles Dickens, you're just making sure you won't make any connections except those other Dickens critics have already made. Instead, go read *Psychology Today,* read Hillary Clinton's memoirs, see a movie, watch a documentary on insect societies, or visit a mortuary.

Most of us do the exact opposite of these four idea-getting principles. We set aside a block of time for thinking, cut ourselves off from the outside world by locking ourselves in a stimulus-free study room, and look within ourselves for a large, abstract topic to write on. If you're doing any of that, you're less likely to be successful.

The following essay by Garrison Keillor, who was inspired to write it simply by going to church, seems to incorporate all of the principles for getting ideas. First, I'm willing to bet that **he didn't start with a topic** (being nice in a mean world). Also, the essay is a result of his noting what was going on around him and **connecting** it to things he'd obviously been **thinking** about a lot, for a long time, which allowed him to **go from little, concrete things to big, abstract ones.**

RENOUNCING EVIL POWERS AND ANONYMITY

GARRISON KEILLOR

I went to church in San Francisco on Sunday, the big stone cathedral on Nob Hill, whose name comes from an old slang term for a rich person, where a gaggle of railroad and mining tycoons built their palaces high above the squalid tenements of the poor back in the Gilded Age, and there with considerable pomp we baptized a dozen infants into the fellowship of faith and renounced the evil powers of this world, which all in all is a good day's work.

The term "evil powers" is one you hear only in the church or in Marvel comic books or Republican speeches, and it isn't something I renounce every day. I am a romantic Democrat, raised on William Saroyan and Pete Seeger and Preston Sturges, and we have faith in the decency of the little guy, and we believe you can depend on the kindness of strangers. But it ain't necessarily so.

Evil lurks in the heart of man, and anonymity tends to bring it out. Internet flamers would never say the jagged things they do if they had to sign their names. Road rage is anonymous; there is no equivalent pedestrian rage or bicyclist rage. (Have you ever yelled vile profanities at a fellow motorist—a spontaneous outburst—and then found that you're holding a cell phone in your hand and a female colleague is on the other end? I have, and it is excruciating.) War requires very well-brought-up people to do vicious things that they are able to do efficiently because the recipients of their viciousness are unknown to them. The bombardier never sees the quiet, shady street of brick houses that he is about to incinerate.

I want to believe in the kindness of strangers. I believe that if voters actually knew gay couples, they would not vote to ban gay marriage. This particular cruelty is the result of social separation, which breeds contempt. I know something about that, having spent time in grad school. When I was 24, I was an insufferable snob, thanks to lofty isolation from the ordinary tumult of life, and what cured me eventually was entering the field of light, frothy entertainment. When you strive to amuse a crowd of strangers, you have to drop your pants, and a man without pants gives up the right to look down on anybody.

We liberals can be as rigidly humorless as anybody else: You learn that writing a newspaper column. Hard-shell Baptists have nothing on us when it comes to self-righteousness. Mostly we look down on Republicans and the iconic small-town values that they have exploited so successfully, and yet, deep down, we share those values. We admire personal enterprise, we are wary of the power and blindness of big bureaucracies, and we do not admire self-pity. When I hear long tales of woe—Poor Me, my benighted life—my inner Republican thinks, "That was you who poured all that alcohol down your gullet. You. Nobody else. And why didn't you work a little harder in school? Duh. Your mama tried to tell you and you sneered at her. You did it to yourself, pal. You got on the train to Nowheresville, and guess what? You arrived."

The center of civility in our society is not the small town but the big city, where you learn to thread your way through heavy traffic and subdue your aggressiveness and extend kindness to strangers. Small-town Republicans are leery of big cities and the anonymity they bestow, but there is no better place to learn the delicate ballet of social skill. Isolation is a difficult trick for a pedestrian, even with music pouring into your ears.

And here, this morning, in a city famous for eccentricity, we strangers in Grace Cathedral embrace other people's children and promise to fight the good fight on their behalf, a ceremony that never fails to bring tears to my eyes. We renounce evil powers. I renounce isolation and separation and the splendid anonymity of the Internet and the doink-doink-doink of the clicker propelling me through six Web sites in five minutes. I vow to put my feet on the ground and walk through town and make small talk with clerks and call my mother on the phone and put money in the busker's hat. We welcome the infants into our herd, and though some of them sob bitter tears at the prospect, they are now in our hearts and in our prayers, and we will not easily let them go.

—Keillor, Garrison, "Renouncing evil powers and anonymity," CHIGAGO TRIBUNE, January 14, 2010. Copyright © 2010 by Tribune Media Services.

Garrison Keillor is writer, musician, storyteller, and the host of Minnesota Public Radio's *A Prairie Home Companion.*

WRITING FROM RAGE

If your due date is near and you're still having trouble finding a topic, there might be a way out: *write from rage.* I've had students write uninspired, boring essays all semester long until something finally makes them angry enough to respond in writing, and suddenly their text springs to life. In fact, one of my favorite pieces of my own writing came about when, after being awakened early one Sunday morning by the neighbor's leaf blower, I went to the computer and wrote a guest editorial for our local newspaper.

Titled "The Monsters of Fall," the piece took to task those hideous machines that I felt were shattering the peace and quiet of otherwise lovely weekend autumn mornings.

Similarly, I recently had a student come to me to apologize for not submitting a paper that had been due the previous class meeting—she said she had no idea what to write about. Something else was bothering her, too: it turned out that she was a former substance abuser (heroin and alcohol, to my astonishment), and was angry at the lack of support on campus. A friend of hers attended a college in a different part of the state and had told her that that campus offered an organized support group, drop-in counseling, and a twenty-four-hour "hot line" for students trying to stay—or to get—sober. "Why can't we have something like that here?" she said, frustrated. "I thought you said you didn't have a topic for your paper," I said. Her face lit up. "I could write about that, couldn't I?" Well, she did, and then turned that short paper into a long inquiry-based end-of-term research paper about how best to start such a program. Last I talked to her, she was working with administration officials to start her own support group here on our campus.

A word of caution: writing from rage can get you in big trouble too. Surely you've been made angry by a friend's email—or behavior—and fired off a response before waiting to cool down and think clearly and rationally. That can happen just as easily in essay writing. While the rage can fuel your writing, you need to be able to step back enough from your subject so that you can see it clearly—and realize the effect you'll have on your reader. Once when Ernest Hemingway was living in Florida, his editor, visiting from New York, commented on the beauty of the area and asked the famous writer why he hadn't written about it. Hemingway responded, "Because I haven't been away from it for ten years." So let your emotions fire you up, but be cool and rational—and try to get some distance from your topic when you write.

FROM FIRST THOUGHTS TO DRAFTS

One way to get into trouble with an essay or academic paper is to expect too much from an early draft. Don't worry yet about what the finished product is going to look like. This stage can be playful, messy, and meandering. For me it's sort of like working on a potter's wheel. You've got an ugly lump of clay spinning round and round in front of you, and you start to give it shape, lift the sides up, then ... nah. Looks like crap. Back down into an ugly lump of clay, then back into a new shape. Hmmm. A little better. You're starting with the same material, but trying out different ways it can work. (Of course, some potters have a very clear idea what their finished product will look like, as do some writers.)

Writing instructors call this early phase "prewriting." You can call it anything you want, or nothing at all. I don't care.

Many people, without saying so, have decided that this kicking-around stage shouldn't have to happen and that if it does, something's wrong. My students are always surprised when I tell them how different my own first drafts are from the final and often published versions. Honestly, you might not recognize that a first and "final" draft were written by the same person, and in fact, you might think that the topics weren't even the same. In that case, you'd often be right. I frequently use drafts to figure out what I want to say, and along the way change my topic altogether. I once (thought I) was working on an essay about how easily and inexpensively one can keep a car in good running condition, but as I worked my way through the first few drafts, the essay sort of took on a mind of its own—like it wanted to be about something else. For a couple of drafts, then, it was about my father teaching me to drive, and from there it became a very personal piece about how painful it was to lose a friend in an automobile accident.

More recently, I was writing a travel essay about a cross-country road trip that my wife and I took, including a very moving visit to the Flight 93 Memorial in eastern Pennsylvania. I had the piece almost done—I'd written five or six drafts—but something was missing. I wasn't sure what. Then one day, we were talking about the memorial with our good friend Francesca, who has lived all over the world, including in France, Senegal, Japan, and the Philippines. The attempts to take back control of the plane, she said, seemed "like a very American thing." In fact her Japanese friend, Tomo, had agreed, at the time telling her he couldn't imagine Japanese attempting such a thing.

And then I had it—not only a conclusion to the essay, but a way to frame the whole piece. Of course, I had to go back through and revise significantly (again!) to make that stuff work, but it did—many people told me that that was the best part of essay. So, another example not only of "thinking all the time" but also of being open to allowing your writing to come to you in ways you can't predict. (I've taken the liberty of reprinting that essay in the back of the book in "A Collection of Good Writing." I hope that doesn't seem arrogant....)

Another analogy: the football teams need to get out there before the game starts so that the players can warm up, but most of the fans just want to see the game, not the players doing jumping jacks. Likewise, you need to "warm up," but most readers aren't interested in reading that stuff. But they want to be there for the kickoff.

Drafting should be as easy as talking, and most of us talk without effort. But it isn't, and the only difference is fear. When we write, we feel there's a lot on the line, and it freezes us. But remember, *one of the main goals of drafting is to keep the words coming—don't worry whether or not they're what you'll end up with.* If you can keep the words coming, you'll write your way to good stuff.

WRITER'S BLOCK: MYTH OR REALITY?

I was once at a journalism conference where there were roughly equal numbers of students, professors, and professional journalists. After one particularly stimulating session about writing editorials, there was question-and-answer time for the panel. A member of the audience stood up and asked a newspaper editor if he ever got writer's block. The editor's answer was honest and simple: "I don't have time for writer's block."

That is, he works on deadline and simply has to get the job done. Can you imagine a plumber stopping suddenly and saying, "Sorry, I can't go on. I have plumber's block"? Or a dairy farmer: "Sorry, I have milker's block." The editor simply sat at his desk and did the work he had to do.

Obviously, writing is different in many ways, but a big part of writing is simply sitting down in front of your computer and writing—it will get done. If you have to wait for the muses, you're likely to wait a very long time. Besides, the muses are much more likely to "speak" to you when you're sitting there writing than when you're in the kitchen making cookies because you're telling yourself—and perhaps others—that you have writer's block.

Conversely, writer's block can be a very real problem, which people get largely because they define writing and their relationship to it in terms opposite to the ones we practiced in Chapter 1. They don't feel like writers. So they try to be someone they're not when they write; they try to fake it. They write to people they aren't comfortable talking to. They equate their writing with their self-worth: "If I write a bad essay, I'm a bad person." So they ask too much of themselves, try too hard, and write to avoid failure. We have to replace those attitudes with healthy alternatives. Here are eleven ways to cultivate them.

Defeating Writer's Block

1. Call Yourself a Writer.   We talked in the Guide to Studying about how important this is (Prologue). If you've been putting it off, now's the time. You can't play good tennis telling yourself over and over, "I'm not really a tennis player; I'm not really a tennis player."

2. Give Yourself a Lot of Time.   How obvious. Yet no rule of writing is broken more often. We wait until the last minute before a paper is due, conning ourselves into believing that we write better under pressure. But we don't. Time pressure always heightens fear. So instead of trying to force out a draft the night before it's due, set a part of your mind nibbling at the project from the moment the assignment is made, and keep nibbling off and on throughout the day, every day, mulling over the assignment and your possible approaches even as you jog through the park or take a shower.

3. Write as Yourself.   The less you have to disavow yourself when you write, the less writer's block will touch you. Writer's block comes from fear of being found out. If you write to convince the reader you're someone you're not, the risk of being found out increases. Mark Twain said the great advantage of telling the truth is that you don't need a good memory. Similarly, if you write as your true self, you can't be exposed as someone you're not. The draft you produce this way may not be ready to hand in, but you'll have the draft, and that's what matters.

4. Write to Your Favorite Audience.   People get tense when they try to talk to strangers. You'll make it easier on yourself if you write to someone you can talk freely to.

Most people choose to write to one of the three toughest audiences in the world: no one, the instructor, or the whole world. No one is hard because you know the writing is pointless. The instructor is hard because she knows more than you, and she's judging (grading) you instead of reading you. (I know that in reality you *are* writing to the instructor and writing for a grade, but there are some realities it's wise to forget, and this is one of them.) Writing to the whole world is hard because there is little you can say that the whole world wants to hear.

The audience that's easiest to write to is small and homogeneous: It's made up of people with the same interests, values, level of sophistication, and education. It knows less than you on the subject. It wants what you have to offer. It doesn't threaten you; it's not made up of people who are richer than you, a higher class than you, academically more advanced than you, or whatever makes you feel at a disadvantage. This audience is pulling for you: friends, family, pen pals, classmates. As always, the draft you produce this way may not be ready to hand in, but you'll have the draft, and that's the important thing. Much more on this later.

5. Don't Write; Talk.   Since most of us are used to being ourselves when we talk, if we talk on the page we'll feel that it's the real us writing. We're also better at talking because we've done so much more of it, so we'll be more successful writing the way we speak. Again, a first draft you've *spoken* may not be ready to hand in, but you can fix that later.

The basic way to write like you talk is to imagine yourself talking and write down what you hear. But if that isn't enough, you can make the talk real. You can talk to yourself, out loud—when you get stuck, stop typing and speak aloud to the air what you're trying to say. Or find a listener: rush out of the room, grab the nearest victim, and dump what you're trying to write into his astonished ear.

Or you can go all the way and literally dictate your text into a recording device and then type a transcript. Once I was asked to edit the narrative for a film on conservation. The author of the text said it didn't sound like a person talking, and he asked me to fix it. Instead of rewriting the text, I read the first paragraph of the text to see what it said, then tried to *speak* the content— without looking at the written text—and then recorded it. I worked my way through the text in this way, and the product was the same text, now in the language of a human speaker, not a stiff and artificial writer.

Remind yourself to use your talking language by using contractions: *can't, it's, I'm.* Every time you write *cannot* or *it is,* you remind yourself that you're not allowed to be you when you write; every time you write *can't* or *it's*, you'll remind yourself that's not so.

6. Take Your Ego Out of the Loop.   We get stage fright because we feel our ego is on the line: if we fail, we've proved we're bad, inept people. The essay *is us*, and we crash if it crashes. To escape that fate, we have to unlearn the ego identification. *You are not the essay.* If it crashes, you can still be a worthy person who occasionally writes essays that don't work. Remember, too, the definition of an essay, from Chapter 1: it's examination, an analysis, a test, an attempt. It's not an answer or the last word. It *invites* conversation, dialogue, even disagreement.

The first step in this unlearning is to realize that we choose to equate our egos with things, and can choose not to. I can go out and play soccer badly and not grieve, because I am not my soccer game, but if I write badly I must hate myself, because I am my writing. But there is nothing inherent in soccer or writing that makes me assign those values to them—I choose it. I have the power to move writing over to the "It's not a big deal" category any time I want.

Second, realize that the result of assigning such import to an action is destructive. I may tell myself that I'm helping myself write well by caring so much, but in fact the only result is that I can play soccer without fear (and therefore boldly, joyfully, and well), but I dare not write—there's too much to lose.

Third, understand how audiences read. *You* think the essay is you, but *they* don't. Imagine a guitar student with extreme stage fright. But the teacher was smart. The teacher said, "You fear because you think the audience listens to *you*. They do not. They listen to Bach, or Villa-Lobos. You are merely a messenger. You are nothing. They don't hear you. Remember this, and you'll disappear. Then there is no reason to be afraid."

7. Don't Demand That You Know Where You're Going.   Geniuses have something in common: a talent for working without rigidly defined goals. They're willing to let the investigation work itself out and discover where they'll end up when they've gotten there. Less creative minds want to know exactly where they're going before they start. The genius wisely says, "How can I know I'm going to invent the laser or discover the theory of relativity when no one knows such a thing exists yet?"

Sometimes school teaches you the reverse, by telling you that you need discipline and structure and requiring you to use outlines, thesis statements, and other tools that force those skills. If someone tells you that, learn to say, "Those tools are nice when I'm revising, but NOT NOW!"

8. Lower Your Standards.   We're talking about the damage done by *feeling obligated*. A football player who chokes because he's anticipating getting clobbered is said to "hear footsteps." Most people write hearing footsteps: the footsteps of their own critical selves, coming to clobber them for not measuring up.

Most writers are burdened with obligations: obligations to the English language, to the spelling system, to the rules of grammar, to the noble art of composition, or to their parents, who are paying for their college education, to instructors, to the demands of the five-paragraph format. All those obligations instill fear and make it harder to write. To silence them, *lower your standards,* fool around, and indulge yourself at every turn. Ask as little of yourself as possible.

It works. Here's how Lewis Thomas, a modern master of the essay, discovered the benefits of not trying hard when he turned from writing medical research and tried his hand at essay writing for the first time:

> The chance to ... try the essay form raised my spirits, but at the same time worried me. I tried outlining some ideas for essays, making lists of items I'd like to cover in each piece, organizing my thoughts in orderly sequences, and wrote several dreadful essays which I could not bring myself to reread, and decided to give up being orderly. I changed the method to no method at all, picked out some suitable times late at night, usually on the weekend two days after I'd already passed the deadline, and wrote without outline or planning in advance, as fast as I could. This worked better, or at least was more fun, and I was able to get started.
>
> (LEWIS THOMAS, THE YOUNGEST SCIENCE)

Three years after that beginning, those essays won the National Book Award.

If your guilt reflex tries to tell you that excellence lies in sweating the details, assure it there will be ample time for that during the polishing stages. Write the last draft to suit others, and write everything else to suit yourself. After all, when in the writing process do you owe other people (audiences, bosses, teachers, grammarians) anything? Not till the moment you hand the essay in. Writing's one great advantage is that none of it "counts" until you say it does. Don't throw this advantage away by insisting you write well from the first page of the first draft. What do you care how good the first draft of *Harry Potter and the Sorcerer's Stone* was?

Once you know your internal voice of self-criticism is active, you can set up a writing regimen that denies it an opportunity to speak. Forbid yourself to reread what you write until you are at the end of the draft. Or use the voice's input to your advantage. Make a rule that you never cross out anything. When the voice says that something you wrote isn't good enough, leave it and write onward, saying it all over again better or discussing what you didn't like about it. That way the voice of criticism becomes a force for *more* writing, not less.

Sheer speed helps, because it prevents you from thinking too much about what you're doing. Good early-stage writers write fast. Your normal composing pace should be as fast as your fingers will move.

9. Quit When You're Hot; Persist When You're Not. Ernest Hemingway is said to have always quit writing when he knew exactly what was going to happen next, not when he ran out of things to say. That way, he was always excited about going to work the next day instead of dreading it. Hemingway understood that every time you stop writing, whether it's for five minutes or five months, you run the risk of finding out you're blocked when you come back. Get around the problem by quitting when you're hot. Take a break on a winning note, not a losing one. Stop writing when things are going well, when you feel strong and know where you're going next—if it helps, write a short note to yourself right there in the text as a reminder. When you're at a loss, don't let yourself quit; stick with it until the block dissolves, words come—even if they're not the ones you'll end up with—and you've triumphed momentarily.

The longer the break, the more important it is to quit knowing what you'll do next. When I break for five minutes, I want to know what sentence I'm going to write when I come back; when I break for the day, I typically finish with a sketchy paragraph summary of where the discussion is going in the next few passages—a map of tomorrow's journey.

10. Sidestep the Thing That Blocks You. Identify the thing that stops you from writing, and figure out a way to go around it.

Do you ever refuse to begin the essay until you sweat out a title? Do you ever refuse to write the body of an essay until you've ground out an opening paragraph that refuses to come? Do you ever write and rewrite a sticky passage, refusing to go on until it's just right? Do you ever interrupt the steady flow of words to check a spelling in the dictionary? All these behaviors may be excuses to stop writing.

There are an infinite number of ways to stop yourself, but three are so common we'll name them.

- *Fear of page one.* Renowned literary scholar Dwight Culler said he used to roll the paper into the typewriter and stare at page 1 in blank terror. Then he got an idea: he rolled the paper into the typewriter, typed "page 10" at the top ... and found he could write with relative ease.
- *Fear of the page limit.* This is where you are assigned a ten-page paper and are terrified you'll never find enough to say to fill ten pages. Attack this in two ways. First, fill pages quickly: double-space, use large margins, and ramble—be as wordy and redundant as you please. Pile up text until you're well past the page limit. Now the problem is no longer how to stretch to fill the assigned space, but how to cut down to fit into it. It may all be an illusion, but you'll feel better nonetheless. Second, don't let yourself know how many pages you've written.
- *Fear of the essay.* This is perhaps the most common source of writer's block. Most of us write lots of things more easily than we write essays—so don't write essays, until the last draft. Instead ...

11. Write Un-essays. Here are seven ways to get writing out of yourself that have friendlier names:

1. *Reactive reading.* We talked about this earlier, but try these specific ways of reacting. You read something stimulating on your chosen issue and jot down all the stuff pouring from you in response. Follow three rules. (1) *Write your reactions down as you read*—don't read, then write down your thoughts, because by then they'll be gone. (As a matter of fact, I'm doing that at this very moment, reading through the eighth edition of *The Writer's Way* looking for things to change for the ninth edition, and, weirdly enough, this very sentence became one....) (2) *Don't write on the prompt,* like in the margins; write on a notepad. Don't tell yourself you'll transcribe the notes later—you won't. (3) *Don't take notes on what the text says;* record the reactions you're having to it. If this is hard for you, force yourself by drawing a vertical line down the middle of the note page and writing text content on the left side of the page and your reactions on the right. Force yourself to fill the right side as well as the left.

2. *Brainstorming.* Brainstorming is chatting, often without apparent direction, with colleagues accompanied by note taking—surely you've heard someone say, "I'm just thinking out loud here," meaning, "Don't hold me to this: I'm just trying to figure it out." That's brainstorming, which differs from the conversations we hold with friends every day in three ways: (1) Brainstorming is unstructured—you try to spit out single words and phrases as well as sentences or whole thoughts, and you take whatever comes, however fragmented, however ill-phrased, however apparently irrelevant. (2) You have no standards. (3) You record everything people say.

3. *Mapping.* Mapping is my students' favorite prewriting tool (and I'll talk about it as an organizational tool in Chapter 7). You can use it to find a seed, but it's usually used when you've found one. Write the seed in the center of a piece of paper and circle it. You don't need a thesis or a great idea—you can start with a word, a suggestive phrase, a visual image, a picture. Now begin brainstorming or free-associating connections between the seed and other thoughts. Let the other bits be whatever they are— words, sensations, questions. As each bit comes, write it down on the paper somewhere, circle it, and draw a line from it to the bit on the page it seems somehow connected to. Work out from the seed in all directions, letting bits cluster as they will. Try to connect everything in the map to something else in the map, so you're making a spider web, or highway system, or whatever you want to think of it as.

   If a bit doesn't seem related to any other bit, don't worry about it; just write it anywhere and circle it. Don't demand that you know what the bits or connections mean. If you momentarily run dry, keep doodling or retrace the spiderweb, so your hand keeps moving and invites your brain to contribute.

FIGURE 4.1 Sample Essay Map

If, as you're mapping, you catch glimpses of essay structure, record them somewhere. If you notice, for instance, that many of your bits concerning industrial pollution are about the history of the problem, many are about public opinion on the issue, and many are about the federal government's role in the problem and its solution, you can try to cluster the bits around three main arteries in the map, respectively labeled "history," "John Q. Public," and "Feds." But you needn't do any of that now. You're *generating*; you can sort, label, sequence, and analyze later.

As you map, keep reminding yourself of the following:

4. *Don't map only nouns.* Map everything—nouns, verbs, adjectives, adverbs, phrases, sentences, pictures, questions....

5. *Circle everything.* Connect every circle to something via a line. Use circles, not boxes—boxes are prisons.

6. *Don't be linear.* Use all 360 degrees of the circle. Wander.

   Don't think you're now committed to writing an essay that follows the map. You don't owe a map, or any other prewriting tool, anything. If you have to prove this to yourself, take a part of the map that you like, move it to the center of a new piece of paper, and map around it.

7. *Journals.* A journal is a notebook or binder where you dump everything you think, feel, or observe. It's written to and for you, and you write in it every day or nearly every day—not just when a good idea strikes. It's the only one of the prewriting tools that you use on schedule, so it gives you a lot of writing practice. But there's more to it than that: it teaches you to monitor your mind and heart constantly, as a part of life, and to value what's pouring out of them. We're always moving, breathing, thinking, and feeling; if we're writers, we observe and record what we think and feel. Most good writers keep journals, at least for a year or so until the monitoring habit is firmly established.

   People who don't keep journals can't figure out what people who do keep journals find to put in them, so here are some entries from the journal of Susan Wooldridge, who kept her journal for more than twenty years, just writing down things she was noticing and recording her reactions to them. Eventually, Susan published her journal as *Poemcrazy*, a wonderful book that is at once insightful, whimsical, and useful—and a great resource for writers.

Happy morning.

Tiniest sprouts in our herb garden. Sunlight on our plants.

Aristophanes—

"Who's there?"

"An ill-starred man."

"Then keep it to yourself."

Perhaps the heaviness will leave soon. Perhaps I can will it away, perhaps it will just lift. All right, why is it here. Heavy dreams. Kent interested in someone else, though not truly, I knew that in the dream. Heavy weather. Anger at myself for having a job so basically useless to the world and to me. Every day. Morning energy lost on it.

André Malraux said of Goya:

"He discovered his genius the day he dared to give up pleasing others."

I urge Smokey into the large field, recently plowed, we trot, canter, turn, figure 8, etc. I watch our shadow galloping across the field and try to convince myself that this, truly, is my childhood dream come true. Me galloping through a green field with my own beautiful horse. Sometimes it feels right. Sometimes I feel guilt. Self-indulgence! Bad Sue. You should be out in the ghettoes carrying bundles of food to the starving and poor.

Doing office work. Typing like an automaton. Breathing stale smoke smells guardedly through my nose, occasionally flailing a broken fly swatter at a spiraling bumpy fly that refuses to land except on fragile typewriter parts.

Cows in the fog, dumb and heavy. Vague clumps of cows, a hog and sows in pale rows in a bog of weeds and grass and cows vacant as glass in the fog.

Words. Reasons, worries, flight. Birds. Nested birds.

We went, with the rent, for another chat with Clarence and Grace. Good folk in their way. Clarence like a big cumbersome child, devilish. Grace somewhat shy, somewhat sly. Real country folk. She had pet pigs once. Cows. Clarence delivered milk during the depression. Real Illinois farmers. Clarence has been to 4 funerals this week, friends.

There will be snow tonight. And perhaps tomorrow I shall speed, skate, spin on thick ice.

Our tree is lying frozen outside.

And oh, this curse of words, endless rumination, introspection and self exposure. Here it is: I am a writer I am a writer I write I write I am a person who writes I am a woman I am a woman who likes to write, who chooses to write. I am a writer. No more fudging on this one, Susan, this drive will not be submerged, this is a need, a want. So follow it. Do it. Hell. Hello. Hell, Hello.

There are two things worth noting here. First, in conventional terms *nothing has happened* in Susan's life. She sees cows, predicts snow. Not much more. As always, it's the watchful eye and heart of the writer that makes things worth saying, not the experiences themselves. Second, these entries aren't mini-essays or proto-essays. They're written for the journal keeper—an audience of one. Writing to others is different.

8. *Letter writing.* Most of us write well when we text, email, and write letters, because we're writing as ourselves to a real audience we feel we can talk to. Write about the events of the day if that's all you feel up to; if you want to ask more of yourself, write, "I've been mulling over this thing for this essay I'm writing for a class. It's about ...," and block out the essay for your reader.

9. *Discovery drafts.* A discovery draft is a first draft that's purely exploratory; you just keep saying things and see where they lead you. You ask nothing, but you hope that by the time you're done, you will have discovered in your writing a sense of what you're going to do. It's sort of like a football team doing calisthenics before a game—just loosening up. No one really cares to watch. It's not for the benefit of the audience/crowd anyway; it's for the benefit of the players, who wouldn't be ready to play without warming up first.

   Writers often call this kind of loosening up "freewriting." In its most extreme form, you write for a predetermined period of time and keep writing sentences no matter what happens. If you have nothing to say, write, "I have nothing to say" over and over until you find something else to say. Write song lyrics, gibberish, "The quick brown fox jumps over the lazy dog," or whatever, but keep writing.

10. *Abstracts.* Abstracts can be intimidating, but they can also be liberating if you have been mulling the essay over, your head is full of what you want to say, and you just try to dash the abstract off, like a cartoon before the detailed drawing. In Chapter 7 I'll talk more about how to write abstracts.

11. *Don't outline, or if you do, do so freely and without regard to formal structure.* Outlining isn't an un-essay because it's an organizing discipline, not a prewriting tool. It's rigid, mechanical, and structured—the opposite of everything we want at this stage. It closes you down instead of opening you up. Map or write an abstract instead.

WRITER'S WORKSHOP

Finding Essays in Your Life

Professor Rawlins once asked his class for a volunteer who "had nothing to say," someone whose life had been "nothing special." He and the volunteer (Sally) talked for twenty minutes and then looked back over their conversation for possible essay topics. Here's their conversation, with the ideas for essays in parentheses.

JR: Tell me about yourself. What do you do?

S: I'm a student. I work in a restaurant, and I enjoy sports.

JR: What kind of sports do you do?

S: I used to compete in track, but now it's for my own enjoyment. (*Compare being athletic in formal competition with being athletic just for fun, arguing that athletics outside of organized competition is healthier, more fun, less stressful.*) I run, play basketball, do cross-country skiing, downhill. I play a little bit of volleyball, swim, play softball. I've only just started cross-country skiing. I really like it because of the solitude; there's more physical exercise. Downhill I like because of the speed and getting accuracy down. (*Write to downhillers, arguing that cross-country skiing is less crowded, cheaper, better for your body, and better for your spirit.*)

JR: What did you do in track?

  S: Shot put and half mile. I had a lot of strength from weight lifting.

JR: Did you ever take any flak for doing something that was as "unfeminine" as putting the shot?

  S: Sure. We were considered jocks. There was a lot of stereotyping.... (*Write to large, strong girls, sharing your experience pursuing a "manly" sport and encouraging them not to be intimidated; or defend the thesis: Even after the women's movement, female athletes still face prejudice.*) I was used as a guinea pig for a program. Since I was a good athlete, they wanted to see how strong they could really make me. But I ended up getting injured. They didn't provide the equipment I needed—belts and stuff like that. I strained my back. From trying to squat too much. (*Write to beginning women weight trainers, offering training tips and cautioning them about the dangers.*)

JR: Tell me about your past. What was your childhood like?

  S: We grew up fairly poor. My mom divorced when I was seven, so it was just the girls in the house: my two sisters, Mom, and me.

JR: What was it like when your parents divorced?

  S: I was happy about it. I was scared to death of my father. He hit us a lot. The way I look on it now, that was the only way he had to communicate. That's the way he was raised. I was scared to death of him and anyone who was ever going to raise a hand to me. It caused many problems with our relationship. To the point where I didn't know him—though he doesn't live very far from my hometown. (*Write to children of divorce, sharing your feelings and the insights you've gained from the experience; or write to children physically abused by their parents, sharing your experiences and your feelings; or defend the thesis: Sometimes divorce is good for the children of the marriage.*)

JR: How did your father's treatment of you affect you?

  S: It made it hard to be affectionate with people—I'm beginning to outgrow that. Also I felt like I was a bad person, but that's also because he would tell me bad things about myself. I wanted to be a lawyer all my life, but he always told me, "Nope, you'll never be good at that, you'll never be good at that." And he told me that so many times, I tell myself that. He wanted a boy. (*Write about what it's like growing up with parents who tell you you're bound to fail; or write about what it's like being a girl in a family where a parent wanted a boy.*)

JR: Did you always live in the same place when you were growing up?

S: No, in high school we moved and I had to change schools. My mom thought I was a little too radical and the neighborhood was a bad influence on me.

JR: Do you agree?

S: No. There was definitely a better grade of education in the new place, but the new high school was in a richer neighborhood and was really into cocaine. The girls were all daddy's little girls, they got everything they wanted, they didn't have to work for anything; the guys all thought they were cowboys, which I thought was funny, since they probably never had been near a horse. (*Write a satire laughing at the foolishness of parents who move to upper-middle-class neighborhoods in the mistaken belief that they're escaping the problems of poverty or the city; or defend the thesis: "Better neighborhoods" aren't always better.*)

JR: Were you doing drugs?

S: I drank a lot, but never when I was playing any sport, because it would screw me up. (*Defend the thesis: We should fight drug abuse by helping kids find something they love so much they won't risk losing it.*)

JR: How did you ever survive long enough to make it to college?

S: I had the influence of my mother, which was very positive, very striving. She works in a field where very few women do, general contracting: multimillion-dollar buildings. She doesn't have a college degree, so she doesn't have a title, but she travels all over the country, part engineer work, part administration; she heads a marketing team.... She's a super-intelligent lady, and the kind of person who, when something isn't supposed to be possible, can get it done. (*Write about your mother and your relationship with her, showing the ways she helped you survive your youth.*)

JR: It sounds like your mom was a very good influence.

S: Almost too much so. I'm in awe. And I have a stepfather who's a doctor and very successful, who's also very intelligent. (*Write about the pluses and minuses of having a stepparent; or write about the pluses and minuses of having parents who are superheroes.*)

JR: What are your plans?

S: I intend to go overseas and teach. That's what I'd like. Teach English for a while. (*Write to English majors, defending the thesis: You should consider teaching English overseas for a year or two.*)

That's seventeen essays in twenty minutes from what Sally was convinced was a "nothing" life. Of course, Sally's life turned out to be anything but ordinary, but the funny thing is that the same thing happens with every life, including yours, when you start looking at it this way.

Now It's Your Turn.   With a classmate, do Sally-type interviews of each other. Have her interview you for fifteen minutes; then you interview her. Together, find as many essay seeds in each interview as you can. Try to find personal essays, informative essays, and arguments. Make sure that none of the seeds is a topic (a noun or a noun phrase).

EXERCISES

1. For two days, record (in a notebook or journal) all the striking prompts you encounter: fragments of conversation overheard in the grocery store, startling ads on TV, unusual moments in class. Take two and recast them as ideas for essays, a sentence to a short paragraph each.

2. Make a list of things that have made you mad recently. Take one and explore its possibilities as an essay, not only as a personal essay but as other forms with other purposes. What kind of inquiry does it lead to for research? What's a possible thesis for an argument paper?

3. On pp. 46–47 is a list of five ways to find essay ideas. Find an essay in your life by way of each item in the list. For example, for the first item, pick some place you've been and describe it to someone in a couple of sentences.

4. Find an essay, in *The Writer's Way* or elsewhere, that sparks a thoughtful response in you. Turn that response into an essay.

5. Find an essay, in *The Writer's Way* or elsewhere, that has a technical feature (lots of dialogue, a flashback, use of second person, etc.) that you like but have never tried. Using the essay as a model, write a short essay mimicking that feature. At the bottom of the page, identify the feature you're mimicking: for example, "I'm mimicking the use of dialogue." My students love to mimic Megan Sprowls' essay "The Dos and Don'ts...." on p. 342 in "A Collection of Good Writing."

6. Identify an idea for an essay. Then do the following things with it:

    a.   Make a map from it.

    b.   Brainstorm it with a classmate for ten minutes.

    c.   Write a real letter to a real friend of yours in which you say something like, "I've been thinking about this essay I'm writing for my comp class. It's about...." Then tell your reader the essay, keeping him interested.

d. Talk the essay into your smart phone; then transcribe the recording. Rewrite it into an essay. Write a paragraph discussing what changes the spoken text needed.

e. Via the Internet or elsewhere, find a piece of writing that addresses your essay's issues. React to the piece, and rewrite your essay to include the new thoughts generated by the reading.

f. Write a half-page essay in which you identify precisely what gives you writer's block. Then write another essay in which you plot ways to sidestep the blocker—ways you can write to avoid it.

g. Keep a journal for a week. Write in it at least once a day. Then take two entries and rewrite them as essay seeds.

h. Start a letter to a friend, in which you plan to give her some good news or to tell her something important. But don't get that far. Stop when you know exactly what you will say next, and then don't write again until the next day. See how you *look forward* to writing when you know exactly what you're going to say?

Chapter 5

Thesis, Purpose, and Audience

Many beginning writers overemphasize thesis in their papers, or at least they tend to think of thesis as something apart from everything else in the paper. In reality, though, you can do very little with it until you think seriously about purpose and audience. I once had a student who was convinced that he wanted to write a paper about Monday Night Football. OK, I said, what's your thesis and purpose and who's your audience? He thought about it a minute (clearly not enough time) and said, My thesis is that watching Monday Night Football is a good way to relax with friends, my purpose is to convince my readers to watch Monday Night Football, and my audience will be football fans. I see, I said. And your audience needs or wants to read this paper, *why*?

We talked about it a while, and he ended up changing his audience to "football widows," urging them to join their husbands in watching the games. And you know what? It was a darn good essay. He had a purpose and a real audience.

This chapter will explore the connections among thesis, purpose, and audience, and how to think about them, and then Chapter 6 will explore style and tone and help you answer questions about voice and levels of formality. For now, take a look at everything that knowing your purpose and audience tells you about how to write.

PURPOSE AND AUDIENCE TELL YOU HOW TO WRITE

Purpose and audience tell us how to structure, how to begin, how to end, how long the sentences should be, whether to use slang or not ... in short, everything. Writing is a constant series of "What should I do now?" questions: Should I state my thesis? Should I begin a sentence with "but"? Should I explain what I just said? Should I summarize in my conclusion? *Purpose and audience answer all such questions, and only purpose and audience can answer them.*

Consider the following:

Example 1: Should you state your thesis in the opening paragraph, elsewhere, or imply it, hoping your reader "gets it"?

It depends on to whom you're writing and why. If your instructor has required you to put your thesis in the opening paragraph, then by all means do so. Likewise, academic papers often have their theses stated up front, so that the reader knows exactly what the paper, which is probably quite long, is setting out to do. On the other hand, if you're trying to be more subtle and your examples will make your thesis clear, then maybe you don't need a thesis statement at all. Remember, "Something Happened a Long Time Ago" (on p. 22)? Imagine how that essay would have been compromised with a thesis ("Live your life fully") in the opening paragraph.

Example 2: How should you structure the essay?

It depends on to whom you're writing and why. How-to essays usually go through a process step by step, because the reader is trying to go through the process herself with the essay as a guide. Technical reports usually begin with summary, conclusion, or recommendations, because they're read by bosses who don't have time to read the whole thing and want *an answer* where they can see it at a glance. Newspaper articles always put their most important information first and their least important information last, because newspaper readers skim the openings of articles, pick the ones worth reading, read until their interest flags, and quit. Arguments often start by declaring that something needs fixing in the world but hold off telling the reader what the thesis is. The idea is to win the reader's attention but to give the writer time to talk him into agreeing with her. In each of these cases, organization is dictated by what you're trying to do to the reader and what he's reading you for.

Example 3: How much background information should you give?

It depends on to whom you're writing and why. I was recently writing a review of the Bruce Springsteen CD *We Shall Overcome: The Seeger Sessions* for a Northern California arts-and-entertainment weekly, whose average reader is probably about twenty-three years old. On the CD, Springsteen covers several songs made famous by Pete Seeger, the hugely important folk singer of the 1950s and '60s, as well as a handful of other songs from the civil rights era. I assumed that most of my readers knew Springsteen's music, but I figured they didn't know much, if anything, about Seeger. So I had to provide some background about Seeger and his time and music as well as talk about what Springsteen did with the songs. For the review itself, see p. 88.

THESIS

Many students who struggle with the word "thesis" have no trouble with "point" or "main point." They see "theses" as things that occur only in school in academic papers that they have to write for classes that they're required to take, and that freezes them up. On the other hand, they understand, and in fact demand, "main points" in stories. Consider the grandfather talking to his teenage grandson: "When I was your age, we played in the woods every day—after school and we didn't need computers or video games or phones to entertain us." Grandson, rolling his eyes, thinking: "What's your point, Grandpa?"

Thesis, main point, claim—all pretty much the same thing. But we'll use the word for "thesis" for now. If you're more comfortable with another word, substitute that one.

Your thesis is the statement at the heart of the essay—the topic sentence, the core, the point, the lesson, the moral, the content in a flash, the *one* thing you have to say. Here are theses for three of the essays in this book:

"Given the Chance" (p. 278): The state of California's commitment to drug rehabilitation programs is so minimal that it's impossible for social service people to help those who need it.

"Why?" (p. 279): Getting sickeningly drunk to celebrate your twenty-first birthday makes no sense, but we keep doing it.

"Why I Never Cared for the Civil War" (p. 359): Traditional ways of teaching school are boring and don't work, but there are powerful, exciting alternatives.

Thesis vs. Thesis Statement.   Don't confuse the two. Your thesis is your essay's main idea or claim, and in much writing it's implied, not stated at all. A thesis statement is that idea or claim actually stated within the essay itself.

Making the Tool

Since the thesis has a great gift for pointing out when we aren't really saying anything, there is a temptation to build it wrong so we can escape its frightening revelations. Obey the following tool-making rules strictly:

1. **A thesis is a complete sentence**—not sentence fragment, however large—and rarely two sentences, because writing a thesis is the moment when you demand to know what's at the *center,* and there can be only one center.

2. **A thesis is a declarative sentence**—not a question, since theses are *answers*. Likewise, a thesis is not "Why you should go to a community college instead of a four-year university" or "Why global warming is the most critical issue facing the planet today." Instead: "You should go to a community college instead of a four-year university" and "Global warming is the most critical issue facing the planet today."

3. **A good thesis often contains or implies the word "should"**—to force you to think about what you're trying to do, not just say, with the essay. Example: You should buy an electric car. (Note: "should not" also works.)

4. **A good thesis usually contains or implies the word "because"**—to force you to have at least one reason. Example: "You should buy an electric car because emissions from internal-combustion engines contribute to global warming and you will save money on gas."

5. **A thesis must fit well into the following template:** "In this essay I say, '_____.' " Thus the sentence "This essay explains how to change the oil in your car" isn't a thesis.

6. **A thesis must summarize the entire essay**—all parts of the essay must serve to support it.

7. **The thesis is frequently not present as a sentence in the essay.** Don't pick whichever sentence in the draft is closest to your thesis and call it your thesis, and don't feel obligated to declare your thesis somewhere in the essay. Make sure the thesis is clear in your own mind, and use it as a statement within the text if the situation (or your assignment) calls for it.

Occasionally, a writer will write out the thesis in a sentence or two and hand it to the reader. In George Orwell's "Shooting an Elephant," he tells how he, as a minor British official in India, was forced by the pressure of an expectant mob to shoot an elephant that had gotten loose from its owner. He tells you exactly what the lesson of the story is:

> And it was at this moment, as I stood there with the rifle in my hands, that I first grasped the hollowness, the futility of the white man's dominion in the East. Here was I, the white man with his gun, standing in front of the unarmed native crowd—seemingly the leading actor of the piece; but in reality I was only an absurd puppet pushed to and fro by the will of those yellow faces behind. I perceived in this moment that *when the white man turns tyrant it is his own freedom that he destroys* [the thesis is italicized].

But you can spread the thesis throughout a couple of paragraphs, imply it indirectly, or keep it to yourself—see "Why?" (p. 279) and "Dad" (p. 210), for examples. Similarly, you can put the thesis in the first sentence of the essay, the last, or nowhere. You're the boss. The only place you're obliged to have the thesis is *in your head*.

Some audiences and purposes demand an explicit statement of thesis, and others don't. Scientific and technical writing always states its thesis up front; fiction rarely states it at all.

8. **Almost every essay has a thesis, including informative essays.** In an informative essay, the thesis may not be the heart and soul of the piece, but it's there, however quietly. For example, the thesis in "Why Falling in Love Feels So Good" (p. 358) is something like "with a little knowledge about your own body chemistry, you can pick a mate wisely and avoid a lifetime of unhappiness or a messy divorce."

Using the Tool

Once your thesis is well made, you employ it by asking it questions and answering the questions. The place to begin is at the beginning: *"Did I say anything?"* If the answer is yes, go on to questions like

Did I say anything interesting? Anything useful?

Did I say anything that at least some readers will challenge?

Anything risky?

Anything new?

Anything important to the reader? Anything important to me?

But don't limit yourself to a set list of specific questions; instead, as with all diagnostic tools, try to look at the thesis and learn from it whatever it can teach you. Ask, What's going on? What can I see here? What is this telling me about the draft? What seems to be going well and what's going badly?

Remember, a diagnostic tool can't tell you what to do (p. 75), so don't assume there are universally right answers to your questions. Not all great essays have earth-shaking theses (the "I hate eggs" essay on p. 48 doesn't). Not all great essays have "should"s in their theses (the ones mentioned on p. 76 don't). Not all great essays have theses that can be stated simply in words ("Dad" on p. 210). Not all great essays have theses (how-to essays often don't).

PURPOSE

While the term "purpose statement" isn't as common as the term "thesis statement," it's just as useful—translate your purpose into a specific statement, which will become clear when you answer questions like

Why am I writing this?

What do I hope to accomplish? What do I want?

What do I want the reader to do?

Like the thesis statement, it's small but mighty, and since it is terrifically revealing, writers will often go to great lengths to escape its lessons.

When we start thinking about why we write, most of our purposes are unhelpful ones:

To complete the assignment

To get a good grade

To write a good essay

To learn about the topic

To practice researching, thinking, and writing

To tell the reader something

The problem with all these purposes is *they don't tell you what to do.* A writer is constantly faced with decisions: How should I say this? Should I put this piece of information in or not? Should I do X, then Y, or the other way around? *The clearer a purpose is, the more it answers such writer's questions.* If I say, "My purpose is to write a great essay," that purpose answers no questions at all. If I say, "I want to make the reader sad," that purpose helps a little. If I say, "I want to capture the essence of my neighbor's daughter, Dee," I can start answering some specific questions about what I want to do. And if I say, "I want to capture Dee's ambivalence. She's absolutely brilliant but is reluctant to let people see that side of her, and I want to use that example to show how conflicted young girls often are in a culture that's afraid of smart females," I've got a purpose that will tell me exactly what to do.

Making the Tool

Here are four rules to follow to ensure you're making the purpose statement right

1. **Make the purpose statement an infinitive verb:** "My purpose is *to expose* the contemptible cowardice of the campus newspaper staff." You can start the sentence many ways: "I wrote in order to … ," "My goal was to … ," "I want to … ," "I intend to … ," "I'm going to...." Any of these phrases will lead you to end with a verb, which is what you want.
2. **Ask "Why?" and keep asking "Why?":** Purposes come in series. The result you hope to bring about by writing will bring about something else, which in turn will bring about something else: my purpose is to convince the reader to vote Republican in the next presidential election, *so that* the Republican candidate will win, *so that* he will increase defense spending, *so that* America will have a strong defense, *so that* we will remain safe from the threat of military attack, *so that* I don't end up in some concentration camp.
3. **Have at least two purposes:** to get something for yourself and to give the reader something he wants or should want. Humans are selfish; if there isn't something in it for you, you won't write, and if there isn't something in it for the reader, he won't read. Ask yourself what each of you has to gain.
4. **Make sure your purpose is a version of the universal writer's purpose:** to do something to the reader.

Using the Tool

Once you've written a well-formed purpose statement, the hard work is behind you. First, ask the central question: "Am I clear on what I'm trying to accomplish?" Then move on to questions like

Is my purpose constant throughout the essay?

Does it account for everything in the draft?

Is it important to me?

Will it be important to the reader?

AUDIENCE

A purpose is always an intent to do something to *someone*. The clearer you are about who it is, the better you'll write. Chapter 2 talked about this. Let's take it further.

Making the Tool

Write a paragraph or so detailing everything you know about whom you're writing to. It sounds simple-minded, but don't sell it short. The audience definition is more powerful than it at first appears. And it's harder to produce than you'd think. The first time you try it, you usually end up saying something useless like "I'm writing to anyone who would like to read this essay."

We're audience-unconscious because a sense of audience in our *reading* is like air: it's always there, so we take it for granted. But the instant a writer fails to take us into consideration or assumes we're someone we're not, the significance of audience becomes deafeningly clear. Here is the opening of an essay from a writer who doesn't know who we are:

> Dance forms are characterized by the use of particular movements. The various forms of dance require differing degrees of body mathematics usage, strength, endurance, practiced ability, innate ability, and mental concentration.

> Butoh dance movement requires all of the above. The precision of body placement, the strength needed for sustained positions, the endurance necessary to sustain positions, the repetitive exercises to build strength and endurance, the natural ability to execute movement, and the high level of concentration are the components of the body and mind for the Butoh dancer. The development of these enable the dancer to tap inner and outer spheres of energy movement. The physical body is the initiator, receptor, and giver of these energy realms.

Our first question may be, what does this mean? But another question must be answered first: who is this for, and how is she supposed to use it?

Once the essay declares an audience and purpose, meaning becomes a manageable problem:

YOUR FIRST BUTOH CONCERT

If you're a long-time lover of dance, you probably think you've seen it all. But the first time you attend a concert of Butoh, the new, exciting blend of Eastern philosophy and Western modern-dance technique, your immediate response may be, "But they're not *dancing* at all!" Well, they really are, but they aren't doing anything you're used to calling dance. Butoh looks odd, because it thinks a different way about movement than other schools of dance do, but once I walk you through it you may find it's something you want to see again and again—and perhaps try yourself.

Here's the first paragraph of another essay, "Make Them Pay," whose writer forgot to think about audience:

> There are many people in this world that are against the death penalty. They think it is wrong, inhumane, cruel, and unusual, etc. They feel that no one has the right to take someone else's life. But what about the life that was taken by the criminal in question? What gave them the right to take an innocent life? I feel that the death penalty is sufficient punishment for violent crimes such as murder and rape. Crimes like these are repulsive and should be considered crimes against humanity. Those who commit them should pay with their lives, not only as punishment for their sick mistakes, but also as a lesson to others that such offenses will not be tolerated in this society.

Naturally, this writer has aimed her argument at people who oppose the death penalty, but she hasn't really thought that through. The writer thinks, for instance, that if she can convince her readers that these crimes are heinous they will agree with her position. But most people who oppose the death penalty would agree that those crimes are "repulsive" and "against humanity." What this writer needs to do is learn about her audience: *what are the reasons* her audience is against the death penalty? Then she can begin to address those arguments.

So the first challenge is to convince ourselves that every piece of writing—from naval histories to menus to rental agreements—has a real and specific audience and that good communicators filter everything they say through a sense of who's listening.

If you doubt this, just take a look at the magazines on the racks at your school bookstore. There are publications for people who show golden retrievers, who restore Volkswagens, who collect baseball cards. Or think of it this way: imagine you've just flunked your first college midterm, and you decide to write three different emails explaining what happened—one to your parents, one to your best friend, and one to the instructor, asking if you can take the test again. Would you write just one letter and send it to all three? I didn't think so.

Using the Tool

Now that you're a believer, follow these guidelines as you write your audience definition:

1. **The audience is never you. That's journal or diary writing.** However much you may feel that you're writing to educate yourself or writing to figure out what you think or writing to get something off your chest, as soon as you give it to someone else to read, you're saying, "I think this will profit *you*." And then you need to know who that someone is.

2. **Audience must always be chosen.** There is no such thing as the only or the right or the inevitable audience for a piece of writing. You choose audience the way you choose thesis.

Let's assume that the trustees of your state university have just decided to raise the tuition ... again. As one of the students, you decide to write an essay decrying this. Your purpose is clear: to stop the fee hike. Now, whom should you write to? There are many groups who have a say in the matter: students, parents, college administrators, state legislators (since they control the state university's purse strings), teachers, and citizens (since they elect the legislators). Within these groups are smaller groups. Within the student body, for instance, there's a group of students who think it's OK for rising costs to be borne in part by the students; there's a group that's vehemently opposed; there's a group that doesn't care; there's a group that hasn't heard about the issue; and there's a group that's on the fence.

Each audience has to be talked to in a different way. The students who are vehemently opposed to fee hikes need to be preached to like brothers; those who think the hike is a good idea need to be persuaded they're wrong; administrators need to be shown alternative ways to pay the university's bills; citizens need to be convinced that it's ultimately to the benefit of society that bright kids can afford to go to college. Writing to all these audiences at once is nearly impossible. So choose, and choose early—at the same time that you're writing your thesis and identifying your purpose.

3. **Smaller means easier.** The narrower your audience, the easier it is to write to, because writing is about controlling the reader—and the smaller the group, the easier it is to predict how they will react. Your easiest audience is the smallest: your best friend. As the audience enlarges, the diversity of experience, tastes, values, and beliefs grows, the reactions become more unpredictable, and the challenge of controlling the audience increases. The hardest audience is "everyone," since "everyone" is almost totally

unpredictable; but oddly, that's the one students are drawn to. Would "everyone" be interested in a review of the new Spearhead CD? Would "everyone" know what you meant if you wrote, "Sometimes you can improve performance by replacing your exhaust manifold"?

Likewise, don't make the mistake, as my students often do, of defining their audience as "Anyone interested in my topic." That doesn't work. My dad, who's eighty-four and a retired engineer, is *interested* in cell-phone technology, and so are my daughters, who are twenty-four and twenty-one. But they are parts of two very different audiences—the essay that you write for my father about cell-phone technology would be very different from an essay that you write for my daughters about cell-phone technology. That's not to say the two audiences might both get something of value from the same piece of writing. See "target audience," below.

There is a kind of writing whose audience is defined no more clearly than "every American citizen interested in social issues." It's what we see in *Newsweek* and *Time*. And since we see such writing all the time, we're in danger of concluding that most writing is to such audiences. But most writing isn't. For every *Newsweek*, there are a hundred specialized magazines that are just for Mac owners, or dirt bike aficionados, or scuba divers. For every national magazine, there are a thousand local club newsletters. For every newsletter, there are a thousand letters to friends. So the vast bulk of writing in our world is to narrowly specified audiences. And the essayists in *Time* and *Newsweek* are the best writers in the country. They have to be, because writing to "everyone" is that tough.

4. **Make the writing easy by choosing an audience like yourself, or make it challenging and useful by choosing an audience unlike yourself.** The more like you the audience is, the easier it is to write, because the easier it is to guess how they'll respond. That's why it's so easy to write emails to friends. Most writers know this and instinctively write as if all readers are exactly like them—thus the number of essays I get about how much fun it was to get drunk last weekend. The problem is that people just like us can't profit much from our writing, because it has nowhere new to take them—they're already where we are (also see Chapter 14). If we're writing against tuition hikes, the administrators are the hardest to write to because they're least like you, but that means there's more to be gained by winning them over.

5. **Aim at a "target" audience.** Just because you're narrowing your audience way down, that doesn't mean that other readers won't find anything of value in your essay. I frequently read magazines in the waiting rooms at doctors' offices: *Golf Digest, Antiquing Magazine, Health,* sometimes even (full disclosure here), *People.* And I enjoy them and often learn stuff. But I am not the "target" audience of those publications.

Another example: Remember Laura Kate James' essay "School Is Cool" (p. 25)? I absolutely love that essay, but I am not among her "target" audience, whom she clearly speaks to: "You imagine your weekends immediately being booked with dinner-movie-coffee-date plans by handsome young males" and "Your clothes and books and CDs and eight pairs of high heels…all packed in big black garbage bags and prune boxes."

6. **Go beyond the simple label.** Most writers, when they first start trying to describe audiences, stop at noun labels: "My audience is college students"; "My audience is working mothers." That's not enough. Think again about magazines. Here's how the editors of *Redbook* magazine describe their readers: "*Redbook* addresses young married women, ages 28–44. Most of our readers are married with children 10 and under; over 60 percent work outside the home."

And here's how *Esquire* magazine sees its target audience:

> "While other men's magazines are written for highly aspirational readers, *Esquire* is geared toward men who have arrived. They dress for themselves; have both the means and knowledge to invest; can order with confidence in a fine restaurant; have a healthy respect and admiration for women; take vacations that enrich their lives and recharge their energy; and have mastered many of life's basics. What they want is a primer on how to lead a richer, better, fuller, and more meaningful life."

So ask questions about your readers:

What gender are they?

How old are they?

How much money do they have?

How much formal education do they have?

Do they have a sense of humor?

How sophisticated are their English-language skills?

How do they feel about seeing the word "asshole" in print?

How conservative or liberal are they?

What is their value system?

How close- or open-minded are they about the issue in question?

How interested are they in this issue?

How well informed about it are they?

What do they need to know from me?

What do they want from me?

How are they going to perceive me?

How will they react to what I'm saying?

There's one question you can't avoid answering: how much does your audience already know? Because every time you tell the reader something, you're assuming she doesn't already know it, and every time you *don't* tell her something, you're assuming she does. If I say, "Next, remove the tire's lug nuts with a tire iron," I must either explain or not explain what lug nuts and tire irons are, and either choice requires a decision about my audience's prior knowledge.

7. **More is better.** Since we want to know as much about our audience as we can, the longer a definition of audience gets, the better it must be. So keep adding detail to your definition as long as you can.

Using the Tool

As you write your first draft, even though you know you'll be making changes later, keep in mind what you now know about your audience—imagine *saying* everything to them as you read, and imagine their reaction: "How will they react when I say *this*?" You can judge the quality of the draft by the clarity of your answers: if you have a pretty good idea what the reader would say in response to every line, how he would feel, then you're off to a good start.

EXERCISES

1. Write down five topics. Then translate the five into thesis statements.
2. Convert the following topics into thesis statements:
   a. Organic food
   b. SUVs
   c. Poverty in the third world
   d. The rising cost of a university education
   e. The effect of TV on children
3. Narrow the following topics. Example: Rock music, Rock's role in society, Rock musicians' involvement in political causes:
   a. SUVs
   b. TV
   c. Education
   d. Child raising
   e. Race in America
4. Revise each of the following so that they work as thesis statements:
   a. You can't legislate morality.
   b. This culture is so racist!
   c. My thesis is that boxing is brutal. It's incredible to me that in a society that bans cock fighting and bear baiting, we permit the same sort of thing with human beings.

    d.   Why do we let TV corrupt our children?

    e.   Why World War II was unnecessary.

    f.   I love the new Ben and Jerry's flavor, Purple Haze.

    g.   Three reasons why everyone should exercise regularly.

5. For each of the theses you revised in Exercise 4, think about at least two potential audiences for each. Write them down, and then describe in a brief paragraph how you would approach each thesis for each specific audience.

6. For each of the following broad audiences, write half a page detailing everything you know about them. When you don't know something, narrow the audience by choosing an audience within the audience. Example: "I am writing to readers of restaurant reviews who live in the Boston area and who are fighting high cholesterol."

    a.   Registered nurses

    b.   Working mothers

    c.   College professors

    d.   Republican voters

    e.   Readers of movie reviews

7. Pick any essay in "A Collection of Good Writing" and answer the following questions:

    a.   What's the topic?

    b.   What's the thesis?

    c.   Where, if anywhere, in the essay is the thesis?

    d.   What's the purpose?

    e.   Who's the audience?

8. Go online and look at the writer's guidelines and/or the reader profile of a magazine that you read. How closely do you fit the profile?

9. Look closely at any magazine. Based on both the articles (subjects, language, length) and the advertisements, write a one-paragraph profile of the magazine's "target" audience. Consider gender, age, income, educational level, and so on. Look on line at how the magazine identifies its readers. How close did you get?

Chapter 6

Style and Tone

Purpose and audience help us determine style—how we say what we say—and also help us know whether the tone we hope to achieve will work.

STYLE

Should you wear jeans to the party or khakis or a suit? Are shorts OK? This old sweatshirt with the torn hood? That sexy black dress? Depends, right? On what? The occasion and how you want to be perceived. Some occasions call for casual wear, some for formal. Same with writing. You decide—after you know not only what the occasion (assignment) calls for but also how you want the other guests (readers/audience) to perceive you.

Writing style is the decorative covering we put over the content.

Example 1: Should you use slang like "sick," "phat, "hella," or "noob"? Should you use contractions like "can't," which tend to be informal, or should you spell out "can not"? It depends on to whom you're writing and why. Slang and levels of formality identify you as members of certain groups, and that might very well be what you want. If you're talking to members of that group, using slang or the level of formality that they use may earn you instant acceptance. On the other hand, using slang to outsiders advertises the fact that you're not one of them and often seriously calls your credibility into question. Slang also has a short shelf life. If you want your work to hold up over time, avoid language that won't be around tomorrow. (Rawlins and I have updated this section of *The Writer's Way* nine times now, and I fear that by the time you're reading this that my preceding examples will already just be a part of linguistic history.)

What Writing Style or Voice Should You Use?

Remember my story about writing the review of Bruce Springsteen's CD *The Seeger Sessions* (p. 75)? In addition to having to decide how much background information to include, I had to determine a writing style, in this case one that would be appropriate to my mostly eighteen-to-thirty-year-old readers interested in popular music. And there was another catch: I was limited to 160 words. This is what I ended up with:

> It's a natural: Bruce Springsteen, the working-man's rock star, meets Pete Seeger, American folk-music icon. Recorded unrehearsed at Springsteen's New Jersey farm, *The Seeger Sessions* captures the Boss and friends—on guitar, fiddle, piano, upright bass, accordion, washboard, tuba, trombone, banjo, and mandolin—playing with joy, passion, and apparently plenty of lubrication. At one point, Springsteen asks, "Anyone else need another beer? Let's loosen up on these vocals." While the party atmosphere makes it impossible not to get caught up in the music, it also risks undermining the political intensity of the original songs. On the other hand, the gospelly "O Mary, Don't You Weep" becomes a rousing call to arms, the entire cast belting out the vocals, painfully punctuated by the high hat that sounds eerily like a cracking bull whip, and the title tune is solemn and stirring, as is the gorgeous "Shenandoah." A "dual-disk," the *Seeger Sessions* includes a remarkable DVD of the recording, with bandleader Springsteen not only calling out solos and key changes but thoughtfully discussing in quiet interviews the songs and the importance of "recontextualizing" the music.

Some Important Style Principles to Keep in Mind

Style Is Independent of Content.   You can say any message in any style, just as you can put any sort of clothing on any body. Anyone can wear a wetsuit or a belly-dancing costume. You may get laughed at or run from, but that's a different issue.

This is the most important lesson about style to learn, because writers defend bad writing by insisting that what they say determines how they say it. "I have to be stuffy and pretentious, because I'm talking about this very serious issue," they say. Never.

Style Is Chosen.   You decide what style to use the way you decide what clothes to wear. Even if you got dressed this morning without thinking much about it, you decided. Oh, this black trench coat? I just threw it on without thinking. Right. You could have worn something else. You're responsible for the choice.

You Can't Not Choose.   You can't write without style any more than you can dress in no way at all. Whatever language you use will have a certain sentence length, be passive or active, use Latinate words or avoid them. Doing what's "in" or what everyone else is doing is still a choice. Since you can't not choose, you want to control your choosing.

Style Sends a Message.   Some believe it shouldn't be that way, but it's true: the way you use language, like the way you dress, is heard as a message by everyone who sees it. Whether you wear your baseball cap backward, dye your hair pink, or wear Wranglers and boots, you're telling people something.

Choose Your Style for the Effect It Has on the Reader.   There is no good or right style, only styles that produce the response you want in the reader and those that don't.

Remember, controlling effect never equals doing what the reader wants. You *may* want to please, but you don't *have to*. You can wear a clown suit, or a loincloth, or your underwear over your jeans to class if you're willing to take the predictable reaction.

Alternatives Equal Power.   The more ways you can dress, the more places you can go, and the more things you can do. If you can wear only a T-shirt and jeans, you can't go to the ball. If you don't own a wetsuit, you can't go scuba diving. Similarly, the more ways you can write, the more responses you can provoke and the more things you can do with your writing.

Most of Us Choose by Habit.   We write the way we dress—the way we always do. This is giving up our power to choose and thus control our audience.

Style Is Fun.   Trying out different words and sentence structures should feel just like playing dress up or trying on clothes at the mall: it's a game. Try on the clown suit, sample a few wigs, slip into the slinky cocktail dress....

How to Master a Style

Style is a series of *choices*: Do you make the sentences long or short? Do you write in first person or third person? To control a stylistic choice, you have to do two things:

1. **Believe you have the choice.** English offers you the options. Everyone knows that English will let you write long sentences or short ones, for instance. Sometimes it isn't so obvious. Not all of us realize that English will let you write passive sentences or active sentences, and almost no one outside the academy realizes that in English you write Latinate words, Romance words, and Germanic words.

   Many writers say, "Sure, I know that English makes it possible to write in concrete language and short sentences, but I can't do it here—I'm writing about serious, sophisticated stuff, so I *need* big words and long, complex sentence structure." Any time you tell yourself that your topic or your message dictates your style choice, you're wrong. You can say anything about anything in any style.

2. **Understand the effect of your choices.** You must know what happens if you do it a certain way. If you make your sentences short, how will readers react? If you make them long, how will they react?

As with all predicting of human behavior, this is an inexact science. If you wear your baseball cap backward, some people will react with "Oooh, he's cool" and some with "What a doofus." If your teacher wears a tie to work, some students will react with "He's a competent professional" and some with "He's stuffy and boring." As always, expect readers' responses to be a lot like your own: how do *you* feel when you read a lot of short sentences?

Let's practice these steps, using three elements of style: sentence length, Latinate diction, and concretion.

Sentence Length.   First we must believe that sentence length is something we can control independent of content. We can prove this to ourselves either by taking a passage of very long sentences and dividing them up (that's easy) or by taking a passage of very short sentences and combining them (that's harder). Here's a passage from a student essay about Buddy Bolden, the legendary blues man, in various sentence lengths from short to very long:

Short There are some things historians agree on. Bolden played cornet. No one could play like him. His fellow band members said so. Even Jelly Roll Morton said so. Morton was egocentric. Bolden worked as a barber. He had his own business. By noon, he was working on his second bottle of whiskey. You had to go to him before noon if you wanted a decent hair cut. He gradually went insane. He was committed to a state mental hospital. That was in Louisiana. He was committed in 1907. He died there twenty-four years later. (fifteen sentences)

Medium There are some things historians agree on. Bolden played cornet like no one before or after him could do, for one thing. His fellow band members said so. Even Jelly Roll Morton said so, and he was egocentric. Bolden worked as a barber and had his own business. By noon, he was working on his second bottle of whiskey, so you had to go to him before noon if you wanted a decent hair cut. He gradually went insane and was committed to the East Louisiana State Hospital. He was committed in 1907 and died there twenty-four years later. (eight sentences)

One sentence (which is how the student wrote it) Historians agree that Bolden played the cornet as no one before or after him was able to do (accounts of everyone from fellow band members to the egocentric Jelly Roll Morton confirm this), that he was self-employed as a barber (one to whom—if a decent haircut was important—you went before noon, by which time he was usually working on his second bottle of whiskey), and that he gradually went insane and was committed in 1907 to East Louisiana State Hospital, where he died twenty-four years later.

Listen to how sentences sound. Short sentences "feel" lots of different ways: earthy, plain, solid, masculine, childlike, simpleminded, choppy, wise, primitive, honest, blunt. Long sentences "feel" the opposite of all those: sophisticated, intelligent, intellectual, scholarly, clinical, educated, fluid, suave, subtle, deceptive, pretentious. Mid-length sentences feel in the middle. Armed with this knowledge, you can decide how you want to be "felt" and choose a length to produce that feeling. We can all break long sentences into shorter ones, but how do you combine short sentences to make longer ones? Consider a simple pair of sentences:

I went jogging yesterday. I saw a dead deer.

How many tools does English give us for combining these into one? The best known is the *conjunction*:

I went jogging yesterday, *and* I saw a dead deer.

But conjunctions are just the beginning. Consider these possibilities:

When I went jogging yesterday, I saw a dead deer. (dependent clause)

Jogging yesterday, I saw a dead deer. (participial phrase)

During my run yesterday, I saw a dead deer. (prepositional phrase)

I went jogging yesterday; I saw a dead deer. (semicolon)

I went jogging yesterday, saw a dead deer, and ... (compound verb)

The dead deer *that I saw* while jogging ... (relative clause)

Any of these can be combined with any others:

When I saw a dead deer *during* my run yesterday ... (dependent clause and prepositional phrase)

Now it's just a matter of forcing yourself to use the tools. Think like a skater in training: spend some time practicing axels, then some time practicing figure eights. Work on turning sentences into participial phrases, then into dependent clauses, and so on.

Latinate Diction.   Few people have ever heard of Latinate diction, but it's perhaps the stylistic choice that packs the biggest wallop for readers. A brief history lesson: English is a Germanic language, which means it is descended from an ancient parent language spoken in Germany perhaps six thousand years ago. As a result, the ancient root of the vocabulary—words like "good," "foot," "dirt," "water," "mother," and "eat"—are all Germanic and have been in the language from the beginning. These are the words that you learned first when you were growing up, the words you use most often and know the best. Later, mostly between 1150 and 1800, English borrowed a lot of words from Latin, words that feel scholarly, scientific, and clinical: "condition," "instinctual," "relativity," "procedure," "effective," "factor," "element," "consideration," "criterion," and "process."

You can say anything either way: "chew" or "masticate," "trip" or "excursion," "spread" or "disseminate."

> **Latinate:** The alleged perpetrator was observed to exit the premises in the company of two unidentified male Caucasian individuals.
>
> **Germanic:** I saw the guy who I think did it leave the place with two other white guys—I don't know who they were.
>
> **Latinate:** Violation of any of these statutes will result in immediate and permanent expulsion.
>
> **Germanic:** If you break any of these rules, we'll kick you out.
>
> **Latinate:** Excrement occurs.
>
> **Germanic:** Shit happens.

The degradation of language is an omnipresent cancer in our society. The disease goes by many names: BS, bureaucratic English, bureau-cratese, political English, Pentagonese. Not surprisingly, the people with the most to hide and the greatest need to impress—the government, the military, advertising, the police, politicians, and all bureaucracies, including your college—use it the most.

And we all fall for it. Here's a highly Latinate passage. See how impressed you are by it, and how unimpressive its Germanic revision is?

> **Latinate:** It can be determined that an herbivorous quadruped of the equine persuasion can be directed toward a chemical compound consisting of two parts hydrogen and one part oxygen; however, the aforementioned quadruped cannot necessarily be induced to partake in the consumption of the previously described aqueous solution.
>
> **Germanic:** You can lead a horse to water but you can't make it drink.

Note how the Latinate is also passive instead of active (see p. 96) and uses mostly abstractions instead of concretions (see below).

The typical Latinate level of U.S. newspapers is 20 percent, which means one of every five words on the page is from Latin. Significantly less—10 percent or lower—will feel earthy or simple when we read it. Significantly more—30 percent or higher—will feel intellectually impressive and begin to impair our ability to understand. Forty percent Latinity (four of every ten words) is incomprehensible to most of us. So unless you're engaged in an intentional snow job, keep your Latinate level below 30 percent. But don't strive for a percentile below 10 percent either, unless you want to sound like a child.

Concretion. *Concretions* are things you can perceive with the five senses—tastes, smells, sights, sounds, touches. The opposite of concretions are *abstractions:* thoughts, opinions, feelings, ideas, concepts. By extension, in language concretions are words or passages that *evoke* sensation—they make you feel like you're smelling, seeing, and so on, when you read them; abstractions don't. Concretions and abstractions can be nouns, verbs, adjectives, or adverbs.

Concretions: swim, jump, door, shoe, nose, crash, prickly, wet, slowly, saunter, trumpet, Hollandaise sauce, CD

Abstractions: idea, think, love, wonder, consideration, problem, anger, threaten, perversely, extreme, honest

As with all style features, we begin by convincing ourselves that any message can be said either in concretions or in abstractions. Most writers think that certain writing tasks are inherently concrete, like describing a car crash or showing how to bake a cake, and certain tasks are inherently abstract, like discussing philosophy or religion. To break down that prejudice, take "inherently" concrete or abstract statements and translate them into the opposite style:

Abstract: Modern society suffers from alienation.

Concrete: All of us walk through this world rubbing shoulders but never really touching.

Concrete: The car skidded off the slick macadam, rolled twice, and folded itself around a three-foot-thick oak.

Abstract: A terrible accident occurred.

Abstract: Gun ownership can lead to the possibility of serious injury.

Concrete: If you buy a gun, there's a good chance you'll shoot your foot off.

Concrete: His eyes were twitching, his hands were trembling, his brow was coated with sweat, and he kept pacing back and forth mumbling to himself.

Abstract: He was nervous.

Concrete language, because it involves the senses, is *emotionally intense*— it makes us feel. It's *easier to understand,* because humans are primarily feelers, secondarily thinkers. It's *compelling*—we believe it— because we feel like we're getting the facts, the actual evidence, instead of just the opinion. Speaking of which: a good friend of mine is a defense attorney, and he told me recently that he uses concretions to help determine whether a witness is being honest or not. The more concrete, the more specific the details, the more believable a story is.

Note, too, that the difference between being concrete and abstract is the exact same as the difference between "showing" and "telling," about which we'll talk much more in Chapter 12.

So where would you ever want to write abstractly? In school, where teachers are trying to get you to master abstract thought. In places where you want to remain rational and concretions would reduce the conversation to an emotional brawl, as in discussions of volatile issues like race or abortion.

In places where clinical objectivity is a must, as in medical writing or reporting on scientific experiments. When you're applying for government grants, and you want to appear as professorial as possible. So as always you need both styles.

To control our concretion level, we first must be sure we can distinguish between concrete and abstract on the page. Begin by asking if you can perceive it with your senses. Be careful: we tend to say things like "I could *see* she was angry," but in fact you can't—you can hear that someone is shouting, see she's red in the face, and feel she's beating you with her fists, so those are all concretions, but anger is a *conclusion* you draw from the concrete data, so anger is an abstraction. And don't assume that if the word makes you feel, then it's concrete; lots of abstract ideas—like *racism* or *Christianity*—evoke strong feelings.

There are other measuring sticks:

> Most concretions are visual, so ask yourself if you can *draw* the word—if so, it's concrete.

> Ask yourself, "How do I know?" If you say, "The door is red" and ask yourself how you know, the only possible answers are "Because I looked" or "Because I have eyes." When you find the "How do I know?" questions producing only obvious or silly answers like this, you're dealing with a concretion. But if I say, "America is becoming more uncivil" and ask myself how I know, I realize I need *evidence* to back that up, and that's a sign that I've got an abstraction.

> Imagine you're serving on a jury and a witness makes a statement under oath. If the attorney can ask the witness to back up the statement with evidence or proof, it's an abstraction; if not, it's a concretion.

Once you know for sure whether a passage is concrete or not, how do you make it concrete if it isn't? Here are eleven ways.

1. **Ask, "What's my evidence? How do I know?"** and write down the answers. You write, "He loves me," ask how you know, and write down, "He leaves little love notes on Post-its in secret places, like in my physics class notebook, so I discover them when I'm in class."
2. **Ask, "Who's doing what to whom?"** Talk in terms of *people*. Almost everything you write is about humans doing things—express it in those terms. "Practice charity" becomes "Hand the next homeless person you see ten dollars." "The usage of a dictionary is encouraged" becomes "I encourage teachers to use a dictionary."

J. M. Barrie, who wrote *Peter Pan*, knew the power of people, so *Peter Pan* begins with this note:

> Do you know that this book is part of the J. M. Barrie "Peter Pan Request"? This means that J. M. Barrie's royalty on this book goes to help the doctors and nurses to cure the children who are lying ill in the Great Ormond Street Hospital for Sick Children in London.

People appear in those two sentences eight times: you, J. M. Barrie, Peter Pan, J. M. Barrie, doctors, nurses, children, and sick children. Take the people out, and the loss hits you like a chill wind:

> All royalties from the sale of this book are donated to further medical research in pediatrics and to help defer the cost of indigent pediatric medical care.

3. **Use "I" and "you."** You and the reader are the two concretions you've always got.

4. **Let people talk.** All quotations are concrete, because they're *heard*. "Ain't no good fishin' around here no more" does a lot more work than "He was an outdoorsman who talked like a redneck." So, quote the speech of the people you mention. Use dialogue in narratives. Keep in mind, too, that when you're using dialogue, you don't have to recall and then re-create the *exact* words that were said, like you would if you were writing a profile of a celebrity for a magazine. What a person *would* have said, or *typically* said, or said something *like* works fine—*as long as you're being honest in your depiction.*

5. **Concretize your verbs.** Verbs are the parts of speech most likely to go abstract, so we want to focus on them and force them to concretize. Abstract verbs are like "is," "are," "continue," "accomplish," "effect," "involve," "proceed," "utilize," "initiate," "remain," and "constitute." Concrete verbs are like "run," "jump," "smell," "fall," "shrink," and "fly."

6. **Particularize your concretions.** Some concretions are better than others— more emotive, more colorful. "Move" is colorless; "slither" is colorful. The difference is one of *particularity*. To particularize a word, ask yourself, "In what way did it happen?" or "What kind of thing was it?"

Less lively	More lively
Move	slither, slink, sashay, saunter, crawl, skip
Car	ragtop, four-door, SUV, lowrider
Horse	pinto, Clydesdale, swayback plow horse
Hairdo	mullet, cornrows

Particulars are more persuasive, as every good salesperson knows: the more particulars, the more we're *sold* on what we read. When you read an ad for a powerboat that says,

> Kurtis Kraft 10-inch runner bottom, blown injected, 1/4-inch Velasco crank, Childs and Albert rods, Lenco clutch, Casale 871 Little Field blower, Enderle injection,

even if you don't know what any of that means, you're probably thinking, "It must be a great boat!"

7. **Tell stories.** Narratives encourage concretion, because they're usually about things *people did.*

8. **Use the active voice.** Passive constructions make the people disappear. In an *active* sentence, the doer is the subject: "George sold the car." A *passive* construction—a form of *to be* plus a past participle—doesn't need to mention the doer at all: "The car was sold."

There is one large exception to this rule. In scientific and technical writing, if you are describing a process—a step-by-step series of events—then *what was done* is all that matters and *who did it* is a distraction, so use the passive voice. Write, "The surface liquid was drained off and the residue transferred to a sterile Petri dish"; don't write, "One of my lab assistants, Pippi Carboy, drained off the surface liquid, and Lance Credance, a postdoctoral fellow, who shares the lab, transferred the residue to a sterile Petri dish."

9. **Use metaphors.** A metaphor is an implied comparison. Instead of stating an abstraction, you state a concretion that the abstraction is *like*. That sounds intimidating, but in fact you use metaphors hundreds of times a day. Instead of saying to your roommate, "Your living habits are filthy and revolting," you say, "You're a pig." You can't articulate clearly on a sleepy Monday morning, and instead of saying, "My mental processes are impaired," you say, "I can't jump-start my brain." Instead of saying, "That rock band is out-of-date," you say, "They're dinosaurs."

Everyday English is stiff with metaphors. In the world of sports, for instance, teams lock horns, fold, choke, run out of gas, get snakebit, and look over their shoulder. Players press too hard, go flat, carry teams, get swelled heads, rest on their laurels, and coast. Quarterbacks pick defenses apart and have to eat the ball, and pitchers throw smoke, pull the string, and nibble at the corners. But the best metaphors are the ones you make up yourself. An interviewer once asked Charlton Heston what Cecil B. DeMille, the legendary Hollywood director, was like, and Heston replied, "He cut a very large hole in the air."

To make up a metaphor, you just take the abstraction and ask yourself, "What physical process is this like? What do I see when I try to visualize it? How does it feel in the body? How would I draw it?" Having your boyfriend terminate your relationship feels like getting your heart ripped out and handed to you; you imagine him booting you out the door and you landing on your butt on the pavement; and so on.

10. **Use similes.** You're probably more comfortable with similes than with metaphors because they're easier to spot. A simile (pronounced "SIMMalee") is a metaphor with the comparison identified with the word "like" or "as":

Writing unrhymed poetry is like playing tennis without a net.

(ROBERT FROST)

Like a bridge over troubled waters / I will lay me down.

(PAUL SIMON)

One of my favorite simile-rich passages is this one, from an April 2007 *National Geographic* article called "My Blue Heaven" by Kennedy Warne. How many similes can you count?

> Descending into the fiords is like landing through smog in an aircraft. For a few seconds everything is brown, and you're driving blind. Then, at the mixing point between fresh and salt, the water starts to shimmer like a mirage, and you emerge like Alice through the looking glass. Projecting from the fiord walls are ten-foot-tall black coral trees. Butterfly perch shoal among their tiny branches like Christmas tree ornaments. Symbiotic snake stars—sulphur yellow, burgundy, spotted, or boldly striped— entwine their arms tightly around twig and trunk.
>
> Wax ascidians—sponge-like encrustations—drip down the rock faces like melting candles. A pea green sea slug the size of a grapefruit rests in corpulent splendor on a boulder. At a site called Strawberry Fields, pimply, red sea squirts turn the rocks into an underwater fruit bowl. Arrays of sea pens stand on the seabed like some kind of alien installation. Cruising them are nosy, in-your-face blue cod, wearing perpetual frowns on their frog-eyed noggins.

11. **Substitute examples.** When you find an abstraction, ask yourself, "What's a concrete example of that?" and replace the abstraction with the example.

    WEAK: *With Google you can find anything you want.*

    STRONGER: With Google, you can find the capital of Borneo (or a recipe for jambalaya, or a golden retriever breeder in Detroit, or Buster Posey's high school batting average, etc.).

    WEAK: *You can use Googlemaps to get directions from Point A to Point B.*

    STRONGER: You can use Googlemaps to get directions from Boulder to Burning Man (or from your house to the closest Macy's, etc.)

    WEAK: *You can use Google to look up the definition of any word.*

    STRONGER: You can use Google to look up the definition of "basorexia" (which I just did).

    WEAK: *With Google, it's easy to get distracted and end up all over the place.*

    STRONGER: With Google, it's easy to get distracted. One minute you're working on your paper for your American history class and the next you're reading about Borneo (or jambalaya, or golden retrievers, or Buster Posey, or Burning Man, or looking up weird words like "basorexia," etc.)

The Bible loves to illustrate abstract lessons with concrete examples. It won't say, "Be generous with others"; it will say, "Take your bread and divide it in half and give half to a stranger."

A final word: we've mastered three stylistic features—sentence length, Latinate diction, and concretion—but that's just the beginning. We can use the same three steps to master dozens of others that remain. For instance:

Do you use adjectives rarely or often?

Do you ever use dashes? Semicolons? Parentheses?

Do you use the active voice or the passive voice?

Which carry the weight, your nouns or your verbs?

Do you use the first person, "I," or the third person, "he," "she," "it," "they"?

Do you use contractions ("can't") or full forms ("cannot")?

Do you use slang or Standard English?

The world of style is all before you. Have fun exploring.

TONE (LOL!)

Anyone who's ever written an email or text and used an emoticon like ;-) or an abbreviation like LOL understands the importance of tone in writing. You *assume* the person will understand that you're being sarcastic, or "just kidding," but you're not sure, so you insert a little blinking, smiling face to ensure the reader "gets it." In essays and academic papers, we don't have that luxury, so we have to be very clear what emotions our words are conveying.

In fact, tone is the emotional mood of the writing and is described by the same *adjectives* we use to describe people's moods or personalities: angry, sweet, frustrated, formal, snide, silly, cold, melancholy, professorial, stuffy, hip, and so on. In a way, tone is the manifestation of style. That is, the style (the words) you use will determine the tone (emotion) that the writing suggests.

In school we tend to be deaf to tone. Odd, since in life mood is the first thing we notice. Yet often students tend to notice tone last, if at all, when they read. They'll talk about an essay's content for hours, but not notice it's funny. And of the five big issues—thesis, purpose, audience, tone, and style—tone is the one students have typically not thought much about. So train yourself to be tone-sensitive when you read and when you write. You already know how to "do" tone—you know how to sound angry or sad. It's just a matter of giving yourself permission.

How important is tone? It's more than garnish—often it's more important than content. People often care more about how others "feel" to them than about what they say. Every time there's a presidential debate, we see that Americans care more about how a candidate's personality comes across (does he seem warm? does he seem trustworthy?) than about his political platform.

Mastering tone begins with the realization that *you can't not have one,* any more than a person can be in *no* mood. If you ask someone how she feels and she says, "I feel nothing," you know she's in denial—and so are you if you say your writing has no tone. Any set of words will create a tone, just as any set of clothes will make some impression, so your only choices are to control tone or be out of control.

Don't strive for blandness unless the boss orders you to. Few people seek to feel nothing, few people say beige is their favorite color, few love plain oatmeal above all other foods, and few people read to feel nothing. So don't strive for tonal neutrality unless you're sure your purposes call for it—as in legal depositions and medical research. For most of us, emotion is good. The most common problem with writing is that it's too flat, *so push toward the brighter colors*—outrage, impishness, absurdity, fright, joy. For an example of tone in writing, see Laura Kate James's essay "Thanksgiving" on p. 351.

Once we grant that tone exists, we like to escape responsibility for choosing the tone of our writing, saying, "My tone is forced on me by my subject matter (or my thesis)." Never. *Tone is chosen*, just like audience. Any subject matter and any message can be presented in any tone. Dramatist Craig Wright has written a comedy about the day after September 11 (*Recent Tragic Events*), and he was also the head writer for HBO's *Six Feet Under*, a television show about undertakers!

Cultivate a large vocabulary of tones. Tones are tools, and the more tools we have, the more powerful we are. Writing everything in the same tone is as impractical as hitting every golf shot with the same club and as boring as always wearing khakis. Anyway, tone is where the fun is. Imagine writing a letter to your bank telling them they've once again fouled up your checking account. Try several different tones:

Sarcastic: I have to hand it to you guys—I never thought you'd find a new way to foul things up, but you have.

Sympathetic: We all make mistakes—I know, I make them myself all day long. I appreciate the load of work you guys are under. I realize how it can happen, but you seem to have gotten my account confused with someone else's.

Indignant: I have never in my twenty-five years as a businessman witnessed anything like the level of administrative incompetence that is the daily norm in your bank ...

Suppliant: I don't want to make a nuisance of myself, but might I ask that you reexamine your records for my account? There seems to be a mistake somewhere, and I know it's probably mine, but ...

Choose the tone that works—which always means the tone that gets the reaction you want from your reader. In other words, tone is dictated by purpose. Sometimes anger works for you; sometimes it works against you. Only a clear sense of purpose (and of audience) will tell you which situation applies in a particular essay. If you're trying to jolt the audience out of its complacency, you may want to be obnoxious, offensive, and profane—that's exactly what the punk music of the 1980s did. If you're trying to soothe a patient just before his open-heart surgery, clinical objectivity is probably called for, since you want the patient as numb as possible.

Making the Tool

A statement of tone often starts with a single adjective: "This essay feels _____"—informal, formal, informative, educational, personal, funny, comic, angry. But a tone is the mirror of a personality talking, and personalities can be very complex. So push beyond the single generic word. As with topic and audience, more is better. If your tone is "funny," ask, "What kind of funny?" Perhaps it's "slightly sarcastic, gently teasing, a little grumpy but basically good-humored and ultimately sympathetic."

Using the Tool

Using a definition of tone comes down to asking two questions. First, "Is this tone intriguing/touching/powerful?" If it isn't, you may need to rewrite the essay in some color other than beige. Second, "How does this tone serve my purpose?" Your answer must be in terms of audience response: "This tone will make my reader react *thus*, and that's the reaction I want." If you struggle in answering, the problem may be in your purpose—if you aren't sure what you're trying to do, you can't tell if the tone will help or not.

WRITER'S WORKSHOP

Thinking About Thesis, Audience, Purpose, Tone, and Style

Here's a first draft that's full of interesting stuff, but the writer doesn't yet know what he's saying, or to whom or why.

NO TITLE WORTHY

ALBERT PIERCE

Student Essay

I think I got the date right. There isn't much else worth remembering. Oh, my thesis! A little advice for all you folks out there who still fall into the category defined by that all too oft-quoted song which I believe says something about those who have not yet accumulated enough scar tissue and believe that they still fit the category label "young at heart" (an interesting little concept when one stops to ponder its complexities): Boys and girls, marriage is for the birds. I could easily use stronger language, but, believe it or not, I'm turning this in as a representation of my consummate skill at argumentative articulation.

And you wonder what revelatory message I could possibly relate that would have any significance to your life? Frankly, I'm not sure that I give a damn if you read this or not.

Perhaps I should explain that it is quickly approaching two in the morning and that I didn't get any sleep last night either. I am perusing the bottom of a bottle of Jack Daniel's (I should have bought two) and my grammar, as well as my sense of good taste, are at a state so low as to not have been experienced before in my lifetime. No doubt, having read this far, you concur.

As to the matter at hand, my wife left me twenty-nine days ago, upon the date of my 37th birthday. So why, I hear you cry, are you still so damn depressed? Because marriages spanning twelve years just don't end that easily. First you have to go through two years of hell while you're still living together but don't know you're going through hell. Then your lady informs you that it's over. Naturally you don't believe it, and in your vain attempt to sway the opinion of your soon-to-be-estranged mate, discover all kinds of things which she never told you about. Excuse me a minute while I pour myself another drink.

At any rate, during the week that it takes you to find an apartment, she discovers that she has made a terrible mistake. And so begins the reconciliation. Now you are totally enamored of each other. You talk incessantly. You have sex in the kitchen. This lasts about two weeks.

After this period begins the stage in which she doubts that the two of you can really make it after all. Wednesday after the Sunday upon which she professed undying love, she tells you she "needs some space" and she hopes you will "always be her friend." This is followed by the Thursday when she won't talk to you except to say that she doesn't want to talk to you. You buy a bottle.

Excuse me, I need more ice.

This last event is quite predictable. It happens within three days prior to the due date of at least three large school projects. No problem!

And now for the first time in your life you discover real pain. I just wrote another poem and put it under her windshield wiper. I will probably never know if she reads it. I will never see her laugh, cry, complain. Twelve years. It wasn't worth it. Don't get married. It's three a.m. I'm going to bed now.

—Permission provided by Steve Metzger

The horsepower is great, but Albert knows he hasn't a clue about who it's talking to or what it hopes to do to the reader. So far it's just personal therapy.

After thinking about it, Albert realized he hadn't really considered an audience for the piece, but he also knew that there was one, out there somewhere. So instead of just writing to get this stuff off his chest, he decided to write to his brother, John, who had just gotten married, and by implication to all other newlyweds. His purpose would be to prepare them for the inevitable agony of divorce. Choosing an audience and purpose led to choosing a structure: the essay would be a letter and a list of tips. Here's how the next draft came out:

BEST-LAID PLANS

Dear John:

I loved your wedding. The flowers were lovely, and the bride looked radiant.

I'm writing to offer you the benefit of my experience as you start out on this new phase of your life. Marriage is a big step. It requires planning and foresight. You should be receiving this about two weeks after the ceremony, so the first flush of love is past and it's time to start planning for your divorce.

You may think I'm being a little hasty, but consider. More than half the people who get married these days get divorced. That means the odds are against you. Wouldn't it be wise to take some precautions? Having some practical experience in this area of the human experience, I will be your mentor.

First off, accept the coming divorce as an inevitability. Begin thinking of your spouse as "your future ex-wife." The agony of divorce is largely in the surprise.

Second, accept the fact that the person you're living with isn't the person you'll have to deal with during the divorce. Your loving spouse will overnight become a ruthless enemy bent on domination. You will be amazed at the similarities between dealing with an ex-wife and a gigantic corporation planning a hostile takeover of your company.

In fact, accept the fact that your spouse isn't the person you think she is *right now*. During the divorce proceedings, she will cheerfully tell you that everything you thought you knew about her was a lie: she never liked you, she always thought your jokes were lame, she really hated sex with you and just did it out of a sense of duty, etc., etc.

Now that you have the right attitude, what practical steps can you take? Prepare for the divorce in a businesslike manner. Do exactly what you would do in a business relationship with a shifty partner. Trust no one. Make sure you have at least seven bank accounts, so when her lawyers find three or four of them you'll be left with something. Make sure everything you own of value is heavily mortgaged. Have no significant liquid assets, except whiskey, which will be tax deductible after the divorce as a medical expense. Don't count on your premarital agreement saving you—all legal contracts can be broken. Most important of all, fight for your own interests. Let the other guy look out for the other guy; she will, I assure you.

Lay plans to handle the sense of worthlessness. Start seeing a therapist *now*, to get a head start. And don't make the novice spouse's mistake of severing all ties with members of the opposite sex. I'm not advising having affairs, but when the break comes you'll need women friends to pat you on the head, say you've still got what it takes, and listen as you say loathsome things about your ex.

Know the traditional behavior of the divorcing spouse and expect it. For instance, there is the False Reconciliation. She discovers that she has made a terrible mistake. Now you are totally enamored of each other. You talk incessantly. You have sex in the kitchen. This lasts about a week. Wednesday after the Monday when she professed undying love, she tells you she "needs some space" and she hopes you will "always be her friend." This is followed by the Friday when she won't talk to you except to say that she doesn't want to talk to you. You go into shock. This will always happen three days prior to the due date of at least three large school projects. Plan ahead!

If you take this advice, divorce, like thermonuclear war, can become an unpleasant but survivable disaster. And incidentally, since these realities have nothing to do with the personalities involved, I'm sending a copy of this letter to your wife, with suitable pronoun changes, to be fair. After all, after the divorce I'm hoping to stay friends with both of you.

—Permission provided by Steve Metzger

Now It's Your Turn. Here's the first draft of an essay that hasn't yet committed itself to a thesis, audience, or purpose. Read it closely, and then brainstorm a list of three potential audiences for it and possible corresponding theses and purposes.

UNTOUCHABLES

DUNCAN THOMSON

Student Essay

Women! Can't live with them, can't get near them, drink another beer. Sweet dreams. Is it in the eyes of the beholder? I think not. You see them every day on campus, do they acknowledge you? Maybe, maybe not. They say that love comes from the heart, for a guy, I think it comes from his zipper most of the time. For a gorgeous girl, I think it comes from her attitude. Maybe you truly just have to know someone until you can truly judge them.

She was my *Cosmo* woman, my runway girl, I still think about her and miss what we once had. I feel so stupid for letting her get away to pursue her modeling career. It's over now but for the longest time I couldn't even think about another woman. Life really didn't seem worth living. Will I ever meet her again? I'm looking and she's out there, I just don't know who she is. Is this her?

It's Friday night and you're ready to hit the town. If you're under twenty-one it's a piece of cake, but if you're over twenty-one that means a night at the bars. Why we go, man, I'll never know. You're getting ready. You pick what you think will make you the most attractive person on the face of this earth. Now I feel like a million bucks. There is so much confidence in this bathroom as I stare into the mirror. You see, Mike's is to many of us guys the ultimate place to meet women. From 9 p.m. till 1, the place is completely packed with both sexes.

This is it, the time to find my Christy Brinkley, Elle McPherson. Anything is possible. This is the place where confidence becomes reality: dance, rate the pairs in the room, buy her a drink, throw some one-liners, anything to strike up a conversation. "Those are the most beautiful eyes I've ever seen." It may be corny but it does lead to an interesting conversation.

I'm all fired up as I wait in line to get in. We're going out to get drunk and meet women. Is this paradise or am I just stupid? The fellas and I head for the bar. "Two pitchers and three shots please." No, why oh why did I order shots? Oh well, here we go again.

There she is, oh god, just look at her. Blonde hair, blue eyes, but that's not where my eyes are wandering. What curves! The complete package. I can feel my body start to shake. "Hey bartender, one more shot please." I feel sick, I start talking to myself: relax, jerkface, you haven't even talked to her yet. I still have this really nervous feeling inside but on the outside I still have that confident 90210 look.

I'm really starting to feel good from the alcohol. That other girl who didn't look so hot earlier is all of a sudden looking good. So many women! Blondes, brunettes, tall, short, skinny, voluptuous, and of course the total packages. Most other women call them sluts but I think they got it so they flaunt it. Why are they so hard to meet? I'm a nice, attractive person with a lot going for me. I stumble over to talk to one. "Do you want to dance?" I say. "Maybe next song," she replies. I turn to say hello to a friend and the snooty little bitch is gone. She was just another untouchable.

Some of these girls are so incredible, most men don't even have a chance with them. You have got to have either money, some kind of title, or something that makes you desirable. Everything you try is wrong. I know I'm probably not going to meet this woman in a bar but it's a good place to start.

Let me tell you, when you get to date one of these women just once, your whole world is great. Each day is bright, the sun is shining. Everyone looks at you with this girl, the other guys are thinking, "What? That little dork with such a hot woman?" The world is your oyster. Your dreams become reality. I know, no woman has enough power to do that. Wrong! An untouchable woman is the best thing in the world.

Then that day will come, she's gone. No heart, no soul, worthless. It crushes you for at least six months. Eventually you get over it. Is that why I'm still in this bar?

I'm heading home, with nothing but a piece of pizza in my hand. I get home and grab that little black book and dial for a girl until I pass out. Women! Can't live with them, can't get near them, drink another beer.

God life is great.

—Permission provided by Steve Metzger

EXERCISES

1. Take a familiar expression, either an old saw, such as "Don't count your chickens before they've hatched," or perhaps an advertising slogan, such as "Just Do It," and write it in a wordy, passive, Latinate style, like we did with "You can lead a horse to water but you can't make it drink." Share them with your classmates. Extra credit if they have absolutely no idea what you're talking about (but they must be familiar with the one with which you're working).

For each of the following tones, describe a more precise tone by adding detail.

   a. Sad

   b. Formal

   c. Informative

   d. Angry

2. Pick any essay in "A Collection of Good Writing" and answer the following questions:

   a. What are its stylistic characteristics (level of formality, sentence length, etc.)

   b. What's the tone?

   c. How does the tone suit the purpose?

3. Do Exercise 2 using an essay of your own.

Chapter 7

Organization: Mapping, Outlining, and Abstracting

O nce you have a general sense of what you're saying, why you're saying it, and to whom you are saying it, you need to ask the next large question: "How can I shape all this stuff so that it makes sense?"

And that's a tough question to answer. Writers organize in a wide range of ways, from "organically," that is, letting the piece of writing take its own shape and more or less figuring it out along the way, to using strict and formal outlines and never deviating from them. In fact, not only do different writers organize in different ways, but also different organizational strategies are better suited to different writing tasks. The "organic" approach might be best suited to a short personal essay, while working from a formal outline might be better for a long research paper.

I'm hoping you're convinced—after reading the first six chapters—that you need raw material to work with, that you're comfortable just writing a lot, including lots of stuff that you'll eventually round-file, and that you really can't organize before you have *something* to organize.

In this chapter you're going to practice making and using three tools that will help you find shape for your work—mapping, outlining, and abstracting. You might find that one or another works better for your particular approach to writing, or you might want to create your own hybrid. Confession: I personally have never been able to make mapping work. I've written seven books and over 500 journal and magazine articles—never working from a map. That said, many of my students and colleagues swear by mapping. They say that they'd be lost without it. So, do what works best for you.

But first let's walk through the process to see what reorganizing looks like and to observe some of these tools in action. Here's a brainstormed first draft describing a student's friend:

> Tony can fill a room with excitement. He's very handsome. He used to have a mustache, but he shaved it off. He tells marvelous lies. He wants to be a professional actor. His eyes mist over when he talks about emotional things. He can talk well on almost any subject. Women melt before him. Tony has worked very hard at karate. He's as graceful as a panther. When he fights, his eyes burn with a passionate wildness. Onstage, he acts with unpolished, startling energy. He sweats when he acts. Last week he told me that he wasn't happy. He said he was burned out. An old back injury had suddenly recurred. He said he feared he was going insane. Today I saw him walking down the street, wearing the latest fashions and beautifully tanned. He smiled a hard plastic smile. He talked excitedly about a potential job and hurried off without a backward glance. He's twenty years old. He lives at home with both his parents. He has no job and doesn't want to go to college. He stays out and parties heavily until two or three o'clock in the morning. His mother always waits up for him.

That's twenty-five descriptive facts about Tony—too many to see at a glance. Let's reduce by summarizing the twenty-five items to five:

Tony is energetic and attractive.
He's an eager conversationalist.
He's an expert at karate.
Last week, he said he was miserable and acted rushed and insecure.
He's twenty and has no prospects.

Now we can see that these five items are really two: (1) Tony has a lot of gifts and (2) his life is a mess. We can now express this as a thesis sentence: *Tony is wasting his great talents.* Now we can see how all the twenty-five original parts have jobs in that large design. Tony has power (social, sexual, physical) but can't find anything to do with it. Karate gave him a bit of an outlet, and acting a bit, but acting is only professional faking, and Tony does too much of that already. With all his gifts, he's burned out and directionless—he's wasting his time in pointless partying, and he can't get it together enough to leave his parents. Now we can *outline* the draft:

I. Tony has power and talent to burn.
   A. Sexual: Women swoon over him.
   B. Social: He can walk into a room and every eye will turn to him.
   C. Physical: He's a panther at karate.
   D. Psychic: He's a dominating force on the stage.
II. But he can't seem to do anything with his power.
   A. He's burned out.
   B. He dresses well but looks dead inside.
   C. His body's failing him.
III. He's twenty years old but still living like a child.
   A. He parties every night.
   B. His mother still waits up for him.

And we can *abstract* the outline:

Tony is so attractive that he can walk into any party and fascinate everyone there in five minutes. He has so much natural energy that he's an expert at karate and a compelling actor. Yet he tells me he's burned out and miserable, and he seems empty, in a hurry but with nowhere to go. He's twenty years old, but without a future; he spends his time going from one meaningless party to another, with his mom always waiting up for him.

THE ORGANIZING ATTITUDE

Before we pick up a tool, let's make sure we have the right attitude:

Organizing Begins with Making a Model

To organize anything, you have to see the entire design at a glance, and that means making a miniature version of it—just like the models of buildings or golf courses architects make before the bulldozers go to work. Maps, outlines, and abstracts are just three different kinds of models.

Organizing a draft is like arranging the furniture in a room. You can do it one of two ways: you can move the furniture itself around, stopping from time to time to see how it looks, or you can make a model, by drawing a diagram of the room and cutting out paper representations of the furniture. Making a map or outlining or abstracting is like using a model—obviously a lot easier, and offering an excellent sense of how the room will ultimately look.

On the other hand, sometimes you just need to push the furniture around to actually experience what the room will ultimately look like. So, as you work on your model, remember that you are still not committed and that it is meant only to help you see the bigger picture. Remember, too, that the beauty of models is that you can do several simultaneously and look at them side by side.

We know how big the model should be initially, thanks to the Magic Number Seven (Prologue): seven or fewer standard sentences. You usually don't need seven; here's an essay in condensed form, shrunk to just three:

> I "did well" in school but was bored and learned little, because school was boring and irrelevant. But it doesn't have to be that way—there are ways to make classrooms exciting and useful. And they work: I still remember about paramecia because of the time my class took a field trip to the pond. ("Why I Never Cared for the Civil War," p. 359.)

As soon as you understand your structure on this basic level, you can start adding details, making the model more complex. When we're completely lost, we want a map of extreme simplicity, but the better we know the territory, the more map detail we can handle.

Organize as You're Working on Your Draft

It's hard to arrange the furniture in a room when you don't have any furniture. You need to produce stuff before you can ask, "What shape should this stuff be in?" In some academic writing—especially very long papers—you might need an organizational template or outline before you start actually composing; but in essay writing you often *discover* structure along the way.

Another analogy: my wife and I recently took a cross-country road trip, from California out to the East Coast and back. We knew exactly where we were leaving from, and we knew exactly where we'd end up. And we had a general itinerary (up through the Black Hills and the Midwest, to the Outer Banks of North Carolina, friends in Atlanta, over to Memphis, down into Austin, friends in Flagstaff, then home), but we wanted to feel free to "discover our organization" along the way. Good thing we did, too, or else we never would have deviated from our planned route to visit the Flight 93 Memorial in eastern Pennsylvania, which truly became the most moving and the defining stop on our trip. (To read the article I wrote about it, see p. 345). Same with writing. Once you have the raw material and a pretty good idea of where you're starting from and where you're ending up, you should feel free to let the writing itself dictate the structure—or at least feel free to try lots of different routes, as suggested by the material.

Experiment Freely

The beauty, and the fun, of this stage of writing is that you can't be wrong, because you haven't committed yourself yet. You really have nothing to lose by moving the couch over by the window to see how it looks there; if it doesn't work, move it somewhere else. Note: Use whatever format will allow you the most freedom. If working on a computer is liberating, then work on a computer. If you feel more free to experiment by scribbling in longhand on a sheet of paper, then scribble away.

Take Time to Reflect

Don't just move the couch over by the window and then immediately decide it looks horrible there. Make another model and look at them side by side. Take a break and fix yourself a cup of coffee or a snack, and then come back for another look. Reflect on your model until that reflection leads to concrete revision strategies: "I think I'll start the essay with the old paragraph 3 and see where that goes."

Learn to Organize by Reading for the Craft

Essay organization is hard in part because we never get much practice in it. A lifetime of talking leaves us unprepared to organize essays, because talk is just one thing tacked onto another. So practice observing structure when you read: Ask yourself, How is this put together? How did the author get it started? How did she end? And remember, only essays can model for you how to structure essays. For an example of an essay with a brilliant structure, see Megan Sprowls' "The Dos and Don'ts ..." on p. 342. Note her use of repetition, both to keep the piece moving forward and to give it overall shape (she actually repeats her introductory sentence at the beginning of her second-to-last paragraph).

We'll practice three diagnostic tools for organizing: mapping, outlining, and abstracting. Each gives us different data.

MAPPING

Making the Tool

Mapping is looser and messier than outlining and abstracting, so you can do it at many different stages in the writing process, though it's most useful when you're *prewriting*, that is, before you've written a single word of your draft, or later, once you've got the rough words of a draft on paper (or screen). Mapping is like taking the pieces of the essay and tossing them into the air. It's freer in four ways. First, you can map in all 360 degrees of the circle, and you can connect anything on the page to anything else on the page via a line, as opposed to outlining and abstracting, which limit you to linear thinking. Second, a map has no starting and ending points and no sequence—there's no order to the spokes on a wheel—so mapping forces you to rethink sequence. Third, you can map anything—fragments, words, pictures—whereas outlines and abstracts work with whole sentences. Fourth, maps have *centers,* but outlines and abstracts don't, so use mapping when you're still tinkering with the essay core.

Using the Tool

With our three organizing tools, the art is in the interpretation of the data. After you make the map, what does it tell you about the draft? Only practice will teach you how to answer that question. Figure 7.1 is the author's map for "Legalize Hemp" (Chapter 10). What does it suggest Todd should think about in the revision? First, Bubble A logically should be an offshoot of Bubble B. Second, Bubble B promises solutions to "political" problems, but the map never shows us any. Third, items in the map are mentioned more than once in the draft—Bubble D, for instance. Fourth, Bubble E hangs alone and unexplained, and it shows up in the draft in the last paragraph without explanation. Fifth, Bubble F seems to be from a different essay. Sixth, Bubbles F, G, and H are all together in the map but spread throughout the draft. So Todd has six decisions to make. Is there a problem here? What should he do about it?

OUTLINING

Of our three organizational tools, the most popular is outlining. We see outlines everywhere: instructors outline their lectures on the chalkboard and in PowerPoint presentations, books are outlined in their tables of contents, weddings and funerals often provide programs that outline events in chronological order, and so on. To outline, you reduce the draft to a series of sentences and list them in a vertical column.

Making the Tool

Outlines are wonderfully revealing diagnostic tools, but can go wrong in lots of ways, so here are several guidelines. To begin, since outlines are rigid, intimidating things that have a tendency to freeze a writer's blood, stay loose by following these four rules:

1. *Outline in three to five parts only.* According to the Magic Number Seven, we could have a few more, but outlining is so rigid that we want to keep things very simple.
2. *Outline in a flash.* Write the entire outline in a minute or less. Don't labor over it—try to grasp how the whole essay works in three or four steps and write them down.
3. *Don't feel compelled to use a formal outline structure (Roman numerals, numbers, letters, etc.) unless you find it particularly useful.* All that stuff can stiffen you up, and it emphasizes the structure over content, the container over the contained.
4. *Stay loose.* Feel free to scribble your outline on a sheet of paper. If you do all your prewriting on a computer, keep it loose. Remember, you're still just playing at this point.

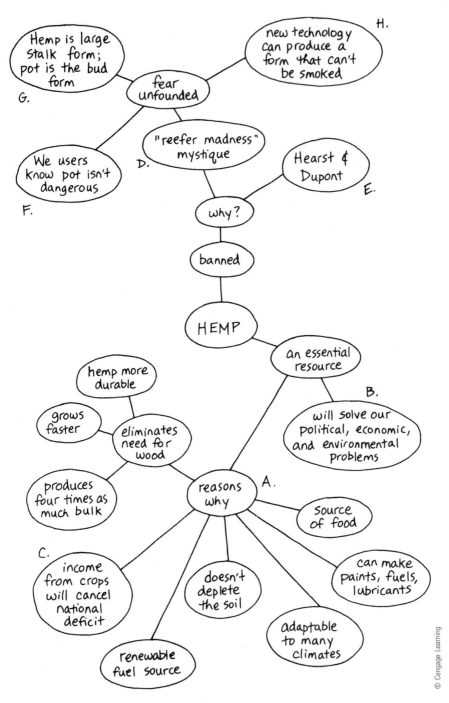

FIGURE 7.1   The Author's Map for "Legalize Hemp."

Some people flatly refuse to do those four things. They like to labor over an outline and make it gleam with Roman numerals and lots of subsections. The finished outline looks very impressive, but the writer has turned into a slab of ice.

Now that we're loose, follow these additional rules:

5. *Don't describe; summarize.* Don't tell the reader what you did or are going to do; instead, speak the essay, in reduced form. Don't say, "I list the causes of the Civil War"; say, "The causes of the Civil War weren't racial; they were economic." You know you're doing it right when a reader can read the outline and feel he has the essay itself in short form—not a promise of an essay.

6. *If you've already got a pretty respectable draft, preserve its sequencing.* Don't rearrange the essay content, because then the outline can't diagnose structural problems. Make sure the first item in the outline is the first large thing the draft says, and the last item is the last large thing the essay says.

7. *Don't quote sentences from the draft.* As with thesis sentence writing, it's rare that the best sentences for the outline can be plucked as is from the draft. Don't *select* sentences for the outline; *compose* them.

8. *Outline whole sentences only.* If you don't outline sentences, you'll outline nouns and fragments only. Here's a nice-*looking* outline:

I. Weapons of mass destruction: the present crisis
II. Historical causes
   A. The fall of the Soviet Union
   B. The Mideast conflict
   C. Cold War mentality
III. Proposed solutions
   A. American proposals
   B. Israeli proposals
   C. Proposals of other nations
   D. Why they don't work
IV. My solution

Looks great, doesn't it? But it's a complete smokescreen. You could do the same thing with virtually any topic, whether you know something about it or not.

Outlining what the draft says turns out to show only half of what we want to know, and the less important half. Remember, we're not in the business of *saying things*; we're in the business of saying things *to do things to readers*. So we need to make two outlines simultaneously, a *content* outline and a *function* outline. The content outline is the kind we just made. We'll write it on the left side of the page. The function outline will run down the right side of the page. For each item in the content outline, there should be a matching item in the function outline, explaining what *job* the sentence in the content outline is doing. Here's a dual outline for the essay called "Given the Chance" (Chapter 15).

Content	Function
1. I met Stacey, a likable drug addict, when I was working at our Group Home.	1. Win reader's sympathy for Stacey.
2. She needs a rehab program, but she can't get into one.	2. State the problem.
3. The State refuses to pay for it.	3. State the source of the problem.
4. The State should give Stacey and me a chance.	4. State thesis.

Function outlining is a continuation of our work with purpose in Chapter 5—now we're just identifying the purpose of each essay *section*. Follow these rules while making function outlines:

9. *Use your favorite synonym.* If the word "function" isn't to your taste, you can use the word "purpose," "intention," "job," or "chore."

10. *Make the function statements verb phrases.* All-purpose statements are inherently verbal. You can use imperatives ("Hook the reader"), infinitives ("To hook the reader"), or participles ("Hooking the reader")—it doesn't matter.

11. *Keep function statements short and familiar.* Most of the time the function of a passage is something short, simple, and well known, because when you get right down to it, there are only a few functions writing can have. You can state a thesis, you can defend it, you can hook the reader with personal narrative, you can marshal facts in support of your argument, you can refute counterarguments, you can consider the consequences of taking action, and so on. Look back at the sample function outline: the four functions are all short, all ordinary. And that's good. If your function statements get complicated and strange, suspect that your intentions are really simpler than you realize.

12. *Don't reproduce content.* This is a version of the point we made about purpose statements (Chapter 5). If you write function statements like "Say what's wrong with affirmative action," "Tell the story about the car accident," or "Describe her parents," you're really just reproducing the stuff from the content side of the outline in altered form. If you do that, the function statements can't teach you anything new. To avoid the trap, *ask yourself, why?* Why are you saying what's wrong? Why are you telling the story? Why are you describing the parents?

13. *Avoid universal function labels like "introduction" and "conclusion."* Such labels don't lie, but they're so broad that they won't teach you anything. Since they'll work for any essay, they can't be insightful

about what *this* essay is doing. To avoid the trap, *ask yourself, how?* How does this essay introduce? How does this essay conclude?

14. *Troubleshoot by asking questions.* If you have trouble grasping the function of a sentence in the outline, ask yourself, "Why is it there?" You can rephrase the question in several helpful ways: What job would go undone if you didn't include that sentence? What were you trying to accomplish by including it? What are you trying to do to the reader by including it?

Using the Tool

The first and largest question to ask of an outline is "Does this structure work?" It's a huge and slippery question, but you will probably know the answer. Beyond that, an outline can teach you a host of interesting things about a draft, so many that I can't list them for you. Each outline will teach its own lessons. So let's practice listening to outlines and seeing what they reveal. Here are three outlines, all of film reviews, to practice on. The outlines aren't perfect, so sometimes the lessons offered are about tool making and sometimes they're about revising the draft:

Outline A

Content	Function
1. The movie *Up* is more than a cartoon; it's a serious look at aging.	1. State thesis.
2. Realistic situations and dialogue add to the reality of this film.	2. Support thesis.
3. There is a complex relationship between the "cartoon" format and the reality that is being portrayed—even though houses can't be lifted up by balloons.	3. State problem.
4. Ultimately, the animation serves to provide both distance from the characters and intimacy with them.	4. State solution.

What looks good? The outline is about something important—about how a "cartoon" can be taken seriously. And the essay moves from the small, particular thing (the movie) to larger issues—a good strategy. What needs work? Content 1 is safe and doesn't say very much, so the writer should probably look for a way to begin the essay with more energy, more risk. Nor does there seem to be much of a logical connection between Contents 2 and 3. If there is one, it needs to be made clearly. Finally, the function statements don't really let us know what the essay's thesis is. We've got a "thesis," a "problem," and a "solution" … which one is the real thesis?

Outline B

Content	Function
1. The movie is *Avatar*	1. Introduce the reader to the topic.
2. Although the movie seems to combine tactics from previous movies, it's a refreshing change from the average movie.	2. Catch the reader's attention.
3. All your feelings and emotions will be experienced during this film.	3. Convince the reader to see the movie.
4. Future movies have a new standard to live up to.	4. Conclude

What looks good? The outline is willing to take a stand; it doesn't sit on the fence. Content 4 has a punchy ring to it. And the outline language is straightforward and clear. What needs work? Content 1 is the weakest of the four, so the writer probably doesn't have to say it at all. Function 1 acknowledges this by admitting that not a lot is going on here. Content 2 seems to contain a contradiction—the movie is simultaneously innovative and familiar—so the writer would want to make clear in the draft how that could be true. Function 2 sounds like the job of an opening, so the writer should probably find a clearer sense of Content 2's job or move it to the front of the draft. When the outline ends, we've been told three times in four sentences that the movie is really good, but we don't have much in the way of a reason. In fact, we really have no idea what the movie is like or even what it's about. Content 3 is a step in that direction, but not enough—the writer should probably shore up her evidence by doing more describing. Function 4 says nothing, so the writer should probably ask, "How?" until she knows how the conclusion is working.

Outline C

Content	Function
1. *Bruno* is a terrible movie.	1. Inform my readers of my opinion.
2. The movie failed in its efforts to be funny; it was just stupid.	2. Give reasons.
3. The first few minutes introduced the characters and what they were doing.	3. Tell audience about the characters.
4. The movie felt like it dragged on forever, wasn't funny, and never made any sense.	4. List faults of the movie.
5. Although the movie is terrible, I would still recommend it just so you can form your own opinion.	5. Recommend the movie even though it's bad.

What looks good? An opinion is stated clearly, without hedging (the movie's terrible), and three solid reasons are given (it's slow, not funny, and incomprehensible). What needs work? Content 1 has no sense of "hook." Content 3 seems to add nothing to the argument, and it also seems to float alone, out of sequence. Function 3 is repetition of content, so it obscures the function instead of revealing it. Content 4 repeats Content 2, and Function 4 is a rewording of Function 2, so the writer should check to see if he's repeated himself. Content 5 should make the writer wonder why she wrote the outline at all. She's just bailing out. I'd take the risk and stand by my judgment: the movie stinks. Function 5 repeats content, so I'd keep asking, "Why say that?" until I got an answer.

ABSTRACTING

Once you've outlined and the outline says the draft looks good, you are *not* done, because writing isn't a list. There's something else, something *between* the items in your outline. Students usually say writing that has it "flows," and when it doesn't have it, they say the writing sounds "choppy." Choppy writing sounds like this:

> I think requiring deposits on soda bottles is unfair. I clean up my own litter. How much is a clean roadside worth to Americans? Glass is not something we're likely to run out of soon. Why should people be forced to do something they don't want to do?

Missing from that passage is what writing teachers call *transition* (or *transitions*). An outline encourages you not to think about the matter, by reducing the writing to a stack of parts. So we need an organizational tool that focuses on transition, and the *abstract* is it.

What exactly is transition? There are lots of ways to describe how it *feels*. In transitionless writing, the separate bits feel isolated, like shy strangers at a party. When you read it, you feel like you're constantly starting and stopping, like when you were first learning to drive a car with a manual transmission. You stopped and started abruptly, without graceful forward movement. Writing without transition is like that. It feels rough, jerky—yes, choppy. Writing that has transition feels smooth, easy—yes, it flows. It's like driving with a manual transmission after you've mastered it (or driving with an automatic transmission). And readers feel just like the passengers in your car: they'll move forward without even realizing you're changing gears.

Transition and Readers

Writing turns out to feel rich in transitions when both the writer and the reader agree that the next thing the text says follows gracefully and naturally what went before. We can describe this in two ways. One way is in terms of the reader's dialogue we tracked in Chapter 2. The writer writes something; the reader reacts with a question, a want, a feeling, a request for clarification; and the writer responds by addressing the want. That response prompts another reaction from the reader, and the back-and-forth continues to the end of the essay. If we try to carry on such an exchange with the author of the piece on recycling, we see the problem—she's not listening to us:

AUTHOR: I think requiring deposits on soda bottles is unfair.

READER: *Why?*

AUTHOR: I clean up my own litter.

READER: *So what?*

AUTHOR: How much is a clean roadside worth to Americans?

READER: I don't care.

AUTHOR: Glass is not something we're likely to run out of soon.

READER: *So what?*

AUTHOR: Why should people be forced to do something they don't *want to do?*

READER: *Because people aren't best for society? HELLO!!? ARE YOU LISTENING TO ME!!?*

Writing with transition is a back-and-forth between attentive equals. Here's Sheridan Baker discussing paragraph structure:

> Now, that paragraph turned out a little different from what I anticipated. I overshot my original thesis, discovering, as I wrote, a thesis one step further—an underlying cause—about coming to friendly terms with oneself. But it illustrates the funnel, from the broad and general to the one particular point that will be your essay's main idea, your thesis.
>
> (SHERIDAN BAKER, THE PRACTICAL STYLIST)

And here's the dialogue between Baker and the reader:

Now, that paragraph turned out a little different from what I anticipated. In what way was it different?

I overshot my original thesis.
Why did you do that?

Because I discovered, as I wrote, a thesis one step further.
What kind of thesis?

An underlying cause.
What was it about?

About coming to terms with oneself.

So your previous claim was wrong?

No, the paragraph still illustrates the funnel.

In what ways?

It still goes from the broad and general to the one particular point that will be your essay's main idea.

What's that idea called?

Your thesis.

Obviously, this approach works only if you *do something to the reader,* from the very first sentence; if you don't provoke a response, the reader is mute, and you have no reason to keep writing.

Transition and Connectors

The second way to think about this notion of "the appropriate next thing to say" is to focus on *connectors*. Connectors are devices that link one clause to another. They look like this:

and	so	but
still	yet	first, second, etc.
because	thus	even though
since	for instance	therefore
furthermore	nevertheless	moreover
however	finally	instead
although	rather than	too
also	in fact	for example
consequently	in other words	on the other hand
while	that	as a result

Connectors express logical relationships between sentences—they say, "I'm putting this sentence after that one for a reason, and here's what the reason is." "But" means "I'm going to qualify what I just said or disagree with it in some way." "So" means "I'm going to draw a conclusion from what I just said." "Instead" means "I'm going to offer an alternative."

The most familiar connectors are conjunctions ("and," "but," "so," "if"), but some adverbs connect ("therefore," "however"), and some punctuation marks do. The punctuation marks that end sentences (question marks, periods, exclamation points) *don't* connect, because they tell us only about what just happened, not how it relates to what's coming. Commas *don't* connect because they give us no specific relationship information. But the semicolon and the colon are highly specific connectors. The semicolon means "The next sentence is the second half of the idea started in the previous sentence." The colon means "Now I'm going to explain or list examples of what I just said." The typical connector is one word long, but connectors can be large blocks of text, like "Despite all that, ..."

Now we have two ways to diagnose the quality of the transitions in any piece of writing in front of us. Writing has transitions (1) if we can write out the reader's half of the dialogue between the sentences, and the product sounds like a smooth conversation, or (2) if we can put connectors between all the clauses, the connectors make sense, and the text reads well. Armed with this knowledge, we're ready to abstract the draft.

WRITING ABSTRACTS

Don't confuse this kind of abstract with abstracts of long academic papers. This is a drafting tool, for the benefit of the writer. Academic papers often include abstracts for the benefit of the reader, to provide an overview.

You can write an abstract simply by writing all the sentences in it one after the other across the page instead of in a column. Or you can look at the essay, say, "What does this say, briefly?" and spew it out. Here are abstracts for three of the essays in this book:

"Grateful" (p. 208):
Mai Thao had just moved to California from Thailand, and I was going to show her around our school. We were both eight. The first week was difficult; she was distant and seemed angry. Finally, she told me how wasteful Americans appeared to her, and she pointed out specific examples. Through Mai's eyes I learned to appreciate how fortunate I am to be an American and to appreciate what I have. We are still friends today, and I still try not to be wasteful.

"The Sprout Route" (p. 356):
If you're interested in your health, you should consider adding home-grown sprouts to your diet. Not only are they a living food supply—full of nutrients and enzymes—but they're very easy and inexpensive to grow, as well as easy to cook with. To start, all you need are some seeds, available in bulk at health-food stores, and some canning jars.

"The Good Mother" (p. 368):
If you're raising a child and it's going beautifully, you may be doing a great job, or there may be another explanation. When I raised my first child, he was an angel and I got rave reviews from myself and other parents. I assumed I was different from those other moms, who screamed and spanked. Then I had my second child, who was difficult. I tried all the right parenting responses, but they didn't work, and he turned me into the cranky, spanking mom of my nightmares. From this experience I learned that children aren't created by grown-ups, and that people (including me)

aren't as simple as they think they are. This knowledge will come in handy when I'm a teacher and it comes in handy now in my relationships with my peers and family— I'm more tolerant, more willing to listen, less sure I'm right.

Abstracting asks more of you than mapping or outlining, but it also tells you more. It's the greatest diagnostic tool an essay organizer has. And since abstracting will do everything outlining can do and more, once you master abstracting you might be able to skip the outlining stage altogether.

Making the Tool

As you abstract, follow these rules, many of which are versions of our rules for outlining:

1. **Summarize; don't describe.** With abstracting even more than outlining, the temptation is to dodge all the hard work by telling the reader what you *did* instead of saying what you *said*. Such abstracts, called *descriptive abstracts* by technical writers, usually begin like this:

   I'm going to …
   This essay is a description of … How to …
   In this essay I said …
   An introduction to …

   Descriptive abstracts have their uses for *readers,* but they tell the *writer* nothing. Prove it to yourself by writing a descriptive abstract for an essay you can't write: "This essay solves the problem of world over-population, suggests a workable cure for cancer, and proves that Elvis is really alive." If you find yourself irresistibly sucked into describing, write, "Next in this essay I say … ," finish the sentence, and then delete those first six words.

2. **Preserve the essay's sequencing.**
3. **Don't quote from the draft.**
4. **Use the voice, tone, and point of view the essay uses.** If the essay is in first person, write the abstract in first person. If the essay is funny, the abstract should be funny.
5. **Write it fairly quickly.** Pondering too long might make you belabor details. Now we're looking at the bigger picture.
6. **Write the abstract in one paragraph only.** The abstract is primarily good for diagnosing flow. A paragraph break is a big interruption in the flow, so it will obscure any transition problems and taint the diagnosis.
7. **Make the abstract about 100 words long.** It's possible to abstract to any length, and each length will teach you something useful. But for most people the abstract is most productive if it's 70–150 words, one-quarter to one-third of a single-spaced typed page, about seven normal-length sentences. Don't make the abstract longer just because the draft is longer—the Magic Number Seven never changes, and every map in

your glove compartment probably is the same size whether it's for your town or your state.

Using the Tool

As with the thesis statement and outline, begin using the abstract by asking any and all large questions about what's going on: Did you say anything? Is it interesting? Did you take any risks? and so on. But since abstracts are primarily good at diagnosing transition, focus on transition issues: Does the abstract flow? Does it read well? Do you feel *pulled through* the abstract as you read?

Let's practice reading the following three abstracts critically:

Abstract A

Mark Twain is the best writer in American literature, because he could do things Cooper and Whitman couldn't do. Cooper's works were inconsistent and unrealistic. Whitman was also very influential, and liberated American literature from taboos about sex and free verse. Twain tackled taboos more successfully. In summation, American literature was shaped by Twain, Cooper, and Whitman. Twain was unique in his tact, the vividness of his descriptions, and his frank honesty. He died penniless and mad, cursing the human race. Hemingway said that all modern American literature comes from *Huckleberry Finn*.

What's going well? The abstract has a lot to say and conveys excitement. The voice seems direct and forceful—not boring. The abstract starts right off with a meaty first sentence that wastes no time and gives itself a worthy task to perform. *What needs work?* The sequencing is shaky. We can get specific about where the problem manifests itself:

1. Sentence 3 seems to contradict sentence 1.
2. The "also" of sentence 3 implies this is the *second* of something, but we can't see the first.
3. "In summation" comes in the middle of things, and it doesn't summarize, since it tells us something new.
4. We can't see how "He died penniless and mad" is logically connected to anything.
5. The last sentence doesn't seem to end anything.

We can fix all these problems by resequencing:

The Rewrite

Hemingway said all of modern American literature sprang from *Huckleberry Finn*. Why would he say that? What's so special about Twain among the other great nineteenth-century American writers? Two things: he did what greats like Cooper and Whitman did, only better—like break social and artistic taboos; and he had things they didn't have, like tact, descriptive accuracy, and, most of all, a willingness to look at the dark side of human nature. That willingness was so uncompromising that it drove him mad and left him penniless.

Abstract B

A favorite way to spend Friday night for many people is to watch hardball. My nephew plays and is talented and confident. I wonder if my five-year-old son will have the chance to build his confidence. Some kids make it through without getting hit by the ball. Many parents oppose the use of the standard hardball because it's dangerous. Cost and tradition are the biggest reasons for not changing over to the ragball. The Little League Association needs to adopt the use of the ragball in this beginning league; it works just as well. Why should a potentially dangerous ball be used when technology has produced a good and safe alternative?

What's going well? The abstract has a strong thesis, a clear sense of purpose, and a passion. *What needs work?* We need to declare the problem earlier, telegraph the transitions, and make only one sequencing change: put the refutation of the opposition's argument ("cost and tradition are the biggest reasons ...") *after* the declaration of thesis. You can't address the rebuttal before you've stated your case:

The Rewrite

A favorite way for my family to spend Friday night is to watch hardball. My nephew plays with confidence, but sometimes I wonder if my five-year-old son will have the chance to build his confidence. Not all beginners get hit by the ball, but many do, and those who do often are injured and quit in fear. But there's a way to avoid that: switch from the conventional hardball to the ragball. It works just as well as the hardball without the danger. Why should a potentially dangerous ball be used when technology has produced a good and safe alternative? The only arguments against it are cost and tradition, but certainly the added expense is worth it and tradition isn't worth the cost in frightened children and injuries.

Abstract C

The search for a golden tan is an annual quest for many white students. Tan skin is risking skin cancer, premature aging, and wrinkles. A tan is a status symbol, but it doesn't necessarily make you a better person. I'm pale and have heard all the pale jokes, but I still don't think a tan is important. The stereotypes applied to pale people are just as bad as those applied to tan people. A tan may be nice now, but it can create wrinkles that will last a lifetime. I may never be tan, but I'll have smooth skin when I'm old.

What's going well? The thesis is clear, the author knows what she wants, she's alive, and she has arguments to support her thesis. *What needs work?* Every sentence seems unconnected to the sentences before and after. A clue is the lack of connectors: only four, and all "but"s. Let's up the number from four to ten (two are colons):

The Rewrite

The search for a golden tan is an annual quest for many white students, *but* tanners don't realize what danger they're in: tanning is risking skin cancer, premature aging, and wrinkles. A tan may make you look great now, *but* it can create wrinkles that will last a lifetime. *Of course,* a tan is a status symbol, *so* not having one means you have to put up with a certain amount of guff. *I know*—I'm pale and have heard all the pale jokes and the stereotypes. *But* you can learn to live with it. *And* there are payoffs later: I may never be tan, *but* I'll have smooth skin when I'm old.

Diagnosing Transition by the Numbers

Often you can just *feel* or sense that transition is missing—and that's all you need to know to fix the problem. But if you want to quantify transition, here's a by-the-numbers diagnostic program:

1. Insert all the connectors between the ideas and points in your abstract.
2. Identify places where connectors are missing between ideas and points. Try to add connectors in these places.
3. Identify all *false connectors*—connectors that promise logical relationships that aren't there. When you start trying to add connectors to your abstracts, there's a huge temptation to make all transition problems seem to disappear by filling your abstract with snappy-looking but dishonest connectors. They sound like this:

   You have to have respect and then you'll be OK; *for example,* when you're a veteran nobody messes with you.

   I was struck by a careless driver who ran a stop sign. I was able to survive; *consequently* the accident resulted in complete damage to my car.

   Wherever possible, replace all false connectors with honest ones: I was unhurt, *but* my car was totaled.
4. (This is the key step.) Any place where good connectors wouldn't go easily is a structural trouble spot. What can you do to solve the problem? How can you resequence the abstract to make the transitions smoother?
5. Check to see if the sentences are combining and thus becoming fewer and longer. If they are, transition is getting better. That's what connectors do—they combine short sentences into longer ones. If you do your transition work perfectly, you'll end up with an abstract that is one huge, complex, but clear sentence. But remember, ungrammatical sentences, empty connectors, and false connectors don't count.

STRUCTURAL TEMPLATES

We've talked about organization as if a writer always starts with a draft and, through tools like abstracting, seeks the essay's own unique, ideal structure. And it often works like that. But there are other ways to organize thought, so essays usually turn out to be versions of conventional essay *templates*, archetypal structures writers have been recycling for centuries. You could approach organization by picking a template and fitting your draft to it:

> **For an investigative essay:** Pose a fascinating question. Gather data toward an answer. Answer the question, and discuss the implications of your answer.

> **For an argumentative essay:** Declare a thesis. Marshal arguments, supportive evidence, and examples to prove it. Finally, discuss the implications of the thesis.

> **For a lab report:** Summarize the experiment and its findings in the introduction, describe what was done in the experiment in the methods section, reproduce the data gathered in the results section, and discuss your findings in a discussion.

This approach works, and it's a lot simpler than what we've been doing, but it isn't much fun and may doom you to a certain mediocrity.

> **For a restaurant review:** Follow the customer through the stages of the meal. First discuss the ambiance, then the service, then the menu, then the salad, the soup, the main course, the dessert, and the bill.

On the other hand (note the transition/connector), some templates do allow you to have some fun, as well as offer an opportunity to rise above mediocrity. I often use a template when I write profiles: I start with a physical description of my subject, in present tense, and then throw in a snippet of dialogue: "Stan Hopkins rolls his swivel chair away from his desk, loosens his tie, and swaps his shiny brown wingtips for a pair of red high-top Chuck Taylors. 'Come on,' he says, draining the last sip of coffee from a Styrofoam cup and dropping it into the trash can. 'Let's get out of this friggin' office.'"

PARAGRAPHING

We all know from our junior high school and high school English classes that a paragraph is the development of one "aspect" of a larger idea or argument—a topic sentence and several supporting sentences. In fact, some instructors are far more prescriptive than that and assign not only a specific number of supporting sentences but also a specific task to each one.

The thing is, it's not that simple.

Some paragraphs are just one sentence long, writers using them to emphasize certain points.

On the other hand, I'm frequently surprised when student essays include paragraphs that go on for a page, a page and a half, sometimes longer. When I ask them why their paragraphs are so long, they tell me about developing that one "aspect" of the paper, and then say something like, "That whole paragraph is about how my brother's schizophrenia tore our family apart" or "That whole paragraph is about the way chickens are slaughtered to take to market."

Remember, though, that you use paragraphs for several reasons, and that one of them is simply to give your reader a break, a chance to consider what he's just read. Surely, you've had the experience of turning the page in a textbook only to see the entire text on the page flush left. Your reaction? "Oh, no! I'll never get through that." So a paragraph break, a little white space, is just another way of inviting your reader into your writing. In fact, in the Middle Ages, when writing was done on scrolls, writers indicated paragraph breaks in the left-hand margins of their texts (the word comes from the Greek "para" for "alongside" and "graph" for "writing") with a pilcrow (¶). This indicated not only changes in direction but also gave readers a sense that they would get chance to rest, and maybe take a long swallow of ale.

So oftentimes, when those students say, "Well, then where should I break up that paragraph," I close my eyes and drop my finger down onto the page and say, "What about here?" And, surprisingly, it frequently works—more typically in narratives than in arguments, for example, in which each paragraph tends to have a more clearly defined purpose. But even when it doesn't work, the students do tend to see the range of possibilities, and the ways they can use paragraph breaks not only to develop those single "aspects" but to help provide their writing with transition.

Using Paragraphs for Transition

We talked earlier about the important of transition. Good writing isn't a list—it's a logical or emotional process. Thus there are no real "stops" along the way—one thing always leads to another. So connect your paragraphs, with transition words and phrases ("Additionally," "On the other hand," "Finally," and others we looked at on p. 119)

Remember, too, that if your paragraphs are all short, it might mean that you haven't found the strong sequencing that allows the reader to keep moving down the road. Use outlining and abstracting to get it. If your paragraphs are too long, it might mean that you just don't like to take breaks. That's a healthy sign, but you need to learn to take pity on the reader, who needs them.

So look at your page-long paragraph and ask yourself not only, "Where's a good place to break this up *logically*?" but also "Where should I let my reader come up for air?" And put your paragraph break, or breaks, there, roughly one every quarter or third of a single-spaced page, unless you want a special effect: short paragraphs for jerky, explosive effects, long paragraphs for tension building. Here's George Orwell doing the first in his essay "Marrakech," where the first paragraph is one sentence long:

> As the corpse went past, the flies left the restaurant table in a cloud and rushed after it, but they came back a few minutes later.

On the other hand, look at how Rosa Levy uses very long sentences in her essay "How to Talk to Your Kids About Drugs" (p. 340) to capture that unstoppable forward momentum of interior monologue and memory.

More Practically

You're right: most paragraphs (and writers) are more conventional and traditional, and modeling them is useful. And, of course, some instructors will demand that you write more conventional and traditional paragraphs—topic sentence followed by support/development. Here's one of my favorite essayists, the naturalist David Quammen, from a piece called "Voices in the Wilderness" from his book *Natural Acts*, doing just that:

> Francis Crick is no common crank. Arguably, he is no crank at all: This is the man who (with James Watson) discovered the structure of DNA and thereby won a share of the 1962 Nobel Prize, whose body of work over the past three decades places him high among the world's preeminent molecular biologists, who has been acclaimed second only to Charles Darwin in the history of British biology. He has always carried the reputation of a bold thinker, a careful scientist, a hard-headed skeptic. Lately, though, there is some cause for wondering whether Francis Crick might have stepped off the curb. It stems from a theory he calls Directed Panspermia.

EXERCISES

1. Pick an essay from "A Collection of Good Writing" and abstract it. Describe in a couple of sentences the organizational structure that abstracting reveals.
2. Pick an essay from "A Collection of Good Writing" and outline it. Describe in a couple of sentences the organizational structure that outlining reveals.
3. Do Exercise 2 using one of your own drafts.
4. Do Exercise 3 using one of your own drafts.
5. Write a critique of each of the following outlines, in two stages: First, describe how well it follows the fourteen outline-making rules of Chapter 7.

Second, rewrite the outline to eliminate any problems. Third, make a list of everything the outline tells you about the draft. Fourth, make a list of concrete suggestions for revision.

Outline A

Content	Function
1. Small-breed dogs aren't real canines; big dogs are.	1. To put different dogs in different categories and explain why some dogs aren't considered dogs.
2. Rocket dogs are Weimaraners, and the author used to have one.	2. To explain what a rocket dog is and her own experience with owning one.
3. Some friends own a black Lab the author hangs out with now.	3. To contrast a Lab owned by her friends with her old dog.

Outline B

Content	Function
1. The institution of marriage has been tarnished in my eyes because of my roommate.	1. Make the reader laugh.
2. Since my roommate got married, he has dropped out of school and become haggard.	2. Win the support for my stance on marriage.
3. Marriage has lost all importance in America.	3. Suggest to reader that marriage is a sham.

Outline C

Content	Function
1. Darwin changed his mind about his own theories.	1. Evolution is not sound science.
2. Scientists hang on to Darwin's original theories.	2. State the problem.
3. Science knows only what it knows.	3. State the source of the problem.
4. It takes just as much faith to believe in evolution as creation.	4. State thesis.

6. Write a critique of the following abstract: which rules for abstract making does it follow, and which does it break?

I describe the parking problem at the university. How the problem came into existence. The administration is responsible for the problem.

Possible solutions. Riding bikes. So we could build a parking garage for students.

Read the following three abstracts. Then follow the instructions in Exercises 8–10.

A. Because information learned in conjunction with music is retained accurately and for a long time, music can be considered an effective learning tool. Rating a child's musical abilities can cause egotism, self-doubt, or total rejection of music. While providing educational benefits, music also promotes creativity and reveals the beauty surrounding knowledge—an essential in the learning process. Music when incorporated into the school curriculum must not be performance oriented or stressful in any way.

B. Most articles on surviving in the back country tell how to live off the land, but I think they ignore prevention. Real survival is knowing how to avoid the dangerous situation in the first place. One survival article showed how a guy snowed in on a deer hunt couldn't start a fire, couldn't retrace his steps, etc. With a little forethought, none of this would have happened. An important factor in survival is keeping your head. Once I went goose hunting without my pack, got lost, panicked, and spent a cold night out. I learned my lesson. To survive, you don't need to know how to live off the land—just take the right equipment and keep your head.

C. Advertising is making all of us hate the way we look. Every company offers products to improve our bodies. We're sicker and fatter now as a result. Bulimia and anorexia nervosa are two diseases commonly suffered by young women and sometimes men. Last summer I got to know my sister's friends. Iris admitted she was bulimic. Iris's problem wouldn't go away. Advertising has made fat one of our ultimate taboos. At an interview I was told to lose fifteen pounds. I wasn't fat then. Have we gone too far? Maybe we should reduce advertising until we become accustomed to imperfect people again.

7. Write a critique of each abstract, and ask if it obeyed the seven rules for abstract making. Rewrite the abstract so that it does.

8. For each abstract, go through the five-step diagnostic program (see p. 124).

9. For each abstract, write a paragraph critiquing it. Make a list of concrete suggestions for revising the draft, such as "Move the anecdote about the wedding to the front." Rewrite the abstract so that it follows your suggestions.

10. Write an essay using a structural template you like, whether in *The Writer's Way* or not. Add to the essay a brief description of the template.

11. Describe someone you know using David Quammen's paragraph about Francis Crick as a model (p. 127).

12. Look at Rosa Levy's essay "How to Talk to Your Kids About Drugs" (p. 340) and identify at least four places where she could have indicated paragraph breaks. Describe what would have been lost and/or gained had she done so.

Part Three

Revising and Editing

Chapter 8

The Spirit of Revising

Now that you've produced a draft, it's time to rewrite it. No other step in the writing process is so badly done by so many writers as rewriting. Shake a tree and a dozen good first-draft writers will fall out, but you're lucky if you get one good rewriter.

Most of us give ourselves rewriter's block by buying into one or more of several bad arguments. Many writers argue that since they rewrite badly, rewriting must be useless: "My rewrites are always worse than my first drafts," they boast. Other writers define rewriting in unhelpful terms and equate it with mechanics: rewriting is proofreading, checking grammar and spelling, and replacing words with better words. Others define rewriting in negative terms: rewriting is looking for errors and blemishes and eliminating them.

As long as you hold any of these beliefs, rewriting will be an unproductive pain. Instead, adopt a new mind-set:

Rewriting is rethinking, experimentation, adventure, boldly going where no first draft has gone before.

Rewriting is positive, not negative: you're enriching and expanding, not correcting; And rewriting, like writing, fries the biggest fish first. You give first priority to the big deals—Do I really believe this? What else does my reader need from me? Does she really need this paragraph?— and last priority to cosmetics like spelling and grammar rules. Rewriting is *liberating*. Feel free to toss out stuff from the first draft; in fact, feel free to toss out most of the first draft and start anew. Feel free to add material that you hadn't even encountered when you wrote the first draft. I recently had a student bring to class a first draft in which she was arguing that despite claims that America's a "melting pot," in reality, people hang with people much like themselves. It just so happened that the day before, the producers of the TV reality show *Survivor* had announced that in the new season the "tribes" would be organized by *ethnicity,* and one of her classmates described an article she read about it. This led to a lively class discussion, and afterward the student writer rushed home to begin revising so that she could include the *Survivor* example as part of her argument.

REVISION TOOLS

Revision is hard because we don't know how to reduce it to concrete steps. We need a recipe ("First, combine all dry ingredients in a large bowl ..."), and we need tools—concrete gizmos like measuring cups and sifters we can hold in our hand and do the steps with. Part 3 of this book is a loose sort of recipe, and it will offer you a series of such tools. All craftspeople know you can never have enough tools, so I'm going to give you the whole hardware store. When we're done, our toolbox will consist of thesis, purpose, audience, tone, and style (Chapters 5 and 6); mapping, outlining, and abstracting (Chapter 7); tools for making drafts longer or shorter (Chapter 8); beginnings, conclusions, and titles (Chapter 9); peer feedback (Chapter 10); and editing (Chapter 11).

What do we know about tools?

1. **Tools are for you, not the customer.** When you sell the chair you made, you don't sell the saw and drill along with it. So don't write the outline for the reader or attach the thesis statement to the essay (unless, of course, the assignment calls for you to do that).
2. **The purpose in using a tool is never simply to use the tool.** Nobody ever said, "I think I'll go run my sewing machine for an hour." You run the sewing machine to make a dress. So if you outline just to make an outline or peer edit just to have a peer-editing experience, you've lost sight of your real purpose. With revision tools, your purpose is always *to produce a better draft,* and if you don't end up with that, you wasted your tool time.

    Rule 2 may sound obvious, but in fact writers make this mistake all the time. They'll take a draft, outline it, maybe even learn some interesting things from the outline, leave the draft largely unchanged, show it to their instructor, and say, "Look at this cool outline," as if the act itself should be admired.
3. **Using a tool takes skill, which comes with practice.** It takes years to learn to use a router well, as apprentice cabinetmakers can tell you. So we have

to expect to put in some time learning to use a thesis statement or peer-editing session.

4. **Tools don't make the project good by themselves.** Even if I'm the world's greatest user of a sewing machine, the machine by itself can't make the dress beautiful. Tools just make the work easier—it's hard to sew cloth or shape wood with your bare hands. So a thesis statement will help you make a great essay, but it won't make the essay great. You still need talent, inspiration, passion, and time.

DIAGNOSTIC TOOLS

Some of the tools we're going to master belong to a special category of tools called diagnostics: tools that provide you with data you use to draw conclusions—the way tape measures, thermometers, CAT scans, and blood tests do. A thermometer tells you if you have a fever. An abstract tells you if a draft has any transition problems.

We know lots of interesting things about diagnostic tools:

1. **Diagnostic tools see things we can't see.** CAT scans see inside your brain. Outlines see inside your essay.
2. **The diagnostic tool makes the problem concrete,** so we can figure out what to do about it. It changes "I don't feel well" into "I have mononucleosis." It changes "This draft seems choppy" into "The sentences are too short."
3. **Diagnostic tools always must be read,** and the reading requires training. First our dad has to show us how to read the thermometer; then we have to know that 98.6 equals normal. Reading writers' tools means answering questions like, What can I learn from this outline? What is the thesis statement telling me about the draft? And that takes practice.
4. **Diagnostic tools don't tell you what to do.** A tape measure tells you how long the board is; it can't tell you how long the board should be. A thesis statement or an outline will let you see what's going on in the draft. That's its only job. It's your job to take that insight and decide what, if anything, you should do about it. Stylistic analysis will tell you your sentences are short. Only you can decide if you should make them longer. But you need to know the sentences are short before you can make that decision.

MAKING YOUR OWN TOOLS

Writers' tools differ from shop tools in one important way: shop tools are made by Black & Decker and other manufacturers; writers' tools you make yourself. You build the thesis statement or the outline. Then you use it, by learning from it and applying what you learned when you revise. This two-step model contains three vital implications:

1. We have to build the tool correctly, or all the information the tool gives us will be unreliable.
2. We have to do *both* steps. Making the saw is merely a preamble to the real work of making the chair. It's easy to do just Step 1, quit, and think you've actually accomplished something (you haven't).
3. A problem can crop up in Step 1, in Step 2, or in the draft. You need to know where the problem lies. If the problem lies in Step 1, you fix it by repairing the tool (rewriting the thesis statement, for instance). If the problem lies in Step 2, you fix it by learning to interpret the data better. And if the problem lies in the draft, you fix it by revising.

Rule 3 is usually obvious in life. If you take your temperature and the thermometer reads 103 degrees, you don't blame the thermometer for reading so high, since the tool is just doing its job and the problem lies in your body. But in writing, we love to blame our tools for revealing problems in our drafts. For instance, when students are asked to outline their essays and then to critique the outline, they'll often say, "This outline is terrible, because it's choppy and confusing and boring." But probably the outline is doing its job, which is to reveal things about the draft, and it's the draft that is choppy, confusing, and boring.

REVISION IN FOUR STEPS

Revision is a messy process, so we're going to reduce it to four steps. Step 1: Troubleshoot thesis, purpose, audience, tone, and style (from Chapters 5 and 6). Step 2: Troubleshoot organization (Chapter 7). Step 3: Get peer feedback (Chapter 10). Step 4: Edit for grammar and mechanics (Chapter 11). The first step is discussed in the rest of this chapter.

Thesis, Purpose, Audience, Tone, and Style

The five most powerful diagnostic tools at a reviser's disposal are the thesis statement ("What am I saying?"), the purpose statement ("Why am I saying it?"), the definition of audience ("Who am I talking to?"), the definition of tone ("What is the mood of the essay?"), and the definition of style ("How do I want to dress this essay to present it to the world?"). These are what the hammer and saw are to the carpenter. You'll use them every day of your writing life.

Of course, you've been working with your thesis, purpose, audience, tone, and style, at least unconsciously, since the essay project quickened in your brain. Now it's time to *re*-consider them. Most writers have a sense of these things when they begin writing, but they never lock them in, and when better ones come along, they welcome them. Staying committed to your first thesis is like marrying the first person you hook up with—it would be a miracle if you ended up with your true soul mate. And demanding that you have a big important message before you start writing is a great way to give yourself writer's block.

How soon you arrive at firm answers to the five questions depends a lot on what kind of writing you're doing. Technical or scientific writing often is sure of purpose, audience, tone, and style long before the writing begins, when the experiment or project is first being designed. In argumentative writing or writing in the humanities, you may not discover the final version of the answers until a very late draft. If you write down your thesis when you start and promise to stick to it through thick and thin, you're just promising to *not learn anything* during the drafting and revising. "How can I know what I think until I see what I've written?" writing instructor James Britten says.

Topic: A Brief Review

We talked about topics earlier. Of course, your essay will have a topic—it's impossible to write without writing about *something*—but topic is next to worthless as a revision tool. The only slight value in topic making comes from *narrowing the topic* by adding detail. Here, more is better. Begin with a topic label for your essay: "Education." Now add detail: "Problems in education." Keep adding detail, making the topic statement longer, until you can add no more: "How to make reading interesting to a generation of students raised on texting and tweeting and Facebooking."

Thesis

Remember, your thesis—whether it's stated or implied—should be a single sentence. Read back over your draft. Can you summarize the essay in one, clear sentence? Is it what you intended? (That might not matter—maybe what you ended up with is better.) We'll get to peer editing shortly, but this might be a good time to let someone read your draft. Don't tell her your intended thesis, but after she reads your essay, have her write down what she thinks it is. Did she get it? If not, where is the disconnect? Could she be right? That you thought you were saying one thing and ended up saying something else?

Feel free to tweak your thesis to fit what your essay's saying apart from your intended thesis, and then of course to tweak what you're saying to make it fit the revised thesis.

Purpose

Your purpose statement tells you *why* you're writing. What do you hope that the essay accomplishes? How do you want your reader to respond? What do you want him to *do* when he's done reading?

Read back through your draft, making sure that the purpose (or purposes) is constant throughout, that it's the reason for everything you've written, and that your reader will understand why it's important.

It might even be useful to write your purpose statement at the top of the draft and glance up at it from time to remind yourself of what you're up to. If you get off track, you probably should rewrite—or cut— so that what you've got serves your purpose.

Audience

Your paper may ultimately have several different types of audiences. For example: I might pick up *Car and Driver* or *Bass Fishing Monthly* while I'm waiting at the doctor's office, but I am not among the target audience the editors and writers of those magazines have in mind. Instead, the articles (and ads) are tailored to those readers, whose interests, levels of income, age range, and so on, the editors and writers have identified. Likewise, the narrower your audience, and the more you know about them, the better. Look at your thesis and purpose again. Are they appropriate to the reader whom you're targeting? Will they find what you say relevant? Obvious? Compelling? Useful?

Style

Now that you've reconsidered your audience, take a close look at the writing style. Is the level of formality appropriate? Could you use the word "meet" instead of "interface," "many" instead of "a plethora of"? Should you use "gastrointestinal disorder" instead of "upset stomach"? Will your reader know what you mean when you recommend a really "sick" study-abroad program?

What about sentence length? Remember that longer sentences "feel" more sophisticated and scholarly than shorter sentences, which feel basic and honest. Should you combine—or break up—some sentences so they're better suited to your reader and sound like you want them to sound?

Tone

As you're reading through your draft, consider its mood, the emotion it conveys, the way the writing will come across to the reader: sarcastic, self-deprecating, mean, and so on. Keep in mind the emotional wallop that words can pack and how a single word or phrase can completely define a tone and in so doing turn your reader off or on. I recently read a letter to the editor of our local newspaper about medical marijuana. The writer described smoking pot with his dying father and how, for the first time in years, his dad had a few hours without pain. It was a moving and compelling story—very convincing. The problem was, the writer concluded by saying, "So all you sanctimonious assholes out there need to think about my father next time you vote against medical marijuana." The effect? His tone totally undermined his argument.

REVISING FOR LENGTH: MAKING THE DRAFT LONGER OR SHORTER

It's time to practice the writer's art of writing to the assigned length.

Beginning writers usually think an essay should be as long as it takes to do the task at hand—you write till you've said it all. That's great in a perfect world, but in the real world—from a first-year writing class to grad seminars, from academic journals and grants to popular magazines—there are almost always limitations, maximums and minimums, word or page count. My wife is a grant writer and is often given maximum numbers of *characters* for her responses to questions (e.g., "How will your school district oversee the distribution of funding?").

When you first start writing for real reasons for real readers, the problem is usually that the draft is too short. But after you've been writing for a few years, the problem reverses itself and the draft is almost always too long.

Remember the road trip I described in Chapters 4 and 7 and the article that I wrote about it (p. 345)? The editor had originally told me to send him "about" 3,500 words. Well, it was an 8,500-mile trip over nearly a month! My first draft was 6,000 words long—and could have been much longer. Holding out hope against hope, perhaps that he might want to publish it in two installments, I sent it anyway. Nope, he emailed back. "Cut it to 3,500 words." So, I went to work—first mostly tightening sentences (Chapter 11). New word count? Just over 5,000. Ouch! Now it was time to ask the question above: "Does my reader really need this?" Or at least to prioritize: "What parts are more important than others?" Once I was honest with myself about the answers to those questions (such as, "Does she really need to know where we'd *planned* to go in addition to where we really went?"), it was pretty easy to cut it back to 3,500 words.

Regardless, however, of whether you'll end up working to make the final draft longer or shorter, it's best to begin by drafting everything you have in you—don't think about length at all. Then compare what you've got to the length you're shooting for and cut or expand accordingly.

Making It Shorter

You make a text shorter in one of two ways: say it all, faster, or say less.

To say it faster, we need to only notice that Chapter 5 reduced essays to single sentences (thesis statements) and that Chapter 6 reduced them to three to five sentences each (outlines) and paragraphs (abstracts), so any coherent text can be reduced to any size. Just to prove it, here are successively shrunk versions of "A Moral Victory?" (see its 500-word form in "A Collection of Good Writing"):

The Half-Size Version:

In 1984, some white male police officers sued San Francisco, claiming they were the victims of reverse discrimination because they had been passed over for promotion in favor of less qualified minority officers. The U.S. Supreme Court has refused to hear their case. This may seem to be a victory for minorities, but isn't it really a loss for us all?

I'm married to a white male, and I've seen a lot through his eyes. He's an engineering professor who has worked in industry for thirteen years. Unfortunately, reverse discrimination is for him a fact of life. Employers are forced by federal quotas to give preference to Hispanics, blacks, and women.

My sister is also an engineering professor in the same system, but basically what she wants she gets, because the quota system makes her a sought-after commodity. It took my sister a long time to appreciate the injustice of this.

Right now her department is interviewing for a new instructor. The department doesn't actually have an open position, but the university has funding for a certain number of faculty who meet "specific criteria." The candidate is black, so of course she's irresistible!

We feel an awful sense of collective guilt in this country for what we've done to women and minorities, and we should. But can we really right past wrongs by creating new ones? I don't propose that we forget our past, but I think it's time to forgive ourselves and move on.

The Quarter-Size Version:

The U.S. Supreme Court has refused to hear a reverse discrimination case concerning San Francisco policemen. Is this a victory for minorities or a loss for us all? My husband is an engineering professor. Unfortunately, reverse discrimination is for him a fact of life. Employers are forced by federal quotas to give preference to Hispanics, blacks, and women.

My sister is also an engineering professor, but basically what she wants she gets, because the quota system makes her a sought-after commodity. Right now her department has a job that's open only to people who meet "specific criteria"—being black, for instance.

Americans feel guilty for past racism and sexism, and we should. But it's time to forgive ourselves, and move on.

The Eighth-Size Version:

Reverse discrimination isn't a victory for minorities, it's a loss for us all. For my husband, reverse discrimination is a fact of life. But my sister gets anything she wants, since she's female, and her department has a job that's open only to minorities. We should feel guilty about our past, but it's time to forgive ourselves and move on.

The Sixteenth-Size Version:

Reverse discrimination is a loss for us all. My husband suffers from reverse discrimination daily, but my sister gets anything she wants, since she's female. Guilt is good, but let's forgive ourselves and move on.

On the Head of a Pin:

Reverse discrimination is a loss for us all; let's forgive ourselves and move on.

To say less, you think differently. You reduce the essay to a short list, and you pick from the list. You think, "I'd like to talk about the San Francisco discrimination case and my husband's experiences with reverse discrimination and my sister's change of heart and the hiring her department is doing, but I just don't have the time, so instead I'll focus on my sister's change of heart and leave everything else for another day."

Making It Longer

Making a text shorter is pretty easy compared to the harder problem you face when the instructor says "Give me five pages" and you've run dry after two paragraphs.

We work on this throughout the book. In Chapter 4 we brainstormed and freewrote to expand a seed into a draft. In Chapter 10 we'll use peer editing to show how the draft could become something bigger and better. In Chapter 14 we'll use a thesis statement as a springboard to an endless conversation. All of these activities are based on the idea that a draft is just a starting place.

You can expand in three ways: filling in, expanding the canvas, and asking the next question.

Making It Longer by Filling In. Saying it in more detail does *not* mean saying exactly the same thing in twice as many words. It means filling in blanks and providing background detail. An essay is like a painted portrait. The one-paragraph version is like a happy face—nothing but a circle for the head, a curved line for the mouth, two circles for eyes. Now we're going to go in and start adding details—lips, ears, irises, pupils. Then we can add details to the details—chapped skin on the lips, ear hair, bloodshot eyes. We can keep adding details forever, like sharpening the resolution on a TV screen by increasing the number of pixels. Remember the suggestion to substitute concretions for abstractions in Chapter 6 (also, "Show, Don't Tell" in Chapter 12)? Same thing. The example:

Not filled in: *When you use Google, it's easy to get distracted and end up all over the place.*

Filled in: *When you use Google, it's easy to get distracted. One minute you're working on your paper for your American history class and the next you're reading about Borneo, jambalaya, golden retrievers, Buster Posey, or Burning Man.*

Note: Despite what my students often claim, the second version is not "wordy." In fact, you could argue that the first version is actually wordy, although shorter, because it hardly gets any work done. The second, however, does a lot of work—all those words serve purposes.

Another example: imagine a passage from an essay on changing a flat tire, in various degrees of detail.

Short version: Remove the hubcap.

Longer version: Remove the hubcap with the tire iron.

Still longer: Find the tire iron. It's a long iron bar. Stick one end under the lip of the hubcap and pry until the hubcap comes off.

Even longer: Find the tire iron. It's a long iron bar and is probably alongside your jack, either in the trunk or under the hood. Stick one end under the lip of the hubcap anywhere along the circumference and pry until the hubcap comes off.

Longest so far: Check to see if you have a hubcap—a Frisbee of shiny metal covering your lug nuts. If you do, you have to remove it. Find the tire iron. It's a long iron bar and is probably alongside your jack, either in the trunk or under the hood. If you want to stay clean, be careful—it, like the jack, is likely to be pretty yucky if it's been used before. Grasping the iron in your left hand (if you're right-handed), stick the end that is flattened and slightly canted under the lip of the hubcap anywhere along the circumference and push hard on the other end with the flat of your right hand. The hubcap should pop off. If it doesn't work, push harder. Don't worry—you can't hurt the iron or the hubcap. Keep prying until the hubcap comes off, whatever it takes. If it's stuck, try different spots around the lip. Above all, DON'T wrap your right hand around the bar when you're prying—if you do, when the hubcap comes loose, your fingers will be crushed between the iron and the tire or fender.

Former Chico State student Mark Wilpolt experimented with this idea by starting with the short sentence "I arrived at the gym" and then turning it into the following paragraph:

Yesterday the rain stopped and the sun came out. I had been doing homework all day, so I jumped on my bike to experience the drying streets. Along the way I decided to turn the bike ride into a trip to the gym. I arrived at the gym and worked out on the treadmill for fifteen minutes. On the way home, I took the scenic route along the creek, enjoying the fall colors, the clear sky, and the foothills, with their new patches of snow, in the background. Who says exercise isn't fun?

Then he turned that short paragraph into this playful little narrative essay:

The entrance to the Sports Club is its own little world. As I walk through the lobby, the day care is on the right. A dozen kids are running around the plastic playground as perfect smiling employees in their twenties look on—a Norman Rockwell scene for the '90s. The beauty salon is next: women with big hairdos and long, fluorescent fingernails giving their customers that extra little something they can't get from the workout floor. Then the big-screen TV, surrounded by comfy sofas, and the snack bar, tempting you to just skip the exercise and veg.

I hand my card to the girl at the front counter. Whoever is on duty, it's always the same: a bubbly smile and a musical "Hello, how are you today?, have a nice workout" as she zips my card through the computer, like she's been waiting all day for me to show up and make her shift. They must major in Smiling, the people who get hired for that position. Tough job.

Next I must negotiate my way past the giant wall of glass and the women in pajamas on the other side in their yoga class. Why the big window? Is it so women can see the class going on inside and feel guilty because THEY don't look like that, or so men can watch the proceedings and get their heart rate up in anticipation of their work-out? Whichever the case, there's a bench right there in the hall inviting everyone to sit and stare.

In the Big Room are dozens of machines, none of which I know the name of, for shoulders, thighs, chest, back, quads, biceps, even a machine to exercise your NECK for heaven's sake. A ten-thousand-dollar machine to exercise your NECK? Also there's a fleet of Stairmasters, a bank of treadmills, a rank of stationary bicycles, and a squadron of rowing machines. None of them going anywhere, but some of them being driven pretty hard. The humorless faces of the exercisers say, "This is serious business."

All the machines call to me, "Me, do me first. No, work on your arms first," but it's hard to hear them because a dozen TV sets suspended in rows where the wall meets the ceiling are blaring, "Watch ME instead!" No way to avoid it—you work out and you watch TV. "Wheel of Fortune" is on. I'm trapped. I get on the treadmill and stare. The clue is "Person," five words. The champ has the wheel.
"I'd like an S, please."
"Yes, two of them!" DING, DING. "Spin again!"
"I'd like an R, please?"
"Yes, there are FIVE R's!" DING, DING, DING, DING, DING. The champ buys a couple of vowels.

The tricky part is realizing that arguments or thought processes can be expanded just like information can. Shawni, the author of "Why I Never Cared for the Civil War" (see "A Collection of Good Writing"), could easily expand it to book length by researching the degree to which American schools use the lecture-and-test approach to teaching, citing successful classroom alternatives to it, and detailing how they work and why they succeed.

Expanding the Canvas.   Another way to lengthen is to ask, "What's the larger issue?" If the first way of lengthening was like adding details to a painting, this way of lengthening is like pasting the original work in the middle of a much larger canvas and painting the surroundings.

Seeing the larger issue depends on realizing that all issues are specific versions of larger issues:

Specific Issue	Larger Issues
Why I deserve an A in English 1	How grades are determined; what grades mean; how are students evaluated?
My father was a brute, and I couldn't do anything about it.	Psychological effects of bad parenting on children; why people have children; children's rights
Why I don't vote anymore	The problems in American politics; America's apathy crisis

Asking the Next Question.   Asking the next question means exactly that: when you finish the draft, you ask yourself, "What's the next question to be asked and answered? What's the next task I need to tackle?" No argument ends the debate; no task completed means the work is over. In writing as in science, answers generate only more questions, and there's always a next thing to learn or do. For instance, if you write an essay arguing that the United States shouldn't explore for oil in the Alaskan tundra, the next question might be, "OK, what *should* we do to solve our growing energy problem, then?"

WRITER'S WORKSHOP

Expanding Essays

Let's practice expansion on some student essays.

SEX AND TV

MARJORIE CROW

Do you hate turning on the TV and all you see are people touching each other sexually and some taking off their clothes? Well, I'm tired of it. There is much more to human relationships than sex. Yes, some people would agree that sex has a lot to do with a relationship, but sex on TV is what I'm most annoyed with. Sex is enticing and sex does make products sell, but the question is, should sex be thrown around like it's yesterday's lunch? I feel that something has to be done. It would be great if the media would monitor the shows that we see, but in reality they want to broadcast what will sell, and sex sells.

Questions for Marjorie

1. Filling in:

    What are some examples of how sex is portrayed on TV?

    How does TV use sex to sell things?

    What exactly are the messages we're being sent about sex by TV?

2. The larger canvas:

    How our culture treats sex

    How TV influences our values and beliefs

    Our culture's portrayal of women

3. The next question:

    How can we stop the marketing of sex?

    Who is ultimately responsible?

    What other ways are there that TV cheapens our lives?

—Permission provided by Steve Metzger

TYRANT!

TRICIA IRELAND

Christopher Columbus should not be regarded as a national hero. He was a terrible man who worked only for selfishness and greed. He was not the first on his expedition to spot land; a man named Roderigo was. But according to his own journal, Columbus took credit because the first to spot land was to receive a yearly pension for life.

When Columbus landed in the Bahamas, he took the natives by force and made them his slaves. Hundreds he sent back to Spain; others were held captive in their own country. He made them bring him a monthly quota of gold, and when they did they received a copper coin necklace. If they were found without a necklace, their hands were cut off and they were left to bleed to death.

I don't know why we teach our children to admire and respect Columbus. There exists a terrible amount of ignorance regarding the truth around him. It's time to teach the truth. Columbus Day shouldn't be celebrated, and Columbus himself shouldn't be seen as anything but the cruel tyrant he was.

Questions for Tricia

1. Filling in:

    What else did Columbus do, good and bad?—consider his other virtues and vices.

What's the rest of his story? How did he get the idea to go exploring? How did he die? And so on.

How did the Columbus myth get started?

2. The larger canvas:

What's a hero?

Tradition vs. truth in history

The European bias in our view of history

3. The next question:

What about other heroes like George Washington—are they fables too? Should we also expose them?

Why does this matter, since it's ancient history? How can we change the way we teach history so it isn't so biased?

—Permission provided by Steve Metzger

Now It's Your Turn.   For each of the following essays, write out ways to expand the draft by (a) filling in, (b) writing on the larger canvas, and (c) asking the next question.

OPEN THE DOOR

PAULA BONKOFSKY

College-level students shouldn't be punished, or worse, locked out of classes if they arrive late. Certainly if it becomes habit the teacher should speak with the student and affect their grade accordingly. But on occasion, students who are never regularly late are late because of circumstances that were out of their control. These students should be allowed to come in and participate with their class. Yes, it really is their class because they paid for it.

—Permission provided by Steve Metzger

SEX, LIES, AND POLITICAL BASHING

KERI BOYLES

Lately, it seems as if you can't turn on the TV without seeing some political campaign commercial blasting the opposition. Instead of telling us what they stand for and what they plan to do in office if they get elected, they spend the majority of their time smearing their opponent. These commercials are exactly the reason why a lot of people are presently disgusted with politicians. Not only are they insulting to the voter, but they skirt the issues as well, focusing on their opponent's flaws instead of informing the voter on what their actual policies are and how they plan to "clean up" the messes that politicians (unlike themselves, of course!) have gotten this country into.

It's time to say enough is enough. These distasteful commercials shouldn't be allowed. Candidates should only be able to state what their beliefs and policies are, without smearing their opponent. Voters would then be able to make logical, rational decisions without being bombarded with all the other pointless garbage they are all subjected to when watching their favorite TV shows. Personally, I don't care if Clinton inhaled or not!

—Permission provided by Steve Metzger

EXERCISES

1. Pick an essay from "A Collection of Good Writing" and rewrite it to half its length in two ways:
   a.   Say it all, but twice as fast.
   b.   Cut the essay's scope in half.

2. Do Exercise 1 using an essay of your own.

3. Describe in one paragraph a recent personal experience; then retell it in two pages, adding as much detail as you can but without changing the scope.

4. Write a one-paragraph argument. Then write answers to the three questions from this chapter: How can this be filled out? What is the larger canvas? What is the next question? Be sure to deal with each of the three. Then rewrite the argument to one to two pages, using the material generated by the questions.

5. Write a one-paragraph argument. Read it to the class and ask them to respond to it, not to the writing style but to the logic. Rewrite the argument to one to two pages, using the material generated by the conversation.

Chapter 9

Beginning, Ending, and Titling

You might be wondering why this chapter belongs in the part of the book about revising instead of earlier, in Part 2, on planning and drafting. Simple, really—because introductions, conclusions, and titles should not be written too soon. If you're convinced you need to write a good introduction, conclusion, and title before the body of the paper is in pretty good shape, then you're risking two things:

1. **Getting stuck.** How do you know what you're introducing, for example, until you've got something to introduce?
2. **Limiting yourself.** If you don't allow that the very last line you write might make an awesome introduction, or that the powerful quote on p. 6 can be tweaked into a title, then you're putting restrictions on yourself and your paper's potential.

Keep in mind that beginnings, endings, and titles are key moments of contact with your reader, and that they provide superb diagnostic tools for revision. Essays that begin well, end well, and are titled well are usually good through and through.

Conversely, trouble in one of those areas of the paper usually suggests larger problems elsewhere. In fact, a writing instructor once told me that if I couldn't come up with a good title for a piece I was working on, the piece probably wasn't done yet.

INTRODUCTIONS

When I read drafts of student work, I often find myself suggesting that the writers begin with their second paragraphs. "But then I won't have an introduction," they say. But they will. It'll just be what's now the second paragraph. Example: One assignment I've worked with over the years asks students to write an essay about what they think constitutes the American experience, or to assert something about what being American (or visiting America) means to them. Over half of the drafts usually begin something like, "America means different things to different people. Some people think ... and some people think ..." Exactly! That's why we want to know what it means to you! If I wanted suggestions on the best way to drive across country, I wouldn't need (or want!) people to say, "Different people have different opinions about the best way to drive across the country." No. I want to hear, "Take the northerly route, and be sure to stop at Mt. Rushmore," or, "You've got to take Highway 66, through the Southwest."

Similarly, if I asked you where the best burritos in town were, I don't need (or want!) to hear, "Different people have different opinions on the best burritos in town." No. I want to hear, "The best burritos in town are at Paco's over on Fourth Avenue. Here's why: ..." Same with the American experience essay. The good ones don't start off by telling their readers that America means different things to different people—that's the given. Just jump right in. Here are some good openers from papers in response to that assignment:

> Recent studies show that America has the highest obesity rate in the world.

> My grandfather put his pipe down, sat back in his chair, and said, "To really understand the soul of America, you've got to taste the ribs at Smokin' Sam's down on Beale Street."

> The year I spent studying abroad in the south of France taught me what it means to be an American.

> The American experience is best captured in the country's music—in a hillbilly fiddle reel, in a Billie Holiday ballad, in a Springsteen rocker, in Hendrix's "Star Spangled Banner" at Woodstock, in a street musician playing "This Land Is Your Land" for coins in his guitar case, and in a garage band's passionate commitment to following its dream.

Making the Tool

The draft's first sentence is a popular place for writer's block. We've all had the experience of staring at the blank page, knowing pretty much what we want to say once that hurdle has been overcome, but not being able to budge. For help with that problem, consider the following five suggestions:

1. **Write the title last.** Or rather, be on the lookout for possible titles from the moment you start the project. A good one will likely come late, but grab it and hold on to it whenever it comes.

2. **Write the introduction second to last.** And keep in mind that many parts of your paper could be moved up to serve as introductions. In fact, in peer-editing sessions in my classes, I often have readers suggest to writers three or more places in the paper that could work as introductions.

3. **If you can't find a good opener, have none.** No introduction at all is better than an empty, formulaic one like this:

> After reading Frank Smith's book *Reading Without Nonsense*, you could tell that the author has very definite views on how to teach people to read. He lets the reader know exactly how he feels about different techniques of teaching children to read.

That's just ghastly.

4. **Cut everything that precedes the first good thing you write.** Instead of trying to write a great opener right off the bat, just freewrite. Then read your draft until you find a sentence that really starts something, and throw away everything above it. Assume that your first few paragraphs will be a warm-up and could be trashed. Remember the football metaphor? The players need to do their calisthenics before the game, but the folks in the crowd (readers) don't want to watch; they just want to be there for the kick-off. Here's a good "kick-off":

> Linguist Frank Smith feels that reading food labels, street signs, and board games is a good way to learn to read, because to learn to read, children need to relate the words to something that makes sense.

Note how he doesn't begin, "Different people have different views on good ways to learn to read."

I was recently working with a student who had written about a beloved childhood pet. Her essay began, "Most everyone has had to deal with the loss of a pet. It's painful and hard, but it's also very real and children can learn important lessons from it..." Then in her fifth or sixth sentence, she had written, "When I was seven, my dad brought Franky home. He was part Labrador retriever, and part wolf, but all you could see was the wolf." "Wait, wait, wait," I said. "That's beautiful. What would you think about starting your essay there?" Apparently, she liked the idea, because not only did she take my suggestion, but she also took it a step further. Her revised essay began, "All you could see was the wolf." It gave me chills.

5. **Use a stock opener.** If you're still stuck, fall back on one of four basic strategies writers have been using for centuries (caution, because of that, it's easy to fall back on cliché when using stock openers):

The thesis statement. You declare up front (usually at the end of the first paragraph) the heart of what you have to say. Beginning writers and instructors like this one because it's easy, and bosses and other people in a hurry often like it because they can grasp the gist of a piece of writing in a minute. But it's unexciting unless the thesis is startling and provocative, like the newspaper article a while back that began, "Americans apparently like reading the newspaper more than sex," and it gives away the punch line up front, so the rest of the essay loses energy. However, much academic, scientific, and technical writing demands thesis openers, so use them when needed.

The question. A question opener has three virtues. It forces you to be clear about your purpose, it's dramatic (it turns the essay into a detective story), and it shows you what to do with the rest of the essay: answer the question. Examples: Where's the best place for a student to spend Spring Break? What can you do with a major in history? Is joining a sorority really such a great idea? Is global warming natural or caused by humans?

The hook. Also known as the grabber or the angle, the hook is the eye-catcher that sucks a reader into the essay like a vacuum cleaner: "When I was 6 years old, living in Vietnam, I saw Mrs. Lau, wife of our family servant, drag herself out of bed only a few hours after giving birth, to bury her newborn's umbilical cord in our garden" (*Andrew Lam*).

There are countless ways to hook a reader. You can start with a paradox, an idea that seems self-contradictory and therefore demands explanation—like "Americans are getting more liberal and more conservative all the time." You can tease the reader with a promise of excitement to come: "No one noticed that the world changed on August 7, 1994." You can drop the reader into the middle of things so that she'll read on to find out how she got there—what Latin poets called beginning *in medias res:* "The President looked unamused as he wiped the pie filling off his face." Newspaper sports sections love hooks:

A World Series involving the New York Yankees would not be official without a controversy. The 75th Series was stamped as the real thing yesterday at Yankee Stadium.

Westside High's Cougars did what they had to and nothing more to hand Central a 24–15 defeat Saturday night.

Don't promise what you can't deliver. Don't hook dishonestly: "Free beer!!! Now that I've gotten your attention, I'm going to talk about brands of tennis shoes."

The narrative. Narrative openers—stories—work because they concretize and humanize right off the bat: "In the middle of the worst depression in our nation's history, one woman decided to leave her comfortable home and head west looking for a better life." "Given the Chance" (Chapter 15) and "Why Falling in Love Feels So Good" ("A Collection of Good Writing") have narrative openers.

One subtype of the narrative opener always works as a last resort: the "how I came to write this essay" opener. Explain what started you thinking about the subject: "I was reading the newspaper the other day and noticed an article about the federal government taking over the Coca-Cola Company. I couldn't help thinking ..." But be careful. You risk having your reader respond with a big, "So what! I don't care that you were reading the paper the other day." Remember what we talked about earlier: you might write this to get yourself started, but then when you go back and look at it realize that it can be cut. In fact, the preceding one could easily begin, "A recent news article announced that the federal government is planning to take over Coca-Cola...."

Here are three things good openers often do:

1. **Reveal, or at least suggest, the topic.** This is easy, so do it fast. A whole sentence is too much because it invariably sounds like "In this essay I'm going to talk about...." Reveal the topic as you're doing more important things:

   If you're an average, somewhat chubby individual wanting to get some healthy, not overly strenuous exercise, you should consider bicycling.

   When you start working as a pizza delivery person, you're going to get a new view of life.

   Most of us, if we're honest with ourselves, will admit we've thought about committing suicide.

2. **Reveal the purpose.** Every reader begins with some basic questions: Why are you writing to me? How can I use this? Why does this matter? Begin answering these questions from the outset.

3. **Say, "Read me, read me!"** An opener is like a free sample of salsa at the grocery store—it says, "Here's a typical example of the way I write; once you sample it, you'll want to read more." So write a first sentence you'd like to read:

   In late July 1982, presidential press secretary James Brady sued the gun company that made the pistol used by John Hinckley.

   Grandpa drank too much beer the day he jumped into the pool wearing his boxer shorts.

   Most Americans do not get to experience the excitement and discomfort of train travel very often.

   If you'd like to murder somebody but receive a penance of one year's probation and a small fine, try this: Get yourself blind, staggering, out-of-control drunk some night and just run over some guy as he walks across his own lawn to pick up his newspaper.

   Many gun control advocates believe in the commonsense argument that fewer guns should result in fewer killings. But it may not be that simple.

   The following openers make you want to stop reading:

Handguns are of major concern to many people in the United States.

   Driving under the influence of alcohol is a serious problem in the United States today.

   Bilingual ballots have been in the spotlight for many years.

You don't have to shout; you can say "Read me!" with dignity and class too. Here's a beauty, the famous beginning of George Orwell's "Shooting an Elephant" (p. 77):

In Moulmein, in Lower Burma, I was hated by large numbers of people—the only time in my life that I have been important enough for this to happen to me.

You can't say "Read me" more quietly or more powerfully than that.

Different kinds of writing value the three tasks differently. Scientific and technical writing values "Read me" hardly at all. As a result, few people read scientific and technical writing for fun.

Academic writing values thesis highly but doesn't think about purpose very much—who knows *why* you write an essay about sickness metaphors in *Hamlet*? Entertainment journalism values "Read me" above all and often has no purpose beyond momentary titillation.

Using the Tool

Begin by asking the central question: "Does this beginning make me want to keep reading?" Next, ask if the other two tasks were accomplished: revealing topic and revealing purpose. If you can't find a sense of purpose, make sure the draft has one and that you know what it is.

Let's practice on two professional openers. How well do the following beginnings do their jobs? Here is the opening paragraph of C. S. Lewis's *A Preface to Paradise Lost*:

The first qualification for judging a piece of workmanship, from a corkscrew to a cathedral, is to know *what* it is—what it was intended to do and how it is meant to be used. After that has been discovered, the temperance reformer may decide that the corkscrew was made for a bad purpose, and the communist may think the same about the cathedral. But such questions come later. The first thing is to understand the object before you: as long as you think the corkscrew was meant for opening tins or the cathedral for entertaining tourists, you can say nothing to the purpose about them. The first thing the reader needs to know about *Paradise Lost* is what Milton meant it to be.

We know Lewis's subject: how did Milton mean for *Paradise Lost* to be used? We know his purpose: to tell us how Milton intended his poem to be used so that we may judge it truly. We know that this should matter to us: until we have what Lewis offers us, he implies, we are doomed to misconstrue Milton's poem.

Does Lewis say "Read me"? That depends on who we are. You can't write to everyone, and Lewis doesn't try. He's writing to college literature students primarily, so he speaks in a voice that is learned—to win our respect—but also personal ("you") and mildly witty (corkscrews and cathedrals) and forceful ("know *what* it is"). I think he does well.

The second example is by Bill Donahue from an article called "Under the Sheltering Sky" from the *Washington Post Magazine* (and reprinted in *The Best American Travel Writing*, 2004). It might be my all-time favorite opening:

> The coolest people in the world do not wear their baseball caps backwards or pierce their navels with diamond studs. They are old and their cool is subtle, carrying hints of wisdom and poise. Johnny Cash, Marlon Brando, Georgia O'Keeffe: we behold their weathered sangfroid and we are ineluctably intrigued.

Does Donahue's introduction say, "Read me"? That depends on who you are and what you want. What he's doing, though, is fascinating: taking a handful of very down-to-earth and familiar images and people and juxtaposing them against rather academic and unfamiliar language. I don't know about you, but I want to read an essay whose introduction links the words "cool," "backwards baseball caps," and "Johnny Cash" to words that I'll admit to having to look up. In fact, the introduction was so compelling that I was hooked and kept reading despite not knowing precisely what two of the words meant. (I looked them up later: "sangfroid" means composure; "ineluctably" means unavoidably or inevitably.)

It turns out the essay is about the author's search in Tangier for ghosts of the American ex-patriot writer Paul Bowles. And by the way, it's an absolutely wonderful piece, instructive in many ways and very worth tracking down.

Finally, perhaps the best "Read-me" introduction ever written: "In the beginning was the word."

CONCLUSIONS

Making the Tool

Conclusions are almost as good at breeding writer's block as beginnings. Anyone who's ever found himself stuck on the porch looking for the right last words after a first date knows that. That's why we've invented lots of get-me-out-of-this formulas for concluding: "Last but not least, I'd just like to thank ..."; "And so, without further ado ..."; "Thank you very much for your attention to this matter"; "I'll call ya."

Concluding is surrounded by lots of toxic myths, so let's begin by clearing them out. Here are some rules for what *not* to do:

1. **Don't feel compelled to summarize the essay or repeat the thesis.** This is a shock to lots of people, but frequently a summary conclusion is a waste of time, a deadly bore, and an insult to your reader. Only do it if your

teacher tells you to or the situation otherwise calls for it. Some academic papers and formal reports do.

2. **Don't seek the last word.** If you write a paper on the national economy, you're *not* going to end all discussion of the national economy. Yet the conclusion must say, "We can stop here for now"—like a campsite on a walking tour, a home for the night. In fact, journalists use the slang term "walk-off" for conclusion. They're basically saying, "That's what I've got for you. Now I'm outta here." Journalists know, too, that they don't have the last word—aren't news stories (and editorials) really places to *begin* conversation?

3. **Remember that a "conclusion" takes lots of different forms.** Don't feel obligated to have a formal conclusion. In fact, your conclusion will be whatever you end up with, so you just have to make sure that it suggests to your reader that your essay's done. Just like with introductions (above), frequently I'll suggest to students that they lop off their last paragraph. "But then I won't have a conclusion," they invariably say. "Yes, you will," I tell them. "Your conclusion will be what used to be your second-to-last paragraph." "Dad" (in Chapter 12) is a good example of an essay that despite not having a formal conclusion ("Thus, it can be seen ...") concludes perfectly anyway.

The list of things to *do* is very short:

1. **Study concluding by reading for the craft.** (See Chapter 1.) As you read essays throughout your life, read with an eye on how each one solves the problem of ending.

2. **Be thinking about your conclusion all along.** The conclusion is the place your structure has been taking you. If you ask a question, you're committed to giving the reader an answer. If you're writing a lab report, you're committed to discussing the significance of what you learned. If you begin with a human-interest story, you're committed to returning to the people in it so the reader isn't left wondering what happened to them. If you begin by stating a problem, you're committed to offering a solution (or confessing that you have none).

Here's how it looks. A student reviewed a local taco stand. His thesis was that it was all right, but that it couldn't compare to the Mexican food he was used to back home in L.A. Here's an abstract of his essay, with his concluding sentence intact:

> When I was young, I learned to love the great Mexican food in L.A., but now that I'm here in the sticks I keep seeking a restaurant that comes up to that high standard. In that search I tried Alfredo's. It was pretty good, but hardly spectacular, and the search continues. Now, if you want real Mexican food, I know a little place not far from Hollywood and Vine....

And here's an abstract of a review of a local counterculture restaurant, titled "Lily's Restaurant ... and More":

> Lily's has a wide range of sandwiches, all tasty and reasonably priced— and more. Lily's has a clientele ranging from student hippie to

lumberjack—and more. It has soups, vegetarian meals, and friendly, casual service—and more. It's also got cockroaches, so, no thanks, I'm not going back.

3. **Use a stock closer.** Conclusions, like introductions, fall into types. If you can't find a conclusion, do one of the following standards, but remember: each one commits you to an essay structure that sets it up, so you can't paste it on as an afterthought—and as with stock openers, they risk cliché.

The answer. "Given the Chance" and "Being a Parent Is a Balancing Act" (both from Chapter 15) do this. If you begin by addressing a problem, you naturally end by deciding what's to be done about it. If you begin by asking a question, you end by answering it.

The full circle. A full-circle conclusion ends by returning to where it started, to one of the very first things the essay said. A student began a paper on a quiche restaurant by referring to the author of the bestseller *Real Men Don't Eat Quiche,* saying "Bruce Feirstein has obviously not been to Quiche Heaven," and he returned to that in his concluding line: "I don't care what Bruce Feirstein thinks; he doesn't know what he's been missing." If you begin with a *person,* return to that person: "Perhaps, if these changes are enacted, no one ever again will suffer the way Alice suffered." The essay on the Mexican restaurant does this, beginning with the author's beloved L.A. haunts and returning to them, as does "Scratch That Itch" ("A Collection of Good Writing"). But notice that coming full circle is *not* summarizing or repeating a thesis. Keep in mind, too, that the "full-circle" and the "answer" conclusions are often the same thing.

Taking the long view. After you've arrived at your destination, you explore the long-term implications of your discovery, consider the larger issues, or raise the next question (Chapter 7). If you've argued that women are getting more into weightlifting, talk about the long-term implications for women's self-image, standards of female attractiveness in our culture, and sexism. This can work with personal writing, too. The long-view conclusion is just about the only way to conclude a thesis-opener essay without summarizing or restating. "A Moral Victory?" and "Why I Never Cared for the Civil War" (both in "A Collection of Good Writing") have brief long-view conclusions.

The punch line. If no better conclusion has come to you, you can usually end with your best line. "How to Audition for a Play" (in Chapter 13) has a punch-line ending.

Using the Tool

There is no fancy diagnostic program for conclusions. Just read the conclusion and ask yourself if it works. If you think it does, it probably does. If it doesn't, assume that the problem is a symptom of a problem in the draft's overall design, and go back to abstracting. If you're not sure, have someone read the essay, looking specifically at the conclusion. As we've discovered, sometimes you get so close to your own work that it's difficult to tell what's working and what isn't. Readers can be an immense help.

Titles

The title is the drive-through of revision, the quickest diagnostic tool a writer has. In about two seconds you can tell if the essay is complete or not.

Making the Tool.   Some people seem naturally gifted at coming up with good titles. Others find it next to impossible. And although it's difficult to talk about titling in general—it's much easier to look at a particular essay and talk about possible titles—here are some things to think about:

1. **Have one.** The biggest problem with titles in school is a lack of one. Nothing's surer to turn off your reader or instructor than an essay without a title, or, perhaps worse, something like "Essay #3" or "Assignment #2."
2. **Do the same three jobs you did in your introduction.** Reveal the topic, imply a thesis, a purpose, or a task to accomplish, and say "Read me, read me!" Any title does at least one of these three; the trick is to do all three.

Some titles just state topic:

Prayer in School

Friendship

Some titles do topic and purpose without much "Read me!":

The Joys of Racquetball

Mark Twain: America's Finest Author

Fad Diets Don't Work

Some do a lot of "Read me!" and no topic:

Give Me *Massive* Doses!

Killing Bambi

What we're striving for is the title that does all three:

Tube Addiction

Yes, Virginia, Leisure Is a Good Thing

Anatomy of the Myopic Introvert

3. **Don't have your title state the thesis,** because it's wordy and dull. It's enough to imply or suggest it:

Title	Implied Thesis
A Gamble for Better Education	We should have a state lottery.
China Syndrome	The food at Lee's is good
In the Long Run	Jogging is good for you.

4. **Use a stock format.** If you shy away from suggesting your thesis in your titles, you can force yourself to by using any of three title formats:

   The question: "School Music: Fundamental or Thrill?"; "What Is Pornography?"

   The "why" title: "Why Advertisements for Prescriptions Drugs Should Be Banned"

   The declarative sentence: "Breast Feeding Is Best"

   Yes, that last one breaks Rule 3—see "How to Feel About Rules," in Chapter 2.

5. **Use a colon title.** We've just said that a good title should declare a topic, imply a thesis, purpose, or task, and say "Read me!" But most titles are two or three words long, and doing all three tasks in such a small space is hard. One way around that is to stick two titles together with a colon. Write a title that does two of the three tasks, put in a colon, and then add a title that does the third. Colon titles are a bit stuffy, but they work. Sometimes you do the topic, put a colon, then do thesis and "Read me!": "Television: The Glamour Medium." Sometimes you do it the other way around: "Rotten in Denmark: Images of Disease in *Hamlet*."

6. **Use language from your text.** Sometimes you can find a snippet from the essay itself, often in the conclusion, and tweak it into a title. Look at the conclusion of "Scratch That Itch" ("A Collection of Good Writing"). Some possible titles are taken from its language: "Fallen Barricades," "Minimizing the Damage," "Your Mother Was Right" (or, "The Truth Your Mother Told You"), "Goldenseal and Onions."

7. **Play with a familiar expression.** Another way to title your essay is by taking a familiar expression (cliché, film title, song lyric, etc.) and playing with its language. I wrote a travel story some years back about skiing in the French Alps—shortly after the film *The Unbearable Lightness of Being* had come out. I titled the piece "The Unbeatable Rightness of Skiing." Just recently I was helping a student research her paper on the long-term effects of youth beauty pageants on the participants, and we came across an article with one of the best titles I've ever seen: "Buy, Buy, Miss America Lie."

   Other (hypothetical) examples: for an informative essay on horseshoeing, "Just Shoe It"; for a piece on etiquette at Fourth of July parties, "Star-Spangled Manners"; for a profile of an exceptional emergency-room nurse, "The Wizard of Gauze." A word of caution: don't let your cleverness get in the way. Obviously (just look at my examples), you at least risk saying "*Don't* read me" by going too far with this. (In fact, in the last edition of this book, I changed Chapter 8's title from "The Spirit of Revising" to "Give Me That Old Time Revision." My editor, wisely, suggested that it didn't work, that it was both too cutesy and that my readers might not get the reference—to the song "Give Me That Old Time Religion.")

8. **Consider how it sounds.** Depending on your subject and tone, you might want to play with language. How about some alliteration? For an informative essay on cooking spaghetti: "Preparing Perfect Pasta." Or rhyme? For a personal essay about blowing it on a job and getting fired: "Lost, Bossed, and Tossed."

A Final Suggestion.   Read newspaper headlines. Good headline writers know how to say "Read me" in interesting ways. Check out sports headlines especially: "Vikings Pillage Panthers in Easy Win"; "Bears Slumber in Loss to Wildcats"; "Forty-Niners Go for Gold in Overtime."

Formatting Titles.   Don't underline or italicize your titles or put them in quote marks. You might want to increase the font size a bit, but generally just center the title double spaced above your introduction (which is what MLA format calls for—see also Chapter 18).

Using the Tool

As with the introduction, ask of the title, "Does this work? Does it make the reader want to read the essay?" You'll know the answer. Next, ask, "Does it do the three tasks of a perfect title?" If the title is faulty, blame the draft. If you can't find a hint of thesis, it's probably because the draft doesn't have one; if you can't find signs of life, it's probably because the draft doesn't have any.

EXERCISES

1. Write a paragraph or two describing how successfully each of the following openers reveals its topic, reveals its purpose, and says "Read me."

   a.   For at least the past 10,000 years, the Grand Canyon has been luring human beings into its depths. From the Desert Archaics, who left behind their split-twig figurines, to the Anasazi, who built villages of adobe; from John Wesley Powell's tumultuous 1869 river adventure to "Uncle Jimmy" Owens's turn-of-the-century mountain lion hunts; from the 40,000 annual visitors (out of four million total) who come to practice their survival skills below the rim to the handful every decade who choose the canyon as the place to end their lives: No one enters the Grand Canyon casually, and no one, I would wager, leaves it without being variously and sufficiently awed.
   (Pam Houston, "The Vertigo Girls Do the East Tonto Trail")

   b.   On our frequent American road trips, my friend Guy de la Valdène has invariably said at lunch, "These French fries are filthy," but he always eats them anyway, and some of mine, too. Another friend, the painter Russell Chatham, likes to remind me that we pioneered the idea of ordering multiple entrées in restaurants back in the seventies—the theory being that if you order several entrées you can then avoid the terrible disappointment of having ordered the wrong thing while others at the table have inevitably ordered the right thing. The results can't have been all that bad, since both of us are still more or less alive, though neither of us owns any spandex.

(Jim Harrison, "A Really Big Lunch")

2. Do Exercise 1 using an essay from "A Collection of Good Writing".

3. Do Exercise 1 using an essay of your own. Rewrite the opener to include any task you find missing.

4. Write four stock openers for one of your own essays.

5. Write critiques of the conclusions in three essays in "A Collection of Good Writing": How do they work? Do they use any of the four stock conclusions? How does the essay design plan for the conclusion?

6. Do Exercise 5 using one of your own essays.

7. Here's a list of titles from essays on censorship. For each title, answer the question "Which of a title's three tasks does it do?" If any titles don't do all three, rewrite them so that they do; make up content if you need to. Example: "Eating" → "Tomorrow We Diet: My Life as an Overeater."

   a.   Why Is Censorship Needed?

   b.   Who's to Judge?

   c.   From a Child's Point of View

   d.   You Want to Read *What?*

   e.   Censorship: The Deterioration of the First Amendment

   f.   Censorship

8. Write four titles for one of your essays, one in each of the four stock formats.

9. Write colon titles for three of the essays in "A Collection of Good Writing".

10. Write three colon titles for one of your essays.

11. Write a one-paragraph critique of the title of one of your essays: does it do the three tasks of a perfect title? If it doesn't, rewrite it so that it does.

Chapter 10

Peer Feedback

Peer feedback goes by many different names: peer editing, peer evaluation, and workshopping, for example. These terms usually refer to sharing drafts of writing in the classroom. It's important to remember, though, that this process occurs outside the classroom as well. I don't know a single writer who doesn't have someone else read a draft of a piece she's working on before sending it out or otherwise presenting it to its real intended audience. I personally always have my wife—or sometimes one or more of my friends—read my work in draft stage. In fact, I often have her read it in several stages—usually fairly early on, which for me is about a fifth or sixth draft, and then again as I'm closer to being done. In fact, in our house it's become kind of a ritual: I give my wife a piece I'm working on, and she goes over to the couch to read it. Then I pretend to busy myself, while in reality I'm watching and listening closely—sometimes peeking around the corner from the kitchen—for her reactions.

Why do we need readers? Because writers know what they're *trying* to do, but there's absolutely no way to know whether they're succeeding without readers who can tell them if their words are having the effect they intended. I usually have some specific questions for my reader: Is the example in paragraph 6 convincing? Is my tone effective? Is the language too slangy? Too formal? Is the pun in the title stupid? A former student of mine, Matt Kiser, recently emailed me a draft of a letter he was sending to *Spin* magazine to apply for an internship. While he wanted my general feedback, he had a very specific question: do I come across as arrogant? (He didn't, got the position, and has been working for the magazine ever since.)

Of course, as human beings we want our readers to say, "This is perfect (totally convincing, incredibly moving, absolutely hilarious) exactly as it stands. Don't change a thing." But as writers we also have to keep in mind that it is in fact a draft and that our reader(s) will most likely make some suggestions for revisions—and those suggestions are at least worth considering.

Peer feedback in the classroom takes many forms. Some writing instructors have students make copies of their work to pass around to the entire class; others break the class into smaller groups. Some instructors have their students submit electronic copies of their drafts and then project the drafts onto a screen (or at individual computers), and the whole class works on one essay together. Regardless, there are certain rules to follow and important things to keep in mind if the feedback session is to be worthwhile. And it's critical that readers have specific things in mind while they're reading— including, ideally, questions for the writer. Otherwise, peer feedback can be a complete waste of time. Writing "I liked it" on a draft is not helpful.

RULES FOR READERS

1. **Make sure you know the writer's intended audience.** If you don't know for whom the writer is writing, how do you know whether something's working or not? Is the language too formal? Should the term "artificial intelligence" in the second paragraph be defined? How about the reference to Pliny the Elder in the third, Newton's first law of motion in the fourth? The answers to these questions all depend on your knowing the writer's intended audience.

2. **Ask the writer if there's anything in particular that you should be looking for.** Usually, writers know that certain parts of their essays aren't working as well as others or that they're stuck in certain places. If you know where the writer is struggling, you'll more likely be of help.

3. **Fry the biggest fish first.** Address the thing(s) that will help the essay the most first and the thing(s) that will help it the least last. If someone asked you to help restore a dilapidated 1957 Chevrolet, you wouldn't first suggest that he polish the chrome on the headlights; you'd probably first recommend he reupholster the seats and rebuild the transmission, then wash and polish the car last.

4. **Don't focus on what's wrong or list mistakes.** Doing so is devastating for the writer, it's not how people learn, and there's no such thing as right and wrong in writing anyway. Instead, do the following:

5. **Tell the writer how the text reads to you.** Say things like, "This paragraph confused me," or "I wanted to know more here," or "The title made me

laugh." This is the one thing the writer can't do for himself. The writer hits the golf ball, but only you can tell him where it lands. You can't be "wrong," since you're just declaring what you experienced while reading. The writer can't argue with you, for the same reason.

If you do this one job, you'll have served your writer well, but there's much more help you can offer.

6. **Identify the source of your reactions.** Find what, specifically, in the text is causing you to feel the way you do. You help a little if you say, "This essay feels cold," but you help a lot if you add, "I think it's because of all the academic jargon" and even more if you can be specific: "particularly the part about the pedagogy of trination and ambiguation in the discourse of post-modern marginalized composition students."

7. **Suggest possible revision strategies.** Show the writer possible ways to work with the essay features you're observing. You help a little if you say, "The opening paragraph seems lifeless," but you help a lot if you add, "Maybe should think about starting the essay with the personal narrative in paragraph 4?"

Rule 7 runs a lot of risks. You must remember that it's not your job to tell the writer how to write, and the writer must remember that she doesn't have to follow your suggestions—she decides what to do, because she's the writer. But if you can both stay in your proper roles, "You *could* do this...," "You *might think about* this...," suggestions can be golden.

8. **Generalize and note patterns.** Make broad statements that apply to the essay as a whole. Note when the same sort of thing happens over and over. Every time you make an observation about a place in the text, ask yourself, "Are there other places where similar things occur?" If you don't do this, feedback tends to be an overwhelming flood of unrelated suggestions.

9. **Give yeas as well as nays.** Give as much energy to pointing out what pleased you as to what didn't. "Keep doing this, this, and this" teaches at least as well as "Dump that, that, and that." And it feels a lot better. Psychologists who study marriages say that in healthy ones affirmations outnumber criticisms by about five to one. You may not be able to maintain that ratio, but you can embrace the spirit of it.

10. **Help the writer see alternatives and possibilities.** Think about what the essay could be that it isn't yet. Ask, Where can this draft go from here? What else could it be doing? What related issues does this open up?

This is the most precious gift you can give the writer, because it's the one thing he's least likely to be able to do himself. To do it you have to stop staring at the draft and asking "What needs fixing?" Instead, step back, and think outside the box. Ironically, this is the easiest part of the feedback process for the reader, because all you have to do is *share your thoughts on what the draft says.* Since you didn't write it, you'll have things to say about it that the writer will never think of, and those thoughts will open doors and make new essays possible.

To do this last task well, both the writer and the reader must remember that the purpose behind peer editing is not to rid the draft of errors but to remake the draft into the best possible essay. That often means developing the draft into something considerably different. Looking for errors to fix creates a tunnel vision that prevents that large-scale growth.

11. **End by prioritizing.** Since a good peer-editing session touches on a dizzying range of issues, avoid overload by ending with a highlighting of the two or three suggestions that have the biggest potential for gain: "Of all the things we've talked about, I think those two ideas about opening with the story about you and your mother and dropping the tirade about rude telemarketers are the best."

RULES FOR WRITERS

While you can do several things to increase the chances of getting good feedback, you must first have the right attitude: you need to be *open* to feedback. If you're too defensive, you're not likely to listen. If you're too submissive, you're likely to assume that you should make every single change your readers suggest. So listen to what your readers say, but trust your own instincts and ideas as well—allow that your readers might be flat-out wrong sometimes.

Also, keep in mind that it's a good idea to let some time pass between getting the feedback and sitting down with it to consider what you want to heed and what you don't. You might want to wait a few hours; you might want to wait a few days. At any rate, you'll probably be more open to listening openly and honestly if you've let some time pass.

Some guidelines:

1. **Let your reader know, as specifically as possible, who your intended audience is.** If she doesn't know that, she can't offer much in the way of feedback.

2. **Let your reader know what you're trying to do with the piece of writing, what your purpose is.** While it might sometimes be good to let your reader come to the essay "cold," that is, without telling him what to look for—an ironic tone, for example—the more your reader knows about what you're intending, the more he'll be able to tell you whether you're being successful.

3. **Provide specific things for your reader to keep in mind while reading.** I always have my students write—at the very tops of their papers—at least one question they have about their work, or a problem they're having with it, for their readers to consider while they read. And, as I suggested with the rules for readers, fry the biggest fish first.

4. **Ask for peer feedback before you're "done."** If you wait until the project feels finished, you'll fight off advice as a parent fights off criticism of her children. The earlier you ask for feedback from readers, the better.

5. **Keep in mind that some readers just won't get it,** especially if you're trying something interesting or different. Some readers dislike the unexpected. Seek out readers who are interested in your work and who are smart enough to recognize and appreciate what you're up to. They might say that what you're doing doesn't work—but it won't be just *because* it's different from what they expected.

6. **Have your work read by several readers.** But keep in mind that different qualified readers will have different reactions to your work. When I was in graduate school, I showed a draft of my thesis to my two committee members. One of them bracketed a long passage and said, "Cut this, and the piece will work better." The other one bracketed the same passage and said, "Great! This really makes your argument effective."

   Of course, you can get more readers, and that's a good idea—to try to find consensus—but you might continue to receive more varying reactions. Ultimately, it will come back to you. It's your work, after all.

7. **When it's over, say "Thank you."** Remind your editors and yourself that they were doing you a favor.

PEER EDITING IN GROUPS

Peer editing in groups can be an effective way for a writer to see what kind of effect his work is having on several readers at once. However, group peer-editing sessions risk becoming chaotic and nonproductive. To that end, here are some rules:

1. **Raise one issue at a time.** Good students violate this rule with the best of intentions. They come to class and want to get on with it, so they start the discussion with a list: "I've got four things I want to say about the draft: first, the thesis is unclear; second, ..." When the lecture is finished, if you're lucky, someone will address one of the issues on the list and everything else will be forgotten.

2. **Stick to an issue once it's been raised.** If someone raises a question about structure, discuss structure until all comments on structure have been heard.

3. **Stay with an issue until clarity is reached.** This doesn't mean grind down all opposition until everyone in the room thinks the same thing. It means talk about it until the group figures out where it stands. If there are different opinions in the room, get clear on what they are, who's on what side, and why they feel that way.

4. **Voice your opinion.** Silence following a comment suggests consensus, but the writer wants to know how the piece is working on the group, not on one reader. So if someone says she thinks something is working particularly well, say, "I agree." Likewise, if you disagree, say so.

5. **Use your organizing tools.** Since group editing is much more fragmented and chaotic than editing one-on-one, you have to work even harder to

organize the chaos by doing the things we've already talked about: look for patterns, connect, generalize, and prioritize. Keep saying things like:

I think what Will is saying ties in with what Eunice said a few minutes ago.

In different ways, we keep coming back to structural issues. I'd like to get back to the question of purpose and audience—that seems crucial to me.

So it sounds to me like some of us like the tone and some of us think it's too folksy.

The Writer's Role in Group Editing

A group needs a leader, and since the writer has the most at stake and knows what he wants, he may as well be it.

This role is fraught with peril. If you can't lead without being defensive, then ask a couple of questions to start things off and say nothing else. But if you have the necessary self-control, you can do yourself a lot of good by following one rule:

6. **Remind the group to follow the rules.** Keep saying things like

    How many others agree with Nell?—a show of hands, please.

    As long as we're talking about structure, what other structural comments do you have?

    So what do you think I should do about it?

    Are there other places where that sort of thing happens?

    How big a problem is that?

    So what does the essay need the most?

Peer Editing for Mechanics and Grammar

Mechanics and grammar—comma placement, sentence structure, spelling— are legitimate topics in peer editing, but most conversations on those topics turn into useless nitpicking and wrangling that helps the writer hardly at all. So before you bring those topics up, be sure you're practicing some of the chapter's now-familiar rules:

1. **Keep frying the biggest fish first.** Discuss mechanics only in those rare cases where mechanical problems are the overriding issue.
2. **Discuss grammar and mechanics only in general terms.** If the problem isn't habitual, ignore it.
3. **Prioritize all mechanical advice.** Tell the writer how serious the problem is. Are you saying, "Since we've taken care of everything that really matters, we'll tinker with spelling," or are you saying, "My God, we've got to do something about the spelling before we do anything else!"?

A Final Piece of Advice

I've found that students respond best when they have specific jobs to do, so I usually give them lists of things to do as they read their peers' papers. The following is a template of a worksheet that I modify appropriately for various assignments. Sometimes I project it onto a screen; sometimes I make copies and have students attach it to the fronts of their essays.

While number 3 might seem obvious, I've found it to be extremely useful. If the writer finds that her reader's one-sentence summary is not what she intended, then she has to find where the disconnect is.

English XX—Section 4 Spring 2013

Please attach this sheet to the front of your essay.

Writer: (1) Identify, as narrowly as possible, your intended audience; (2) identify some questions or problems you have with the draft as it now stands. Be as specific as possible.

Readers:

1. Read the essay carefully, with the intended audience in mind; then, on one of the attached sheets of paper:
2. Address the writer's question(s)/problem(s).
3. Summarize the essay in one sentence.
4. Describe the degree to which the essay is appropriate to its intended audience, considering level of formality, definition of terms, etc.
5. Identify the most convincing piece of evidence.
6. Identify any counter ("yeah, but ...") arguments that the writer hasn't considered.
7. Make one concrete suggestion for revision.
8. Sign your name.

Notes: (A) Initial any in-text comments; (B) read as a writer—you can both provide feedback and learn from the writer's work; (C) feel free to talk about these and to consider aspects of the writing not specified above.

WRITER'S WORKSHOP

Peer Editing a Peer-Editing Session

Let's practice peer editing. Here's a draft that was submitted by Todd Burks, one of Professor Rawlins's composition students. Following it is the peer-editing conversation that took place after Burks had shared the draft with the class. The italics in the margins are Rawlins's notes about the degree to which the readers were following the rules.

LEGALIZE HEMP: AN ESSENTIAL RESOURCE FOR THE FUTURE

TODD BURKS

Student Essay

Hemp, falsley known to many as marijuana, is an essential resource for the future of the planet. In today's age of environmental awareness it seems silly that we are not taking advantage of such a valuable commodity. Not only would the legalization of hemp save our forests, but it would stimulate the presently ailing economy.

Although both marijuana and hemp are derived from cannabis sativa, you can't get "stoaned" from hemp. You see, hemp is the large stock form while marijuana is the small "budding" form. Unfortunately, negative stigmas have been placed on hemp since marijuana became a popular street drug back in the late thirties. "The flower was said to be the most violent inducing drug in the history of mankind." Those of us who have experimented with the marijuana form Know this to be false.

The legalization of hemp (marijuana) for personnal use does not concern me. However, the legalization of hemp as a valuable resource would alleviate many political, economic, and environmental ills that plague the world.

To begin, hemp legalization would virtually eliminate the need for wood in paper products. Four times the amount of hemp can be grown on an acre of land than wood. The hemp takes only four months until harvesting, compared to nearly ten years for trees. Furthrmore, hemp paper is more durable than wood paper, lasting four times as long, and it's cheaper to produce.

The adaptibility of hemp to many soils and climates would allow for extensive growth worldwide. Unlike many rotation crops that degrade the soil, hemp roots actually permeate the soil, allowing for more productivity.

Hemp seeds could also develop into daily diets around the world. "The hemp seed is the second most complete vegetable protein, second only to soybeans. However, hemp seeds are more easily synthesized by humans due to the high content of enzymes, endistins, and essential amino acids." The seeds can also be used to make margarine and a tofu-like substance.

Almost one-third of the hemp seed is oil. Hemp oil can be used in paints and varnishes, eliminating the need for petrochemical oils. The biodegradable hemp seed can also be used for diesel fuel and lubricant, causing less environmental pollution.

Finally, the rapid growth rate of hemp makes it the number-one renewable biomass resource in the world. "Biomass is fuel, whether it be petroleum, coal, or hemp." Therefore, hemp can be used in place of fossil fuels. Rather than carbon monoxide hemp gives off carbon dioxide which is naturally synthesized by our atmosphere.

It is obvious that hemp has gotten a bad rap due to the popularity of marijuana as a street drug. Not to mention the false propaganda headed by Hearst and DuPont early in the twentieth cent. However, with today's technology in genetic engineering, we can produce a plant that is purely stalk and is not possible to smoke. Finally, with government regulation and taxation we could virtually wipe out the trillion-dollar deficit hanging over our heads.

Here's the classroom conversation. "Remember to ..." in the margin indicates the rule is being broken.

*Remember to begin with
the writer's questions.*

Fry the biggest fish first.   It seemed like you jumped right into your argument, and you could hold off on that a little more—like in your introduction, explain what hemp is, what you're going to use it for, then start saying, "But this is the reason why it's not being used ..."

*Remember to stick with an
issue once it's raised.*   There was one sentence I'd take out: "Those of us who have experimented with the marijuana form know this to be false." That could weaken your case, because we could say, "Oh, it's a pot smoker, he just wants it legal so he can smoke it."

*Remember to stick with an
issue once it's raised.*   He says legalization for personal use doesn't concern him, but I think it does concern him, because I don't see how you can start reforesting the fields of hemp for commercial use without some people doing it for personal use too.

*Remember to stick with an
issue once it's raised.*   He needs to make more of how he just wants to legalize the genetically engineered plants.

*Remember to raise one
issue at a time.*   A couple of things I thought when I read it: If we have all this hemp, what do we do with the pot? Do we legalize that as well? And this fossil fuel thing: I've heard there's about fifty or so alternatives to replace fossil fuel; the only problem is it's really expensive to do so.

Maybe you could argue, "The fossil fuels are limited, this is replaceable...."

That gets around the cost issue.

It ends up you can still grow it in Mexico for a tenth the cost. There's no way we can compete with Third World countries where it grows wild along the road.

Connect with previous comments. If you disagree, say so.

As far as throwing out the "those of us" sentence, I don't know. Because obviously in the back of the reader's mind they're saying, "Wait a minute—some people have experimented with it, and I'm sure they have something to say about it." But I think that could be a potentially strong argument.

Stay till consensus is reached.

Everyone seems to agree that the essay should either drop that aside about personal use or develop it more. Let's get a show of hands: How many think it should be dropped? And how many want to develop it? *(Rawlins)* (The vote is to drop it.)

Todd, didn't you tell me that it's just the stalk that makes the paper and stuff, so there's no reason to even worry about it being misused as pot?

You can certainly breed out the THC content—they've been intensifying it for twenty years, so I'm sure you can reduce it by the same genetic engineering.

I'm sure if I'm a farmer I'm going to grow hemp when I can grow pot for twenty times the money.

Tell the writer how the text reads to you.

I'm confused about whether hemp and marijuana are the same thing, because in the first sentence you say "hemp, falsely known as marijuana," and in the third paragraph you say "hemp (marijuana)."

Remember not to explain or defend yourself.

Well, they're both *Cannabis sativa,* but one is the long stalk form and the other is the flower form. *(Author)*

So they're from the same family but two separate plants?

Connect, generalize, prioritize.

Same plant, different breeding. *(Author)*

That issue seems to be an important one. Does the group agree that that issue needs to be clarified? *(Rawlins)* (Signs of agreement throughout the room)

Tell the writer how the text reads to you.	I don't understand that bit about Hearst's false propaganda.
	Don't you remember the "killer weed" business in the fifties?
	What's that got to do with Hearst and DuPont?
	At the time hemp was the second biggest crop after cotton, and they were going to use it as an alternative to paper products. Hearst and DuPont rallied against it, because DuPont has the patent on sulfuric acid, which breaks down wood into pulp, and Hearst had huge tracts of forest land, so they didn't want hemp to hurt the wood paper market. That's when they started all this reefer madness thing. *(Author)*
Suggest revision strategies.	That all sounds like great stuff—I'd put it right into the essay. *(Rawlins)*
Remember to fry the biggest fish first.	I'd just prefer "cent." to be turned into "century."
	Me, too.
	How do you spell "stoned"? "S-t-o-n-e-d"?
Prioritize mechanical issues.	Is spelling a problem in the essay? *(Rawlins)*
	Yes. *(Several voices)*
	Like what? *(Rawlins)*
	"Falsley." "Personnal." "Furthrmore." *(Several voices)*
	Also there are two "finally"s. When I hear the word "finally" I think, you know, "finally," so when I hear it again I go "Whoa... ." I just deleted the last "finally."
	You could say "sorta finally" and "really finally."
Fry the biggest fish first.	Before we turn to grammar and mechanics, are there any larger issues anyone wanted to talk about? *(Rawlins)*

In the last paragraph when you say "bad rap" I could tell it was your voice. The essay seemed so technical, when I got to "bad rap" I thought, "Gee, it's not so technical anymore."

Turn comments into concrete revision suggestions.

Are you saying you *like* "bad rap" and want more of it, or that you *don't* and suggest Todd take it out? *(Rawlins)*

It just seems like a contradiction—it sticks out.

So you'd like the tone to be more consistent. *(Rawlins)*

One question that I have: There are three large quotes in the paper and you don't say where they come from or who said them or anything. They're just kind of there, so ...

Remember to stick with an issue once it's raised.

On the first page you talk about "political, economic, and environmental" benefits of hemp. You talk mostly about environmental, and you mention economics at the end, but I really didn't see much about political.

Is that the thesis of the essay there? Because I thought the end of paragraph 1 was the thesis.

Remember to generalize and connect. Several of the comments address structure.

You know, you talk about "negative stigmas" twice, in paragraph 2 and the last paragraph. I wonder if you need to do that.

Remember to fry the biggest fish first.

Should this be two sentences: "Not to mention the false propaganda headed by Hearst and DuPont ..." Maybe it should be a comma.

Prioritize.

Is punctuation a problem in the essay? *(Rawlins)*

No. *(Several voices)*

Tell the writer how it reads for you.

You say it can be used for diesel fuel and lubricant ... I'm sorry, I just don't get that. I don't work on cars.

I need to know more about hemp roots penetrating the soil. It's not that I don't agree—I'm just not going to buy it until I know what it all means.

Generalize and connect.

I hear several of these comments addressing the same issue: you'd like *more information*—what exactly the roots do to the soil, how exactly hemp and marijuana are different, how hemp can be used for diesel fuel. *(Rawlins)*

Remember to fry the biggest fish first.

I've been playing with this sentence in paragraph 2: "You see, hemp is the large stock form, while marijuana is the small 'budding' form." I tried, "While hemp is the large stock form of *Cannabis sativa*, marijuana is the small budding form."

You could just cross out "you see," couldn't you?

The only sentence I had trouble with was "The flower was said to be the most violent inducing drug in the history of mankind." I'm not sure what a "violent inducing drug" is.

Remember not to defend.

That's a quote from a book. *(Author)*

I still don't understand it.

I think it should be "violence-inducing drug."

Generalize and prioritize.

OK, we're nearing the end. What are your biggest and most important suggestions to Todd? *(Rawlins)*

Explain yourself more—like the roots and the soil.

Make it clearer what the difference between pot and hemp is, and how you can grow one without running the risk of growing the other.

Tell us more about Hearst and DuPont— that was interesting.

Connect, generalize.   You know, many of your comments relate to structure. For instance, the way the essay talks about stigmas twice, and the two "finally"s, and the two thesis sentences, and the way it promises to discuss politics in paragraph 3 but never does. If we were going to restructure, I thought the very first comment of the day gave us a good design: first list the virtues of hemp, then explain why we're prohibited from using it, relate the history, and *then* argue that the ban should be lifted. That suckers the reader into agreeing before he knows what he's in for. *(Rawlins)*

Now It's Your Turn. Have a classmate distribute copies of his draft to the class. Peer edit the draft as a group, in the manner of Chapter 10. Then individually write a one-page essay in which you critique the group's performance by answering the following two questions: Which of the chapter's rules did the group and the author follow? Which did they break? Then write down two resolutions: what two things are you personally going to do differently the next time you peer edit?

Chapter 11

Editing

Now it's time to polish, to go over the text line by line—word by word—to make sure it's as clean and shiny as you can make it. Remember that '57 Chevy? You've spent the last two years rebuilding the engine and redoing the interior. Now the day of the big car show is approaching. You want to clean the glass, polish the chrome, and shampoo the carpeting. Of course, this is all superficial stuff, but it's what will impress the judges. That new engine might purr like a kitten, but the judges will still dock points for that coffee stain on the rear seat.

GETTING THE EDITING ATTITUDE

The trickiest part of editing is doing it for the right reasons. To do that, embrace the following five principles:

1. **Editing is not writing.** Many people believe that if you follow all the mechanical rules, you're writing well. That's like believing that if you're never offside, you must be a great football player.

   In fact, writing is the original multitasking activity, which is why it's challenging. To write, you must have thoughts, express them, organize them, polish your language, clarify your thesis, be aware of your audience, and follow mechanical rules. You must play well *and* never be offside.

2. **Editing is different from creating.** A writer's tasks fall into two groups, creative tasks and obedience tasks. Everything we've done so far in Chapters 1–9 is creative, and rules have been something we've chosen to follow or not. Now we have to become obedient rule followers. That means we literally have to shift into a different part of our brains.

If you don't make that shift, you can't edit. If you try to create and correct at the same time or try to edit out of your creative brain, all that will happen is that the creative brain will rule and you won't edit. That's why every publishing house employs line editors, people who do nothing but read closely for correctness only and who aren't allowed to tinker with the creative side. So follow their lead, and create a step in the writing process when you redefine yourself as a line editor and then *edit, and only edit.* Obviously this line-editing step must come dead last, since if you do anything else afterward you'll have to line edit again.

3. **Editing is like cleaning windows.** Think of the printed page as a window. Your job as a writer is to show the reader what's on the other side of the glass. We talked earlier about how pretentious writing is like stained glass that the reader can't see through. Poorly edited writing is like a *dirty* window. You want the glass to *disappear* so that the viewer doesn't get distracted by streaks and fingerprints—that is, by run-on sentences, misspelled words, incorrect punctuation, even typos that call attention to themselves. You want 100 percent of the reader's attention on what you're saying. Trai reedign tHis, sentecne and yew'l see wut ii; meat. Every mechanical oddity is a tiny tug on the reader's sleeve pulling her focus away from your content.

4. **Stripping to the skeleton makes fixing mechanical errors easier.** Most of us write problematic sentences, not because we don't know the rules, but because when the sentences get complex we can't see how the rules apply. Nobody would write *"It's a problem for I," but lots of people do write *"It's an ongoing problem for my husband, Andy, and I." The problem is simple busy-ness, and you fix it by simplifying the sentence until you can see what is basically going on. Strip the sentence down to its skeleton—its basic framework—and ask if the skeleton looks good by the rules you already know. If *"It's a problem for I" is incorrect, then *"It's an ongoing problem for my husband, Andy, and I" is incorrect, and we fix both sentences the same way, by changing *I* to *me.* (The asterisk in front of the sentence, which you'll see throughout this chapter, means the sentence is incorrect.)

   To strip to the skeleton, toss out all the unnecessary parts of the sentence: prepositional phrases, all adjectives, all adverbs, all introductory phrases.

Original: *Watching the reflection of the sun and mountains bouncing off the lake as I fed the horses is an image that can never be forgotten.

Skeleton: *Watching is an image that can never be forgotten.

Rewrite: The reflection of the sun and mountains bouncing off the beautiful lake as I fed the horses is an image that can never be forgotten.

Sentences that use *which* clauses often cause problems, and they frequently need extra help. Take the *which* clause by itself, replace the *which* with a personal pronoun, and reorder the words to make a sentence:

*The Board has set two ground rules which only one must be followed by manufacturers.

Skeleton of the which clause: *Only one they must be followed by manufacturers.

Rewrite: The board has set two ground rules, only one of which must be followed by manufacturers.

*Children aren't familiar with print and it becomes a challenge to them, a problem in which they can and must make sense of.

Skeleton of the which clause: *They can make sense of in it.

Rewrite: Children aren't familiar with print and it becomes a challenge to them, a problem they can and must make sense of.

5. **Frequently, mechanics can't be explained.** The rules are more complex than words can say. Consider the commas in these two examples:

A tall, handsome, unmarried stranger

A typical pushy American tourist

Why commas in the first sentence and none in the second? It's almost impossible to put into words, so *all handbook rules lie by oversimplification,* including the ones in this chapter. (Actually, later in the chapter I will explain the rule at work here: basically, if you can use "and" between the adjectives, like you can in the first example, then you use commas. If not, don't use commas.) In the end, though, the only thing that will steer you right is a sense of how English "goes," and *that* you get from years of reading.

"GRAMMAR"

The thing to remember about rules is that they didn't come first. It's sort of like driving. Long before U.S. vehicle codes mandated that people drive on the right side of the road, people were driving on the right side of the road. Later, it was codified, to decrease the chances of accidents.

Likewise, no one sat down and created a list of, say, comma rules and then invented writing. Instead, people wanted to write clearly and consistently; they wanted their readers to know what they meant. For example, if I write, "After eating my brother and I drove home," you're going to have to pause to make sense of what I meant. But if I write, "After eating, my brother and I drove home," you'll know exactly what I meant, and you won't pause to think, "If he knew how to punctuate his sentences, he wouldn't be writing about eating his brother."

Now you have a comma "rule" at work (use a comma after a prepositional phrase before the main clause), but that's not what's important. What's important is that the reader knows what you're saying or at least that she doesn't stop to question your credibility. And, naturally, you care far more about being clear—and credible—than you do about whether commas should follow prepositional phrases.

Nonetheless, it is helpful to know some grammar, basically a combination of at least three different types of rules: conventions, rules of logic, and rules of clarity.

Conventions

Conventions are rules that can't be figured out or explained or are sometimes used to make sense but don't anymore—they're "just the way it's done." Language is conventional; so are lots of things. Think about driving, for example: conventionally (and legally), we drive on the right side of the road in the United States; conventionally (and legally), they drive on the left side of the road in England. That's "just the way it's done." Conventionally, we say, "She gets on my nerves," but that doesn't make much sense. In fact, perhaps, "She gets *in* my nerves," as a Japanese student of mine once wrote, makes *more* sense. But when I tried to explain to her why we say "on" instead of "in," all I could really say was, "That's just the way it's done."

Unless you're learning English for the first time, you already know at least one set of English conventions—the set used by your parents or peer group—and the only question is whether you need to learn additional ones. Any convention is as good as any other as long as everyone in the group agrees to abide by it, so there's nothing wrong with the ones you know or better about the ones you're trying to learn.

Most of us know the conventions of Colloquial English (CE), but the conventions of formal Essay English (EE) are occasionally different:

CE: Everybody has to bring *their* own pencil and paper.

EE: Everybody has to bring *his* own pencil and paper.

CE: Try *and* get some rest before the big game.

EE: Try *to* get some rest before the big game.

CE: *Can* I go now?

EE: *May* I go now?

CE: *Who* is this intended *for*?

EE: *For whom* is this intended?

Do we ever use colloquial English in writing? Sure. As usual, knowing your audience will help you make the call. For example, I'm in regular email contact with a bunch of my high school buddies, none of whom are English teachers, writers, or particularly concerned with the correctness of language (actually, since "none" is a contraction of "not one," that should read, "*not one of whom* is an *English teacher, a writer, or particularly concerned* ..."). So when one of them writes asking me if I'd like to meet them at a San Francisco Giants baseball game—as we do regularly—I write back using appropriately informal and sometimes "incorrect" language. If I used "whom," even if the "rule" called for it, they probably wouldn't let me sit with them! On the other hand, when I'm writing letters of recommendation for students who are applying to graduate school, I use very formal language. If the "rule" requires "whom" instead of "who," I use "whom."

In writing essays for college classes (as well as for some publications—note the difference in level of formality between the language in the *New Yorker* and in *Transworld Snowboarding*), you need to be as correct as possible—not only because your professors expect it but because even the tiniest of glitches can give your readers reasons to question your credibility.

How do you know whether "who" or "whom" is correct? Good question. And though writing handbooks try to explain this and other grammar rules, they unfortunately have to rely on readers already knowing a lot about how language works—with "who" and "whom," for example, the difference between the subjective objective case. So even detailed explanations aren't always all helpful. The bottom line, again, is exposure: you simply need to read lots of professional essays to get a feel for the language. Eventually, you'll soak it up and do it naturally.

A Final Word on "Who" and "Whom."   Trust me here: when in doubt, use "who" instead of "whom," since "whom" when it should be "who" sounds way worse than "who" when it should be "whom."

Examples:

This is my brother, whom loves to fish. (Wrong: And sounds really stupid.)

There are many people who I would love to invite to the party. (Also wrong: But doesn't sound so bad. Plus it's likely you'll have more people at your party if you don't use the word "whom" around them.)

Rules of Logic

Some people think that all grammar is logical. We now know better, because many conventions have no logic, but there is a small pocket of grammar that is logic based.

All of the following examples are illogical.

*Q: Do you mind if I sit here? A: Sure.

*That's a very unique sweater.

*He won't do nothing about it.

*I could care less if he quits.

Here are the logic problems:

"Sure" must logically mean "I do mind!"

"Unique" means "unlike everything else," so it's logically impossible to be very unlike something—either it's unlike or it isn't.

If he won't do nothing, then logically he must do something.

If you could care less, then logically you must care some.

Parallelism

The heart of language logic is consistency, which grammar calls *parallelism*. Once you start doing it one way, you must keep doing it that way:

> If you're making a list and the first item in the list is a verb, make all the items in the list verbs; if it's a participle, make all the items participles. The same goes for nouns, adjectives, full sentences—anything.
>   If you start telling a story in the past tense, stay in the past tense.
>   If you start talking about *parents* in the plural, stay in the plural.
>   If you start referring to a hypothetical person as *her/him*, continue calling the person *her/him*.

The four most common parallelism problems are unparallel lists, tense changes, subject-verb agreement, and noun-pronoun agreement.

Unparallel Lists

*I gained organization and speaking skills, along with thinking quick.

The first item in the list is "skills," which are things you possess; the second item is "thinking," which is an action. Things you *have* aren't parallel with things you *do*. You could fix it in several ways:

Rewrite: I gained organization and speaking skills, along with the ability to think quickly,

or

I gained the ability to organize, speak well, and think quickly,

or

I got good at organizing, speaking, and thinking quickly.

Tense Changes.   The law of parallelism says, Stay in the same verb tense unless your meaning has shifted tense too.

*A spelling game *may* excite the children and make learning fun. The class *will be* split in half. The first half *will* continue reading and writing while the second half *plays* the game. The group playing the game *would* line up across the room. Each child *is* given a chance to roll a set of dice.

Here's a revision in present tense:

Rewrite: A spelling game can excite the children and make learning fun. Split the class in half. The first half continues reading and writing while the second half plays the game. The group playing the game lines up across the room. Each child is given a chance to roll a set of dice.

Subject-Verb Agreement. Subjects and verbs are supposed to agree in number—they should both be singular or both be plural. Most agreement problems occur when the subject and verb get separated by distracting business in between:

*If a child is made to write on a topic of little interest to him, the *chances* of his learning anything from the experience *is* slim.

Rewrite: *If a child is made to write on a topic of little interest to him, the chances of his learning anything from the experience are slim.*

*The price of letter-quality printers have fallen dramatically.

Rewrite: *The price of letter-quality printers has fallen dramatically.*

Note: This is another place not to rely on your spell/grammar checker, which might actually make this mistake for you. That's because your word-processing program might assume that "printers" is the subject of the phrase instead of "the price of printers."

Pronoun Agreement. Pronouns refer to nouns: in "George said he could," "he" refers to "George." A pronoun has to follow four rules: (1) The noun it refers to must be physically present on the page. (2) The noun must precede the pronoun. (3) The noun must be the first noun you reach, reading back from the pronoun, that can logically be the pronoun's referent. (4) And the pronoun and noun must agree in number: they must both be singular or be plural. Colloquial English violates the fourth rule in two cases:

1. Pronouns like "anyone," "anybody," "everybody," "no one," and "nobody" are logically singular, so possessive pronouns that refer to them must also be singular:

   *Everybody has to bring *their* own juice.

   Rewrite: *Everybody has to bring her own juice.*
2. Anonymous single people ("a student," "a parent") need singular pronouns:

   *The key to writing success is choosing subject matter *the child* is familiar with and a vocabulary level *they* are familiar with.

   Rewrite: *The key to writing success is choosing subject matter the child is familiar with and a vocabulary level he is familiar with.*

Note: Some writers use "their" or "they" to refer to a preceding noun in order to avoid sexist language, obviously a good idea. Purists (myself among them), however, shudder at the thought. Purists who want to avoid sexist language have several options. Consider the following sentence in which the pronoun doesn't work:

*Everyone should bring their own camping gear.

1. Switch to plural: All campers should bring their own camping gear.
2. Use the feminine pronoun: Everyone should bring her own camping gear.

3. Use "his or her": Everyone should bring his or her (or her or his) own camping gear.

   Note: If you do it this way, you must keep the sentence parallel throughout, and this often leads to problems: Everyone should bring his or her own camping gear, unless he or she doesn't own any, in which case he or she might be able to borrow some from one of his or her friends.

4. Alternate use of feminine and masculine pronouns. Naturally, you don't want to alternate midsentence or in a way that would confuse your reader: Everyone should bring his own camping gear unless she doesn't have any. But you can do this in longer passages. Maybe you've noticed that I've been doing this throughout *The Writer's Way*. Sometimes I use "he," and sometimes I use "she."

   Interestingly, this can backfire on you. Consider this sentence: A student who doesn't understand her homework might want to find a tutor. Uh oh! I was writing an article for a skiing magazine several years ago and, trying to be sensitive, wrote something like, "The ramp at the top of this chairlift is steeper than most and a skier unloading from it needs to be careful that she doesn't fall." So much for Mr. Sensitive. What, only women fall? No, no! That's not what I meant! So I changed it to "Skiers unloading from this chair need to be careful that they don't fall."

5. Finally, sometimes you can simply rewrite the sentence so that it avoids pronouns altogether: Camping gear is the responsibility of individual campers; or Camping gear must be provided by individual campers.

The Limits of Logic.   The only problem with approaching language logically is that it often doesn't work—logic will talk you into error almost as often as it will help you out of it. Here are two examples.

1. Essay English disapproves of *"A crowd of people are outside," because "crowd" is a singular noun and requires a singular verb: we should write "A crowd of people *is* outside." But if that's so, then, since "lot" is also a singular noun, it too should take a singular verb, so we must write *"A lot of people *is* outside," which is nobody's English.

2. "It's raining" violates the first three rules of pronoun usage above, but everyone agrees it's good English.

   So remember, *convention always trumps logic*—if the two are in conflict, be guided by convention.

Rules of Clarity

Pronoun Reference.   Some language rules try to prevent confusion and misreading. We've already mentioned one set: the rules governing pronoun use above, which are designed to prevent confusion like this:

   *I placed my order at a counter *that* looks like a regular fast-food restaurant. (The counter looks like a restaurant?) *It* is partially blocked off so *it* didn't bother me while I was eating. (The restaurant is blocked off? What didn't *it* bother you?) After I ordered and paid for *it*, I sat down. (What did you pay for?)

Rewrite: *I placed my order at a counter that looks like the counter in any fast-food restaurant. It's partially blocked off so I wasn't bothered by sights of food cooking while I was eating. After I ordered and paid for my food, I sat down.*

Misplaced Modifiers.   A modifier is any word, phrase, or clause that modifies (roughly, "tells you something about") a noun or verb. When words modify other words, make sure the reader is in no doubt about which words modify what. Most of the time it's obvious and there's no problem: if I say "As the sun was sinking in the west, the tall Texan slowly lowered himself onto the stool," "tall" modifies "Texan," and "slowly," "onto the stool," and "as the sun was sinking in the west" all modify the verb "lowered." But modifiers get unclear in two positions.

First, when a modifier ends a sentence, it can be hard to tell which preceding noun or verb the modifier refers to:

*County Sheriff Wayne Hamilton this morning discussed where to put prisoners arrested for drinking with the Jefferson County Commissioners.

"With the Jefferson County Commissioners" modifies some verb, but we can't tell which one, so the sentence ends up implying that people are getting drunk with the Commissioners. To solve the problem, *move the modifier:*

Rewrite: *County Sheriff Wayne Hamilton this morning discussed with the Jefferson County Commissioners where to put prisoners arrested for drinking.*

Second, when a modifier begins a sentence, it's often unclear what part of the sentence it refers to, so Essay English lays down a rule that it must always refer to the subject of the sentence.

*As a future teacher, censorship seems to me to be an overblown issue.

(Sounds like *censorship* is planning on becoming a teacher.)

Rewrite: *As a future teacher, I think censorship is an overblown issue.*

*Despite having spent $1.3 billion since 1992 on county jails, the need for more jail cells is still strong.

(Sounds like *the need for more jail cells* spent the money.)

Rewrite: *Despite having spent $1.3 billion since 1992 on county jails, we still need more jail cells.*

*Driving to work this morning, a cat ran out in front of my car. (Sounds like *a cat* was driving to work.)

Rewrite: *As I was driving to work this morning, a cat ran out in front of my car.*

Or: *Driving to work this morning, I almost ran over a cat.*

Or: *Driving to work this morning, I had to avoid a cat that ran out in front of my car.*

PUNCTUATION

While there are in fact punctuation "rules," the truth is you use punctuation for one simple reason: to tell your reader how you want your words to sound, so that she'll know what you mean.

I was working with a student the other day who had written the following sentence:

"America offers many opportunities, for example, you can get grants to help pay for your education."

There's a problem there, right? And while an English teacher would call it a comma splice, the real problem is that I didn't know how the student wanted me to hear it, which would tell me what she meant.

Did she mean, "America offers many opportunities, for example. You can get grants to help pay for your education" or "America offers many opportunities. For example, you can get grants to help pay for your education"?

Of course, I assumed she meant the latter, but her job—the writer's job—is to use punctuation so that the reader's not left guessing or, worse, confused.

Most handbooks or Web sites that include punctuation rules are guilty of overkill. No kidding, some handbooks list twenty, thirty, or *more* comma rules—and too many other rules for punctuation. Way too many. Here at *The Writer's Way* Bar and Grill, we honestly believe that all you need to know are eight rules: five comma rules, two semicolon rules, and one colon rule. Unfortunately, we're going to talk about grammar a bit. Sorry about that. But if you manage to stay awake, you'll be surprised how useful grammar can be.

The Comma

The response I nearly always get when I ask students to identify a comma rule is, "Put a comma where you pause." True enough. But then I remind them that you also pause where there's a period, a dash, parentheses, a colon, between paragraphs, and so on. So that rule doesn't work. Here are five that do:

1. **The introductory comma.** Commas mark when a long introduction is over and the main clause begins:

   After the town had been battered by high winds for seven straight days, the rains came.

   If the introductory bit is short, the reader probably won't need the comma's guidance, and you can leave it out:

   After dinner I went to bed.

How long is long and how short is short? Sometimes it's a judgment or even a stylistic call—some writers might use it, and some might not. On the other hand, you simply need the introductory comma for clarity. Remember the one we looked at on p. 177? "After eating, my brother and I drove home."

At the risk of oversimplifying, I'm even going to suggest that this rule is why you put a comma after a single-word transition such as "however" before the main clause: "Additionally, some feel that the increase in forest fires is a direct result of years of mismanagement by the Forest Service."

2. **The conjunctive comma.** Commas mark when one independent clause ends and a coordinating conjunction begins another:

The rage swept through him like the angel of death, and he stooped and picked up the knife.

The loss of Flanagan will certainly hurt our offense, but we've devised some trick plays to make up for that.

There's a trick to remembering all the coordinating conjunctions: the acronym FANBOYS spells them out: for, and, nor, but, or, yet, and so.

As with the introductory comma, this comma can be dropped if the clauses are short and the reader is unlikely to get lost:

The rage swept through him and he picked up the knife.

3. **Parenthetical commas.** Commas set off information that can be omitted *without the meaning of the sentence changing.* They often come *in pairs,* like parentheses. The way to determine whether you need them or not is to look at the clause, phrase, or word and try reading the sentence without it. If the meaning changes, or becomes unclear, then you need the commas. Examples:

History 101, a required course, is one of the easiest on campus.

He stood over Ragnalf, sword drawn, and exulted.

I backed the old Rolls, inch by inch, into the narrow parking space.

Professor Ann Brown, who got her degree from MIT, will be teaching the course.

Note: This is the same rule that tells you to put a comma after the main clause and before nonessential information added to the *end* of a sentence, often in the form of a "which" or "who" clause.

My favorite novel is *Moby Dick,* which was first published in 1850.

My favorite author is James Joyce, who wrote *Ulysses.*

Also, lots of minor comma rules that you've been taught are simply versions of this rule, another reason why some handbooks list so many rules:

We visited Salem, Oregon, last year.

She was born November 7, 1991, at 2:45 p.m.

4. **Series commas.** Commas punctuating a series of *three or more* go between each pair, including the last one:

We visited Salem, Eugene, and Portland last year.

The reading list includes the Bible, the Koran, and *The Writer's Way*.

He turned slowly, sensually, and seductively.

He worked for Apple, he worked for General Motors, and he worked for Hawaiian Airlines.

Generations of students were taught to leave that last comma out, or that it's "optional," and in fact many newspapers and some other publications may not include it. You should use it, though, in formal essays and papers.

5. **Parallel adjectives commas.** Put commas between adjectives of equal weight. This is kind of a tricky one, but it gets easy if you run either one of two simple tests: (1) If you can use "and" instead of a comma, then use the comma. If you can't, don't. Or, (2) If you can reverse the order of them, use commas. If you can't, don't.
So:

He lived in a blue, yellow, and green house on the corner. You could say, He lived in a blue and yellow and green house on the corner—so, use commas (if you don't use the "and"s). Or you could reverse the order of the colors.

And:

He lived in a big blue stucco house on the corner. You wouldn't say, He lived in a big and blue and stucco house on the corner—so, no commas. Nor would you say, He lived in a stucco blue big house on the corner.

The same is true even with two adjectives:

Alaska is known for its massive, towering mountains.

When the U.S. economy collapsed in 2009, there was a somber, despairing mood on Wall Street.

They bought some beautiful creek-side property outside Ashland (you wouldn't say "beautiful and creek-side property" or "creek-side beautiful property").

Fun with Commas (No, I'm Serious Here!).   Believe it or not, you can actually have fun with comma rules, or at least punctuation geeks (such as I) can. At this point, feel free to skip directly ahead to Things Commas *Don't* Do, but if you're interested in seeing where this goes, come along.

Question: How can both of the following sentences be both true and punctuated correctly?

My sister, Peggy, lives in California.

My brother Rick lives in Idaho.

Think about that for a little bit.

Now consider these two sentences:

Bruce Springsteen's CD *We Shall Overcome: The Seeger Sessions* is his best yet.

Bruce Springsteen's most recent CD, *We Shall Overcome: The Seeger Sessions,* is his best yet.

Both are correct.

See how it works? If your reader will still know what you mean when you take the information out, then you need to put commas on both sides. If your reader needs the information, you don't want the commas. So if I remove the title of the CD from the first sentence, my readers won't know which CD I'm referring to, but if I take it out of the second one, they would.

OK. How can the sentences about my brother and sister both be true and punctuated correctly? Anyone get it? A show of hands, please.

Answer: I have one sister but two brothers. So I can take "Peggy" out of the first one but I can't take "Rick" out of the second one.

Ah, but you didn't know that, you say. Exactamundo! Remember: You use punctuation for one simple reason: to tell your reader how you want your words to sound, so that she'll know what you mean—you use punctuation to provide meaning. I used commas, or didn't, to give you information about my brother(s) and sister.

So, if I wrote, "My wife Liz is a grant writer," a perfectly logical follow-up question would be. "Really? And what does your other wife do?" No, no! That's not what I meant! My wife, Liz, is a grant writer!

Things Commas *Don't* Do

Beyond putting commas where they belong, you have to make sure you don't put them in the wrong place.

First, commas do not go between a subject and its verb, even if the subject is long:

*The reason I didn't tell you about cracking up the car and having to spend the night in jail, is that I simply forgot.

Rewrite: *The reason I didn't tell you about cracking up the car and having to spend the night in jail is that I simply forgot.*

Second, commas do not go between conjunctions and their following clauses:

*I never showed up because, my parents wouldn't let me have the car.

Rewrite: *I never showed up because my parents wouldn't let me have the car.*

Third, commas do not go between two sentences with no conjunction:

*The teacher cannot teach children to read or write, this can be learned only through doing it yourself.

Rewrite: *The teacher cannot teach children to read or write; this can be learned only through doing it yourself.*

*Paella is a traditional rice-and-seafood dish from Barcelona, it is also popular in other parts of Spain.

Rewrite: *Paella is a traditional rice-and-seafood dish from Barcelona, and it is also popular in other parts of Spain.*

That no-no is called a *comma splice*—the splicing together of two sentences with only a comma. It gets a huge amount of attention in school and from some readers outside school, so it's worth learning to avoid. Say to yourself, "A comma isn't big enough to join sentences by itself; I need more." *You don't need to reword the sentence;* you can replace the comma with a semicolon, colon, or dash, or keep the comma and add a conjunction.

A popular comma splice is the *however* comma splice:

*I'd really like to come, however my scheduling just won't allow it.

Rewrite: *I'd really like to come; however, my scheduling just won't allow it.*

"However" (and words like it—"nevertheless," "therefore") is really an *adverb*. Since it's not a conjunction, it and a comma can't join independent clauses. You need a semicolon.

Fourth, commas do not go between *pairs* joined by conjunctions, except pairs of sentences:

*He stopped walking for a moment, and picked up something shiny from the gutter.

Rewrite: *He stopped walking for a moment and picked up something shiny from the gutter.*

Fifth, commas do not surround "anything that can be taken out of the sentence." Use your oral-reading sense to tell you where there's a sense of interruption or turning aside:

The Boston Red Sox, who are my favorite team, seem determined to break my heart.

The Boston Red Sox who trashed that reporter's car should be heavily fined.

Finally, commas don't go "where you pause." Sometimes they do, but it's a rule that will lead you astray as often as it pays off.

The Semicolon

The semicolon does two things:

1. **It joins two independent clauses.** This semicolon joins sentences that are halves of a balanced pair. It says, "Don't think the thought is over just because the sentence is over. Keep reading; you're really only half done":

   Personal writing isn't trying to sell you anything; it's just trying to share a part of the writer's life.

If it's above 70 degrees, he's too hot; if it's below 70 degrees, he's too cold.

The semicolon is correct if a comma *and* a coordinating conjunction (FANBOYS) would work but there's no coordinating conjunction.
2. **It clarifies lists or series that have other punctuation**: Consider this sentence:

The panel included Celine O'Malley, a doctor, Georgia Nilsson, an attorney, and Hannah Rose, an art professor.

How many people are on that panel? Six? Three? Actually, according to the list (and our comma rule: commas between items in a series), there are six, or perhaps five. If, however, I meant that Celine's the doctor, that Georgia's the attorney, and that Hannah's the art professor, then I need to separate them, and I do that with semicolons:

The panel included Celine O'Malley, a doctor; Georgia Nilsson, an attorney; and Hannah Rose, an art professor.

So here's the rule: Use a semicolon to separate items in a series when the items themselves use commas.

The rule applied to other examples:

We visited Prescott, Arizona; Salem, Oregon; and Tempe, Arizona.

They read several novels, including *The Art of Fielding*, by Chad Harbach; *Body and Soul*, by Frank Conroy; and *Pnin*, by Vladimir Nabokov.

Things Semicolons *Don't* Do

Semicolons do not join sentences and following fragments—use a colon or dash instead:

*There is only one reason the new sex education program will never succeed; parental objections.

Rewrite: *There is only one reason the new sex education program will never succeed: parental objections.*

Semicolons do not come before a list. Use a colon or nothing, depending on how you set it up.

*The panel consisted of several experts including; a doctor, an attorney, and an art student.

Rewrite: The panel consisted of several experts: a doctor, an attorney, and an art student.

or

The panel consisted of several experts, including a doctor, an attorney, and an art student.

The Colon

The colon comes *after a complete sentence* and announces that what follows will list or explain something the sentence *promised* but didn't specify:

> Every time we try to make the relationship work, we run up against the same two obstacles: my personality and her personality.

> There are three secrets to a successful business: location, location, location.

Many people say a colon precedes a list, which is OK as long as you remember that it can be a list of one *and* that it must follow a complete sentence:

> She knew what she needed: chocolate.

> He suddenly had a wonderful idea: why not hold the show right here?

Things Colons *Don't* Do

Colons do not follow sentence fragments. When you feel the urge to do that, either use no punctuation or rewrite the opening so it's a sentence:

> *The three main problems facing the Middle East today are: poverty, Iraq, and religious fanaticism.

> Rewrite: *The three main problems facing the Middle East today are poverty, Iraq, and religious fanaticism.*

> or

> *The Middle East today faces three main problems: poverty, Iraq, and religious fanaticism.*

OTHER PUNCTUATION

The Dash

The dash is not only the most loosely defined punctuation mark, but it is also characteristic of a relatively informal level of writing. It works in most essays—I've seen it in the *New Yorker* and the *Atlantic Monthly*—but you probably would want to avoid it in a formal master's thesis, for example.

Most dashes come in two places. The first is between a sentence and a following fragment:

> He either had to say yes or tell her why not—a hopeless situation.

> It's already raining outside—pouring, in fact.

The second use of dashes is to surround a drastic interruption in the middle of a sentence:

> Suddenly there was a noise—it sounded more like a cannon than anything else—and the south wall disappeared.

It was Shakespeare—or was it Madonna?—who once said, "All the world's a stage."

If your word-processing program doesn't have dashes and you need to use them in your writing, substitute two hyphens—otherwise it will look like a compound word. It should look like this, "word—word," not like this, "word-word."

Parentheses

Everybody knows that parentheses indicate a whispered aside, but punctuating around them can get confusing. Punctuate the sentence without the parentheses; then put the parentheses in, leaving all other punctuation untouched:

He was tall and mean-looking.

He was tall (very tall, in fact) and mean-looking.

He was tall, but his legs were short.

He was tall (very tall, in fact), but his legs were short.

Question Marks

Put a question mark after any sentence that is syntactically a question, whether it "feels" like a question or not:

Why don't you come over tonight and we'll order pizza?

Will you be kind enough to reply as soon as possible?

The Hyphen

The hyphen is a word-making tool. It lets us combine words and affixes to make three kinds of words:

The Compound-Adjective Hyphen. The hyphen adds words together so they can be used as adjectives.

five ten-gallon hats

a nine-to-five job

a soon-to-be-fired-for-his-incompetence employee

In practice it's hard to tell if a familiar two-word adjective should be written as two words, a hyphenated word, or simply one word: is it *red hot*, *red-hot*, or *redhot*? Just look it up in a dictionary. If the word isn't there, hyphenate.

Another way to check is to see if using it changes the meaning. Consider:

Used car salesman

Used-car salesman

In the first one, the car salesman is used; in the second one, his cars are. Recently, the editors of our local newspaper apparently forgot how a hyphen can change meaning, in this case humorously, and ran a headline that read "Topless Bar Owner Arrested." See? According to the headline, the owner of the bar was topless, when they meant to say that he owned a bar with topless waitresses.

Sometimes, on the other hand, convention tells us to ignore the rule. Technically, you'd hyphenate "high school students"; otherwise, it'd mean that the school students were "high." But I rarely see that phrase hyphenated, even in print, probably because we're so used to seeing, and saying, the words "high" and "school" together that there's not much chance of misunderstanding.

The Verb-Phrase Noun Hyphen.   This hyphen adds a verb and its following adverb together so they can be *used as a noun:*

The car needed a little touch-up.

The hyphen says, "Take this group of words and think of it as a single word." The key is that *the phrases have been moved from their natural position.* In their natural positions, they have no hyphens:

The hat held ten gallons.

I worked from nine to five.

The employee was soon to be fired for his incompetence.

We were going to stake out the house.

I asked him to touch up the paint on the car.

The Prefix Hyphen.   Hyphens join prefixes to words if the joining is an awkward one:

ex-husband vs. extinction

pro-choice vs. productive

The Apostrophe

There are three kinds of apostrophes.

The Contraction Apostrophe.   This apostrophe marks places where letters have been dropped out in contractions and reductions:

could not → couldn't

I will → I'll

I expect he is swimming about now. → 'I 'spect he's swimmin' 'bout now.

The apostrophe goes exactly where the letter dropped out, and you need one for each place where a letter or letters used to be:

Write *doesn't*, not **does'nt*.

Write *rock 'n' roll*, not **rock 'n roll*.

The same is true for numbers, such as decades. Write '60s, not 60's.

The Possessive Apostrophe. This apostrophe marks possession, which is a loose kind of ownership:

The pitcher's absence forced the cancellation of the game.

The men's room is locked.

The book's disappearance remained a mystery.

The rules for positioning the apostrophe are inflexible:

1. If the noun is singular, add -'s:

one dog's collar

Do this even if the noun ends in -s already:

one dress's hemline

2. If the noun is plural and is pluralized with an -s, add the apostrophe after the -s that's already there:

some dogs' collars

some dresses' hemlines

3. If the noun is an irregular plural, add -'s:

the men's department

the octopi's mittens

4. If the word showing ownership is a *pronoun,* use no apostrophe at all: "his," "hers," "theirs," "yours," "ours," and especially "its." Memorize it: "Its" means "belonging to it"; "it's" means "it is" or "it has."

5. If the noun is singular and ends in -s, sometimes the possessive looks or sounds funny, in which case some people give you permission to drop the second -s:

Ted Williams's batting average

or

Ted Williams' batting average

The Odd Plural Apostrophe. This apostrophe separates a plural noun from its pluralizing -s only if it would be confusing to the eye to use a normal plural form:

I love the Oakland A's.

Give me two 10's. (Some style guides, however, ask for 10s.)

How many *e*'s are there in *separate*?

Quotation Marks

Quotation marks do four things.

1. They surround someone else's exact words when you quote them:

   I can still hear Monique saying, "But I didn't *mean* it!"

   Her exact words were that she didn't "have a clue" about his whereabouts.

   Use quotation marks even if the speaker or speech is imaginary:

   I can just imagine what my father would say: "How are you going to pay for that?"

   Nobody ever said, "Have a lousy day."

2. They create ironic distance: the punctuational equivalent of a wink. They surround language you use but want to disown—language representative of the way *someone else* talks:

   Doctors never like to talk about pain. When I'm sick, I don't "feel discomfort"—I *hurt*!

   Unions are always talking about "parity."

   I don't want to meet your "special friend."

3. They surround minor titles: titles of little things or parts of things, like chapters from books, songs, essays, short stories, or newspaper articles. The titles for the big, whole things (books, anthologies, newspapers) are *italicized*.

   "The Telltale Heart" vs. *The Collected Works of Edgar Allan Poe*

   "Man Bites Dog" vs. *the New York Times*

4. They surround words as words:

   How do you spell "necessary"?

   I hate the phrase "special education."

   Sometimes italics do this job.

Things Quotation Marks *Don't* Do

Quotation marks don't surround the title at the head of your essay. They don't give emphasis to words or suggest heightened drama:

   *Win a free trip to "Paris"!

   *"Special" today, broccoli 35 cents/lb.

   This a common mistake and like so many others can lead to unintentional humor. Every August an apartment complex near the college where I teach erects a huge sign that says Welcome Back "Students."

Spacing and Positioning

Follow periods and all sentence-ending punctuation marks with one space. Follow all commas, semicolons, and colons with one space.

Parentheses surround words without internal spacing (like this) (*but not like this).

Dashes and hyphens have no spaces around them—like this—but not— oops!— like that.

Quotation marks always come outside commas and periods; they come inside colons and semicolons; and question marks and exclamation points go wherever the sense dictates: if the question or exclamation is a part of the quotation, put it inside (He said, "Why?"); if the question or exclamation is the whole sentence, put it outside (Why did he say "ragmop"?).

SPELLING

Bad news: first, the world has decided that spelling matters enormously. If you can't spell, most readers will conclude you're illiterate, stupid, careless, or all three. Also, the world's spelling standards are very high. My brother recruits computer science and accounting majors for a large national oil company, and he recently rescinded a very generous job offer to a graduating senior after seeing misspellings on the student's personal Web page—not because the company wants good spellers but because the company wants employees who pay attention to detail and how they present themselves to the public.

Unfortunately, spelling English is fiendishly hard, and nothing can make it easy. And your spell-checker computer programs won't save you, because a misspelled English word often looks just like another word (*their/there, planning/planing*). The only good news is that spelling is one of the world's most fascinating games.

The four most common ways people try to spell don't work. Let's rule them out now:

1. **Don't rely on your computer's spell-checker.** Spell-checkers can't determine context, so all they can do is tell you that a word doesn't exist—in their own dictionaries, that is. A student of mine was working on a paper on Duke Ellington, and he simply did a global "search and fix" before he submitted it to me. Because his computer didn't recognize "Ellington," he ended up with a paper about "Duke Wellington." I handed it back without reading past the first paragraph.

   My personal pet peeve, though—and, honestly, I see this a half dozen times a semester—is when a student submits a paper that she thinks uses the word "definitely" but that she has misspelled as "definately," and the spell checker then "corrects" it to "defiantly."

Note: Spell-check programs can be useful. Just don't *rely* on them. Look closely at the word the program is suggesting as a replacement. Make sure it's what you want.

2. **Don't try to spell by rule.** There are a few rules that help you spell (see below), but each will solve only one problem in a hundred.

3. **Don't try to spell phonetically (by sounding words out).** Most of the words you use a lot don't follow the rules.

4. **Don't overrate mnemonic devices.** A mnemonic device is a trick, jingle, or story to help you remember something: "the princi*pal* is your *pal*"; "I shot *par* on two se*par*ate golf courses." Mnemonic devices work, but they're slow and cumbersome. I learned to spell *receive* via the famous mnemonic "*I* before *E* except after *C*," and thirty years later I still have to stop and recite the jingle every time I write the word.

So much for what doesn't work; here are six techniques that do:

1. **Spell for fun.** Fall in love with language and words and become fascinated by how they work. Trace interesting etymologies in the dictionary. Play spelling games like Scrabble, Boggle, and Password; do crossword puzzles. There are also some wonderful spelling and other word games online, including Word Sailing at shockwave.com, and several versions of Scrabble and Boggle, where you can either play alone, set up games with friends, or let the sites find opponents for you. Check out fun-with-words.com, pogo.com, and games.com for starters. Or download some of the apps out there, and play with your friends on your smart phone (not in class, of course!). One of my favorite is Words With Friends, which I play with my daughter (who usually has about six games going at once with her own friends).

2. **Make your own list of demons.** Most of us misspell only forty or fifty words (and that includes *misspel*!). It doesn't take long to make a list of them; then you can drill on them.

3. **Memorize a few rules.** These rules are worth learning:

   1. *I* before *E* except after *C*, or when sounded like *A*, as in *neighbor* and *weigh*.

   2. In stressed nonfinal syllables, double the consonants after short vowels; keep consonants single after long vowels. *Matting* needs two *t*'s; *mating* needs one.

   3. Final *-e*'s disappear before suffixes starting with vowels; they don't disappear before suffixes starting with consonants: *manage → managing, management; consummate → consummation, consummately*.

   4. Final *-y* becomes *-i* when followed by a suffix: *pity → pitiful, rely → relies, controversy → controversial, family → familiar*. Exception: *-y* before *-i* or after a vowel stays *y*: *pity, pitying; stay, stayed*.

DON'T SIDESTEP MECHANICS PROBLEMS

Many students deal with mechanical problems by avoiding any situation in which they might arise. If a word is hard to spell, they just don't use it. If they aren't sure how to use a semicolon, they don't use it at all. Once they realize that long sentences risk structure problems, they use only short, simple sentences. In a way, this approach works, but it's the worst thing that can happen to you, because once you start writing with the purpose of avoiding error, the logical end result is to not write at all. Writing is inherently risky, like snowboarding or driving a race car. That's why it's a rush. Embrace the risk, the way a race car driver looks forward eagerly to the twisting stretch of road.

REMEMBER THE TIGHTENING

Cut excess language; you want your writing to be as tight as possible. You don't want your reader to waste time and energy reading unnecessary verbiage. So tight writing is the key. Here are five tools to help you do that (note how they often overlap):

1. **Use strong verbs.** Frankly, I never got it when my teachers told me that verbs were "action" words. "Sleep" an action word? "Consult"? "Is"? "Cause"? Those didn't seem very action filled to me. Here's a more useful way to think about it: verbs are the motors, the engines, of your sentences; they're what provide the power, what *drive* them. It stands to reason, then, that you want strong verbs, especially in long sentences. A thirty-six-horsepower VW motor is not powerful enough to pull a semi up over the pass.

   Banning pesticide use is [verb] one of the first steps to sustainable farming. (12 words)

   Sustainable farming begins [new verb] when pesticides are banned [verb phrase]. (7 words)

   Or:

   Ban [verb] pesticides and farm [verb] sustainably. (5 words)

2. **Use the active voice.** Changing passive sentences to active sentences does several things, among them simply eliminating words.

   Passive: The course was taught by a dynamic professor. (8 words)

   Active: A dynamic professor taught the course. (6 words)

   Note: The names "passive" and "active" refer to the subjects of the sentence. In an active sentence, the subject (the professor, in this example) is acting. In a passive sentence, action happens to the subject. Sometimes, the passive voice is preferred (that's an example), for example, when you want to emphasize what *happened* to the subject as opposed to what it did.

   The dog got hit by a car.

   Or when it's less important who's acting than what's happening:

   The course will be offered again this semester.

3. **Avoid sentences that begin "There is/are" "It is/was,"** etc. Not always of course—after all, you also want sentence variety—but if you find yourself doing it a lot, try tightening some of them.

It is clear that Professor Brown needs to retire. (9 words)

Clearly, Professor Brown needs to retire. (6 words)

There were sixteen students who had enrolled in the course. (10 words)

Sixteen students had enrolled in the course. (7 words)

4. **Avoid "nouniness."** Nouns are the opposite of engines; they're the heavy trailers that need to be pulled along. Often you can turn a noun into a verb to make for a much more effective sentence.

He enjoyed the consumption [noun] of liquid refreshments. (7 words)

He enjoyed consuming [verb] liquid refreshments. (5)

There are several ways to facilitate the instruction [noun] of writing. (10 words)

Writing can be taught [new verb] several ways. (6 words)

Note that we're also applying Tools 1 and 3 in that example.

5. **Avoid "filler."** We talked about this some in Chapter 6—this is all about writing *style*. Remember, though, that "due to the fact that" just means "because" and "at this point in time" means "now."

Using the Tools

Take a look at this sentence:

The flooding of the fields was caused by the overflowing of the river. (13 words)

Let's apply Tool 2 first and make it active:

The overflowing of the river caused the flooding of the fields. (11 words)

Better? Now let's apply Tool 4 ("overflowing" and "flooding" are nouns) and Tool 1 (both could be verbs that would be much stronger than "was caused," the verb phrase in the original):

The river overflowed [now a verb and flooded [ditto] the fields. (7 words)

You could also turn "overflowing" into an adjective:

The overflowing river flooded the fields. (6 words)

You might even argue that the field couldn't have flooded if the river hadn't overflowed, and so it's redundant to say both (a kind of filler):

The river flooded the fields. (5 words)

In the Exercises section at the end of the chapter are some more wordy sentences. Try tightening them.

FOLLOWING FORMAT

A format is a set of rules about how an essay is laid out on the page: how big to make the margins, whether to type the title in full capitals or not, where to put the page numbers, and so on. Some students consider such matters too trivial for their attention, but editors and publishers don't. In fact, editors and publishers consider them *very* important and often will not even bother with a piece—no matter how profound or compelling—if it doesn't follow their format. If you're thinking of submitting a piece for publication, take a look at the publication's writers' guidelines, usually available by calling and asking or by going to the publication's home page and clicking on "writers' guidelines."

There are no universal formatting rules, so the only way to know the "correct" format is to ask the boss. Use this format for school papers if your instructor hasn't mandated one:

1. Use only one side of standard size (8½" ×11") paper of medium weight (20 lb.) or heavier.
2. Print—never handwrite—using a quality printer with good ink/toner.
3. Proofread carefully, and make all handwritten corrections or additions neatly, in black ink.
4. Keep a margin of one inch on all four sides of the page. Don't center your text—and it should be flush left, ragged right.
5. Center each line of your title. Don't italicize it or put quotation marks around it (unless it's a quote). Don't use full capitals; capitalize the first letter of only the first word and all important words: all nouns, verbs, adjectives, adverbs, and anything over four letters long. Put more space between your title and the text than there is between the lines of text themselves: if you're double-spacing the text, triple-space between title and text. Don't have a separate title page unless you're told to or the essay is more than thirty pages long.
6. Put in the upper right-hand corner of page 1 the following information: your name, the course *number* (e.g., Anthro. 210B), and the date. Note: MLA calls for the upper left-hand corner.
7. Connect the pages with a staple in the upper left-hand corner. Don't fold the pages or dog-ear them.
8. Double-space.
9. Indent the first line of each new paragraph one tab stop, which should be set to five spaces. Don't put extra space between paragraphs.
10. Number all pages after page 1. Put the page numbers in any one of three places: upper right-hand corner, top center, or bottom center.
11. Use no eye-catching fonts or letter sizes. Be simple, conventional, and understated.

PROOFREADING

Proofreading is reading over the text to look for places where your fingers slipped and you typed *ration* instead of *nation*. It's the very last thing you do before printing the final copy. For a hilarious send-up on relying on spell-checkers, see slam poet Taylor Mali's "The The Impotence of Proofreading."

(Warning, or perhaps further encouragement, the bit contains some borderline in appropriate language.)

To get in the mood, begin by realizing four truths:

Proofreading matters. You become a zealous proofreader the day you grasp how destructive a typo is to your reader's concentration. A single typo can undo all your hard work. How do *you* react when you read about "thirf graders," "shot stories," or "censoring textbools"?

Proofreading problems can be fixed. Spelling problems are problems of *knowledge,* and you fix them by *learning;* typos are just finger slips, and you fix them by learning to *look.*

Your word-processing program's spell-checker won't save you. Spell-checker programs make typo problems *worse,* because they lull you into thinking they've fixed the problem when they haven't. The program will catch all the "hte" typos, but it leaves all the ones that produce other words and phrases, such as "The red penis your friend," instead of "The red pen is your friend," as Taylor Mali points out.

Proofreading is hard. It's because all your life you've been practicing the art of *not looking at the letters.* Good readers read by skimming and guessing—experts estimate you're actually seeing perhaps 25 percent of a text.

Suggestions for effective proofreading:

To proofread well, you stop *reading* and start *staring.* Here are nine principles to guide you:

Proofread from hard copy. Most people simply do not see the mistakes on a screen that they will see on a piece of paper. So print out a copy, proofread, make the corrections, print out another copy, make the corrections, and keep doing that until you've got it.

Assume there's at least one typo per page. If you don't, you'll never find any.

Set aside a time for nothing but proofreading—you can't do it and anything else too, since it uses your eyes and brain in a unique way.

Ignore content. As soon as you start listening to what the text is *saying,* you'll start seeing what you expect and not what's there. You can do this by **reading backward,** to prevent yourself from predicting (i.e., read sentence by sentence backward, not word by word).

Go slow. Any attempt to hurry and you'll start guessing and skimming.

Don't just proofread individual words; proofread phrases and clauses. Otherwise you'll miss goofs like these:

*I would explain that in our society there correct and incorrect forms to use.

*The little cap just pulls off it you put enough effort into it.

*After two weeks, it is evident that the that the consistent and continual printing errors are the result of a defective printer.

After making editing changes, carefully proofread the new text and everything surrounding it. That should ensure that you haven't introduced new problems.

Get help. It's easy to get so close to your work that you just don't see it clearly anymore. I've proofread and proofread and proofread and, finally, thinking I've caught everything, shown it to my wife for one more go-over. Almost every time she catches something: *You don't need the second "the" in "the the best way to proofread,"* she'll say.

EXERCISES

1. List three mechanical *facts* (not principles or attitudes) you didn't know before you read Chapter 11. Begin each with "I didn't know that ..."

2. Line edit a page of manuscript in class as a group. Have a volunteer distribute a double-spaced page of essay to the class. Divide the readers into teams of two. Have each team make a list of three mechanical problems in the text, each with a repair and a clear, concrete explanation for why it's a problem. Have each team identify one problem, repair it, and explain it in front of the class. Discuss each presentation to see if the group agrees.

3. Make a list of mechanical topics covered in this chapter: format, parallelism, semicolon usage, and so on. Have each member of the class sign up as class expert on that topic. Line edit a classmate's essay page as in Exercise 2, with each expert reporting on any problems in her area of expertise that appear in the draft.

4. Using the five sentence-tightening tools (p. 197–198), revise the following sentences. You can rearrange, break into two or more, and so on, but keep all the information and don't change the meaning. The first number in the parentheses is how many words the original contains; the second is what I tightened them to (on p. 202—don't look until you've tried them all).

   a. The failing of the proposed activity center was most likely the result of a massive amount of lobbying on the part of the owners of health clubs and of students' opinion that the legacy they'd be leaving was not worth the price tag that they would have to paid. (49/21)

   b. One of the results of the Drug War has been to increase the number of people doing time in federal prisons for nonviolent crimes such as the growing of marijuana for the purposes of selling it to buyers. (38/21)

   c. It is clear that the issue of the legality of online music downloading is a complicated one and that anyone looking into it will realize that there are valid arguments to be made on both sides of the matter. (39/11)

   d. After much consideration about Smith's future in the sport of football with regard to possible permanent injuries, I came to the conclusion that it would be in his best interest not to continue his pursuit of playing football anymore. (39/10)

e.   Compared to most university courses, this course would be categorized as virtually basic and simple; however, what the course lacks in rigor, it makes up for by providing the students with an enriching learning experience. (35/11)

f.   There are so many seaside spots to watch the waves, surfers, and even some amazing wildlife. Dolphins are a common sight off the Santa Cruz coast, in addition to harbor seals, sea otters, and sea lions. (36/18)

g.   The lack of clouds allowed us to see Alcatraz without any fog or anything else blocking it. (17/5)

h.   For the number of you out there who think there is no significant difference between taking a vitamin and not taking one, you may want to think twice. (28/12)

i.   It is not inconceivable to imagine that students partake of writing in wordy and passive ways for two reasons, one being to attempt to have an effect on their teachers and the other being because they have been in the habit of writing in this way since they first began their educational careers. (53/27)

j.   Throughout the many studies that have been done in recent years, it has become a known fact that teenagers aren't morning people. (22/8)

Part Four

Forms of Writing: Three Key Genres

Chapter 12

Personal Writing

Not so long ago, if you were taking a writing class, you'd most likely have written a series of papers that writing instructors call rhetorical modes, and in fact many writing textbooks were—and some still are—organized by these modes: narration, cause-and-effect, extended definition, classification, compare-and-contrast, description, argument, and so on. In reality, though, these are artificial designations. Effective writing is not about some predetermined form. It's about *content* and is rarely limited to just one mode. Writers incorporate many different modes into their essays, papers, articles, and columns.

A restaurant review, for example, will be largely descriptive but with either an implied or stated argument: don't eat there. Also, a narration might in fact actually *be* at the same time a cause-and-effect essay. Even a "compare-and-contrast" article looking at two teams' centerfielders will most likely use description, narration, maybe cause-and-effect, and in fact is also probably also an argument. On the other hand, a science paper might call for pure classification or extended definition—yet might include cause-and-effect. Even here in the field of composition, academics write definition papers, including ones that attempt to redefine words such as "recontextualize"—but still they're frequently buoyed by narration, cause-and-effect, and description.

So emphasizing mode (or form) over purpose is bass-ackwards. I seriously doubt any writer—except those taking writing classes—ever sat down and said, "Today I'm going to write a compare-and-contrast essay."

That said, we here at *The Writer's Way* World Headquarters have identified three specific forms—or genres—of writing that are frequently seen in both schools and the real world: personal writing, informative writing, and argumentative writing.

Important note: *These are not mutually exclusive. Personal writing informs and frequently has an argumentative edge. Informative writing often uses personal experiences and observations to advance a thesis. And argumentative writing often includes personal examples and, of course, lots of information.*

PERSONAL WRITING—START BY READING

When you're doing personal writing, the basic rule is the same as for all writing everywhere: you can't do it if you haven't read a lot of it. So the easiest way to write a good personal essay is also the most pleasant: read all the personal essays in A Collection of Good Writing and then *write one like them*.

What's Personal Writing?

Personal writing is both the easiest kind of writing to do and the most difficult. That is, it's easy to write about your experience, to recall details from your life, to jot them down on paper. Plus, you can't be wrong! Yet, you need to make that experience—those details from your life—*matter*, to a real reader.

That's why the what-I-did-last-summer essay has become a joke. Who cares? Not I—unless you somehow *make* it matter, or, as my students like to say, make it so readers can "relate to it."

Frequently, students will respond to a peer's essay by saying they can "relate to it" because they've had the same experience. Perhaps a student has written about his parents' divorce, so half the class (statistically) can relate because their parents, too, are divorced.

That's not what writing's about, though. Good writers can make readers who *haven't* had the experience "relate to it." If you've been to Maui and so has your reader, it's easy to write a piece that will make her "see" the island. But the writer's job, in this case, is to describe Maui in such a way that the reader who *hasn't* been there can "see" it. The same is true for the divorce essay. If the reader can "relate" because his parents are also divorced, that's the subject at work, not the writing.

So just how do you make personal writing matter?

That's what's difficult: there must be something bigger than the topic. That is, the divorce paper might become a paper about loss or disappointment or perhaps even about how odd it feels to become a statistic. I've talked off and on in this book about the importance of the bigger picture. That's what personal writing must somehow consider. While the what-I-did-last-summer essay is indeed a joke, in reality, if handled properly—if it connects to a bigger picture—it can be quite powerful. In fact, it's a classic subject of literature, as well as of many excellent films. Consider a film we've all seen, *The Wizard of Oz,* the story of an adolescent girl who runs away from home (or dreams she does), gets transported by tornado to a distant land, meets some weird characters, and then ends up back at home. Now I don't know about you, but I've never met a talking scarecrow, tin man, or lion (let alone a witch or flying monkeys)—nor am I an adolescent girl. So why do I—in fact why does almost everyone—"relate" to Dorothy's story? Because, of course, there's a bigger picture. Haven't we all felt, at one time or another, that people don't understand us? Haven't we come to realize, at some time or another, that what we've been looking so hard for is "right in our own back yard"?

How do you connect to the bigger picture? There's no easy answer. The best thing you can do, of course, is to read lots of personal essays as models. Look at what's going on in them, at what the writers are doing to make the subjects more than just what would amount to diary entries. Sometimes the writer steps away from the subject and comments directly. Consider, for example, Yer Thao's essay on p. 208, in which she concludes by telling us that she'll never again waste even a single grain or rice. Or look at "Daddy and Donuts" on p. 215, in which Danny Dietz points out the similarities between choosing donuts and the "important" choices we have to make later in life.

Some writers find the bigger picture through style and tone. Look at Laura Kate James' essay "Thanksgiving" (p. 351), in which her sentence fragments serve to convey the sense that her relationship with her sister is growing "fragmented." I don't smoke, and I don't have an older sister who paints her fingernails black, but I can "relate" to being saddened by a relationship that is changing—and about which I can do absolutely nothing. I'm sure you can, too.

Personal writing doesn't teach the reader something utilitarian, like how to crochet or what to do with bored children on a rainy day. It doesn't argue the reader into buying a thesis, like "We should immediately offer economic aid to Russia." Instead, it's a sharing of the self, or a reaching out. When Kris Tachmier wrote the wonderful personal essay about how much she hated eggs (Chapter 4), she wasn't trying to teach us something new about eggs that we could put to practical use, and she wasn't trying to convince us that we should hate eggs too. She's just kind of poking fun at herself for having this irrational—but very real— hatred of eggs, and we can "relate" to it because irrational feelings are universally human. The fact that they're eggs doesn't even much matter. We also simply like the writer. Since she's self-deprecating instead of preaching, we feel a real connection to her, as though we've made a friend. And what could be more universal than the joy of new friendship?

Most personal writing is in one of three forms:

Narrative: "This had an impact on me ..." (The first time I realized my dad was wrong about something.)

Character sketch: "Bob is an interesting person ..." (My hippie philosophy professor who used to be a Marine.)

Personal symbol: "This car/necklace/merry-go-round has an interesting significance ..." (See "Daddy and Donuts" on p. 215.)

Where Do We See Personal Writing?

Personal writing is actually very common outside the classroom. Most magazines and newspapers have at least one columnist who regularly writes a first-person piece, and some magazines, including *Newsweek,* have pages set aside for guest contributors—these are more often than not personal essays. Travel writing is often personal—at the same time, usually, very informative—and longer, book-length essays, called memoirs (French for "memories"), have become hugely popular of late.

We can usually do good personal writing as soon as we know that anyone cares. Take a look at the following essay. It was written by my student Yer Thao after a class discussion, on the fifth anniversary of September 11, about what it means to be American. Yer was self-conscious about her language ability—her first language is Hmong—but she obviously had something to say. Note, too, that while the essay is about something very personal, she also connects that experience to the bigger picture.

GRATEFUL

YER THAO

Student Essay

They say that some friends come and go in your life without much of an impression, but others will leave footprints that will last forever. Mai Thao is one of those footprint leavers. She has not only taught me what it means to be a true friend, but she has also taught me what it means to be an American.

Plop, plop, plop ... I awoke on that typical Monday morning to the sound of raindrops dripping from the bare branches outside my window to the puddles on the lawn. Yawning, I stretched my arms and looked at my clock. It was 6:45 a.m. Sitting up, I could already smell the aroma of mushroom and onion filled omelets wafting from the kitchen. Smiling, I jumped out of bed, grabbed my towel, and rushed to the bathroom for a quick morning shower.

After breakfast, Mom told me to hurry up and get ready because we also have to pick up Mai today. Mai and her family had just arrived from Thailand a week before so today was her first day of school in America.

She was eight too, so we were going to be in the same class. I was supposed to show her around and help her adjust to her new life. Nodding, I washed my breakfast dishes and ran back to my room to get my backpack. In ten minutes, we had picked Mai up from her house and were on our way to Wyandotte Elementary School. During the ride to school, Mom tried to make little conversations, but Mai just answered whatever question that needed to be answered. Then she was silent again.

After we were dropped off, I led her to our third grade class. She was silent the entire way. At first, I tried to make conversations with her, but it was no use. She wasn't interested in talking. "Here's our classroom," I told her as we stood outside room 9. And then, with a comforting smile, I told her not to worry because Mrs. Bloomingcamp was a very nice teacher. She smiled bravely back at me, and then we opened the door and we both stepped through the threshold.

At lunch, I invited her to eat with my friends and me, and she sat down with us, but five minutes later, she got up and walked away. My friends looked at me questioningly, so I got up and followed her. I found her sitting alone outside on a bench eating a green apple. I walked over to her and sat down. The rain had stopped and the sky was just starting to clear. The November air felt so fresh and clean that I couldn't help but smile. At first, she didn't even notice me. She was staring at the other kids and, strangely, at the trash cans. "What are you looking at?" I asked her. "Nothing," she replied. Then she got up and gathered her books and walked away. I looked at her and with a shrug got up and walked back to my friends.

For the entire week, we carried on that same routine. She would arrive to class with me every morning, but since she was assigned a desk three rows ahead of me, we hardly got to talk. After the first day, she started disappearing at lunchtime, so it wasn't until Friday that I actually saw her at lunch again. I had just thrown away my half-eaten fries when I spotted Mai walking out the door. Curious, I followed her out into the playground but lost her in a crowd of students playing dodge-ball. It was five minutes later when I found her in the back of the playground sitting in a hidden corner with her knees pulled up and her face hidden behind them.

"Are you okay?" I ask her.

"Go away!" she snapped.

"What's wrong? Are you sick?" I asked.

"Go away, you stupid American." She yelled at me as she raised her head up and glared at me through angry, teary eyes. "You are the most spoiled people I've ever met! You wake up, go into a room, turn silver knobs and clean warm water squirts out to wash you! You have free education and you are encouraged to get it. You drive to school like kings and queens even though the weather is fine. You waste perfectly good food every day! And worst of all, you're still complaining all the time! You all don't even see what you have! Back in Thailand, we wake up before dawn every morning to walk twenty minutes to the nearest well to bring water back to boil for usage. We don't waste water the way you Americans do. Many children would love to have the opportunity to get an education, but most can't afford it and are needed in the fields. Even after a hard year of toiling in the fields, food is still scarce! You are the most ungrateful pigs I have ever seen!"

Astonished at her outburst, I stood in front of her, speechless, for what seems like hours. Finally, I was able to utter the words, "I had no idea."

All this time, she had been quiet because she was watching and listening to everything and everyone around her. It was true that kids all around her complained about their parents and homework and friends all the time. It was true that Americans are tossing out billions in food each year. It was true that we sometimes act as though electricity and indoor plumbing are a right and not a privilege. It was then that I realized how fortunate we Americans are. Most of us don't even know the true meaning of starvation, even though we always complain even before lunch time. We're spoiled and take everything for granted!

It's been ten years since we first met, and Mai and I are still best of friends. Even though her family moved to Sacramento in the middle of high school and we both have our own different schedules now, we still keep in touch as much as possible. Just this Thanksgiving, my family and I, as well as a few other relatives, were invited to have dinner with her family in Sacramento. The first thing I told her, after I gave her a hug, was about this paper. We both laughed remembering that day long ago when we first came to understand each other. Then we made a plan.

After everyone around the enormous rectangular wooden table had said what they were thankful for, the Thao family started to pass around the beans and ham and rice. But they didn't get far before Mai and I stood up, with our glasses full of Sunny Delight, to declare a toast.

"A toast," Mai began, "to our good health, our refrigerator full of bountiful food, and this society with numerous opportunities for a man to create his own fortune."

"A toast," I began, "to none of us wasting not even a single grain of rice." Then squinting my eyes at everyone around the table, I ended, "GOT IT?"

"Cheers," everyone agreed heartily and not a single grain of rice was wasted that night. Thank you, Mai, for opening my eyes. I will continue to try my best to never waste even a single grain of rice for as long as I live.

—Permission provided by Steve Metzger

Generally, personal writing has little visible sign of structure, thesis, or purpose, but often that's the fun of it. Some writers can keep you reading—with their attention to detail or perhaps their idiosyncratic voice—and you don't realize until you get to the end that there was a whole lot going on. Read the following piece and note how the structure of the last three sentences—short, simple, even naïve—provides resonance to the rest of the essay.

DAD

MICHAEL CLARK

Student Essay

I remember he used to take forever in the bathroom. Some mornings I could get up, eat breakfast, get ready for school, and leave without ever seeing him. I'd hear him, though: coughing, spitting, and gagging himself. Anyone else hearing him in the morning would probably think he was going to die. But he had always done that, and I figured it was just the way all grown men got up in the morning.

When he came home in the evenings you could tell he was glad not to be at work any more. It was always best not to ask him questions about anything or make any kind of noise. Mom would ask him a couple of things while she was fixing dinner. He'd answer her. Otherwise he'd just sit at the dining room table with his martini, reading the newspaper.

At dinner, Mom would make most of the conversation. He generally reserved his participation for when we kids got too lighthearted or proud or disrespectful or something and needed trampling.

When I played in Little League, he'd drive me. The Conservation Club was next to the park. He'd hang out there until practice was over. Once he ambled over a little early. He interrupted the coach and insisted on explaining the infield fly rule—not just once but three times. He'd have gone on like a broken record if the coach hadn't stopped him and thanked him and quickly dismissed the team.

I always hated riding home with him after he'd been at the Club. Winter was the worst. We'd take our trash to the town dump. The dump was also right next to the park, so naturally we'd stop in at the Club. We'd always stay past dark. On the way home I always wanted to tell him you shouldn't drive so fast on a day's accumulation of ice and snow, but I never did. The couple of times we slid off the road didn't convince him. He'd just rock the car out, get back on the road, and drive on as if nothing had happened.

As time went on, he'd come home later and later in the evenings. Often he'd come through the door all red-faced and walk straight into the bedroom, where we'd hear him moan a little and talk to the dog. Then he'd pass out and we wouldn't see him again until he came home the same way the next evening.

With my brother in the Army and my sister at college, I was the only one around to see that Mom was spending her nights on the living room couch. Though it didn't surprise me, the divorce came as kind of a blow.

I've seen him a couple of times since then. He's remarried. I think I called him last Thanksgiving.

—Permission provided by Steve Metzger

Sometimes a little chaos just adds to the believability:

Well, the big news is I'm pregnant. Boy, do I hate that word—PREGNANT, sounds so harsh. "With child" sounds positively smarmy. "Expecting" always makes me want to say, "Expecting what?" It's not that I'm not pleased about this—I just don't think I'm comfortable with the jargon yet. And oh boy, is there jargon! La Leche League, Bradley, Lamaze, LaBoyer, transition period, episiotomy, and baby blues. In my naive way I assumed I'd have this baby, take a week off, and then jump into student teaching. Then I read the books, became acquainted with the terminology, decided to take the whole semester off. What I'm slowly realizing is that I'm not just PREGNANT, I'm having a BABY—that books about the next twenty years. This is going to CHANGE my lifestyle! AAAGGGHHH!

Burn out. I've been doing this for too long, and it seems like everyone around me feels the same way. I want to go beyond bitching this semester, so like the last three semesters I've told myself I'm going to take it easy. This time I mean it. I really do.

I can already see I'm lying. I want to audit the modern poetry class. And I want to keep tutoring. And I need to keep a few hours on the job. The money will be nice, and if I stop I'll have to start at $3.35 an hour when

I go back. Then there's the newspaper. That ought to take a couple hundred hours. And I want to save time for my own writing. I've told myself I need to keep Tuesday and Thursday afternoons free. I'll probably have to tutor at one of those times, but if I'm lucky I'll be able to keep the other one free.

Planning. That's the key. I've got to stop bitching and start planning. If I'm still bitching two weeks from now, I'll have to say it's hopeless.

If personal writing doesn't need coherent organization or thesis, what *does* it need? First, dramatic intensity: the reader feels he's in the scene, living it along with the writer, feeling the wind in his hair and catching the tang of gunpowder in his nostrils. Second, a sought effect: the reader senses that everything in the essay adds up to one thing and takes us to the same end point. Let's look at ways to get each one.

SHOW, DON'T TELL

I know, I know—you've heard this before. But bear with me; it's hugely important.

There's a paradox about drama: the worst way to communicate to the reader how you're feeling is to tell him. Yer wouldn't strengthen "Grateful" by saying "People should be careful not to take for granted the things they have"; she would weaken it. Michael wouldn't strengthen "Dad" by saying, "My father was a pathetic drunk, and I *feel* like I lost out on having a father as a result"; he would weaken it. Instead, Yer puts us at Wyandotte Elementary School and lets us *feel* Mai's anger. Michael lets us *watch* his father act out his life so that we witness his isolation.

So writing teachers traditionally express this insight by the ancient incantation, "Show, don't tell." These are just different words for the basic lesson of the concretion section of Chapter 5. To get life, concretize and particularize. Avoid generalized abstractions: "He was really weird"; "It was the most exciting class of my life"; "I was so scared." Replace them with concretions.

Imagine you're directing a movie, and you've just filmed an actor doing a scene conveying her sadness over the loss of her father. As a director, you don't get in front of the camera and say, "Look! Isn't she sad?" You let the particulars, the details, do the work, and you trust your audience to understand why you've chosen to use them.

Remember, too, how subjective those kinds of abstractions are. Surely you've had the experience of saying something like, "I met this totally hilarious guy at a party last week—he was in the dining room doing impressions of Saddam Hussein as a Catholic priest!" only to have your listener/audience say, "That's not hilarious; that's disgusting." So it's better just to describe the person *acting* and to leave the generalizing/interpreting to your reader. This passage from a first draft does it wrong:

She was impulsive, funny, and highly irresponsible. I liked her because she did things I wouldn't do. I was reliable, down to earth, and boring. She was spontaneous. I looked up to her. In my eyes, she was a leader because she did things I was afraid to do. In many ways, she was immature. She had no concept of responsibility. I loved being with her, though, because she was fun. Being with her was like being on a vacation.

We understand perfectly, but we feel nothing. When the author re-wrote to *show,* the new version began,

"Hey, Cathy, I'm dying for an In-N-Out burger and fries and, you know me, I don't want to go alone. I'll pick you up in ten minutes." "But Nikki, it's ... CLICK ... ten o'clock at night," I respond to a dial tone.

Later in the new draft we get this:

During the freshman initiation ceremony in high school, our friendship was born. We were dressed in costume (unwillingly) and instructed to do something totally silly and asinine in front of the entire student body. Nikki, dressed as Pinocchio, was told to tell a lie. "I love this school," she blurted out emphatically. Everybody booed.

Now we really *get it.*

More is better. "He didn't respect his students" doesn't say much. "He would always tell his students they'd never amount to anything" is better. Better still is "He scowled, dropped our math tests in the waste-basket, and said, 'See you losers Monday.'" Here's a good more-is-better description of an eatery:

I was living in Laguna Beach and working at Tip's Deli. Tip's served beer and wine, chopped chicken liver, lox and bagels, pastrami on Jewish rye, and imported cheeses to a colorful clientele. Wally Tip was a short, plump, balding Jew originally from Toronto who claimed to have been a pimp in Las Vegas and made one believe in the possibilities of a Jewish Mafia. I liked him a lot. On Sunday morning he cooked breakfast himself, sweating and swearing over his tiny grill as he made his Tip's Special Omelet, which he served for a ridiculously low price to local businessmen and hippies and outsiders from Los Angeles who bitched about the fat on the pastrami, compared the place unfavorably to Ratner's, and left look-ing pleased. There was usually a long wait. Every time an order was turned in, Wally looked dismayed and muttered that the bastards would have to wait.

One of the best ways to "show" is to use dialogue. It's a great way to reveal character. Consider the following: "He was a redneck who didn't care about school" versus "I ain't got time for homework. Me and Dan are gonna change the oil in my pickup and then we're goin' squirrel huntin'."

In fact, just think how frequently you use dialogue in conversation, often to describe someone's personality. Most likely, you've recently described someone you've met by "quoting" him—or using dialogue: "This guy came up to me after class yesterday and said ..."

Keep in mind, though, that there should be a reason for using dialogue. Apparently, some students have been told "Show, don't tell" and to use lots of dialogue but not to think about why. There's little that's more annoying than pointless dialogue. Well-chosen dialogue, however, can go a long way. In fact, it can even result in a "movie" (and plays are *all* dialogue, save for minor stage directions), which the writer doesn't need to interrupt at all.

FORGET HOMEWORK

JENNIFER WISSMATH

Student Essay

"Jen, please!"

"Jeez, Darron, relax—I'm coming."

"I called you three times; this food has been sitting here forever!"

"I was taking an order and it hasn't been here that long. Where's the ticket for this order? I don't know where it goes."

"Table three. Hurry up ..."

Man, he gets on my nerves. This plate is really hot. Hurry up, lady, move your stupid salad plate. "Here you go. I'll run and get you some Parmesan cheese. Do you need anything else?"

"Is our bread coming?"

"Oh, yes, it should be right out."

Okay, Parmesan, water—whoa! I almost slipped. There's a puddle in here the size of Lake Michigan. This whole station is a mess! You could never guess that there were two other waitresses who were supposed to do sidework before they left. I'm going to be here until way after 10—shoot, it's 9:45 right now. I guess my homework will just have to wait. "Here you go. Enjoy your meal—I'll be right back with your bread. Darron, I need the bread for Table 3."

"I already sent that out!"

"Well, Table 3 didn't get it. Hurry, the man on that table has been waiting forever."

There's the door—oh shoot, more people. Why are they coming in so late? I'd love to tell those jerks to leave—we could all get the hell out of here a little sooner. Let's see: Table 3—bread; Table 2—eating; Table 11—almost finished, they'll leave first; Table 8—okay; Table 16—take order.

"Hello, how are you doing this evening? Are you ready to order?"

"Yes. Honey, you go first."

"Um, okay. I think I'll get the eggplant."

"Oh, I was going to get that. Hmmm, I guess I could get lasagna and we could pull the old switcheroo."

("Jen, please!")

"But, hmmm, I'm not sure I really feel like lasagna."

Oh, God, could you please hurry up?

"Okay, she'll have the eggplant and I'll have the raviolis." "Honey, I don't like raviolis."

"How about ... well, I'll just stick with the lasagna."

What a revelation. Don't waste my time or anything. I don't think I'll ask them if they want salads. "Would you like any garlic bread?"

"Oh, yes—Honey, let's get it with cheese?" "I don't like it with cheese ..."
("Jen, please!!!")
"Will that be all for you?"
"Honey, don't forget the wine."
"Oh, yes, we would like a liter of White Zinfandel."

Oh, please, make my night longer. I don't have anything else to do. I don't really need to read those three chapters for my history quiz, and I'm sure my teacher wouldn't mind my handing in a late paper. This job is too much. If I didn't need the money so badly, I would probably get straight A's.

"JEN PLEASE!!!"

Damn. Let's see—this goes to Table 8. Oh my gosh, they don't even have their drinks. I just love getting a late rush. "Here you go—I'll be right back with your drinks. Do you need some Parmesan cheese?"

Okay—drinks, drinks, Parmesan. Then deliver food, check water, pick up plates, pour coffee, add tickets, clear tables, be civil, do sidework, fill Parm holders, fill sugars, clean station, clean salad bar, mop floor, go home, *forget homework*, go to bed.

—Permission provided by Steve Metzger

DADDY AND DONUTS

DANNY DIETZ

Student Essay

Donuts have always played a large part in my life and there's a large part of my life I owe to donuts, mainly my midsection but as I see it, that's a small price to pay for a decade's long relationship with something so warm and so wicked it warrants the words you're wandering through right now.

As a kid, it was Winchell's Donut Shop at the Fontana Square that got me hooked and that I hold responsible for my current addiction and bulging belt size. It was a rare Sunday morning that we didn't stop there usually after church as a reward for going, I guess. The small corner shop had gleaming glass windows and gooey, glazed, goodies that begged loudly to be eaten, so loudly in fact no one could resist, not me then and certainly not me now.

Thursday mornings I sleep in a bit and take Maddie to day-care. We've made a tradition out of stopping at the Donut Wheel and I'd have to say Maddie has done well at weaving the sights and sounds and smells of the local donut shop into the fabric of her young life. I couldn't be more proud. Some people have mile-stones marked in granite. I'm OK that ours are marked with chocolate, maple and strawberry frosting. Who remembers a granite milestone anyway? Who can forget a fancy, French donut dripping with warm and wicked maple frosting?

The first girl I ever got up enough nerve to ask out on a date worked at Helen's Donut Nook in a small town in northern California. "Can I have a maple bar and coffee please," had to be repeated countless times before I was able to squeeze in the "and would you like to go out sometime" part of my donut shop experience. A guy never forgets the name of his first girlfriend, Elaine, or the taste of his first donut, delicious. I don't want to come off sounding like some donut fanatic—I'm no Homer Simpson—it's just that for whatever reason, donuts have always been present in pivotal parts of my life.

Maddie likes to eat the frosting off the top first. Pink strawberry is her current favorite. I can't help but wonder if there's some little boy at day care she likes and will always remember and associate with the Donut Wheel and pink frosting the way her daddy can't eat a maple bar without visions of a long gone Elaine dancing around in his head.

All different shapes and colors and flavors seem to easily overwhelm Maddie as she stands wide-eyed and wondering at the many confusing choices laid out before her. As she grows older, will the choices that lie beyond the gleaming glass of the display case come easier for her? If given the opportunity, will she dig deeper into the issues that she'll face in her life or simply scrape away at the surface like she does now with the pink frosting?

Will she even remember it was her daddy who held her hand and lifted her up so she could see all the choices she has to make today and into tomorrow? Those won't be as easy as a choice between a maple bar and a cake donut. Some will have outcomes not nearly as sweet as pink frosting, but God willing, I'll still be around to hold her hand and lift her up to see her tomorrows filled with options so much more abundant.

Permission provided by Danny Dietz

Chapter 6 gives you a list of ways to concretize an essay. But they are revision strategies—they think in terms of *adding* concretions to something you've already written. Instead, build the essay up from concretions. Instead of brainstorming by asking abstract questions ("What sort of a person is he?" "How do I feel about her?"), begin by listing objects, gestures, or fragments of dialogue that capture the spirit of your subject. Ask yourself questions like this:

How does she dress? Birkenstocks? Red Converse high tops? Hemp necklaces?

What kind of car does he drive? Raised Ford F-350 with a Ducks Unlimited bumper sticker? Toyota Prius with a "Think Green" bumper sticker?

Does she have any verbal idiosyncrasies? Remember, using dialogue is a great way to "show" a person's character, so if he says "ain't," use it. If he, like, habitually uses, like, a certain word, use it.

What does he own that is meaningful and that defines him? A German shepherd named Spike? An Elvis lunchbox? A $4,000 mountain bike?

Is there a specific story about her that people tell when describing her? Did she organize a car wash to raise money to send to needy children in Nicaragua?

"Dad" might have begun with a list like this:

Coughing and spitting in the bathroom

Explaining the infield fly rule to coach

Talking to the dog

The Club

Sliding off the road in the car

CHOOSING AN EFFECT

Once we have good concretions to work with, we need a rationale for putting them together in some way. Don't outline—it will just drive away the spontaneity. And don't begin with thesis, though thesis may emerge, because it forces you back into telling instead of showing.

Instead, think about effect: what are you trying to do to the reader? That effect may involve a thesis or a moral, but it doesn't have to. You can leave it pretty vague in the beginning: "I'm trying to capture what it feels like to play in a rec-league softball tournament"; "I want the reader to meet my father." The sought effect will become more specific as you work. Here are specific effects for some of the essays in this chapter:

"Dad": to capture the miserable alcoholic isolation my father lived with, and my inability to get near him.

"Forget Homework": to capture how hysterical, frustrating, and dehumanizing my nighttime job is, and to show how infuriating it is to have it ruin my schoolwork.

"Daddy and Donuts": to capture the ambivalent feelings of growing up—and of watching my daughter growing up.

THESIS IN PERSONAL WRITING

Does personal writing have a thesis? Not always, and not in the same way that traditional arguments do. If someone's telling you a story and you sense he's trying to teach you something, you'll probably get annoyed. On the other hand, you want there to be some kind of point to the story he's telling you. Otherwise, why bother?

Then again, some personal writing has a very clear thesis, which is usually implied as opposed to stated. Remember "Something Happened a Long Time Ago" in Chapter 2? There's not only a point to that story but a thesis as well, which Carroll playfully summarizes by quoting the poet Wendell Berry: "Practice resurrection." Additionally, essays like "Forget Homework" and "Dad" don't teach, but they do have theses. The thesis for "Dad" is "My father was cut off from the human race and his family by his alcoholism." The thesis in "Forget Homework" is something like "My wage-earning job often prevents me from being the best student I can be." And if we wanted to, we could *turn any personal essay into an argument* by drawing larger conclusions from the experience. We could use "Dad" to make the argument that our culture teaches males to deal with their emotional pain through silence and self-inflicted isolation. We could use "Forget Homework" to make the argument that it's to society's advantage to support student aid programs, so worthy students can concentrate on getting the most out of their education. Chapter 15 has two essays that use personal narrative in this way, "Given the Chance" and "Why?"

SEEING THE MODE

Figure 12.1 shows an image that's etched in the minds of hundreds of millions of people around the world—at least, those who were six or seven years old or older on September 11, 2001. What do you remember about that day? What memories does this photograph recall? Are there "bigger issues" that you could address by writing about that day in your life? The importance of family? A child's confusion? The power of the media? Or even the loss of innocence—of a child, of a nation?

Sean Adair/Reuters/CORBIS

FIGURE 12.1   They say a picture is worth a thousand words. Some inspire millions of them. Some leave us speechless

WRITER'S WORKSHOP

Concretizing Abstract Generalizations

Let's look at how a student writer revises a very "tell-y" character sketch so that it "shows" instead.

MY MOTHER

LORI ANN PROUST

She is understanding and always there for me. She listens and is full of positive support. I am lucky to have someone who is both a close friend *and* a mother. Not everyone has this kind of a relationship.

I could find endless words in the thesaurus to describe my mother, but the one word that stands out above the rest is "incredible." She is my sole support system. Whenever something exciting happens or there is a crisis in my life, she is the first person I turn to. I have seen many friends come and go in my life, but my mother is different. For eighteen years of my life she has always been there for me. No matter the distance in miles between us, we are always close. She understands me and knows me better than anyone else I know. She doesn't make demands nor does she pressure me with school and my future. She has complete faith and trust in me that I am doing the right thing with my life. I make her happy by letting her know I am happy and like who I am and where my life is taking me.

Every day I count my blessings and think about how grateful I am to have a mother who loves me. Not once do I take this for granted. I cannot imagine my life any differently without her. One thing is for certain: it just wouldn't be the same.

—Permission provided by Steve Metzger

Lori Ann's classmates said they simply didn't *believe* the essay—it felt like a sales pitch. They encouraged Lori Ann to start from concretions. She said, "Well, I just had a phone conversation with her that was pretty typical—maybe I could use that." She did, and this is what she got:

MOTHERS ... ?!!

"Hello?"

"Hi, Mom. How was your day?"

"What's wrong?"

"Nothing is wrong, Mom. I just called to tell you I found an incredible place to live next year! It's an apartment in an antique house. It has hardwood floors, high ceilings, it's close to school, has lots of potential, and the rent is *only* ..."

"Does it have summer rent?"

"Yes."

"Forget it then."

"Fine, Mom."

"I already told you that neighborhood is dangerous and full of rapists."

"Mother, I've lived on this street for the past *three* years now." "And what about the fraternity boys across the street? Do you know what you're in for?"

"Mother, these guys are my friends and I have also lived across the street from a fraternity house before ..."

"Forget it."

"Fine, Mom. Would you rather pay $225 a month for me to live in a two-bedroom apartment instead of $150 a month? You'd also have to buy me a car because the only apartments available in September are five miles from campus."

"Does your friend Denice know what a slob you are? Does she know *you're* the reason why you had cockroaches in your apartment last year?"

"Mother, that's because I lived in a *dive!* I found cockroaches before I even moved in ..."

"Oh, are you suddenly scrubbing floors now? I just don't see why you can't wait until September to find a place to live. I'm *not* paying summer rent."

"Fine, Mom. I just thought you might *appreciate* my consideration in letting you know what I am doing with my life before I sign the lease."

"Well, it sounds like you're going to do it anyway."

"Thank you for your support, Mom."

"Bye." Click.

"Good-bye, Mom; I love you too."

To think that mothers are understanding is the world's ultimate illusion. I had to sit in the bathroom as I was talking to my mom because there were thirty screaming girls in the hallway; stereos were blasting, and if this wasn't enough, the smoke alarm was going off because the cooks were burning dinner. I had to control myself from sticking the phone down the toilet and flushing it. That's how understanding she was being.

My mother can be full of positive support but not when you need to hear it the most. "I'm sure you can find something cleaner, can't you? You're such a slob—I guess it wouldn't matter anyway." Right, Mom. To my mother's dismay, I am an immaculate person—just ask any of my friends. She is practically married to the Pine Sol man. She thinks her house is as sterile as the hospital. Well, I have news for her ...

Whenever something exciting happens in my life, my mother is usually the first person I turn to. I don't know why because she always shoots down my dreams. I sent her flowers and a poem I wrote myself for Mother's Day and what does she do? She acts irrational over the telephone. "Why can't you wait until September to find a place? I'm not paying summer rent." Right, Mom. I already told her twice I would pay summer rent myself. Anyone with common sense would realize that it's an advantage to find the best place *now*. That way you don't have to pay storage over the summer.

For eighteen years of my life she has raised me. She knows me better than anyone else I know. It just doesn't make sense why she can't be more sensitive and supportive of my dreams. All I wanted was to hear her say, "It sounds great!" But it was obviously too much to ask.

The phone rang as I was finishing this paper tonight.

"Hello?"

"Hi. I've been talking to your father about that apartment, and he said he would pay half your summer rent. That way we don't have to pay for storage." (What did I tell you, Mom …) "So go ahead and sign the lease." (I didn't tell you before, but … I already did!)

"I'll see you soon, Mom. I love you."

My mom will never know this, but I went ahead and signed the lease yesterday, without her approval or support. I felt good about it, knowing I did the right thing. Today's phone call reassured me that I had done the right thing. Although my mother can be irrational sometimes, she is still my mother and I love her dearly.

—Permission provided by Steve Metzger

The phone conversation forced Lori Ann to come out from behind the safety of the first draft's clichés and face some complex, feisty realities. There's much more to say now, and the essay crackles with the energy of conflict.

Now It's Your Turn. Write a draft of a personal essay. Highlight every abstraction (telling). Replace the abstractions with concretions (showing). Then delete the abstractions.

EXERCISES

1. Find a published personal essay and bring it to class to share. Look at and discuss the degree to which it "universalizes" or connects to a "bigger picture." How does it manage that? Identify examples in the piece of "showing" detail. Does the writer "tell" at all? If so, where, and why?

2. List the objects, verbal expressions, and behaviors that capture the essence of someone in your life. How does he usually dress? What are his verbal tics? What possessions matter to him? And so on. Write a paragraph showing how one item on the list reveals the heart and soul of the person.

3. Make a list of three abstract generalizations about someone in your life, such as "He's very generous." Imagine how a director would film scenes to show that the person is what you say she is. Then write an essay showing those scenes without telling. Share it with your classmates. See if they can guess what abstraction you were trying to convey. Notes: (a) Don't set it up like a riddle. You're trying to be clear, not to trick your reader. (b) Don't use synonyms. (c) Remember that not everyone will guess the same abstraction, which is exactly the point: what's hilarious to one person is disgusting to another; what's proud to one person is self-centered to another.

4. Write a half- to one-page monologue or dialogue that reveals the character of someone in your life.

5. Use one of the personal essays in "A Collection of Good Writing" as a model and write one like it.

6. Describe a setting from your life that matters to you, like the deli earlier in this chapter, in a paragraph or two. Then rewrite it to twice that length by doubling the specific concrete detail.

Chapter 13

Writing to Inform

Every time you give directions to your house, give someone a link to a Web site, write down the ingredients in your favorite smoothie or chocolate-chip cookies, you're doing informative writing. Your resume is informative. Your tweets are probably informative writing. A progress report you write on the job is informative writing. Your Facebook page is an example of informative writing.

That means you're probably already pretty good at it. I guarantee, assuming that you *want* that person to find your house, that the writing's going to be pretty good: clear, concise, reader appropriate, with a built-in purpose. Of course, because there are different kinds of informative essays, you should read a lot of them if you want to learn to do them well. Start by taking a look at the ones in "A Collection of Good Writing."

WHERE DO WE SEE INFORMATIVE WRITING?

Informative writing is probably the most common writing you see outside of school. It accounts for about 95 percent of newspaper writing, from the front page to the sports section, writing in newsmagazines (Time, Newsweek, etc.). You see it in lots of other places, too, though—in gardening magazines, home-improvement Web sites, and *Consumer Reports* magazine, where the reader is going to go out and *do* something practical with the information: plant a garden, install a new water heater, get a good deal on a used car. In fact, most of the writing that's earning money in the real (and online) world is informative: cookbooks, technical and scientific reports, encyclopedias (including Wikipedia), textbooks, travel guides, and Web sites such as WebMD.com and Allmusic.com

Profiles

A profile is an objective description that attempts to capture the essence of—or sometimes one specific part of—a person's character, and it's one of the most common kinds of informative writing that you come across. You've most likely read more of them than you realize. For example, your college newspaper probably publishes one or more in each edition: a profile of a particularly interesting student (reentry, foreign exchange, single mom, etc.), a successful student athlete, or a faculty or staff member. You also see "celebrity profiles" in popular magazines, profiles of CEOs and entrepreneurs in business magazines, and profiles of athletes in magazines such as *Sports Illustrated*. And profiles are fun to write—and an excellent way to work on your writing skills, especially keeping in mind what we've talked about in terms of knowing your audience.

Profiles are different from character descriptions, which tend to be more personal, because you usually don't know your subject; you *get to know her*—through interviews, background reading, and other research—and then write up your "findings." (Hmmm, sounds a lot like a "research paper," doesn't it? Well, it is—and it's a great way to practice for a more "academic" one.) Also, you generally want to keep yourself out of profiles—the focus should be on your subject. I frequently write profiles of faculty and former students for my university's alumni publication, and while there's a subtle, implied persuasive edge (this guy's doing great things; send the school some money so we can help more students go on to similar great things), they're pretty much straight informative writing.

Here's an example of a profile that is the introduction to a longer piece of informative writing about the history of the King James translation of the Bible. It's by Adam Nicholson and was published in the December 2011 issue of *National Geographic* (a great place to see lots of examples of excellent informative writing). Note how Nicholson does exactly what we talked about in the chapter on personal writing (and elsewhere). He *shows* using lots of specific details, letting his readers draw their own conclusions:

Rome Wager stands in front of the rodeo chutes on a small ranch just outside the Navajo Reservation in Waterflow, New Mexico. He is surrounded by a group of young cowboys here for midweek practice. With a big silver buckle at his waist and a long mustache that rolls down on each side of his mouth like the curving ends of a pair of banisters, Wager holds up a Bible in his left hand. The young men take their hats off to balance them on their knees. "My stories always begin a little different," Brother Rome says to them as they crouch in the dust of the yard, "but the Lord always provides the punctuation."

Wager, a Baptist preacher now, is a former bull-riding and saddle-bronc pro, "with more bone breaks in my body than you've got bones in yours." He's part Dutch, part Seneca on his father's side, Lakota on his mother's, married to a full-blood Jicarilla Apache.

He tells them about his wild career. He was raised on a ranch in South Dakota; he fought and was beaten up, shot, and stabbed. He wrestled and boxed, he won prizes and started drinking. "I was a saphead drunk."

But this cowboy life was empty. He was looking for meaning, and one day in the drunk tank in a jail in Montana, he found himself reading the pages of the Bible. "I looked at that book in jail, and I saw then that He'd established me a house in heaven ... He came into my heart."

The heads around the preacher go down, and the words he whispers, which the rodeo riders listen to in such earnestness, are not from the American West: They are from England, translated 400 years ago by a team of black-gowned clergymen who would have been as much at home in this world of swells and saddles, pearl-button shirts and big-fringed chaps as one of these cowboys on a Milanese catwalk. "Second Corinthians 5. 'Therefore if any man be in Christ, he is a new creature: old things are passed away; behold, all things are become new.'"

(REPRINTED BY PERMISSION FROM ADAM NICOLSON)

That's not really writing anyone is going to *use* but it is informative, and though it discusses a sensitive and often contentious subject, Nicholson is making no argument at all about religion—if there's a thesis, it's little more than "Rome Wager is a fascinating guy full of contradictions."

Tips and Suggestions for Writing Profiles

1. Using present tense can be very effective, even though what you're describing—your interview, for example- happened in the past: "Johnson reaches for a magazine on the coffee table and says ..." On the other hand, profiles in newspapers, say of a town's new police chief, are frequently written in past tense: "'I really hope I can make a difference here in Deadwood,' Larson said."

2. Convention calls for using the subject's first and last names the first time you refer to him, and then only the last name there after (unless you need to clarify—for example if there's someone else with the same last name mentioned in your profile). As always, though, do what works. Note, however, that both Anders and Solvejg use their subjects' first names in their profiles (below), and both work just fine.

3. Use quotations. What people say and how they say it reveals a lot about who they are.

4. Don't overuse quotations. For example, you don't need to write, "'My favorite movie is *The Big Lebowski*,' Johnson says." Just write, "Johnson's favorite movie is *The Big Lebowski*." But if the way Johnson says it reveals something about him, then quote: "'Dude! *The Big Lebowski*'s the best movie on the friggin' planet,' Johnson says, lacing up his bowling shoes." (This is also true for using quotations in conventional college research papers, which I talk about in Chapter 17.)

5. Use physical description, not only so that your reader can visualize your subject, but because how people look—especially how they dress, wear their hair, and so on—says a lot about who they are. And try to work the physical description in along the way, instead of devoting a paragraph or section of your profile to it: "Anderson smiles and reaches for a Red Bull, the sleeve of her blue blouse inching up to reveal a dolphin tattoo on her left wrist."

6. Keep yourself out of it. Readers don't need your questions, for example. No need to write, "I asked her what the significance of the dolphin tattoo was," or, "When I asked her what the significance of the dolphin tattoo was, she said ..." Just write, "... inching up to reveal a dolphin tattoo on her left wrist, which she got in Hawaii when she visited with her boyfriend." Nor do you need to comment or pass judgment: "In his spare time, Thompson loves to surf, *which is totally cool*" or, even worse, "*and so do I.*"

7. Note that points 2–5 are just variations of "Show, don't tell."

Take a look at the following profiles, and try to identify in them the tips listed above.

AFTERNOON WITH THE COBBLER

ANDERS NIENSTAEDT

Student Essay

There are shoes everywhere. High heels, cowboy boots, steel-toes, fashionable Eskimo-style mukluks. They have a kicked-off, carefree look, as if there's a huge footy-pajama slumber party happening in the back of the store. Each pair waits with its own scrap of yellow cardstock with a customer's name and phone number written in cursive. They line every counter surface and a large portion of the floor.

In most ways, Randy looks exactly the way you might expect someone who repairs shoes for a living to look. He's in his fifties, mostly bald, with a big, stern mustache. He wears glasses and a checked shirt and an apron with an "I love downtown Northfield" pin. When he doesn't smile in pictures, it's a staid and respectful lack of smile, not an unfriendly one. Randy holds a shoe with a broken heel, and he gestures with it as he talks. To Randy, working and talking are two separate jobs, and he prefers to tackle one at a time.

"Well, I don't like to tell people this, but the economy has actually been really good for my business," he says. Randy is soft-spoken, but in a course, Midwestern way. He says this with an almost confidential sheepishness.

"When cash is tight, people start looking into fixing things. Yeah, the last couple of years have been great."

Randy begins dressing the shoe he holds on a machine he calls "the finisher." The finisher is a man-height amalgamation of brushes, grinders, and belts that looks like the giant, upturned bottom of a fancy vacuum cleaner. He pushes a button, and after a momentary lag the machine whirs to life.

Randy Malecha works with the brusque, estimated precision of a skilled tradesperson. In thirty seconds, he has ground the two cork blocks glued to the bottom of a pair of shoes into seamless reconstructions of the missing heels. He paints them black with an evil-looking brush/can setup that looks and smells like something British factory orphans might have used in the mid-1800s, then sets both on a special grilled part of the finisher that sucks away the fumes. He says that the finisher is the most important tool in the shop.

Randy has a hard time pinning down exactly why he bought Willie's Shoe Service from a man named Willie Wolf in 1986. Willie had opened the shop in 1948, and he still squints from a few black-and-white photos on the shop wall, a cowboy hat on his head, a probable wad of tobacco under his lip. Randy had moved back to his hometown Northfield after a stint as a salesman and some earlier work on farms and in a cheese factory. He had never fixed a pair of shoes in his life, but Willie was ready to hang up his ten-gallon hat. Sure, Randy wanted to own something for himself. After thinking for a while, he comes up with another motivation.

"I like the machines for some reason," he says.

There really are a lot of machines. Besides the finisher and the sewing machines in front, there are hole-punchers, sole-pressers, rubber-cutters, and two nailing machines. They all blend together to create a vague mechanical backdrop that looks cozy in his small shop. A few stairs lead into the back room, a veritable garden of sewing machines, saws, and big fabric-store style rolls of leather.

Randy neatly shaves off the bottom of the shoe with a band saw, and the room is filled with a little cloud of rubber dust. He switches the machine off with the toe of the shoe he's just cut and turns to survey the shop. The machines are all gray and shine with machine oil. They have the names like "St. Louis" and "The Nibbler" cast into their sides in bold letters, and they're all at least fifty years old.

"They don't even really make any of this stuff anymore," Randy says as he points out a stitching machine for horse harnesses. The thing is massive and partially disassembled. Springs and cogs and ratcheting wheels litter the machine and the floor around it. Randy points to a large section of cast brass that gleams inside the gutted harness-maker. "Those things always wore out. I bought this machine because I always wanted one—I had to pay an Amish guy a thousand dollars for that part to get it up and running." According to Randy, there used to be two different people in the Midwest who repaired shoe-repair machines full-time. They're both dead now (as is Willie and most of the shoe repair community, it would seem) but they used to tour the Midwest, going from shop to shop, fixing machines as they went. One of the men had cataracts and had to hire a driver to take him on his rounds. It sounds almost mythical—the blind shoe repair oracle and his mortal companion.

—Reprinted by permission from Anders Neinstaedt

VICTOR

SOLVEJG WASTVEDT

Student Essay

On a beautifully clear spring day, Victor brings a four-foot-tall white tank outside and props it up on a pallet. The tank smells a little strange; this morning it is full of apple cider vinegar. In a room off the kitchen reserved for vinegar-making and growing lettuce, Victor cultivates bacteria in large vats and pours the final product in the white tank. Then he bottles his creation and sells it to his friends and neighbors. Spring isn't the season for apples, though, so today the tank will be re-purposed. Victor fills it with muddy plastic bags, runs water inside with the hose, and stirs his concoction with a long pole.

With the wind ruffling his loose t-shirt and an old baseball cap on backwards, Victor looks disheveled and resembles a witch over a cauldron, or maybe a hippie. In fact, he would identify as none of these things, but he would proudly assume the label "ecologist." Looking into his "office," a set of shelves off the kitchen crammed with broken and disused items, some might disagree. Perhaps "pack rat" would seem more appropriate. But he reuses compulsively. To drink tea with breakfast, he puts yesterday's tea bags in today's mugs of hot water. If it's the third or fourth time a bag has been used, he puts two in a cup at once. Squeezed against a spoon for the last drop of potency, they come out looking very tired. Nevertheless, Victor sees this refusal to throw things away as part of the permaculture philosophy that makes him an ecologist.

Depending on your viewpoint, permaculture can be a religion, a cult, a science, or just something to keep in the back of your mind. Its basic principle is taking advantage of all the products that come out of a process, whether economic, aesthetic, nutritional, spiritual, or otherwise. The plastic bags came to Victor's farm last year, filled with dirt, and he used them to make impromptu gardens. Their bright red color stood out against the green foliage, and they looked lovely. Now, though, they just look faded and sad, so the idea is to clean them and reuse them as stuffing. Possibly for cushions or pillows, but Victor is excited about the prospect of giant sculptures shaped like people and animals. Aesthetics, check. Reducing landfill size, check. He positions the tank so that water draining out the bottom runs into the flowers. Another product utilized.

And one final product: while the plastic soaks, Victor stands by a separate faucet rinsing something that looks like stained white rags. It is the layer of bacteria that drives vinegar-making and has reposed in the bottom of the tank until today. Slimy, with a consistency like the colored foam used for stickers and elementary school craft projects, it now hangs on the clothesline drip-drying. Victor hopes to make a painting using it as canvas.

Victor's way of thinking, in which all products have a purpose, requires astounding creativity and circumspection. He always notices the possibilities around him: How a job could be done better, how more products could be used, how beautiful the contrasting greens look the morning after a rainstorm. Raking up leaves for compost, he only takes from the center of the path and deposits the debris in a nearby hole. If you asked him, he would tell you that water runs down the path to humidify the leaves, which fall from a certain tree in the legume family and therefore have nitrogen-fixing properties perfect for compost.

Removing the thicker twigs, he saves them for firewood. Leaves piled in the hole mix with accumulated moisture and compost. If he can't plant in the resulting compost, Victor tosses in worms—which love compost—and feeds it to the chickens. "In nature," he says, "nothing is extra."

—Permission granted by Solvejg Wastvedt

Now, here's one more. This one I wrote it for our local newspaper after meeting the guy at my gym. I was impressed with his story and his unassuming nature. I got the introductory material from watching the Youtube clip of his band performing the song. Interestingly, I used present tense when I wrote it ("Marshall recalls"), but the editors changed it to past ("Marshall recalled"). By the way, you can check out the Youtube clip by writing "Chantays Pipeline Welk" in the search box.

SURF'S UP

STEVE METZGER

It's May 1963 in Burbank, Calif. A terrified 17-year-old high school student stands on the stage of *The Lawrence Welk Show* holding a Fender Stratocaster. He looks nervously into the television camera and thanks the audience for making his band's song No. 1. Then The Chantays—in matching collarless jackets, too-short pegger slacks and pointy black halfboots—launch into the distinctive and familiar notes of the surf anthem "Pipeline."

Welk's orchestra looks on from behind, not quite sure what to make of the choreography—the corny dance steps and the synchronized waving of the sunburst Fenders of the three boys up front. To the right of the stage is the keyboard player, dancing to the beat and smiling broadly as he plays the distinctive chords on his Wurlitzer.

Rob Marshall retired as a speech and English teacher in 2003. For the past two years, he's worked part time at Chico Sports Club, washing towels and doing general maintenance. Forty-four years ago, "Pipeline," which Marshall co-wrote and on which he played keyboard, was at the top of the charts. "Pipeline" has been covered by The Ventures, Dick Dale (with Stevie Ray Vaughan), even Anthrax, and many more, and the song has been used in movies, television shows and commercials. The Chantays also recorded two albums: *Pipeline*, in 1963, and *Two Sides of The Chantays*, in 1964. In 1996, the Chantays, along with the Ventures ("Walk, Don't Run") and the Surfaris ("Wipeout"), were inducted into the Hollywood Rock Walk. They are also included in the Rock and Roll Hall of Fame Museum in Cleveland. Two years ago, the name of the street in front of Santa Ana High School was changed to Chantay Boulevard.

Marshall was a sophomore when he was approached by Bob Spickard on the Santa Ana High School track, where Marshall was practicing pole vaulting. "I didn't know who he was and I have no idea how he knew me," Marshall recalled. "But he said, 'I hear you play piano. We're getting a garage band together, and we want you to play with us.'"

Though Marshall had taken a year of piano lessons, he was largely self-taught. "I just played by ear," he said. "Even at my lessons, I didn't play from the sheet music. I just mimicked what I heard my teacher playing."

Soon, The Chantays were practicing twice a week after school in Marshall's parents' front room, and "driving the neighbors crazy." Mostly they played covers, but all were talented, creative musicians. "One day Bob said he had an idea for a song," Marshall said, "and he played a little bit of it, but he said he didn't know how the middle should go. I said, 'How 'bout this?'"

"It seemed to fit pretty naturally. And that was it. 'Pipeline.' We wrote that song in half an hour." Marshall shook his head softly, smiling as though he still had trouble believing it all really happened. "It was such a fluke," he said.

Not to some, however. In his 1963 Santa Ana High School yearbook, classmate—and fellow high school choir member—Diane Keaton wrote: "You guys are so bitchin'."

Shortly after they wrote "Pipeline," The Chantays heard about a series of Saturday-night teen dances at Lake Arrowhead. "We went up there and asked the disk jockey, Jack Sands, if we could play live. So we played two one-hour sets, and afterward he came up to us and said, 'What was that one song? I want to record a promo.'"

Two weeks later, they recorded "Pipeline" at a studio in Cucamonga, but Sands didn't like the quality of the studio, so The Chanteys recorded it again at Downey Studios. Just two takes. The 45 was released in January of 1963.

Sands began playing the song on his station, KFXM-FM in San Bernardino, and getting "massive requests" for it. Within a week it had made the station's charts, and three weeks later it was picked up by a Los Angeles AM station. Two weeks after that "Pipeline" was on the Billboard charts.

"We were aghast," said Marshall. "We were 17. We were juniors in high school!"

Soon the money was rolling in. "We all bought new cars. I even bought a boat. That year I paid more income tax than my dad did, and he was working two jobs." Marshall's parents suggested he invest in land. "But what kid is thinking about that?" he said. "We wanted cars. This was 1963. In L.A."

Marshall says the band felt out of place on Welk's show but that Welk was a "nice guy" who introduced them by saying how "proud he was of us for being clean-cut American kids."

"Look at that YouTube clip," he said. "Our drummer didn't have a foot pedal—he was just tapping his foot. The guitars weren't even plugged in." He laughed. "What fun."

With the success of "Pipeline," the Chantays joined the ranks of some of America's best-known bands of the early '60s, touring the country with the Righteous Brothers and Roy Orbison. "The toughest thing, though," said Marshall, "was when we were invited to tour Australia, New Zealand and Europe. All of our parents said, 'Absolutely not.' They all felt that our educations were too important, that we shouldn't be pulled out of high school to tour the world. We were *so* mad."

Marshall did in fact go on to college, Santa Ana Junior College, where he studied music theory and helped The Chantays work out their vocals, three- and four-part harmonies. After a tour of Japan in 1968, Marshall quit the band and moved north to Chico to attend Chico State, originally declaring a music major but soon changing to education. He graduated in 1970, with a multiple-subject and a single-subject (English) teaching credential and in 1971 was hired at Los Molinos Elementary School, where he taught for a year before moving to Los Molinos High School, where he taught English and coached varsity track and junior varsity football. Two years later, he went to work at Vina Elementary School, where he taught seventh and eighth grade until retiring four years ago.

The Chantays, with three of its original members, continue to record, and they perform regularly in Southern California and state fairs. Two years ago, they contacted Marshall and asked him to come to Las Vegas for a show.

"They said they'd fly me down there, pay me, put me up, fly me home. But that's not me any more," said Marshall, clearly content in shorts and a loose-fitting Chico Sports Club sweatshirt. "I've got a different life now." And while that different life means playing in public is "kind of on the back burner," he still has a piano at home, and still loves music.

"All of it," he said. "From Mozart to Travis Tritt."

—Permission granted by Steve Metzger

USING YOUR EXPERIENCE: THE HOW-TO ESSAY

In informative writing most of what you say isn't a matter of opinion, and your relationship to the audience is different from what it is in writing an argument. For example, when you argue, you're trying to talk your reader into giving up her opinion and accepting yours, and she doesn't want to go along, but in informative writing the reader grants that she needs what you're offering—a musician who wants to record a song on Garageband doesn't need much persuading to convince him that he should learn to use the program's tools. Aaron Kenedi's chicken-slaughtering experience, below, could easily have been turned into an argument—perhaps making the case that Americans have lost touch with the eternal verities like birth and death and need to get their hands bloody once in a while.

Since purposes are independent of content, the same material can be turned into any kind of essay. Aaron wanted to write about his memories of watching his grandmother slaughter chickens, but he couldn't decide if he wanted to focus on his relationship with his grandmother or teach the reader the practical ins and outs of chicken slaughtering. He decided to try two, one personal and the other informative. Both are good. Here's the personal version:

INVITATION TO A BEHEADING

AARON KENEDI

Student Essay

When I was about nine, my grandmother came to visit us on our little farm in California. She was from Freeport, Long Island, and if you couldn't tell by her accent, the way she dressed would have given her away, in pleated polyester slacks and a loud plaid shirt, complete with long red nails and a sprayed coif like plaster of Paris. Thus attired, she turned to me one day and out of the blue said, "Ya neva know when ya might need to kill a chicken" and headed for the hen house. After a moment of reflection I decided she had a point, and so, partly horrified and mostly fascinated, I followed her. The chickens we raised were strictly for eggs, so it was all new to me.

She prepared herself like a Zen master—meditation, deep breathing exercises, and stretching. In her thick Hungarian/New York/Jewish accent, she told me, "Chickens aw de tastiest boid in de land when dey aw fresh. Yaw grandfathah loved de chicken in goulash, paprikash, you name it. Oy, dat he didn't have dose triple and double and God knows how many bypasses. It vas de cigars dat kilt him, lemme tell you …"

"Foist thing you do," she explained, "is get yourself a pair of gloves, an old shirt, a plastic bucket, a shawp ax, and some running shoes. Nikes are de best—dey got dat little swoosh on de side, makes you look fashionable. It's impawtant to always look good." When I asked her why running shoes, she looked at me blankly and said, "You ever tried to catch a chicken dat knows it's about to die?" I stepped aside and let Grandma limber up.

Next she stepped into the chicken coop, looking like some sort of lunatic surgeon—yellow gloves, black boots to her knees, and an apron reading "Party Animal." She propped a cardboard box up on a stick with a string tied to it, handed me the string, and gave chase. She was indefatigable, unyielding. It was a scene out of Monty Python, but it worked, I pulled the string, and finally the chicken clucked nervously under the box.

I brought the chicken over to the chopping block. Grandma felt the edge of the ax blade in her hands. I thought maybe I could see a slight grin on her lips when she declared it "not quite shawp enough" and proceeded to hone it with a stone until it glinted in the sunlight. She took some practice swings, saying, "Ya don't vant to botch de first try. Ya vant clean, quick cut right through de old neck. Nothing woise than a howling chicken." She didn't need to convince me.

She set aside her thick glasses and I held the bird carefully. Summoning all her might, she perfectly separated the head from the body. Before I realized it was dead, the bird got up, flapped its wings as if merely startled, and took off in circles around the wood pile. The blood spurted from its neck in thick streams, and it would convulse with each spurt like some avant garde modern dance student. "Dat's nawmul," Grandma said as she leaned on her ax and wiped her brow. "Dey usually jog around a bit afterward."

After the chicken fell in a heap in front of her, Grandma wound its feet together and hung it on an oak branch to let the rest of the blood drip out. "It's a bit like drip-drying the wash," she told me. "Only you vant to make sure the dogs and cats—or the flies—don't get at it."

We moved the operation into the house, and Grandma changed out of her bloody shirt and into an apron. She dunked the bird in a pot of boiling water, sat down on a stool on the front porch with a big garbage bag next to her, and began pulling out clumps of feathers like she was petting a shedding cat. "De hot water loosens up de hold de quills have on de feathers, just like a chuck key does a drill," she explained. Pointing to the now-naked bird, she said, "Heah's de tricky pawt. You see doze little bristles where de feathehs used to be? Vell, ve don't vant to eat dem. So ve got to singe dem off." And she pulled out a Zippo lighter, flicked it on smoother than any movie gangster, and ran the flame lightly over the skin.

The next step was harder to take. Grandma set the bird on its back on the cutting board, took a cleaver, and hacked the neck off with such force that it flew across the room. Then she put on a rubber glove, gritted her teeth, and stuck her hand down the hole where the neck used to be. It sounded like mushing a banana around in your mouth, which was bad, but the smell was horrendous, like a rotten deer carcass in the woods. She pulled out the heart, giblets, and liver and showed them to me like a Mayan priest at a sacrifice. Next came the gizzard. "Chickens swallow all sawts of crap," Grandma explained excitedly. "You never know vat you'll find in a gizzard. Once yaw great grandmother found a gold ring." We tore it open and there before our eyes were some roofing nails my dad had used to build the chicken coop, one of my Matchbox cars, and a penny.

I wanted Grandma to cut off the feet, but she insisted they were delicious to "suck on." "Now ve boil the whole damn thing and make soup—make the best chicken soup you've ever had," she said. "And tomorrow I'll show you how to make a zip gun."

—Permission granted by Steve Metzger

Here's the informative version:

YOUR FIRST KILL

AARON KENEDI

Student Essay

Foster Farms no longer raises chickens. Instead, they raise large-breasted mutants so juiced on hormones they make Hulk Hogan seem normal. Armour raises its poultry in an environment so unspeakably inhumane that it makes you ashamed to be a human being when you hear about it.

You probably know all this—that's why you've decided to raise your own chickens. You're willing to do the work it takes to eat meat that's tastier, cheaper, healthier, and easier on your karma. But chickens don't come chopped up and packaged, so eventually (around the time of the summer's first barbecue) you're going to have to butcher a chicken yourself. Here's how. The method you're about to read is my grandma's, so you can rest assured it's quick and safe.

The first thing you need to know is that, unless you get emotionally attached easily, it will be easier to kill chickens than you think. Chickens aren't cuddly or adorable, and they aren't loyal—they'd do the same to you if the roles were reversed. And they can't cluck, poop, or peck when they're dead.

Roosters are okay to eat, but hens are better, because they're plumper and you'll have more of them in the coop. But before you grab your least favorite and start whacking, do some things first. Dress in old clothes you can throw away, because killing a chicken is about as dirty a job as it sounds. Wear comfortable shoes, preferably running shoes, because a chicken that senses doom is as difficult to catch as an Elvis concert. Consider laying a trap: Tie a string to a stick, use the stick to prop up a box, and chase the chicken until she chances to pass under—then pull the string.

Now comes the icky part. You can do it two ways: Either swiftly and violently twist the bird's neck until it snaps, or sharpen your trusty ax, have a friend hold the little bugger on a chopping block, and unleash a mighty whack on the bird's neck. Cut cleanly the first time, because a half-beheaded chicken makes a sound you've never heard before and will never want to hear again. Snapping is cleaner, but it takes some strength. Axing is easier, but the bird will run around for a few minutes. It's a shock at first to see a headless bird sit up and start jogging, blood spurting out of its neck causing it to shake and convulse, but you have to drain the blood anyway, so this method kills two birds with one stone (sorry).

After the chicken has exhausted itself, tie its feet together and hang it on a branch or clothesline over a bucket to let the remaining blood drip out—about two hours. Don't let dogs, cats, or flies get at it. Meanwhile, boil a large pot of water, prepare some table space, and sharpen your cleaver or largest knife. Put the carcass in the boiling water for about one minute *only*. This will loosen the quills and make picking the bird much easier. Pull out all the feathers, containing them immediately, while they're still wet, in a large trash bag or something similar.

Now you have a naked bird covered with little bristles where the feathers used to be. You can't eat them—it's like eating the rough side of those two-sided kitchen sponges—so you must burn them off. Light a gas burner or a cigarette lighter and, without cooking the chicken, carefully singe off each bristle. It's the most time-consuming step in the process, but it's essential for your gastronomic well-being.

Your chicken now looks a lot like the thing you buy in Safeway. Except on the inside. Now comes the other icky part. If you opted for the snapping method earlier, you first must chop off the head where the neck meets the body. You can also cut off the feet at this point, though Grandma swears they're the tastiest part. Now put on a rubber glove, take a cleansing breath, stick your hand down the hole where the neck used to be, and pull everything out. It's gross, it's messy, it smells like death, you'll feel like a brute, but it must be done. An alternative is to take your knife and split the carcass from the butt to the collar and pry the breast apart with your hands. This method is cleaner because you don't have to grab and squeeze any entrails, but the smell is just as bad. Once laid open, the inside of a chicken is practically designed for disemboweling—just remove everything. Throw the organs away like I do, or fry them up and eat them like Grandma does. The small thing that looks like a Hacky Sack footbag is the gizzard, where the chicken grinds to dust what she eats. If you're curious, cut it open and see what the chicken's been eating. Grandma insists her mother once found a gold ring in one.

Now rinse the bird under cold water and decide how to cook it. Chop it into pieces (that's another essay) and prepare a nice Kiev or marsala sauce, or plop it whole into a large pot, add vegetables, and make the tastiest, cheapest, healthiest chicken soup you've ever had. Grandma would be so proud.

—Permission granted by Steve Metzger

THE THREE CHALLENGES

How-to writing offers the writer three challenges: (1) we don't feel knowledgeable enough, (2) it's boring, and (3) something called the COIK problem is ever-present. Let's find ways to deal with each.

You Don't Feel Knowledgeable Enough

It feels fraudulent to set yourself up as the expert. This is entirely a problem of audience definition. You are the instructor the moment you're talking to people who know less than you do. If you know how to play Words With Friends or how to serve a tennis ball and the reader doesn't, you have knowledge she wants.

You've been learning all your life. And for everything you've learned, there's someone who doesn't know it and would profit from learning it. If you've been in Mrs. Mercer's twelfth-grade English class at Holy Name High School, there's someone coming into the class for the first time who doesn't know how the class works and who could benefit from your expertise. If you watch hockey on TV, there's someone who doesn't and who would benefit if you explain what he's seeing.

To make sure you and your reader know your respective roles, lay them out in paragraph 1. Tell the reader up front that you know something she doesn't know and that she will profit from knowing it:

OK, so your boyfriend dumped you. If your relationship was anything like mine, you probably feel like the lowest, most good-for-nothing human being on earth. Well, I'm here to tell you that you can and will survive your breakup. Here are some things you can do to speed your recovery.

Is there central heating and air? Does the place have a dishwasher? Is the rent reasonable? Of course they're important considerations. But when looking for a place to rent, in our obsession with the inanimate, we often overlook one of the most important questions: what's the landlord like? If you're looking to rent, you should be asking yourself some key questions about your potential landlord.

Warm Up with a Mock-informative Essay.   If the role of teacher feels awkward, warm up by doing a teacher *parody*. Write a *mock-informative essay,* a send-up of informative essays where you take something dead simple (or silly)—chewing gum or putting toothpaste on a toothbrush—and pretend it's as complicated as building a space station. Here are two wonderful examples. The first, by Oscar Villon, a professional journalist, is a hilarious look at thumb wrestling, of all things, that along the way manages to take some jabs at the sport of boxing. Note how Villon uses subheads, which can be very useful in informative writing. The second, by Isabelle Wattenberg, offers tongue-in-cheek advice for taking care of fish, but read between the lines and you'll see that there's more going on than just that. (Compare it to Megan Sprowls' "The Do's and Don'ts..." on p. 342 and Laura Kate James' "How to Be Younger" on p. 352.)

THE SEMI-SWEET SCIENCE: ONE, TWO, THREE, FOUR. I DECLARE ...

OSCAR VILLALON

This happened to me some years ago.

I was in a deli in the East Village. Behind the counter was this plump, short guy with a little mustache, wearing a white butcher's coat. He calls out my number. I lean over the counter and hand him my paper ticket. As he takes it from me, he says, casually, "Nice hams."

I thought I misheard him, so I gave him an "excuse me?" look. He then holds up his mitts, his palms out toward me. He tilts back and moves his hands up and down for me, like a stumpy T-Rex. "Nice hams," he said. "You know?" No, I didn't know. He then pinched his fat palm. "Your thumbs, brother. They got thick hams." I had nothing to say to that.

Later, eating my hot pastrami sandwich, holding the greasy thing away from me between bites, I couldn't help but study what he called my "hams." He was right. That knotty bulb of muscle anchoring my thumbs looked ... tough. Pronounced, even, like the calves of a bodybuilder. I guess you could call them nice, but so what?

But physical gifts account for only a fraction of my or anybody else's success in competitive sports. Dedication and technique must be part of the mix, too, for mastery of the semi-sweet science of thumb wrestling. The allusion to boxing isn't frivolous. Many of the techniques that make boxing "sweet," that is, those things I'm guessing make it sweet, in an ironical way, are prominent in thumb wrestling, which, in truth, should be called thumb boxing. However, thumb boxing conjures the unfortunate image of fighters throwing very awkward punches, followed by the even more unfortunate image of a roundhouse connecting to an opponent's forehead and a thumb snapping off. So thumb wrestling it is.

The Approach: Cocked Like the Hammer of a Colt

There's a reason why people shake hands, and it's not merely because it's a cheap, if rather work-intensive, means of waging germ warfare. It's because you can size up a person in a way that the eye simply can't. Is this person confident? Equivocal? Sick? Granted, you should be able to tell all these things by sight. But what if your eyesight isn't so hot? Then you have a problem. But the truth can't ever hide when skin touches skin.

How you grip your opponent's fingers at the incipiency of the match can set the tone for the battle ahead. It's all about gaining a psychological edge.

First, be sure to grip your opponent's fingers firmly, but take care not to dig your nails into his joints. That signals nervousness on your part, or lack of feeling in your extremities. Either one is bad. Remember: The vibe you want to send is, "I'm no stranger to these parts." Not, "I think I'm having a heart attack."

Second, be sure to keep your thumb ramrod straight, but do make it sizzle a little, like a live wire waiting for a wet foot to step on it. By that I mean let it pulse side to side a couple of times so it gives your opponent something to think about, thus throwing him off his game.

The Haka

New Zealand is home to two great and proud peoples: Crowded House fans and the Maori. The Maori were fierce warriors, much more so than any of the lineage connected to the Finn brothers, and their martial traditions have been incorporated into that antipodean nation's general culture. The rite of facial tattooing didn't really take hold, unfortunately, but performing the war chant of the haka did.

Before rugby matches, soccer games, and possibly even bridge tournaments, teams will greet each other with ritualized dance and ancient song, expressing respect for an opponent along with an unreconciled need to terrorize them before a match.

Thumb wrestling, too, has its haka, and it's as necessary to the competition as, say, hands. Its beauty is its simplicity: "One, two, three, four. I declare a thumb war!" Remember, savor this ritual and use the time it takes to execute the chant to assess your opponent's thumb strength, mental focus, and sense of rhythm.

The Attack: Establish the Jab

Passivity has never won the day in thumb wrestling. Only an onslaught of aggression has ever meant a damn to the sport, and the fuse that lights the touch hole that sets off that cannon of flying fingers is the jab. Remember, as soon the haka is over, you must keep your thumb busy, preferably by attacking your opponent's thumb. Don't try to go for the one-hitter-no-quitter. Instead, keep your opponent off guard by going to his thumb continuously. Keep at him and you'll find out if he's the kind who just curls up and dies or if he's got fight and jabs you right back.

The Volley

If your opponent has got heart, that means you'll have to keep jabbing. This is called the volley, just like in tennis, and this is good. Just like tennis, if there isn't a volley going on, then nobody's going to watch the game. This brings us to a dirty secret about thumb wrestling: It's not only a sport, but it's also entertainment, and you have got to put on a show for the crowd. Even if you know you can take out an opponent in the bat of an eyelash, toy with him. Do it for the children, if you must.

Don't Believe Your Eyes

When you're in a fight, do you spend the entire brawl looking at your fists, trailing them with your eyes to see where they will land? No, you do not, unless you're very drunk or are fighting with boxing gloves 10 times too big for your hands. The same applies to thumb wrestling. Don't be one of those people who look down at what I like to call "the arena of flesh," mesmerized by the speed of their opponent's thumb, trying to keep apace, all slack-jawed and drooling. Instead, look your opponent straight in the eye and jab away. You can do it. This is the closest mortals like us living in the Milky Way are ever going to come to using the Force. Don't be afraid. Turn off your brain. Be the Yoda. Remember, every victory worth attaining should be a no-looker.

The Take Down: Give 'em a Nail for Knuckle

So the fight has been going your way. Your opponent has no answer for your jab. Your reflexes are such that he's afraid to go for you lest he get pinned. Your eyes are watering from drilling your stare into him, and the children are nodding their approval at each other. It's time to put him away.

Here's one way: Trade him your nail for his pride.

A rank rookie mistake made in thumb wrestling is trying to pin an opponent by his thumbnail. That's never going to work unless you have a little bit of stickum on the pad of your thumb, which is illegal in North America but fine in Southeast Asia, where they like to mix things up a bit. Your thumbnail is nature's linoleum, which means it's slick most times, but after 15 seconds of sweaty tangling, it is positively margarine-like.

First, hesitate for just a second, and let your exhausted, deluded opponent think he's worn you down and triumphed. Second, in a wolverine's heartbeat, you slide your thumb right out from under him and thunk it on either the first or second knuckle of his thumb. I prefer landing on the second knuckle; that way if he's strong enough to resist, your thumb will slide down on the first knuckle. By then the ref will have counted to three, and that's that.

Playing Possum

But what if your opponent is smart, or crafty, even? What if he doesn't go for the nail? Then you go to Plan B. It is, however, risky. This strategy follows the boxing axiom of "taking leather to give leather." Willfully ignoring the S&M subtext,

I take it to mean that you sometimes have to lay it on the line if you want to win. So if you can't beat the opponent outright, if his skills demand respect, then you're going to have to offer up your very flesh for bait. This works just like the nail trick, but the potential for backfire is high. You must have the speed and strength to pull out from under a solid pin and turn the tables on your opponent. It's a moment of truth for all thumb wrestlers. It's what separates the wannabes from the champions.

Gut It Out

So what happens if you try both of those and no pin?

What if, instead, you and your opponent are going back and forth, attacking and counterattacking, the tendons in your forearms swelling, the sweat coming down over your faces like a sacred scrim, the air slowly leaking out of the room, and a vision swirls into form in your mind's eye, and you see the girl you loved when you were in the second grade, waving to you from the top of the slide, the airy tinkle of the ice cream man's truck reverberating in your skull, the music coming from afar?

Then, my friend, you have stepped into the zone the ancient Greeks thought could be occupied only by the gods. This is your chance at glory, and for you to seize it, you must will it toward you. Iffy officiating and a partial judge have been known to be factors. But still, you must have the will to win, because it's that cussedness, along with a reputation for awful impulse control, which may intimidate the judge into steering the stalemate your way.

—Villalon, Oscar, "The Semi-Sweet Science," SAN FRANCISCO CHRONICLE, p. D-1, December 3, 2006

Oscar Villalon is a San Francisco writer, editor, publisher, and thumb wrestler.

HOW TO FEED A FISH

ISABELLE WATTENBERG

Student Essay

Find a respectable pet store. Do not agree to take care of your friend's fish while she's vacationing in Sydney and realize three years later that you still have it. Before getting the fish, get the tank or bowl, and set it up with rocks and aquatic plants, letting the nitrified bacteria grow in the gravel that costs three seventy-nine a pound. Or forget the gravel and leave the aquatic plants to gasp for sustenance, growing frail and bitter because you forgot the only thing they really needed. Go ahead and buy the fish, so that at least one of the entities floating around in the tank is alive. Promise yourself you will not forget to do anything else.

Take four months to get used to the fish. By then, you will automatically greet the fish when you return from work. You will speak to it about deep philosophical matters, you will complain to it about your coworkers, and you will receive a look, in the small beady eyes of the creature, that says, *I understand, and I want to know more about you. Because you are someone who has ideas, and while I may only be a fish, you can tell me these things, because my gills filter out untruths, and so I will hear what you mean to say regardless of how you say it.* But because the fish does not say these things and instead only looks at you, you are never quite sure if it truly feels that way. So sometimes when you come home, you focus solely on the fish and ask how its day went and if the tank is clean enough for it. Regardless of its response, scrub at the walls with an algae pad.

Begin to notice that the fish's answers are short and disinterested. Ask fewer questions. In time, begin to wonder if the fish really likes you at all. Become more reserved, because you are afraid the fish will mock your feelings. Ignore it for a few days until you feel lonely enough to sit and stare at it a while, even though it swims away. Give it five dollars and some homemade cookies in an attempt to win its affection. Become confused when the fish sometimes accepts its food agreeably, and sometimes sullenly, opening and closing its mouth without really saying anything at all. Become angry; ask yourself why you put up with this when you are sure other fish would recognize your talent and your kindness. Begin to wonder if you really are kind at all.

Buy another fish. This one swims up eagerly, too eagerly. Become disinterested, simply because it likes you so much. Occasionally acknowledge and appreciate its dark orange scales and similar taste in movies, but forget again when your other fish swims up. Wonder why you don't like this new fish, since it seems to enjoy watching you siphon debris from the tank floor and greets you when you return, bobbing up and down in its pale home. Wonder why, when you arrive home, you always search for the other fish, the fish who rarely emerges from its slimy stone castle. A castle you bought for it, ages ago. Wonder why you didn't buy a castle for the new fish.

Feed the old fish less. When you do feed it, overturn the carton and let its contents fall out in a large clump as you walk away. You used to be careful, strategically placing flakes about the tank in the hopes that the fish would appear and begin nibbling not out of necessity, but in order to be with you. And when you left the tank, you used to feel a sense of self, having given something to the fish, but received something as well. Now, realize that feeding it takes up time and that the fish rarely seems to care whether or not the small flakes break the surface and dangle below its flat nose. Notice that your words to the fish, void of weight, float away to rest beneath a liverwort plant, and that the fish seems more interested in the ripples formed by the food, chasing them as they broaden and broaden until they break against the side of the tank. Stop looking it in the eye because you are not sure if its eyes are open or closed, their opaque lids a mirage that invites you to talk to thin air. Keep feeding it less until you feed it nothing at all, don't even glance at the tank as you return home from a day that appears to be getting fuller and fuller, though you are not sure why since you have freed up the time usually spent with the fish. Time not even spent in company with the new fish, who would offer to fill the void, if only you asked. Ignore both fish, though you watch the old one from the corner of the room, wondering what its gills are detecting.

Return home one day to find it belly-up. Break down into sobs because, even though it was only a fish, you knew that a small child could have kept it alive. Wonder why you ended up incapable of keeping the fish alive when, you are pretty sure, you loved it. Concede that perhaps it was the secret nature of your love that let the fish slip away, because you hid your feelings and, perhaps, if you had openly offered your affection, the message might have resonated enough for the fish to hear through the watery walls and agree to stay alive. Know that the pain of the fish's death is worse for it than for yourself. Secretly ask if this is true. Come to terms not with the death but with the acknowledgement that you chose this ending.

—Permission provided by Isabelle Wattenberg

Mock-informative essays are great fun, but they're good only as ice-breakers, because they dodge the teaching challenge. The joke lies in making simple (or silly) things difficult (or serious), which is the opposite of what good informative writing tries to do.

It's Boring

While informative writing might sometimes lack the emotional wallop of a personal essay or the intellectual drama of an argument, it has its own distinct advantage: ostensibly anyway, the reader *wants* the information. That is, she's not likely to put down the instructions for setting her new atomic clock because the *writing* isn't riveting—she'd do so only if it's unclear.

That's not to say you should write lifeless prose, letting the subject itself do all the work—and forget that your reader is a living human being who wants to read the words of another living human being. On the contrary: you want your informative writing to be lively, specific, distinct, even humorous, if appropriate. Keep in mind, however, you don't want the writing to take center stage, to take the attention from your subject.

Sometimes, on the other hand, you can have fun with the writing itself (like Villon did in his pieces), using it to draw attention to your subject.

COIK Is a Constant Problem

Surely you've noticed the Idiot's Guide series. Bookstores are packed with them: *The Idiot's Guide to Starting a Rock Band, The Idiot's Guide to Learning Italian, The Idiot's Guide to Creating a Web Page, The Idiot's Guide to Buying and Selling a Home.*

Of course, they're not for idiots at all, just for people who don't know much about that particular topic. What the books' writers do, generally, is take knowledge and language that are known to a specialized group and make them accessible to a broader audience. And that's more difficult than it seems it would be, because of a little problem called COIK, which stands for "Clear Only If Known."

COIK writing can be understood only if you already understand it before you read it. Almost all the informative writing you see is COIK writing. You can't understand the auto manual unless you already understand auto repair; you can't understand the book on home wiring unless you already know how to do home wiring; you can't understand the chemistry text unless you're a chemist.

COIK problems are inherent in the way informative writing is made. You, the writer, know the information already—otherwise, you can't teach it. But because you know it, you can't remember what it's like to not know it. So you talk to the reader as if she already knows what you have to teach. Here's an extreme example of COIK, part of some instructions for adjusting a carburetor, from a GMC-truck repair manual (published by Chilton Book Company):

Intermediate Choke Rod

1. Remove the thermostatic cover coil, gasket, and inside baffle plate.
2. Place the idle screw on the high step of the fast idle cam.
3. Close the choke valve by pushing up on the intermediate choke lever.
4. The edge of the choke lever inside the choke housing must align with the edge of the plug gauge.
5. Bend the intermediate choke lever to adjust.
6. Replace the cover and set as in the following adjustment.

What? Was that English? To a mechanic, or someone who's worked on cars a lot, absolutely. But to most of us, these instructions are, well, baffling. They're "clear only if (the terms are) known." And for that reason, they work. The book is intended for mechanics, not you and me.

So how do you avoid COIK problems? Here are four suggestions:

Realize that COIK Problems Are Inevitable, so you must maintain constant vigilance against them.

Define Your Audience's Level of Expertise Precisely, and keep it ever in mind. Constantly ask yourself, "Will my audience understand this?" "What have I assumed they know, and am I right to assume it?" Hear them asking you questions like "What does that mean?" and "How exactly do I do that?"

Get Yourself Some Real Readers. Spotting COIK problems is hard for you but easy for them. Ask them to tell you where they're confused or what they were left wanting to know.

Finally, Remember that It's Usually Better to Explain Too Much than Too Little. At the risk of talking down to your reader, if you're unsure about his level of expertise, give him more information than he might need instead of taking the chance that he won't understand something. If he already knows that a specific step should be taken next, for example, or knows the definition of a term, he can skip ahead, but if he doesn't, he's in trouble.

EIGHT TEACHING TIPS

Now that you feel like an instructor, here are eight teaching techniques that help people learn.

1. **Give an overview.** An overview is a summary, a simple map of the territory you're about to traverse. If I'm going to take you through the thirty steps of a tricky recipe, you'll appreciate knowing that overall you're going to

a.   make the stuffing,
b.   stuff the meat,

c.   make the sauce, and

d.   bake the meat in the sauce.

Overviews often use lists: "First, ... second, ... third ..."; "There are three things you must do ..." The typical overview is one sentence long, so it's in essence a thesis sentence. Here's an overview of "How to Audition for a Play":

> Scoring at the audition comes down to four things: knowing what you're getting into, doing a little homework beforehand, dressing the part, and acting confident when you're on.

Overviews are most helpful when they come early in the essay. Overviews as conclusions usually are too late to be of much use.

2. **Give examples.** No generalization or abstraction ever existed that isn't easier to understand with a following "for instance." Here's an abstract definition:

> A thesaurus, like a dictionary, is arranged alphabetically, but instead of definitions it lists words that are synonyms or antonyms of your source word. It offers alternatives to words you feel are used too often, are too bland, are not descriptive enough, or contain connotations that do not apply.

That would have been COIK writing if the writer hadn't gone on to give an example:

> For instance, let's say you're writing about the desert and you realize you've used the word "hot" nine hundred and thirty-two times. Look up "hot" in the thesaurus and it will give you a list of similar adjectives: parching, toasting, simmering, scalding, scorching, and blazing.

If you need a crutch, force yourself to write *for example* and *for instance* a lot, but keep in mind that readers don't need these links and they can usually be cut out in the rewrite.

3. **Use analogies.** An analogy says that X is like Y: writing is like playing tennis in the dark; style is like the clothing your essay is wearing; cannelloni are like Italian enchiladas. Analogies are great instructors because they make what the reader is trying to learn familiar by translating it into terms she already understands. Here's an analogy for how to breathe while singing:

> To use the diaphragm correctly, you must imagine your midsection is being pumped up like a tire.

Most analogies use the words "like," "as," or "as if," but not always: "Imagine that your diaphragm is a tire being pumped up." "Cannelloni are Italian enchiladas."

4. **Tell the reader what not to do as well as what to do.** Warn the reader away from common errors he's likely to make. List the five most popular

ways to screw up, and tell the reader not to do them. Among the best examples of this are the recipes in *Cook's Illustrated* magazine. While some recipes include only what *to do, Cook's Illustrated* goes to great lengths to tell its readers what can possibly go wrong. In fact, the recipes are often parts of narratives in which the writers themselves admit to botching dishes by not preheating the oven or by using the wrong kind of beans.

5. **Tell the reader why.** For several years, I lived and worked at Lake Tahoe, where it gets very cold in the winter. When people would come to visit me, I'd always tell them not to set their cars' parking brakes at night, and they'd look at me like I was crazy. But when I added "because you're likely to get moisture on the cable, which will freeze, and then you won't be able to release the brake in the morning," they always followed my advice.

To force yourself to say why, write "because" after every instruction, and go on to explain.

6. **Use illustrations.** Informative writing frequently calls for illustrations—charts, tables, graphs, drawings, and photos. If you're describing things you can see—how to tie a clove hitch, how rainfall is annually distributed over certain areas—your writing will be much more effective if you include an appropriate graphic. Food writers, travel writers, technical writers, and other professionals all know the value of illustrations and use them freely, but for some reason, students think using them is cheating. It's not. It's smart.

It's also easy. Not only is there almost an infinite number of illustrations that you can download to use in your own writing (as always, be sure to document your sources), but most computers come with programs that will help you convert your data into tables. A good example is Microsoft Excel Chart, which you can open directly from a Word document. In fact, with the click of a mouse you can view material that you have gathered in different forms—as a line graph, bar graph, table, pie chart, and so forth.

7. **Use imperatives.** Imperatives are commands: "Do this!" "Don't do that!" Shy writers find imperatives pushy, so they avoid them with passives and other roundabout ways of saying things. Don't:

The plugs should be tightened. → *Tighten the plugs.*

A deep mixing bowl and a pair of chopsticks are needed for mixing. → *Get a deep mixing bowl and a pair of chopsticks for mixing.*

8. **Seek to persuade.** Informative writing is almost defined by its lack of persuasive purpose—what's persuasive about how to change your spark plugs?—but we always write better if we're trying to convince. It takes only a slight twist to recast a purely informative intent into a persuasive one:

Subject	Thesis
Gardening	A backyard garden will provide you with cheap, healthy food, good exercise, and an opportunity to spend lots of time outdoors.
Choosing a landlord	Picking a landlord may be the most important part of renting an apartment.

SEEING THE MODE

A bar graph is an excellent way to present to readers material you want them to compare. Figure 13.1 is a single-bar graph—for West Side Unified School District. While the writer conveyed this same information in the text of a grant (where the writers provided the actual numbers), she wanted readers to be able to see the percentages at a glance.

Note: She could have also easily shown other comparisons—gender, ethnicity, income, geographical location of family homes—in a multiple-bar graph. If, for example, there were a difference in the numbers of boys and girls qualifying for free or reduced lunches, she could have indicated that with a second bar, colored or shaded differently, at each school year.

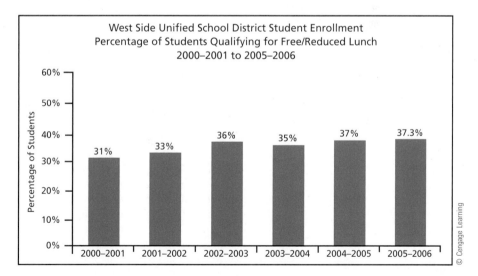

FIGURE 13.1   Single-bar graph—for West Side Unified School District

WRITER'S WORKSHOP

Informative Strategies—Action

Let's read through an informative essay and note when and where many of the teaching tips are used. I've marked such places with numbers and labeled each in the right margin.

HOW TO AUDITION FOR A PLAY

STEVE WIECKING

Student Essay

You're standing in the center of a room. Dozens of people surround you, watching intently your every move. You are told what to do and you do it. Sound like the Inquisition? It isn't, but some might call it a close relative: the audition.

Every few months of every year your college's drama department offers every student the chance to audition for a part in a

1. Persuasive purpose

stage production. (1) As a theater arts minor who was cast with no acting experience in a one-act play last October, I can tell you that auditioning for a play is a truly horrifying, but ultimately rewarding experience. Who wouldn't want to show their stuff up there behind the footlights? Auditioning is open to anyone, and the best way to go about it is to prepare thoroughly and go into it with a feeling of confidence.

2. Analogy

3. Overview

(2) Just as if you were going to a job interview at your local Burger King, (3) you have to know some practical information before an audition. First, what kind of an audition are you going to? If the audition announcement calls for a "cold reading," you're in for performing any given scene from the play unprepared. Well, almost un-prepared—there is

4. Imperative

some accepted cheating. (4) Go to your main library or the Drama Department's script

5. Example

library and check out the play. (5) Find out what that Macbeth guy is up to or what's bug-

6. What not to do

ging Hamlet. (6) Don't try to memorize; just be happy with the head start you'll have on the material because you know what's going on.

7. *Imperative*

8. *Imperative*

9. *Example*

10. *What not to do*
11. *Why*
12. *Analogy*
13. *What not to do*
14. *Why*

15. *Example*
16. *Why*
17. *What not to do*

18. *Example*

19. *Overview*

20. *Imperative*

21. *What not to do*
22. *Why*

Instead of a cold reading try-out, you could be going to one that calls for a monologue. (7) In that case, prepare, *memorize,* a two- to three-minute scene of a single character speaking from any play of your choice (unless instructed otherwise). This requires some hopefully obvious rules. (8) Choose a character that suits you. Be as realistic as possible concerning age, sex, and situation. (9) Freshman girls not yet over the trials of acne should not attempt the death throes of Shakespeare's King Lear. (10) Avoid overdone roles like Romeo or Juliet— (11) to the directors, these have become (12) like hearing "Hello, Dolly" sung without cease. (13) And above all avoid Hamlet. (14) Each director has his own idea of what he wants Hamlet "to be or not to be," and it usually comes in the form of Sir Laurence Olivier— stiff competition at its worst.

Once you know where you're going and what to expect, the proper clothing is necessary. Dress subtly and comfortably in something adaptable (15) like jeans and tennis shoes. (16) You have to be able to move well, and (17) you don't want to be so flashy and singular that the casting director sees only a paisley tie or psychedelic tights instead of a possible character. (18) I recently watched a girl audition in a red, white, and blue sailor suit with spiked heels. If the directors had been casting "Barnacle Bill Does Bloomingdale's" she would have been a shoo-in, but otherwise it was man overboard time on the Titanic.

(19) Once prepared, at the audition nothing is more important than confidence. Present yourself well. (20) Eye the surroundings as if to say you know where you are and have control of the room, and greet the directors pleasantly to show them you want to be there. Handed an unfamiliar script? Make a quick choice as to what you're going to do and stick with it. (21) *Don't glue your eyes to the script.* (22) I guarantee no one has ever been cast for having a wonderful relationship with a Xerox copy. When your turn is over, exit graciously with a smile and a "thank you" that let people know the chance was appreciated.

Of course, this all sounds easier than it really is, and you may say that I've left out one key requirement: talent. But talent you either have or you don't, and if you've seen many college drama productions you'll know that it isn't exactly a huge prerequisite after all.

Now It's Your Turn.   Do to an informative draft of your own what we did to Steve's essay: identify in the margins any places that do any of the eight teaching tips we've looked at. If there are any of the eight the draft hasn't done (and you should do most of them more than once), rewrite, adding passages that do them.

—Permission provided by Steve Metzger

EXERCISES

1. Read back through "The Semi-Sweet Science" and "How to Feed a Fish" identifying as many of the teaching tips as you can. List any that the essays don't use.

2. Write a one- to two-page mock-informative essay.

3. Prewrite an informative essay by writing a list of every possible question your reader might want answered.

4. Tell the class your informative essay topic, and ask them to generate every possible question they would like answered or other readers might like answered.

5. Using the information from Exercises 3 and 4, write the essay.

6. List all possible questions a reader might have after reading the following restaurant review:

   Carmelita's is a pretty good Mexican restaurant. I recommend it if you like Mexican food. I especially like the carne asada, though it may be a little picante for your taste. The prices are low and the portions are ample. My one complaint is they don't have flan, which is something I really go to Mexican restaurants hoping for.

7. Interview someone in your class—or a roommate, professor, etc.—and write a profile of him or her intended for publication in your school newspaper.

Chapter 14

Writing an Argument, Stage 1: Thinking Critically

With argumentative writing, the basic rule is the same as for all writing: you can't do it if you haven't read a lot of it. So the easiest way to write a good argumentative essay is also the most pleasant: read all the argumentative essays in "A Collection of Good Writing" and write one like them.

WHAT'S AN ARGUMENT?

In an argumentative essay you try to convince people to agree with you. That said, the easiest mistake to make, and the most common—and best way to write an unconvincing argument essay—is to think that you have to "win" the argument. Don't think of it as you do an argument with your parents or roommates—which often end up with both sides getting irrational and neither listening to the other. Instead, think of it as a position you're taking and which you're inviting intelligent people with differing (or neutral) positions to consider—and in fact to join in an ongoing dialogue about the subject.

Keep in mind, too, that an argument isn't just a belief or an opinion, such as "I like Mumford and Sons," because an opinion gives the reader no grounds to agree or disagree, and it doesn't urge the reader to join you. An argument is an opinion with reasons to back it up and intentions to sell itself to others. As soon as you say, "Violence in contemporary films is making our culture more violent, and I'm going to try to get you to agree with me," you've got an argument on your hands.

Nor is an argument a sermon, which preaches to the converted. Its listeners don't need persuading; instead, it *celebrates* a message the audience has already accepted, allowing them to renew their faith by agreeing all over again. Most so-called arguments are sermons in disguise, because they assume the reader grants exactly what they purport to be arguing for. Most arguments against gun control, for instance, assume that gun control equals gun prohibition, that the Constitution guarantees U.S. citizens the right to own handguns, and that citizens' ownership of handguns is a deterrent to crime—exactly those things your reader *doesn't* grant and will have to be convinced of.

If you're in doubt about whether you're writing an argument, reduce it to a thesis statement (Chapter 5) and apply two tests. To avoid merely stating an opinion, use the *Should Test:* does the thesis have the word *should* in it or at least imply it?

> You should buy your groceries at a local market, not at a chain store, because the owner cares about you, and your money stays in town.

> You should go see Steven Spielberg's latest movie—it's marvelous.

To avoid the sermon trap, use the second test, the *Stand-Up Test:* how likely is it that a substantial number of the people in the audience will stand up after you state your thesis and say, "I disagree"? If you can't imagine more than a scattered few doing it, you're preaching. Go find something that will make more people want to stand up and challenge you.

WHERE DO WE SEE ARGUMENTATIVE WRITING?

Newspaper editorials, movie reviews, letters to editors, "open forum" pieces in magazines, positions on political candidates and issues—all, usually, are arguments. Your "personal statement" on your college application was an argument ("Please accept me at your school"), as was the email you wrote to your parents asking for more money for school clothes. (You've very likely written and/or read arguments at ratemyprofessor.com or similar sites, although those entries kind of pretend to be informative writing, don't they?) In short, we see argumentative writing in a wide range of publications and serving a wide range of purposes.

FINDING AN ARGUMENTATIVE PROMPT

Finding an argumentative prompt is easy—arguments seek you out every minute of every day. You're being handed a prompt for an argument every time you eat in a restaurant and like it (in which case you can argue that other people should eat there) or don't (in which case you can argue that other people shouldn't); a teacher or the university frustrates you or betrays you or treats you shabbily (in which case you can argue that something should be done so you and other students don't have to suffer like that anymore); you notice as you walk around campus that students seem to hang out in ethnic groups (in which case you could argue that even though we like to think of the United States as a melting pot, where diversity is celebrated, in reality Americans are not comfortable with people unlike themselves); you spend a semester in your school's study-abroad program, have a great experience, and try to convince friends and roommates to consider signing up.

That is, the world is constantly presenting us with evidence that Things Aren't the Way They Should Be, or at least that Things Could Be Improved, and we should feel moved to try to Fix the Problem by arguing those who Don't See It into doing what We Think They Should Do About it.

THINKING CRITICALLY VERSUS SELLING THE CASE

Let's assume you've found your argument. The work that remains can be divided into two stages. Stage 1 (this chapter) is thinking it through—thinking critically to reason your way to a position you firmly believe in and that really holds water. Stage 2 (Chapter 15) is selling the case, where you take the thought-through position and find ways to sell it to your audience.

The main problem people have making arguments is trying to argue and think at the same time. You must think before you argue, because if you try to do the two together, the second poisons the first. Seeking the truth is a process of exploration, risk taking, and discovery. It requires openness and a willingness to look stupid and fail a lot. Convincing others is about selling and winning. People trying to sell and win stop their ears to everything that doesn't strengthen their position. If you're selling a car, any sense of the car's weaknesses makes you a weaker salesperson, so you convince yourself that the car is a treasure. Most people, however much they tell themselves they're thinking, are in fact selling an idea to themselves, shouting down all thoughts that threaten to complicate the initial close-minded position. Here's an example: you've decided you need a new computer, and you're going to do some research, and read and listen to all the arguments for and against different models and brands. Of course, you've already pretty much decided on that MacDell x-2000, although you might not actually admit it to yourself. So you do all your researching and thinking and then—incredibly!—it seems like the MacDell is the logical choice.

WHY THINKING IS HARD

We can't think well until we understand the obstacles in our way. Thinking seems to be an extremely difficult act, judging by the small number of people you and I know who do it well. How many friends do you have who impress you by how well they reason? I rest my case.

But thinking isn't hard the way juggling is hard. It's simply that we don't *want* to think, for a number of reasons, which we might as well face:

1. **Thinking is unemotional:** emotions blind us to reason. Since we are at the core emotional creatures, forsaking our emotions feels like forsaking our

very selves. In science fiction, humans are defined by their emotionality, and the alien races are always scientific, sterile, and unfeeling. *Star Trek*'s Mr. Spock is lovable only because despite all his talk about hating feelings and being glad he doesn't have any, we always know he has them and that's what makes him (part) human. Most of us are devoting our lives to learning to honor our feelings better and getting others to respect them, so telling our emotions to take a hike feels like a step backward.

2. **Thinking is impersonal and objective:** objectivity means that what's true for me is true for you. Though it's easy to give lip service to that idea, we all know it isn't so. You and I are fundamentally different—I'm me and you're not. If you're late, you should apologize; if I'm late, you should learn to be less rigid. Critical thinking says we don't get to be the center of the universe anymore.

3. **Thinking is consistent:** what's right and true now is right and true tomorrow and the day after, and what's right and true in one situation is right and true in another. Thus if Country X can invade Country Y because Country Y has the potential to make weapons of mass destruction, then any country can invade any other country that has that potential, at any time. If one president should be impeached for lying, any president who lies should be impeached. We hate having to embrace consistency. We want to use whatever "rules" prove the case we want to prove at a particular moment, but we don't want to have to live by those rules when they don't get us our way. Thus a political party out of power uses underhanded tactics to block the political appointments of the party in power, then complains when the tables are turned and the other party, now out of power, does exactly the same thing. Not fair! What's sauce for the goose is sauce for the gander, as the old folks used to say.

4. **Thinking is debilitating:** it makes us weaker in a fight. Anyone who tells you that critical thinking will make you a winner is mistaken. Just look at U.S. politics—does the better thinker win the election? No, the election is won by the person with the warmest speaking style or the best haircut or the catchiest slogan. Reagan was one of the most popular presidents in history, and not even his staunchest fans claim he was a thinker. Any politician who makes the mistake of actually *reasoning* in a public debate watches her ratings plummet. (Incredibly, some of Obama's opponents claimed that he's actually *too* smart, and that that was reason to vote against him—"We don't want some elite academic; we want one of *us*.") And no scientist or academician ever won an election without disguising his background. (Obama's a legal scholar but emphasizes his love of basketball and drinkin' a cold one with the guys...) That's because people are persuaded by emotions and affect. Critical thinking (CT) strikes them as cold and clinical—inhuman, in short. Persuading is selling, and the best sellers, used-car salespeople, don't use logic.

So if you want power over others, the ability to manipulate them or control them, critical thinking isn't your friend. As you are about to crush your opponent with the killer argument, CT will rear its ugly head to remind you that you're being inconsistent and subjective.

So why put effort into thinking? Because life isn't always a battle for power or control. Because you want to know who you are and what's going on in your head. Life is about gaining self-knowledge. Your thinking is a huge part of who you are. Thinking badly is like shooting baskets badly in your driveway by yourself—there's no worldly penalty, but it's a crime against a universal rule: do things well.

These four principles come down to one fact: thinking demands a subjugation of the ego. If your ego is weak, you won't want to do this chapter's work. The ego is a good thing, but it isn't the only voice running your life. Do what you must to strengthen your ego; then, when it's strong enough to allow you to think clearly, give it a rest and experience the pleasures of ego-free living. Now you're ready to think. And once you truly *want* to think, I promise that you'll think well if you follow the steps of this chapter. (And no doubt end forever your chances of getting elected president.)

HOW TO THINK: A TEMPLATE

In order to think, you need something to think *about*, so we'll begin by free-writing a draft and reducing the draft to a thesis statement, like we did in Chapter 5. Now we can reduce the amorphous thinking process to three operations to perform on the thesis, in this order:

1. Eliminate language problems in the thesis.
2. Examine the principles and the consequences of the thesis.
3. Perform seven cleanup tasks (I'll explain later).

Eliminating Language Problems

Language problems in the thesis statement are anything in its wording that gets in the way of our thinking. If I say something and mean something else, or say something that can mean lots of different things, or say something that is so negatively worded that it judges the issue before I get a chance to think it through, my reasoning will be fatally corrupted before I begin. Language problems must be corrected before going on to Steps 2 and 3; otherwise, they'll keep reinfecting you, like poison ivy–infected clothing you keep putting on every morning.

We'll break the job of troubleshooting language into two steps:

a. Make a well-formed assertion.
b. Eliminate ambiguous language.

Making a Well-Formed Assertion

Before we start doing hard thinking, we must make sure we've got a thesis we can work with. When we make arguments, it's dangerous to be too bold or too definite, so we make *ill-formed assertions* that take little or no risk.

Behind such remarks lie hinted-at arguments, and we must bring those arguments into the light of day:

> The police in England didn't even carry guns. (What are you implying? That not carrying guns will prevent crime? Or that the English police were fools?)
>
> Almost all of the world's great chefs are men. (What are you implying? That women are inferior to men? Or that women are discriminated against in the restaurant business?)
>
> Skateboarding is not a crime. (What are you implying? That skateboarders should be allowed to do anything they want? Or that skateboarding should be a crime?)

The two most popular ill-formed assertions are *rhetorical questions* and *reasons*.

The *rhetorical question* asks a question and hopes the reader will take the risky step of translating it into an assertion for you:

> Who are you to decide when someone should die? (*Implied assertion:* capital punishment should be stopped, because no one has the right to decide when someone should die.)
>
> Why shouldn't young people be allowed to have a good time and blow off steam once in a while? (*Implied assertion:* the police should stop trying to break up parties, because young people should be allowed to have a good time and blow off steam once in a while.)

To translate a question into an assertion, do one of two things: *answer the question* or *turn it into a declarative sentence*:

> Don't skateboarders have a right to be heard? (*Answer:* skateboarders have a right to be heard.)
>
> If people are so concerned with animal rights, why do they wear leather shoes? (*Declarative sentence:* people who profess to be concerned with animal rights yet wear wooden shoes are hypocrites.)

The *reason* is harder to spot, because it *is* an assertion—it's just not the final assertion. It's an assertion that states a *reason* and lets the reader do the risky work of arriving at the conclusion. It's the "because" clause that follows the unstated thesis. It's a popular ploy in conversation: "Sure, you're a man" means "You don't have any understanding of what women's lives are like and aren't qualified to speak on the subject, *because* you're a man."

Verbal fights are often nothing but a series of reasons without conclusions: "But you said you'd pick me up at 3 p.m.!"; "Well, you forgot to pick me up yesterday!"; "Yeah, well, I got called to a meeting I didn't know about"; "Well, you never even tried to call me." Entire political campaigns have been waged through them: "A woman has a right to choose" is a *because* in defense of the real thesis "Abortion should be legal"; "Skateboarding isn't a crime" is a *because* in defense of the real thesis "Skateboarders should be allowed to skateboard on the sidewalks." And some people use them to avoid making decisions: "Do you want to go to the movies tonight?" gets the response "Well, we haven't been out of the house for a while ..."

To expose a reason posing as a thesis, put the word "because" in front of it and try constructing a "should" clause that can precede it and feels more like *the thing you're really trying to get*:

Step 1: Smokers have rights too.

Step 2: _____ because smokers have rights too.

Step 3: Smoking in bars should be allowed because smokers have rights too.

Eliminating Ambiguous Language

Now that you have a well-formed assertion, ask yourself what it really says. Language is *ambiguous*—most words can have a dozen meanings or more, and when we combine words in sentences the possible meanings multiply. We're wonderfully blind to this; we're always pretty sure we know exactly what we mean—but we're wrong. A student writes:

American children are really spoiled, and the schools are encouraging it.

That seems clear until we think about it for a minute. What does "spoiled" really mean? I could say that a spoiled child is one who has been treated too nicely and thus has come to ask for things he doesn't deserve. But if I think about it I have to ask: How can you be too nice to someone? How does being nice to someone harm him? Some people think it spoils a child to let him cry, listen to his complaints, or give him a voice in how a family or classroom operates. Others consider such things basic human rights and think it's unjust to deny them to children. If "spoiled" means "selfish," isn't everyone selfish—aren't you always doing exactly what you want to do, and isn't that a good thing? And if "spoiled" means "thinking you're something special," isn't it good to think you're special, and aren't you? And how much does a person deserve, and who decided that? If "spoiled" means "never learned you can't have it your own way all the time," well, some people do seem to have it their own way all the time, so are they spoiled?

The more familiar and accepted the assertion, the more likely that your meaning will go unexamined. "TV is mostly garbage" is a statement all of my students grant, but the more you think about it the harder it becomes to say what it really means. How can art or entertainment be "garbage"? Is TV supposed to be doing something and failing? What is "good" art? Is TV garbage because it's stupid (in which case, what's the intellectual level of an hour spent playing basketball or gardening?), or because it's full of ads (in which case, is all selling garbage, or just the highly manipulative selling, or what?), or because it's bad for you (in which case, how can art be good for you?)?

None of this is your fault. Language is inherently cloudy, for at least two reasons. First, *no one teaches you what words mean*—you just figure it out, by hearing others use them. Thus your sense of what a word means is quite literally your own invention, and not surprisingly, other people, who think differently and have different experiences with the word, come to different conclusions. Second, *words' meanings drift through use*. As people use words, they use them in slightly new ways, and those slight meaning shifts, multiplied through millions of uses, mean a word may mean something today it didn't mean last week or last year. There is no way to fix or stop either of these processes, no way to make language unambiguous; you can only work hard at damage control. And there is no step-by-step way to do that, beyond looking hard at language and asking "What does that really mean?" repeatedly. But there are two kinds of cloudy language we can be on the lookout for, loaded language and clichés:

Loaded Language.   Loaded language is language that contains judgment within it—it says "That's good" or "That's bad":

Neutral language	Loaded language
women	babes
attractive	hot
expert	elitist
cops	pigs
southerners	rednecks
sexually active	promiscuous
sexually explicit	pornographic

Like loaded dice, loaded language predetermines the outcome of the thinking process by assigning positive or negative value up front. If I say about a politician, "He conferred with his advisers," I've remained neutral; if I say, "He conferred with his *cronies*," I've damned him as a crook, and if I say, "He conferred with his *henchmen*," I've damned him as a thug.

Fixing loaded language is in theory easy: look for any words that evoke strong "yea" or "nay" responses and replace them with neutral substitutes.

Clichés.   A cliché is a phrase you've heard so many times you don't stop to think what it means anymore: *dead as a doornail, until hell freezes over, the bottom line, dumb as a post, you can't fight city hall, tip of the iceberg, last but not least, and so in conclusion, in the fast-paced modern world of today, farm-fresh eggs*. Politicians don't want you to think too hard, so political positions tend to get reduced to clichés: *law and order, pro-choice, he's one of us, freedom isn't free, reach across the aisle, show the politicians who's boss, new world order, compassionate conservatism*.

Clichés put your brain to sleep and prevent clear thinking by inviting a reflex response, like waving the flag at a political convention:

College students have a *right* to *have a good time* and kick back once in a while.

We must support the soldiers *fighting for our freedom* in the Near East.

The university should do everything it can to encourage *diversity*.

Ambiguity increases with use—the more a word is used, the less sure its meaning becomes. So clichés, which are used constantly and everywhere, come to mean everything and nothing.

Clichés are easy to spot: if it's a word or phrase you hear everywhere, it's a cliché, and you've learned to stop thinking about it. With that in mind, sometimes it's fun to turn a cliché on its ear so that your reader/listener *has* to think about it. If it's an analogy, try tweaking it: *life is like a box of chocolate-covered crickets.* Or play with the language: *the darkest hour is just before Sean.*

Since all words are ambiguous, the task of eliminating ambiguity in an argument would be never-ending. Instead, look at your assertion and ask, "Do any of these words pose *serious* ambiguity problems?" There is a set of hugely vague, heavily loaded American buzzwords that are guaranteed to bring any argument to a standstill: words like "sexist," "racist," "American," "equality," "freedom," "liberty," "rights," "fascist," "liberal," "natural," "environment," "diversity," "feminist," and "conservative." If you use any of them, it's pointless to continue until you break through the fog and figure out what you're really saying.

Examining Your Assumptions

Now that we have a well-formed assertion relatively free of cloudy language, we've got something we can think about.

Thinking about a thesis comes down to two tasks: understanding where the thesis comes from and understanding where it leads. Imagine the thesis as a step in a process or timeline: the thesis *emerges from* or *rests on* principles or assumptions, and it *leads to* consequences:

Principles → thesis → consequences

If we accept the principles on which a thesis is based and accept the consequences of supporting it, we truly support the thesis; if we don't, we don't.

Every thesis rests on basic principles or assumptions:

Thesis: Americans should never accept public nudity, because it would rob making love of all its intimacy.

Principles: *Making love depends on intimacy; intimacy in love-making is good.*

Thesis: The government has no right to tell me to wear seat belts, because it's up to me if I want to kill myself.

Principles: *The government does not have the right or obligation to protect citizens from themselves; suicide is a right; my death would affect only myself.*

Thesis: Meat is good for you—that's why Nature made us carnivorous.

Principles: *Whatever is "natural" is "right." We cannot or should not alter our primitive makeup.*

Thesis: Americans have the right to own and use automatic weapons because the Constitution says so.

Principles: *The Constitution is always eternally right; the language of the Constitution is unambiguous; "arms" means "any kind of arms."*

Principles are merely larger theses, the big beliefs that justify your smaller belief: "*Since* I believe that the Bible is the literal word of God [large belief], I *therefore* believe that the universe was created in seven days [smaller belief]." All thinking goes like this, from larger beliefs to smaller ones, so until we articulate those larger beliefs and see if we really buy them, we don't know if we believe the smaller theses or not.

Principles are beliefs or values, and there is no such thing as a true or false belief. So you'll never find yourself simply agreeing or disagreeing with the principle, unless you're a zealot. Every principle begins a slippery and fascinating conversation about *when, in what situations, and to what extent* you accept it. Let's begin that conversation with each of the four theses above and their underlying principles. If clothing promotes intimacy, does a member of a nudist colony feel less intimate with other members than clothed people do? If your own death is really just your business, why buy life insurance? If we should eat meat because we ate meat a hundred thousand years ago, should we also live in caves and kill our neighbors? If the Constitution is always right, why did it condone owning slaves and prevent women from voting? All principles produce such interesting conversations. To get started critiquing a principle, ask two questions.

"Where Do I Draw the Line?"   Since principles are never a matter of true or false, the real question is how far will you go in supporting them, and when do you bail? Everybody is for free speech … up to a point. Everybody thinks protecting the environment is good … up to a point. Everyone thinks the Constitution is a good document … up to a point. Everyone thinks we should be natural … up to a point. The question isn't whether you believe, but where you draw the line. Take the underlying principle, make up more and more extreme applications of it, and discover when you say "Enough's enough."

Thesis: We need special university admissions standards for minority students. After all, they didn't ask to be born into disadvantaged environments.

Principle: *Standards should be proportional to a candidate's advantages.*

Where do you draw the line? Should graduate schools have higher admission requirements for graduates of "good" colleges, since they've had the advantage of a good undergraduate education? Should personnel officers have hiring criteria that rise as a job applicant's family income rises? Should disadvantaged students in your class be graded on a grading scale less rigorous than the one used on you?

"What's the Philosophical Antithesis?"   Another way of discovering where you draw the line is to imagine your principle as one-half of a pair of opposites—an *antithesis*—and ask yourself to what extent you believe the *other principle* as well.

All principles come in opposite pairs: "Nature knows best" versus "We should evolve and rise above the level of beasts"; "The Constitution is a perfect document" versus "Governments should grow and evolve as we become wiser"; "I have a right to run my own life" versus "Society has a right to curb individual behavior for the good of all." Only zealots can pick one side of the antithesis and call it the right one; the rest of us find a working compromise, a spot on the spectrum connecting the two. We say, "I'm all for freedom of speech, but there are limits …" or "Sure, you have the right to live the way you want, but you have to consider your neighbors too."

Remember the Jon Carroll essay, "Something Happened a Long Time Ago" (Chapter 2)? His thesis was basically, "Take chances; live life on edge." Imagine all the people out there—smart, rational ones— who'd say, "No, it's good to be cautious in life." Both are true, right?

Conversely, a student of mine once wanted to advance the thesis that kids shouldn't bully younger/weaker/less popular kids. When she realized that there was no antithesis ("Oh, sure they should"), she reworked it a bit: "Kids who might think they're just teasing their classmates in good fun are actually doing harm to them that can last a lifetime." Much better.

Like two magnets, the two ideals pull at us, and we move between them until the forces are balanced. If you don't see the merit of both sides of the argument, you're missing something. If there's no antithesis, you don't have an argument.

Imagine concrete scenarios where the principles come into play. For instance, we all believe that customers should be responsible for their own purchasing decisions—and that companies who make and sell things should be responsible for their products. So where do you stand between those two conflicting beliefs? Who's responsible when a boater ignores storm warnings, takes a dinghy out into the ocean, and drowns? Who's responsible when a tire manufacturer makes a flawed tire, knows it, covers up the fact and continues to sell the tire anyway, and drivers are killed? Who's responsible when a customer buys a cup of very hot coffee at a drive-through and spills it on herself? Who's responsible when tobacco companies tell customers that cigarettes cause cancer, then spend millions in advertising to persuade customers to smoke, and a smoker dies of cancer?

As you work with antitheses, guard against two popular mistakes. Don't work with the antithesis of your *thesis;* instead, work with the antithesis of the *principle.* And don't equate the antithesis with the simple negative of the principle—the principle with a "not" added. Notice that in every thesis/antithesis pair in our examples, the antithesis is more than the principle with a "not."

Examining the Consequences of the Thesis

Every time you argue for something, you have to think about what will happen if you get what you're asking for. All actions have consequences.

If you can't accept the consequences of your thesis, you can't accept your the-sis. If you see no consequences to your argument, you aren't arguing.

All actions have *an infinite number of* consequences, so some of those consequences must be good and some bad: AIDS reduces population pressure; recycling increases pollution from paper- and plastic-processing plants. If you see only one consequence to your argument, you're missing the others. If you see only good consequences to your argument, you're missing the bad ones. The question you must answer is, do the good consequences outweigh the bad or vice versa?

Weighing pros and cons is laborious, so we like to reduce our workload by pretending that actions have one and only one consequence: "Vote for A—he'll give us a strong military defense"; "Vote for C—he's a newcomer and we'll show the incumbents we're fed up." Single-issue voting is just another name for not seeing the *other* consequences of an action.

There are two kinds of consequences, logical and practical. Logical conse-quences are *the conclusions you are logically forced to accept if you accept your original thesis.* If an idea is true, then a host of other ideas that follow from it must also be true. For instance:

> If you argue that the cops shouldn't have arrested your friend Bill when he got drunk and began shooting off his shotgun at midnight because he wasn't trying to hurt anyone, **then** you are logically committed to arguing that no one should be held accountable for her actions if she doesn't intend to do harm, and **thus** the person who gets drunk and wipes out your family with his car can't be held accountable either, since he didn't mean to do it.

> If you argue that you should get a good grade in a class because you worked really hard, **then** you are logically committed to arguing that one's grade in a course should be determined by effort, and **thus** you must agree that you should get a lousy grade in any course where you get A's on the tests without trying hard.

> If you argue that the death penalty in the United States is racist because most people on death row are black, **then** you're logically committed to arguing that any system in which a group is represented beyond its demo-graphic percentage is biased, and **thus** the NBA is racist and the death penalty is sexist against men.

Practical consequences are easier to grasp. They are the other events that take place if the action you're arguing for takes place:

> Thesis: Sex education is a bad idea because it undermines the authority of the nuclear family. (It may have that one bad consequence, but it may also have good ones: it may help stop teen pregnancies and save people from AIDS. Are more people suffering from unwanted pregnancy or a nonauthoritative family?)

> Thesis: We desperately need a standardized national competency test for high school graduation, because high schools are graduating students who can't even read or spell. (Such a test might mean that graduates spell

better, but the other consequences might create a cure worse than the disease. More students would drop out, student fear would increase tenfold, and vast sums of money would be diverted from teaching to testing, just for starters. Overall, would we be better off or worse off?)

Seven Cleanup Tasks

If you crafted a well-formed assertion and thought through its underlying principles and its consequences, you've done an honest day's work. But if you have energy left, there are seven cleanup tasks you can perform.

Ask, "How Do I Know?"   A belief has to come from somewhere. Ask yourself where you got yours:

> You lived through it.
>
> You heard it on TV.
>
> Your parents taught you.
>
> Logic led you to that conclusion.

A belief is only as sound as the soundness of its place of origin. Arguments about morality that are defended by "The Bible says so" have only as much authority as readers give the Bible, which varies from total to none.

Ask, "What Are The Facts?"   For almost all arguments, facts matter, and if you don't have any, then you're guessing:

> Thesis: Most welfare recipients would jump at the chance to get off the dole and support themselves. (Research question: *what percentage of welfare recipients say they would jump at the chance if they were offered a job?*)
>
> Thesis: You shouldn't wear seat belts, because you don't want to be trapped in the car if there's an accident. (Research question: *how many people die in car accidents because they are trapped in the car by their belts, and how many die because they aren't belted in?*)

Ask, "Like What?"   Force yourself to concretize all abstractions and generalizations with at least one "for instance":

> Thesis: Schools should censor books that are clearly harmful to children. (*Make a list of those "clearly harmful" books, and ask yourself how you know they're harmful.*)
>
> Thesis: Punishment in schools is never necessary. (*Make a list of specific imaginary disciplinary situations in the classroom and invent nonpunishing ways of handling them.*)

Ask, "What Should Be Done?"   Most arguments contain a call to action: "Somebody should *do* something about this." If your thesis doesn't have one, ask yourself what you want done and who you want to do it:

> Thesis: TV is a waste of time. (*What do you want me to do, shoot my TV? Limit my children's TV time? Organize boycotts of advertisers who*

sponsor violent programs? Do you want Congress to legislate guidelines for children's TV?)

If you are arguing *against* a course of action—"We *shouldn't* do X"— ask yourself, "OK, if we don't do X, what are we going to do *instead?*":

Thesis: It's a crime to hand out condoms in high schools. It just encourages the kids to have sex (*What are we going to do instead? Kids are having babies at age fifteen. Do you know something that will work better than handing out condoms?*)

Ask, "How Will It Work?"   If you're asking that something be done, ask yourself exactly *how* it will be done:

Thesis: College professors should be hired and promoted on the basis of their teaching, not publication, because teaching is their primary job. (*Nice idea, but in fact no one knows how to measure good teaching. Should we test students to determine how much they learn during the term? Should we ask them how much they like the instructor?*)

Thesis: Salaries should be determined by the principle of comparable worth. Jobs that demand equal skills and training should pay equal wages. (*How do we determine the worth of a job? How does the worth of an English professor with ten years of college who writes critical articles about unknown dead poets compare with the worth of an unschooled baseball player who swings a piece of wood at a ball? And which is harder to do, write a great essay on Keats or hit a curve ball?*)

Avoid Black-or-White Thinking.   When we think, we like to make things easier on ourselves by pretending there are only two possibilities, black or white, and our job is to choose one. *This is never true*; there are *always* other alternatives, shades of gray. Black-or-white thinking is also called "playing either/or" or thinking in absolutes. When you find yourself doing it, ask yourself, "What are the options I'm *not* considering?"

Sometimes the words "either" and "or" are actually used:

Thesis: We can either spend some money and live in a healthier environment, or we can let the ecosystem get worse and worse. (*What are the other alternatives? There may be ways to help the environment that don't cost money, and there may be better ways to spend our money than this proposal.*)

Thesis: The national parks have to charge user fees or they'll have to close. (*What are the other alternatives? There are other ways for the state government to fund the parks—taxes, for instance.*)

But often the either/or is disguised and we have to learn to see the implied dichotomy:

Thesis: I had to spank her—I can't let her think it's OK to smear peanut butter on the carpet. (The implied either/or: *You have two choices, either to spank your kids or to let them run amok. What about other forms of reacting to negative behavior, like discussing it, modeling, or rewarding good behavior?*)

THE CLASSICAL FALLACIES

Fallacies are violations of logic that result in unsound reasoning and faulty argumentation, although on the surface they often sound logical. There are dozens, including what rhetoricians call "formal" and "informal" fallacies—and they range from "appeal to emotion" to "straw man" (oversimplifying your opponent's argument and then attacking that view). You'd probably study them closely if you took a logic or critical thinking class or a speech-and-debate class, and of course, the study of law requires an intimate under-standing of them. My daughter took a film class at a community college here in California that used the classical fallacies as a basis for watching, and ana-lyzing, movies. The final assignment asked the students to pick a contempo-rary film and identify at least four fallacies in it.

Because your readers should be able to identify fallacies in your argu-ments, you want to avoid them—you want to convince your readers with sound reasoning instead. You also want to be able to identify them in your background reading/research and in considering your opponents' counter arguments. Therefore, a knowledge of the fallacies is useful in writing con-vincing arguments. That said, the field is vast—entire textbooks, semesters, college majors, even careers are devoted to the study of the classical fallacies. Going over them all here would be more distraction than helpful, I think, but I have identified a handful that are particularly common and worth watching out for in your own reading and writing.

Ad Hominem Reasoning

If you ignore the points that a person—or essay—is making and instead claim that the argument is unsound because of who the person *is*—or who the writer of the essay is—you're guilty of ad hominem (literally "against the man") reasoning. Example:

You can't trust him to think clearly—he's a member of the Tea Party.

Appeal to Authority

While it makes perfect sense to rely on authorities to help you support your arguments, you must make sure that their authority is legitimate and relevant. It's easy to fall into this trap, too, with so much apparently authoritative information available on the Internet. Always examine your sources closely for credibility. See also the CRAAP test for source credibility on p. 296.

Appeal to Common Practice

This fallacy is based on the suggestion that because most people do something that that makes it good/right/moral/practical, and so on. Of course, our parents saw right through our early appeals to common practice when they replied to our pleas by saying, "I don't care if everyone in your whole class gets to stay out after midnight; your curfew is still eleven o'clock!"

Hasty Generalization

This one's pretty self-explanatory—but easy to commit as well as to overlook in your reading nonetheless. It refers to drawing a conclusion without enough evidence, for example, from a too-small sample or from insufficient or biased sources/data. Example: Professor X's American Folklore class should be an awesome course, because her Introduction to American Studies class was.

Post Hoc Reasoning

This fallacy (Latin *post hoc ergo propter hoc,* for "after this therefore because of this") refers to the assumption that because event X *preceded* event Y, X necessarily *caused* Y. That's not always so. An obvious example: legalizing gambling leads to crime, as evidenced in New Jersey, where in the sixteen years since they legalized gambling, the crime rate has increased 26 percent.

A less-obvious example: trial marriage doesn't work because statistics prove that people who live together before marriage are more likely to get divorced than people who don't. (The *post hoc* assumption: *Since the divorces followed the trial marriages, the trial marriages caused the divorces. The logical weakness: It's also likely that the sort of person who is willing to flout society's customs by cohabiting also gives herself permission to leave a bad marriage.*)

Slippery Slope

One of the main reasons for the United States' involvement in Vietnam in the 1960s was the idea that if we didn't stop the Communists there, that they'd gradually take over other countries and eventually end up invading us. This is a classic example of the slippery slope fallacy: if one thing happens, a series of events will follow, leading to something else happening. Another example: if they outlaw assault rifles, next thing you know they'll outlaw handguns, and before long it will be illegal to own a knife.

SEEING THE MODE

Graphic illustrations have been used widely in the discussions on climate change. Former Vice President Al Gore used graphs and tables to great effect in *An Inconvenient Truth,* the 2006 documentary that argued that humans have been largely responsible for global warming.

Figure 14.1 is a very effective photograph, taken to illustrate a story about the effect of human-caused climate change on the environment, particularly the dwindling polar bear population as a result of diminished habitat. Interestingly, similar photos have been used to make the case that annual

FIGURE 14.1 Polar Bear Walks Across Melting Ice Field

spring thaws occur naturally and that global warming is historically cyclical, not caused by humans at all.

WRITER'S WORKSHOP

Using the Tools

Here's a thesis followed by the kind of conversation you might have with yourself about it, armed with the tools we've used in this chapter. Whenever I've used one of the tools, I've italicized it.

> Thesis: Capital punishment is wrong because we say murder is wrong and then we murder people for murdering. If we execute a criminal, we're as guilty as he is.

The first thing we need to do is reformulate the thesis to follow the principles of Chapter 5. Doing that gives us

> Capital punishment should be abolished, because murdering a murderer makes us as guilty as he is.

Now we're ready to get to work.

There's a question about ambiguous *language* here: what does "murder" mean? It usually means "killing I don't approve of," which only postpones the question of whether I should approve of state executions or not. If "murder" means "illegal killing," executions aren't murder because they're legal—but should they be? The language is also *loaded,* since murder is inherently bad. "Execute" isn't much better, since it's a euphemism that obscures the graphic ugliness of the act and is therefore loaded positively. Maybe "killing" is the only neutral word. The thesis is also a *cliché,* since the opinion has been expressed in these exact words a million times, so I might try to say it in fresher language or at least realize that it will be hard for me to be open-minded about language so familiar.

There are several *underlying assumptions:* that all killing is wrong, that all killing is murder, that killing by state decree is the same as killing in passion and for individual profit, that performing an act to punish a guilty party is morally identical to doing it to an innocent victim for personal gain.

Also, where do I draw the line? I'd better *see where I draw the line.* Let's take the first one. Almost no one really believes that all killing is wrong, and neither do I. Killing is acceptable in some circumstances and under some kinds of provocation. Some people tolerate killing in battle; some don't. Most people grant police officers the right to kill, but only under the most strictly defined circumstances—what are they? Euthanasia is often favored precisely by the people least willing to grant the state the right to kill. Few people would call killing someone who was trying to murder you murder. So where do I draw the line? What are the features of acceptable killing that separate it from unacceptable killing?

It's not easy to say. Even if I decide that individuals can take life to protect themselves from danger, how immediate and life threatening does the danger have to be? Can I shoot someone who has just shot me and is reloading? Someone who is aiming a gun at me? Someone who is carrying a gun? Someone who has threatened to kill me? Someone who has tried to kill me is now running away, but will probably try again?

I'm struggling here with a *philosophical antithesis* between two abstract principles: the belief that human life is sacred versus the belief that individuals and society have the right to protect themselves from grave threat. When does the threat become grave enough to justify killing the threatener? A few people say "Never" and will die without raising a hand against their killers. Some people say that individuals never have the right to take life, and that when the state takes life in war or law, that act represents the collective will and is therefore OK. That may be a moral cop-out—maybe every soldier should take personal responsibility for every death he causes. At the other extreme are totalitarian states that execute people who might someday cause the state inconvenience.

If I claim that killing is justified when innocent parties are under immediate threat, there are *other consequences* to that logic that aren't pleasant. Example: a state execution that takes place two years after the crime is unjustified, since no one is directly threatened.

Another *underlying principle* working here is that executing a convicted murderer is like murdering an innocent person. Do I believe that? If the criminal has committed a heinous crime, does that terminate his rights as a human being? And if he has been judged by a supposedly impartial legal system, and there is no passion or personal gain influencing the decision, doesn't that make it unlike murder? In fact, if killing a murderer is wrong, then a *logical consequence* of believing that is that we must question the entire morality of punishment: Why is it wrong to execute a murderer but OK to fine a traffic speeder or deprive a child of his dinner for mouthing off? All these principles and consequences are as open to questioning as the original thesis, of course.

If I abolish capital punishment, *what's the alternative?* I could lock murderers up for life, but is that really more humane? If killing criminals makes me no better than criminals who kill, doesn't imprisoning criminals make me no better than criminals who imprison? Lifelong imprisonment is certainly punishment, so if I convinced myself I didn't have the right to punish, I wouldn't like this any better than execution. If I resolve not to punish, what methods are left to me to deter violent crime? People talk about "rehabilitation," but that's a loaded cliché and *how will it work?*

Notice how the discussion doesn't lead to final answers, but rather to more questions. That's always how it goes.

Now It's Your Turn.   Pick one of the following statements and write a page of critical thinking about it, using all the tools of the chapter.

a.   Prohibition proved that you can't legislate morality—if people want to do something, they'll do it.
b.   Intelligence tests are racist. Blacks consistently score lower on them than whites.
c.   Boxing is brutal. It's incredible to me that in a society that bans cock fighting and bear baiting, we permit the same sort of thing with human beings.
d.   I didn't want to hurt him, but I had to say it or I wouldn't have been honest.
e.   Twenty-five years ago the public schools abandoned sound-it-out reading approaches, and the nation's reading scores on standard tests like the SAT have been dropping ever since.
f.   Marijuana isn't so bad in itself, but it leads to heavier drugs. Most cocaine and heroin addicts started out on pot.
g.   If my neighbors want peace and quiet, why do they live in a student neighborhood?

h. Female reporters have to enter male athletes' locker rooms. If they don't, they can't do their jobs.

i. Don't get mad at me—I didn't mean to do it.

j. Of course she deals drugs—how else can you make a living if you live in the projects?

k. He started it!

l. Vote for Jimenez—he's for the family!

m. You never bring me flowers anymore.

EXERCISES

1. Using the three generic prompts for arguments (see Finding an Argumentative Prompt on p. 248) as models, form two seeds for argumentative essays you might write.

2. Write a one-page essay exploring the ambiguities in one of the following italicized words. Don't grab at a quick, simplistic answer; explore the complexities.

    a. When he never called me again, I felt *used*.

    b. School libraries shouldn't include *pornography*.

    c. I have the *right* to not breathe other people's smoke.

    d. It's not *fair* to be graded down for being late when your car won't start.

    e. I use only *natural* cosmetics.

    f. The American legal system is *racist*.

3. Do the exercise in "Now it's your turn" using a thesis from an essay of your own.

4. Use a thesis from one of your own essays to answer the following question: what is the one step in the critical thinking process, from avoiding questions as assertions to avoiding fallacies, that poses the greatest challenge to your thesis and promises to generate the most insight into it? Write a one-page essay applying the question to the thesis and reaping the benefits.

5. Do the following tasks with a thesis from an essay of your own:

    a. List two principles it's based on.

    b. Write out the antithesis of each principle. Make sure it isn't the negative of the principle.

    c. Pick one principle; describe one hypothetical situation where you support that principle and one hypothetical situation where you don't.

    d. In a half-page essay, discuss where you draw the line.

    e.   List two good practical consequences of accepting the thesis and two bad ones.

    f.   Write down one logical consequence of accepting the thesis.

    g.   Identify any fallacies inherent in the thesis.

6. Listen to a local politician—or find a politician speaking on Youtube—and try to identify examples fallacies in his argument.

Chapter 15

Writing an Argument, Stage 2: Selling the Case

Now that you've thought through your position, it's time to think about ways of selling it to your audience. You have to do four things:

Define your objectives realistically.

Identify your audience as specifically as possible.

Establish a positive relationship with your audience.

Find a dramatic structure.

DEFINE YOUR OBJECTIVES REALISTICALLY

Many writers, when they undertake an argument, set out to do impossible things. They try to have the last word, to say the pure truth that no one else has ever said and that ends debate forever. That only gives you writer's block.

Instead, think of arguing as making your small contribution to the ongoing debate. The contribution isn't "truth"; it's your personal view of things. It doesn't end debate; it generates it by stimulating thought in other people. It needn't even be the only opinion you have—it can be just one of the many thoughts you have on the matter.

Think of this as the Stew Theory of argumentation. Imagine a gigantic pot of Argument Stew always cooking on the Stove of Our Culture. Every citizen is responsible for contributing something to this stew. The more varied the contributions, the better the stew gets. No contribution—no individual potato or carrot—is the "true" one, the "right" one that makes all the other ingredients unnecessary. So don't try to toss in the potato that ends the stew; toss in *your* potato to enrich the mix. And it doesn't help to go up to the stew and say, "I really agree with the potato that last guy threw in," so simply agreeing with someone else's argument doesn't count. Arguing isn't voting.

You can see the stew-making process in online forums. You toss in a potato by posting a thought you've had, and it may provoke a hundred thoughtful reactions in a day—most of them of value, most adding to the ongoing discussion (of course, some people don't "get it" and try to have the last word, the one that shuts everyone else up). For example, in an online class I taught several years ago, I gave my students a prompt and asked them to respond and then to respond to each other's reactions. Here are the prompt and the first few minutes of response.

The Prompt

A California School Board member has suggested that schools ban homework. He has two reasons: (1) homework is interfering with the family by taking the child away from family life, and (2) homework is discriminatory, because students with access to the best technology have an unfair advantage over students who don't. What do you think?

The Response

ERIC: If we can't have homework because some people have computers and some don't, how can we have anything? Lectures are obviously "unfair" because some people hear better than others.

LINDSAY: I find it hard to believe that there are absolutely no resources for these children who lack computers. If this is indeed the case, then the rules should be changed, so that assignments could be handwritten.

JILL: I babysit a seven-year-old whose parents are poor and don't have the money for a computer—but the kid has a Sega system and dozens and dozens of games. So is it a problem of resources or priorities?

ERIC: Trying to "fix" America's family or social problems by banning homework is like trying to clean up our toxic dump problem with a toothbrush. We're always looking for the quick fix, the regulation that will make our world a healthy, happy one. No such thing.

LINDSAY: I loathed homework just like any other kid. But the plain and simple fact is that homework teaches responsibility. Every child is going to have to learn this sooner or later.

AARON: The new family structure is part of the problem. My aunt is a single parent, and she cannot say no to her son. She tells him to do his homework, he begs to play Nintendo, and she gives in. It's emotional blackmail, and lots of single parents feel it.

ADAM: I can see how it is unfair if one kid turns in a paper with amazing graphics and a pretty cover page and gets an A even if the paper isn't very well written. I have seen this injustice, and it must stop!!

JOAN: Stop the discrimination, sure, but stop it by stopping grading, not homework.

AARON: If families are worried about homework interfering with their together time, why don't they help little Timmy do his homework?

LORI: Why do we assume that homework is boring and unrewarding?

They continued this conversation off and on for several days, and at the end had more to talk about than we did when we started. Nobody "won."

IDENTIFY YOUR AUDIENCE AS SPECIFICALLY AS POSSIBLE

While all writing requires you to identify your audience, it's probably most critical in writing arguments. That's because to convince your reader to consider your position, you need to know as much as possible about hers. If you're trying to convince your readers to shop at locally owned stores instead of big-box discount stores, you need to know all the reasons they will come up with for not shopping locally, thank you very much. (See What Is the Opposition's Argument? on p. 276.)

Along the same lines, it's usually best to *narrow* your audience, and to keep in mind what we talked about on p. 83 about a "target" audience. There's no way you can write a convincing argument about the merits of shopping locally for everybody (or, as my students like to say, "anyone who shops at big-box stores"). But narrow your target audience to college students, say, and you're more likely to be convincing. Narrow your target to male college students, and it's even easier. Now narrow it to male college students in your community, and you can really get some work done.

Why? Because in addition to the generalized points you might make about the value of supporting small businesses and keeping money local, you can be very specific in addressing your counterarguments, one of which, in this case, would be that big-box stores have lower prices, which of course they do.

However, one recent Sunday morning, I was replacing the washers in the stems of my garage-sink faucets. It was early and our local hardware store wasn't open yet, so, reluctantly, I headed out to a chain home-improvement store. Of course, they had a huge selection of replacement parts, but guess what. They didn't have just the washers I needed, which should have cost about twelve cents each. Instead, I had to buy entire replacement stems. And guess what? They didn't have exactly the ones I needed, but they had ones that were close ($7.95 each) and would, the nice man assured me, work.

They didn't.

But by the time I'd installed them, and water was squirting in every direction, my local hardware store was open. I took my original faucet stems downtown, showed them to the man behind the counter, and within about three minutes I had my twelve-cent washers, and half an hour later had my old stems reinstalled.

Of course, I could use that story in an argument that I was writing for a broad audience, but if I were writing for a local audience, I'd point out that the hardware store I was talking about was Collier Hardware, at the corner of First and Broadway. While prices might be a bit higher there than at Home Depot or Lowe's, out by the freeway, you can *save* money at Collier. Not only can you buy just the parts you need, but the workers—owner Sal and his sons, Mark and Steve—are also far more knowledgeable than the employees at Home Depot or Lowe's.

ESTABLISH A POSITIVE RELATIONSHIP WITH YOUR AUDIENCE

The Chair Theory of arguing says imagine your reader sitting in a room full of chairs, each chair representing an argumentative position. She is sitting in the chair that represents her opinion. You're sitting in your own chair, some distance away. Your goal as arguer is to convince her to get out of her chair and move to the chair next to you. What makes a person willing to move toward someone? Does a person come toward you if you tell her, "You're an idiot for sitting in that chair. I can't comprehend how anyone with the intelligence God gave a dog could sit in that chair"? Does she come toward you if you tell her, "Only an evil or cruel person could sit in that chair"? Does she come toward you if you coldly and impersonally list several strictly logical reasons why she shouldn't be in that chair? No. Yet most arguers approach their reader in exactly this way, and they harden her heart against them by so doing.

Let's take another approach. Let's agree that when you argue, you want to be the kind of person people find it easy to agree with and be convinced by. To be that kind of person, you have to do three things: be human, be interesting, and empathize.

Be Human

People aren't convinced by facts and logic; they're convinced by *people*. Every politician who makes the mistake of reciting lots of facts and figures loses the election. But most people do everything they can to hide their humanity when they argue.

A typical experience: a student of mine turned in an essay that began like this:

> Attempts to correlate murder to punishment rates have been made for a long time. Most of these studies were full of errors because they were showing the correlation between murder rates and the presence or absence of the capital punishment status, not to the actual executions, which are what really matter. Others failed to properly isolate murder rates from variables other than punishment, even when these variables are known to influence murder rates.

So it went for three pages—conventional dehumanized argument style. I asked her, "Why are you writing about the effects of incarceration anyway? What's it to you?" When she told me, I said, "Wow! Put it in the essay!" and the next draft began:

> I was in prison for four years. True, I was an officer there, but at eight hours a day, sometimes more, for forty-eight weeks a year … well, I put in more time than most criminals do for their serious crimes. My opinions certainly did change while I worked there.

Now we're ready to listen.

Be Interesting

There's a myth out there that says scientists are convincing. So when we argue, we put on our imaginary lab coats and get as boring as possible. It doesn't work. Go the other way. Perform. Give the audience a good time. Instead of beginning a movie review with a thesis plop like "*Problem Child* is a hackneyed film that offers the viewer little more than a rehash of previous films in the genre," one reviewer began like this:

> *Problem Child* is the story of a misunderstood and unwanted boy who finds love from a caring adult who discovers a side of himself he didn't know as he deals with the child's painful struggle to be accepted.

Interesting? Not!

Empathize

If you ask people what they most want from the people they argue with— their spouses, partners, friends, parents—the usual answer is "I want them to understand my point of view." Instead, most of us go the other way and advertise our lack of empathy: "I can't imagine anyone thinking that way; how can you possibly believe that? You can't mean what you're saying," and so on. A simple "I see where you're coming from" can bring down a host of defenses.

You can do this as a ploy, but it's better if you see the truth of it: the other guy's no fool, and he has valid reasons for thinking as he does— remember the Stew Theory. As long as you believe that only a moron could disagree with you, you need to do more critical thinking (Chapter 14) to break out of your narrow-mindedness.

This is a hard truth to grasp in our culture, because our model for argument is the two-party political process, which thrives on demonizing the opposition. But that's not *arguing*; that's *fighting*. So ask yourself, Is the fact that Democrats are encouraged to think Republicans are idiots and monsters, and vice versa, really doing the country any good? If you think not, don't add to the problem by doing it yourself.

Here's a wonderful example of the writer empathizing, in fact going so far as to pretend he's at a bar sharing a beer with his "opponent" (us). These are the first few paragraphs of an argument written by Al Seracevic and published in the San Francisco *Chronicle* a few days after the San Francisco Giants won the 2012 World Series.

Here's the premise: Buster Posey has had the greatest start to a career in major-league history.

I know, I know. It sounds crazy. But pull up a bar stool and let's talk about this. Really, it's not that nutty. In fact, it just might be true.

Consider the evidence: In his first three seasons of big-league ball, Posey has won two championships, a Rookie of the Year trophy, a batting title and will likely become the National League MVP for this season. In that short span, he's also managed to overcome one of the most gruesome baseball injuries in recent memory, and should pick up a Comeback Player of the Year award for his troubles.

All this while playing the most demanding position on the field, handling an all-league pitching staff. We knew Posey was going to be good. But this good?

Go ahead, order another one. Let's talk.

What's that? Derek Jeter? Well, sure. He's the only guy you could compare Posey to in the same generation. Jeter came up with a talented class of Yankee farmhands, started winning immediately, and hasn't stopped. He's a lock first ballot Hall of Famer.

But did he outdo Buster? Let's see. Jeter's first full year was 1996. He won Rookie of the Year. And the Yankees won the Series. Not bad. Jeter batted .314 that first year. Posey hit .305. Their slugging and OPS numbers were comparable. Posey had 18 homers, to Jeter's 10. Sounds like a wash, although Posey received MVP votes in his first year. A harbinger, indeed.

Their second years were similar, even with Posey's injury. Jeter's Yankees didn't win the title in 1997. And Posey's Giants missed the playoffs. Their batting averages were eerily equal, but the whole thing's off due to that play at the plate. Jeter played more, but the result was the same for both guys.

Fast forward to year three. Posey goes off, winning the batting title, (likely) MVP and the World Series. He won the Hank Aaron award. And will win the Silver Slugger, for top-hitting catcher in the National League. Jeter wins the Series with the Yankees, but he's not the only straw that stirs the Yankees' drink, if we may quote Reggie. Buster's the drink, the straw and the ice for the Giants. Their statistics are similar and the end result is the same, but ...

POSEY VS. JETER: ADVANTAGE POSEY

Take it easy, take it easy. I know. Captain Clutch has an argument there, but I'm going to stand behind Posey's MVP and batting title. Case closed. So, pull another one, barkeep. Let's keep going down this road.

(PERMISSION PROVIDED BY SAN FRANCISCO CHRONICLE)

Get Some Support

While your writing instructor might require outside sources and citations for a formal argumentative paper to help you support your claim, this is not strictly an academic exercise, or something you do only in school. Think about it: you're trying to convince a friend to go to Tres Hombres for Mexican food instead of Tacos de Acapulco. You make your case, based in large part on your experience. But what if you know someone who works at Tres Hombres and can vouch for the freshness of the ingredients? Or someone who ate there last week and swears by it? There you go—credible support for your argument: "Tom Smith, who has worked as a chef at Tres Hombres for three years says ..." Surely, you've suggested going to a movie and pointed out the review it got in your paper. Same thing. Support (outside sources, citations) for your argument.

Keep in mind, too, that credibility—or expertise—is determined by context. That is, ordinarily your eight-year-old neighbor probably wouldn't be a credible source (an expert) for an argument you were making, but what if you were trying to make the case that parents should home-school their kids, and this eight-year-old was home-schooled himself and just happened to be reading at the ninth-grade level? There's your expert; interview him, and cite him. (Of course, his being home-schooled might have no bearing whatsoever on his reading level ...)

Note how in the following essay a few brief quotes and statistics help provide support for her argument—as well as provide a powerful counterweight to the context for the essay itself, a letter to her daughter.

I, TOO, AM OPTIMISTIC ABOUT OUR RACIAL FUTURE

CYNTHIA TUCKER

For my daughter:

You came into my life a little more than a year ago, just after the nation elected its first black president. I was confident then that you would live a life unfettered by the crude stereotypes, racist assumptions and self-imposed ceilings that have hindered black Americans for generations.

Since your birth, however, we've seen the limits of the "post-racial" transformation that President Obama's election was supposed to have ushered in. A group of slightly unhinged voters, supported by a few shameless politicians and media figures, continues to insist that the president wasn't born in the United States and is therefore illegitimate.

An angry movement of conservative "populists" has brought its cause to the capital—along with ugly images of Obama as Hitler or a witch doctor. A well-known Ivy League professor, who happened to be black, was arrested in his own home for discourtesy toward a white cop—and Obama was denounced for criticizing the arrest.

The United States is not yet "post-racial," and it may never be. Because human beings have a primal instinct for fearing and hating "the other," even this diverse country may never completely outgrow the invidious distinctions of color and class.

Still, I'm optimistic about the future—about your future. You were born at the magical moment when the distant dream of two little brown-skinned, kinky-haired girls running across the White House lawn suddenly transformed into the reality down on Pennsylvania Avenue.

Most black Americans share my optimism. Fifty-three percent believe the future will be better, according to a new survey by the Pew Research Center.

Pew staffer Scott Keeter told me he attributes that hopefulness to "the Obama effect," and I agree. It is hard to overstate the pride, the relief, the sheer joy sparked by Obama's presidency—a sense that, at long last, we share the full bounty that this great nation has to offer.

Black Americans are all too painfully aware, of course, of a lingering racial animus that has its roots in leftover biases, many of which people don't even know they're subconsciously holding. Even individuals with well-intentioned motives sometimes engage in crude stereotypes, as Senate Majority Leader Harry Reid showed when he spoke of a "Negro dialect."

Reid's gaffe reminded me that your grandmother was oh-so-wise when she insisted that we speak standard English, and I'll apply the same rule to you.

(Your grandparents had other cardinal rules, too—simple things like work hard, pray often and pay your bills on time. I'll be passing those on, as well.)

As for Reid's remark about Obama's skin color, it's certainly true that four centuries of American racism favored lighter-skinned blacks—an unfortunate prejudice that black Americans eagerly adopted. Just as research has shown that whites are more comfortable with lighter-skinned blacks, so generations of accomplished black lawyers, teachers and doctors judged their dark-skinned brothers and sisters unworthy of high social status.

But I don't worry that your skin color—a lovely chocolate brown—will be a burden for you. Michelle Obama wouldn't pass the paper bag test, but her intelligence, grace and elegance are helping Americans, black, brown and white, expand their definition of beauty.

As if a brown-skinned first lady were not remarkable enough, Disney has released an animated film, "The Princess and the Frog," with its first-ever black princess. You wouldn't understand the excitement, but another wall of cultural exclusion was knocked down.

I am not so naive as to believe that you'll never confront racism. I know the day will come when I'll have to console you after some slight or slur that only parents of black children would ever have to explain.

Yet, Obama's election did signal a new racial climate, one in which a little black child and a little white child and a little brown child might dream the same dreams.

—Tucker, Cynthia, "I,too,am optimistic about our racial future," ATLANTA CONSTITUTION-JOURNAL, January 15, 2010, http://blogs.ajc.com/cynthia-tucker/2010/01/15/i-too-am-optimistic-about-our-racial-future/

Cynthia Tucker is a Pulitzer Prize–winning author and the Washington, D.C., correspondent for the *Atlanta Constitution-Journal*.

Four Diagnostic Questions

To push yourself toward our new healthy relationship with your reader, answer the following diagnostic questions and put some form of the answer in the essay:

1. What is the opposition's argument? Keep in mind that your reader has valid reasons for his position. Don't condemn or ridicule him for them. Rather, anticipate them. And, respectfully, counter them. That is, say, "You're right" or "Good point ... However ..."

In class, I like to call the counterarguments the "yeah-but" arguments. You suggest your roommate try a particular restaurant because the burritos are so good. "Yeah, but they're so expensive," he counters. Your counter to that? "You're right ...," or "Good point ... However, the portions are *huge*. Ask the waitress to box up what you don't eat, and then have it for lunch the next day."

Frequently, you acknowledge the counter ("yeah-but") argument right in your text and in fact use it for a transition: "Granted, the burritos at Tres Hombres are expensive. However ..."

2. What would my reader most like to hear me acknowledge about her? If you're writing an essay addressed to the university administration and defending the thesis that the threatened fee hike for university students is unfair and shouldn't be enacted, what would your reader (the university administrator) most like to hear you acknowledge about her? Probably that administrators aren't fiends who just like to rip off students. So you add a passage reassuring her: "I know that administering a university isn't easy, especially in these hard times. You aren't raising fees just for the fun of it. We both want the same thing: to see the university be as good as it can be. I think we can avoid student hardship *and* keep educational quality high."

3. What is my reader's most likely fear in response to my argument? You're writing an essay arguing that the Green Tortoise, a counterculture, low-rent bus line, is an attractive alternative to planes, trains, or conventional bus lines. What is your reader's most likely fear in response to your argument? Probably that the buses are full of winos and creeps and driven by drugged-out slackers who aren't safe on the road. So you add a passage reassuring him: "I know everyone's image of cheap bus travel: being sandwiched between a wino in the seat to your left and a pervert in the seat to your right. But the Green Tortoise isn't like that. The customers are people like you and me: relatively clean, sober, normal people just trying to get some-where without spending a fortune. Nor are the drivers and other employees your stereotypical space-case flakes, though my driver did wear a tie-dyed T-shirt; every employee I dealt with was sober, professional, and competent."

4. How is the reader likely to dislike me for saying what I'm saying? When you try to talk people out of their beliefs, they often resist by defining you in ways that justify their not hearing you. Ask yourself what form that dislike will take; then reassure them: "I'm not who you fear I am." For instance, if you're defending a thesis that says, "Formality is a dying art; people don't know how to dress up and be formal anymore," the most likely negative image your reader will get of you is that you're a snob. So you add a disclaimer: "I'm not one of those people who think Levi's or pants on women is a crime against nature. I love being casual, and I wear jeans most of the time. I'm not saying formality is better than informality; I'm saying that every once in a while knocking out a really fancy recipe, getting dolled up, and inviting friends over for grown-up time is *fun*."

FIND A DRAMATIC STRUCTURE

Many arguers figure that since an argument is won by cold facts and logic, the structure should be as rigid as a scientific experimental write-up: thesis at the end of the first paragraph, supportive arguments in numbered series, and so on. That doesn't work, because arguments are won by people, so go the opposite way: avoid stiff, logical structures at all costs, and look for dramatic alternatives. Consider the following examples, noting especially how the writers empathize with their readers.

BEING A PARENT IS A BALANCING ACT

RUBEN NAVARRETTE

I often describe it as my most important job. It's the one that is the most difficult, and yet the most fulfilling. It consumes the most time, and it's the one where I most often feel as if I'm in over my head. It's also the one where the stakes are highest.

The job is being a parent to my three young children—ages 3, 5 and 7. And this New Year, my resolution was to do it better.

There are no raises, promotions or awards for good parents. In fact, if you earn the title, most people won't even notice. The only evaluations that matter will come from your children, and the jury could be out for years.

But if you're a bad parent, the effects will be obvious and felt long after you're gone. As your children go through life, they'll be like a human billboard that announces your parenting "score" to the world.

There are countless ways to be a bad parent. Abandoning or failing to provide for your kids tops my list. Yet you can also get there by abusing, neglecting, smothering, bullying or belittling.

Yet what has me worried lately—both with my own kids, and with the rest of the society—is that we're producing in the next generation a sense of entitlement. We're teaching kids that desiring something is the same as deserving it. Along the way, we're diminishing the importance of what experts call "earned happiness" and replacing it with a system that gives awards and rewards across the board based solely on needs and wants.

These days, it seems as if parents and teachers are more reluctant to reward good behavior in children, let alone punish bad behavior. In fact, in an era where building a child's self-esteem is the ultimate goal, we've become terrified of words like "good" and "bad."

The problem seems to be that we're confusing good or bad behavior with being a good or bad person. We must never tell our children that they are bad people—i.e., "You're a bad boy." But we can't be afraid to explain to our kids what it means to engage in bad behavior, and make clear that we expect them to refrain from it. In trying to not be too hard on our kids, I fear we've gone too far in the opposite direction.

I knew this was happening in our society—that too many parents were surrendering their expectations, throwing in the towel and forgetting how to be parents. I recognized that the word "bad" had been shelved along with a host of other negative words that many parents today are reluctant to use—"no," "don't," "stop."

But I needed to hear it from a third party. When listening to a radio show, I recently heard a professor of psychiatry insist that even Santa Claus has been co-opted.

He noted that it used to be natural for Santa to sit a child on his lap and ask: "Have you been a good girl?" This doesn't seem to happen much anymore, he said.

He's right. I crossed paths with several Santas during this holiday season, and I don't remember a single one making that inquiry. Instead, children—mine included—would walk up and Santa would ask only one question: "What do you want for Christmas?"

What happened to the idea of a child earning his or her present through good behavior? You know, the difference between being naughty and nice.

That idea is gone.

In our shopping-mall culture of materialism and consumerism, every child gets a present. Just like, in sports, everyone gets a ribbon.

We can't leave anyone out, so we no longer expect anything from anyone. In fact, now the tables have turned, and it is the recipient who expects something for nothing. This parenting business is tricky. You want to give your kids nice things, but you have to be careful not to give them too much.

You don't want to tear them down, but you can't demand too little.

Being a good parent is a balancing act. It's more art than science. A pinch of this, a dash of that. Most of us will never get it exactly right. Mistakes come with the territory.

Even so, this year, I've got to do a better job of it. And it starts not with settling for less but with expecting more—from my kids, and from myself.

—Permission provided by Ruben Navarette

Ruben Navarrette is a nationally syndicated columnist and regular contributor to National Public Radio's "Tell Me More with Michael Martin."

GIVEN THE CHANCE

MELISSA SCHATZ

Student Essay

I met Stacey three weeks ago, when she came to live at the Group Home where I work as a counselor. I liked her immediately. She's a bright, friendly, attractive sixteen-year-old. She's on probation for two years for petty thefts, and she has a two-year-old son. But her biggest problem is that she's a speed freak—she's addicted to shooting methamphetamine directly into her bloodstream.

After spending a month in Juvenile Hall, where she went through withdrawals, Stacey came to the Group Home in fairly clean condition. But she has run away from here twice since then, staying out several days each time. She admits that she was "using." She says she's been an addict for several years now. Her parents are drug addicts too. Stacey wants to quit, but she needs help. She says she needs to go through a drug rehabilitation program. I believe her.

Unfortunately, I can't get Stacey into one. I've tried, but everywhere I've turned I've run into a wall. You see drug rehabilitation programs cost big money—two to three thousand dollars for a one-month stay. And absolutely no one will pay for Stacey to go into a program.

Of course Stacey herself doesn't have any money. Nor do her parents. And addicts don't have medical insurance. This doesn't surprise me. What does surprise me is that the State, which has taken custody of Stacey, placing her in a group home in the first place, refuses to pay for drug rehabilitation. It makes me angry. I feel as if the State has said, "Here, hold on to this," and then chopped my hands off.

Now, I know that drug rehabilitation programs aren't cure-alls. It takes more to kick a drug habit and keep it kicked, especially a mainline habit. It's a day-to-day struggle. Yes, I've known addicts who make their annual trip to the drug rehab. But I have also known addicts who *did* turn their lives around on such a program. Doesn't Stacey deserve the chance? While the State has her in custody, the opportunity is perfect. We're at least obligated to try. And isn't it money well spent, if it saves us from having to support Stacey in prison in the years to come?

Given time, the Group Home could help Stacey work through her behavior problems, get through high school, and learn some social and emancipation skills. But the fact is that unless she kicks her drug habit, she probably won't stay long. Her probation officer told me the next time she runs away he'll put her back in Juvenile Hall to clean out. We both know this doesn't work. Just taking the drugs away isn't the answer. But apparently the State has decided the real answer is too expensive. They tell us to fix these kids, but won't give us the tools. They're not giving Stacey or me a chance.

—Permission provided by Steve Metzger

WHY?

DANA MARIE VAZQUEZ

Student Essay

I looked forward to it for months. I began the countdown in March. Only thirty-five days, only twenty-three days, only fourteen days. As the days passed and it got closer, my excitement grew. Finally it was the night before. I counted down the hours, minutes, and even seconds. "The time is 11:59 and 50 seconds—beep—the time is 12:00 exactly," the recording said as my friends yelled, "Happy birthday" and I popped the cork on my bottle of champagne. It finally happened: I was now twenty-one years old. My friends insisted that I drink the entire bottle of champagne myself. Why? Because it was my twenty-first birthday.

As I was guzzling the champagne, my friends were encouraging me to hurry because it was already 12:15 and the bars would be closing at 2:00. Oh yeah, I just had to go to Safeway and contribute to the delinquency of minors by buying for my twenty-year-old roommate. Snapping pictures the entire time, my roommates cheered me on until I reached the finale at the check stand and the clerk ID'ed me and announced to the entire store that it was my twenty-first birthday.

After a round of applause and much cheering in Safeway, I was dragged out the door and shoved into a car. "We've got to go to Joe's," they exclaimed as we raced towards my downfall. Once inside, I was given a drink that contained every alcohol known to Man. As I sucked mine down, my roommate kept refilling it. Why? Because it was my twenty-first birthday.

"It's her twenty-first birthday," my roommate shouted to a guy across the room she knew. "Then come join our game," was his reply. This dice game was quite easy. The rolls of the dice were counted and whoever reached twenty-one drank a shot. Lucky me—I was chosen to drink a shot of vodka and a shot of a Russian apple. Did my dice roll equal twenty-one? No. Then why did I have to drink? Because it was my twenty-first birthday.

"Yeah," my roommates shouted as I barely downed the vodka. "Let's go to Riley's," they laughed as we ran down the street. "Just a beer, all I want is a beer," I pleaded as we entered. Why was I still drinking even though I didn't want anything, even a beer? Because it was my twenty-first birthday.

So we all chugged a beer and raced on to the Top Flight. "It's her twenty-first birthday," they shouted at the doorman as he checked my ID and I swayed to the pounding music.

"Go tell the bartender and you'll get whatever you want," he screamed at me. I followed his command and ordered a Long Island iced tea. This wasn't a very wise choice because it also had many different types of alcohol in it, but at that point I really wasn't thinking. They were getting ready to close the bar, so I pounded my drink and we left.

About a half hour later—BOOM—it hit me. I began removing everything I had put in my stomach in the last three days. I did this, I'm told, for close to two hours. I was so hung over the next day that all I wanted to do was crawl into a hole and die. But did I go out to the bars still? Yes. Why? Because it was my twenty-first birthday.

I've thought about my birthday a lot lately, and I don't understand the rationale I and everyone else used that night. I don't like it, but I don't think it will change. You'd think I would be the first to want to change it ... but it was my roommate's twenty-first birthday three days ago. We took her out to the bars and made her drink and drink. She got sick at Riley's, puked at Top Flight, and vomited at Shell Cove. She could barely walk, but we still took her to the Bear's Lair. Why? Because it was her twenty-first birthday.

—Permission provided by Steve Metzger

SEEING THE MODE

Editorial/political cartoons can be immensely powerful. Indeed, David Wallis, editor of *Killed Cartoons: Casualties from the War on Free Expression* (Norton, 2007), quotes longtime *Washington Post* columnist Art Buchwald as observing that "dictators of the right and the left fear the political cartoonist more than they do the atomic bomb."

Figure 15.1 shows a not-so-subtle cartoon. Look at how much work gets done in a simple drawing—and, importantly, how much opinion is conveyed in a single glance.

FIGURE 15.1   Like this one, most political cartoons make very clear arguments

What do you think? To what degree do political cartoons present arguments in the ways we've been talking about? Does a political cartoon "establish a positive relationship with its audience"? Does a political cartoon consider the opposing argument? Do political cartoons use "loaded language"?

WRITER'S WORKSHOP

Using Models

Chapter 2 showed how to use models to open doors and inspire yourself to try experiments you'd otherwise never think to undertake. Nowhere is that more useful than in arguing, where our internal paradigm can be so constipated. Go read the newspaper and magazine columnists who have to hold readers' interest day after day or they don't get paid—read Maureen Dowd, Cynthia Tucker, George Will, Thomas L. Friedman, Anna Quindlen, or anyone who writes a regular column in a major newspaper.

Now It's Your Turn.   Read the following essay. Note how Barry has very narrowly identified his "target" audience, while the essay is enormously relevant to readers outside that group. Consider, too, how Barry empathizes with his readers—largely by poking fun at himself. Finally, note that while Barry's topic and thesis are deadly seriously, his approach and tone are hilarious (though some find them offensive), which is why the piece is so effective—remember, no one likes to be lectured at.

Using Barry's piece as a model, write an argument using an approach unlike one you ordinarily would think of yourself.

A JOURNEY INTO MY COLON—AND YOURS

DAVE BARRY

OK. You turned 50. You know you're supposed to get a colonoscopy. But you haven't. Here are your reasons:

1. You've been busy.
2. You don't have a history of cancer in your family.
3. You haven't noticed any problems.
4. You don't want a doctor to stick a tube 17,000 feet up your butt.

Let's examine these reasons one at a time. No, wait, let's not. Because you and I both know that the only real reason is No. 4. This is natural. The idea of having another human, even a medical human, becoming deeply involved in what is technically known as your "behindular zone" gives you the creeping willies.

I know this because I am like you, except worse. I yield to nobody in the field of being a pathetic weenie medical coward. I become faint and nauseous during even very minor medical procedures, such as making an appointment by phone. It's much worse when I come into physical contact with the medical profession. More than one doctor's office has a dent in the floor caused by my forehead striking it seconds after I got a shot.

In 1997, when I turned 50, everybody told me I should get a colonoscopy. I agreed that I definitely should, but not right away. By following this policy, I reached age 55 without having had a colonoscopy. Then I did something so pathetic and embarrassing that I am frankly ashamed to tell you about it.

What happened was, a giant 40-foot replica of a human colon came to Miami Beach. Really. It's an educational exhibit called the Colossal Colon, and it was on a nationwide tour to promote awareness of colo-rectal cancer. The idea is, you crawl through the Colossal Colon, and you encounter various educational items in there, such as polyps, cancer and hemorrhoids the size of regulation volleyballs, and you go, "Whoa, I better find out if I contain any of these things," and you get a colonoscopy.

If you are a professional humor writer, and there is a giant colon within a 200-mile radius, you are legally obligated to go see it. So I went to Miami Beach and crawled through the Colossal Colon. I wrote a column about it, making tasteless colon jokes. But I also urged everyone to get a colonoscopy. I even, when I emerged from the Colossal Colon, signed a pledge stating that I would get one.

But I didn't get one. I was a fraud, a hypocrite, a liar. I was practically a member of Congress.

Five more years passed. I turned 60, and I still hadn't gotten a colonoscopy. Then, a couple of weeks ago, I got an e-mail from my brother Sam, who is 10 years younger than I am, but more mature. The email was addressed to me and my middle brother, Phil. It said:

"Dear Brothers,

"I went in for a routine colonoscopy and got the dreaded diagnosis: cancer. We're told it's early and that there is a good prognosis that they can get it all out, so, fingers crossed, knock on wood, and all that. And of course they told me to tell my siblings to get screened. I imagine you both have."

Um. Well.

First I called Sam. He was hopeful, but scared. We talked for a while, and when we hung up, I called my friend Andy Sable, a gastroenterologist, to make an appointment for a colonoscopy. A few days later, in his office, Andy showed me a color diagram of the colon, a lengthy organ that appears to go all over the place, at one point passing briefly through Minneapolis. Then Andy explained the colonoscopy procedure to me in a thorough, reassuring and patient manner. I nodded thoughtfully, but I didn't really hear anything he said, because my brain was shrieking, quote, "HE'S GOING TO STICK A TUBE 17,000 FEET UP YOUR BUTT!"

I left Andy's office with some written instructions, and a prescription for a product called "MoviPrep," which comes in a box large enough to hold a microwave oven. I will discuss MoviPrep in detail later; for now suffice it to say that we must never allow it to fall into the hands of America's enemies.

I spent the next several days productively sitting around being nervous. Then, on the day before my colonoscopy, I began my preparation. In accordance with my instructions, I didn't eat any solid food that day; all I had was chicken broth, which is basically water, only with less flavor. Then, in the evening, I took the MoviPrep. You mix two packets of powder together in a one-liter plastic jug, then you fill it with lukewarm water. (For those unfamiliar with the metric system, a liter is about 32 gallons.) Then you have to drink the whole jug. This takes about an hour, because MoviPrep tastes— and here I am being kind—like a mixture of goat spit and urinal cleanser, with just a hint of lemon.

The instructions for MoviPrep, clearly written by somebody with a great sense of humor, state that after you drink it, "a loose watery bowel movement may result." This is kind of like saying that after you jump off your roof, you may experience contact with the ground.

MoviPrep is a nuclear laxative. I don't want to be too graphic, here, but: Have you ever seen a space shuttle launch? This is pretty much the MoviPrep experience, with you as the shuttle. There are times when you wish the commode had a seat belt. You spend several hours pretty much confined to the bathroom, spurting violently. You eliminate *everything*. And then, when you figure you must be totally empty, you have to drink *another* liter of MoviPrep, at which point, as far as I can tell, your bowels travel into the future and start eliminating food that you have not even *eaten* yet.

After an action-packed evening, I finally got to sleep. The next morning my wife drove me to the clinic. I was very nervous. Not only was I worried about the procedure, but I had been experiencing occasional return bouts of MoviPrep spurtage. I was thinking, "What if I spurt on Andy?" How do you apologize to a friend for something like that? Flowers would not be enough.

At the clinic I had to sign many forms acknowledging that I understood and totally agreed with whatever the hell the forms said. Then they led me to a room full of other colonoscopy people, where I went inside a little curtained space and took off my clothes and put on one of those hospital garments designed by sadist perverts, the kind that, when you put it on, makes you feel even more naked than when you are actually naked.

Then a nurse named Eddie put a little needle in a vein in my left hand. Ordinarily I would have fainted, but Eddie was very good, and I was already lying down. Eddie also told me that some people put vodka in their MoviPrep. At first I was ticked off that I hadn't thought of this, but then I pondered what would happen if you got yourself too tipsy to make it to the bathroom, so you were staggering around in full Fire Hose Mode. You would have no choice but to burn your house.

When everything was ready, Eddie wheeled me into the procedure room, where Andy was waiting with a nurse and an anesthesiologist. I did not see the 17,000-foot tube, but I knew Andy had it hidden around there somewhere. I was seriously nervous at this point. Andy had me roll over on my left side, and the anesthesiologist began hooking something up to the needle in my hand. There was music playing in the room, and I realized that the song was *Dancing Queen* by Abba. I remarked to Andy that, of all the songs that could be playing during this particular procedure, *Dancing Queen* has to be the least appropriate.

"You want me to turn it up?" said Andy, from somewhere behind me.

"Ha ha," I said.

And then it was time, the moment I had been dreading for more than a decade. If you are squeamish, prepare yourself, because I am going to tell you, in explicit detail, exactly what it was like.

I have no idea. Really. I slept through it. One moment, Abba was shrieking "Dancing Queen! Feel the beat from the tambourine ..."

... and the next moment, I was back in the other room, waking up in a very mellow mood. Andy was looking down at me and asking me how I felt. I felt excellent. I felt even more excellent when Andy told me that it was all over, and that my colon had passed with flying colors. I have never been prouder of an internal organ.

But my point is this: In addition to being a pathetic medical weenie, I was a complete moron. For more than a decade I avoided getting a procedure that was, essentially, nothing. There was no pain and, except for the MoviPrep, no discomfort. I was risking my life for nothing.

If my brother Sam had been as stupid as I was—if, when he turned 50, he had ignored all the medical advice and avoided getting screened—he still would have had cancer. He just wouldn't have known. And by the time he did know—by the time he felt symptoms—his situation would have been much, much more serious. But because he was a grown-up, the doctors caught the cancer early, and they operated and took it out. Sam is now recovering and eating what he describes as "really, really boring food." His prognosis is good, and everybody is optimistic, fingers crossed, knock on wood, and all that.

Which brings us to you, Mr. or Mrs. or Miss or Ms. Over-50-And-Hasn't-Had-a-Colonoscopy. Here's the deal: You either have colo-rectal cancer, or you don't. If you do, a colonoscopy will enable doctors to find it and do something about it. And if you don't have cancer, believe me, it's very reassuring to *know* you don't. There is no sane reason for you not to have it done.

I am so eager for you to do this that I am going to induce you with an Exclusive Limited Time Offer. If you, after reading this, get a colonoscopy, let me know by sending a self-addressed stamped envelope to Dave Barry Colonoscopy Inducement, The Miami Herald, 1 Herald Plaza, Miami, FL 33132. I will send you back a certificate, signed by me and suitable for framing if you don't mind framing a cheesy certificate, stating that you are a grown-up who got a colonoscopy. Accompanying this certificate will be a square of limited-edition custom-printed toilet paper with an image of Miss Paris Hilton on it. You may frame this also, or use it in whatever other way you deem fit.

But even if you don't want this inducement, please get a colonoscopy. If I can do it, you can do it. Don't put it off. Just do it.

Be sure to stress that you want the non-Abba version.

—"Colonoscopy", from I'LL MATURE WHEN I'M DEAD: DAVE BARRY'S AMAZING TALES OF ADULTHOOD by Dave Barry, copyright © 2010 by Dave Barry. Used by permission of G.P. Putnam's Sons, a division of Penguin Group (USA) LLC.

Dave Barry's *Miami Herald* column is syndicated nationally.

EXERCISES

1. Find an argumentative essay in *The Writer's Way* or elsewhere that uses an unconventional technique and use it as your model—write an argument that uses that technique. Attach a copy of the model to the essay, and at the bottom of the essay tell which technical feature you're imitating.

2. Write an anti-cliché—an essay that argues *against* a trendy belief people hold without thinking about it: argue that cotemporary movies aren't violent enough, that speed limits should be done away with, that exercise is unwise, etc. For a great example, see "School Is Cool" on p. 25. *Don't make it a joke*—mean what you say.

3. Take an argument from A Collection of Good Writing and write a one-page essay answering the four diagnostic questions we discussed earlier. How many of them did the essay address?

4. Do Exercise 3 using an argumentative essay you found outside *The Writer's Way*.

5. Do Exercise 3 using an argumentative draft of your own. Rewrite the draft, adding passages to address any of the four diagnostic questions you didn't address.

6. Write an essay using one of the following essays from Chapter 15 as a model:

   a. "Being a Parent Is A Balancing Act"

   b. "Why?"

   c. "I, Too, Am Optimistic About Our Racial Future"

Part Five

Academic Writing

287

Chapter 16

Research

We talked some in Chapter 3 about academic writing, which is more about gathering and synthesizing data than about observation and personal opinion, so you need research skills. Data may be found in the field (interviews and questionnaires) or in the lab (experiments), but these days it's most commonly found online (Surprise!), in databases, scholarly articles, newspapers, and Web sites. That's not to say that your library, with its stacks and stacks of books and bound periodicals and drawers full of microfilm and microfiche, should be ignored, but these days you can find vast amounts of current and credible sources with a few clicks of your mouse—sometimes so vast that it's easy to get overwhelmed. In fact, hard-copy newspapers and magazines around the world are shrinking and in some cases disappearing altogether, as text has become more accessible and convenient—and certainly greener—by way of the Internet, iPad-type tablets, and various smart-phone apps.

So naturally, you probably want to go electronic very early in your research.

Before you do, though, consider some perhaps less obvious sources:

Your instructor. She works with the research materials in your field every day and can probably recite them off the top of her head for you.

Librarians. These wonderful people go to school for eight to twelve years just to learn how to help you find what you're looking for. Don't be reluctant to ask for help—they love this stuff.

Your library's support system. Any academic library should have student tours, free research guides in various disciplines (often called something like

"How to Find Information on a Poem"), live seminars on topics like using the electronic databases, and online tutorials in research methods.

Your classmates. Often the majority of the students in a class are working on similar research projects. Share your findings with one another. Point your classmates to articles, Web sites, and databases that you found useful (just as you would if you and a friend were both looking to buy new flat-screen televisions or laptop computers).

ONLINE RESEARCH

Keep in mind that many online sites and documents are commercial, intended first to make money, not to provide useful information; some are bogus; many are plagiarized themselves. So you need to determine which sources will be credible and most useful for your paper. (See CRAPP test, at the end of this chapter.)

If you're uncomfortable doing electronic research, ask for help. Reference librarians now spend most of their time helping people find useful indexes, databases, and full-text articles. Additionally, most academic libraries have tutorials on how to do effective electronic research. Go to your library's Web site and look for a "Help" or "Tutorial" link.

Databases

This is where most of the serious, academic research is published. A database is essentially the old periodicals section of the library in digital form. It's typically available only by subscription, so your library will buy rights to use it and you will access it through your library's Web site, often using a password. The database may be an index—a list of titles—or it may be a collection of abstracts, in which case you get paragraph summaries of entries. But more and more databases are *full text,* meaning you can call up the complete text of an entry at a mouse click.

Your library may offer you a choice among fifty databases. Which ones should you use?

Ask the librarian. Tell him what you're working on, and ask him to recommend a database. He'll steer you to the most user-friendly, comprehensive one available at the moment.

Start with full-text databases only. They'll cut your work time by about 90 percent. If and only if what you need isn't there, use the abstract indexes next and the plain indexes as a last resort.

Choose a degree of breadth. Each database covers a certain territory. Some, like Academic Search, survey all academic fields. Some, like Science-Direct, are devoted to broad areas like science or the humanities. Some are devoted to single disciplines or issues like literature or feminism. Some are indexes to individual journals or newspapers. The more you know what you're looking for, the more focused a database you want.

Look at the time frame. What years does the database cover? In the old days, the problem with bibliographical tools was they were often months or years out-of-date. Now we have the opposite problem: since the data is so vast and is coming in constantly, databases often chuck older information before it's really old—and include data before it's been thoroughly credited and/or peer reviewed. Many databases contain entries only from the last few years. And some databases, believe it or not, contain no entries from the most recent few years. Depending on your project, you may find these databases useless.

Use more than one database. No database searches all available documents on a topic, so if you want to be thorough you'll use several of them.

Choose a level of sophistication. Some databases cover only cutting-edge academic and professional articles. Some cover popular magazines. Some cover newspapers. Pick one that talks at your level. If you're writing on the politics of radical mastectomy, there's no point in trying to decipher the *Index Medicus* when *Newsweek* or *Women's Health* will speak your language.

Once you're inside the database, you order it to search in one of two ways. You can do keyword searches, the way you do in an Internet search, where you pick a word or two central to your project and ask the search to retrieve every entry that uses those words. Just as often, you'll want to work from the topic *index* at the beginning of the database, select a topic ("English literature" or "sports"), which will lead you to a list of journals in the field, and then search individual journals by the keyword method.

Web Sites

Web sites range in credibility from serious academic publications to commercial trash, which is what often come up first when you do basic Google-type searches. They're also usually free, as opposed to subscription databases.

By far the most important thing to remember about using the Web is that no one screens what you're receiving, so you'll have to judge the value of a site yourself. Any psychopath can build a Web site and distribute her ravings, so never assume that the content of a site has any inherent credibility whatsoever.

Subject gateways. While search engines, especially Google, have become more or less the default places to start online research, subject gateways can be more useful for academic papers. They're directories devoted to narrow fields, typically run by editors who are specialists—thus the quality is very high. If you can find one, start your research here. Find them by looking at your library's list of research tools under a topic like "Anatomy" or by asking someone in the field, like your instructor.

Narrowing your search. Once you've found a search tool and gotten to the keyword stage, you're ready for the moment of artfulness: designing the search parameters. When people first use search tools, they're excited by the fact that a three-second search can turn up 100,000 documents. Soon they realize that this deluge of information is a curse. You don't want 100,000 documents; you want the five useful ones. The trick is to design a search that calls up as few pages as possible without missing any important ones.

Here's how novices do it wrong: you're writing a paper on Captain Cook's influence on native cultures. So you type in "Captain Cook Native Cultures Influence," and you get back a list of every page with any one of those words used prominently, all 50 million of them, including all references to captains, chefs (cooks), natives, cultures (probably stuff about strep throat), and influences (probably including ads for attorneys specializing in DUI representation). Here's how you do it right: you learn the database's search language, a short series of instructions about how to conduct searches, instructions communicated by words and symbols: most commonly +, −, "", *and, or, not,* *, and capitalization. With many search engines, typing in *"Captain Cook"* + *"native cultures"* will bring up only those pages with *both* of those complete phrases. Five minutes spent learning two or three rules in the search language can reduce a hit list from 100,000 to 4. Languages differ from one search tool to another, and each tool should have a help page with the necessary tutorial. If you can't find one or get help from a librarian, consult the Purdue Online Writing Lab (Web).

The most powerful search tool on the Web, and the easiest to use, turns out to be none of the three we've seen so far; it's the links contained within Web sites. Almost every site on the Web has several links to related sites—the virtual equivalent of a recommended reading list. If you can find one useful Web site, its links will probably give you several more, and each of those will give you several more. Sometimes the links are *hyperlinks,* highlighted keywords throughout the Web site text that automatically take you to other sites; sometimes they're listed in a "Related Web Sites of Interest" list at the end of the site or in the main menu.

USING THE LIBRARY

Think of the library as being made up of two parts: (1) the texts, those books, articles, and encyclopedia entries that contain the actual material you need; and (2) search tools, instruments like catalogs, indexes, and bibliographies that help you scan the texts and find the ones that contain your information.

The Texts

Libraries traditionally divide their holdings into five sections: books, references, newspapers, government publications, and periodicals. You find your way around each by means of its own search tools.

Books are the part of the library we think of first. They reside in the *stacks,* and you find your way around them by means of the *main catalog,* which is probably electronic and accessed through a keyboard in the library's reference area or through your computer at home. You can look in the main catalog under the author's name, the book's title, or the subject. Unless you seek a specific title or author, you'll be most interested in the *subject catalog.* You type in keywords, just as you do surfing the Web. You might consult the nearby *Library of Congress Subject Headings,* a big book that helps you use keywords the catalog recognizes. For instance, if you look under "Home Heating," it may tell you to type in "Heating—Home."

Books are the easiest part of the library to navigate, but they're a poor source of information, for two reasons. First, since it takes years to write, publish, and catalog a book, any information in the book stacks is at least several years old, so the information is likely out-of-date. Never use a book as a research source without checking the publication date and deciding if it's too old to be relevant. Second, books are aimed at wide audiences, so they're usually broader in scope than a journal article, and you have to wade through lots of pages before you know if a book includes the information you seek. Use books when you want a broad introduction to a subject, like the history of England, but in more detail than an encyclopedia would give you.

One good thing about books is that they're physically present on the shelves and grouped by topic. So when you find one book that's helpful, the books on either side might be helpful as well. Always examine the books to either side of any book you take from the stacks. You can't always do that in a database.

Unfortunately, **reference sections** of libraries might be going the way of dial telephones. The reference section used to be the place you went to find out how to say hello in Swahili or when Omaha, Nebraska, was founded, or to get a list of Beethoven's complete works. Not anymore. Most such facts are now available online and *very* easy to find. Naturally, it's also easy to get the wrong information (see below for information on determining the legitimacy of online sources), so you need to be careful, but for the most part you can get current, accurate almanac-type information with the click of a mouse.

Having said that, I still recommend familiarizing yourself with the reference section of your library. Sometimes you'll run across information there that you wouldn't find online, largely because of the way the material is organized. As with books in the main catalog, reference materials are grouped by disciplines and topics, and you're likely to discover a resource you didn't even know existed right next to one you were looking for.

Newspapers usually have their own section in the library. The virtues of newspapers are obvious: they're up-to-date, the articles are about very specific topics, and they're written in plain English. But they have two major drawbacks. First, they're very hard to find your way around in, because they're almost impossible to index. Second, they're undocumented—you rarely can tell who wrote something or where the data came from. I suggest you use newspapers only if you're looking for something you know is there—if you know that the *Los Angeles Times* had a big article on your topic on page 1 on April 12 of this year—or if the newspaper has a good index. The move to electronic databases has helped here. It used to be that only newspapers like the *New York Times* and the *Christian Science Monitor* were indexed, but now even my local small-town weekly is.

Another use for newspapers is to provide historical context for a paper you're working on. Let's say you're writing a paper about your community's reaction to President John F. Kennedy's assassination on November 22, 1963. You could look at a newspaper published the next day (either hard copy or microfiche; something from that long ago probably won't be electronically archived) to find out what the weather was like that day, what was playing at theaters, how much a loaf of bread cost—all of which would help both you and your readers imagine that day.

Governments produce a constant stream of publications on everything under the sun. These **government documents** are usually a world unto themselves in the library, a maze of pamphlets, fliers, commission reports, and the like, often without authors, dates, or real titles, often identified only by serial number, usually listed only in their own catalog and not in the main catalog. This section of the library, like the others, is converting rapidly to an electronic format. Using the government publications is an art. Often one reference librarian specializes in them; start with his help.

The **periodicals**—the magazines and journals—are by far the most useful section of the library for most researchers. The information is up-to-date, specific, and usually well documented and well indexed. If the library has a print subscription to a periodical, the very recent issues are usually out on racks for people to browse, but the older ones are collected—usually all the issues from a single year or two together—bound as books, and shelved in their own section of the stacks. More likely you'll access the articles through an online database to which your library subscribes. Soon all scholarly journals will be available only electronically, while libraries will probably continue to subscribe to hard copies of popular magazines.

Library Search Tools

The best article or book in the world is useless if you don't know of its existence. The academic world knows this, so it has developed an industry that does nothing but produce tools to help you find what you're looking for. All these search tools come in print form (books) and electronic form (Web sites and databases). There are four basic sorts: bibliographies, indexes, abstracts, and research guides.

A **bibliography** is a list of titles of works on a subject and publication details that tell you how to find them. Often indexes are called bibliographies, which may be confusing.

An **index** is like a bibliography except it's usually a multivolume, ongoing project, with a new volume every year or so. The 2013 volume lists publications in the field for 2012, which means that if you want to see what's been published over the last ten years, you may have to look in ten different volumes.

Bibliographies and indexes just list titles and information on where to find them, but an **abstract** will give you a one-paragraph summary of the work, which can save you from frequent wild goose chases.

The best of all is a gift of the computer age, the **full-text database**. This is an enormously helpful bibliography that contains the complete text of the articles it lists. When you find an entry that looks promising, you click on it and it appears on your screen. If it's useful, you can print it out right there—glorious! So you want to use full-text search tools when you can, abstracts as a next best choice, and bibliographies and indexes as a last resort. Any electronic database your library owns will tell you if it's full text always, sometimes, or never. Some databases are "full page," which means you're looking at a photocopy of the original printed page, and some are "full text," which means they merely scan and reproduce the written words, so you may not get graphics.

Search tools, like encyclopedias, have subjects, and they range from very broad to very specific. The broadest are bibliographies of all topics, like *The Reader's Guide to Periodical Literature*. It will tell you what has been published on your topic in any given year in any of several hundred popular magazines and journals. Use it if you want to know what *Redbook* or *Esquire* published on your topic.

Some search tools are devoted to broad academic areas:

The Humanities Index

The Social Sciences Index

Business Periodicals Index

Others are devoted to specific disciplines:

Music Index

Index Medicus

Biological and Agricultural Index

Child Development Abstract and Bibliography

Psychological Abstracts

Abstracts of English Studies

There are search tools in subdisciplines, like Victorian poetry, movie reviewing, and neuroenzyme chemistry. Often the leading journal in a discipline publishes a yearly index of work in the field.

A **research guide** does more than list entries; it's a real instruction manual on doing research in the field. It may summarize or critique the sources it lists, review the bibliographical materials available, give an overview of what's being done in the field, and even suggest fruitful new lines of inquiry. Research guides are sometimes devoted to very specialized topics, such as the one on minor nineteenth-century novelist Elizabeth Gaskell. If you can find a reference guide to your subject, and it isn't out-of-date, begin your research there.

The most underutilized research tool in the library is the special kind of index called a **citation index**. It lists every time one author or work has been referred to by another—in other words, it's a bibliography of everyone working on your research question.

EVALUATING THE CREDIBILITY OF YOUR SOURCES

Because so much information (and noninformation) is available both in hard copy and online, you must be vigilant about determining what's credible and what isn't. Most libraries' tutorials include guidelines for making sure that a source is current, credible, and valid. I like the one developed by Sarah Blakeslee and Kris Johnson at my library (Meriam Library at California State University–Chico)—and not just because of the unusual acronym.

The CRAAP Test

The **CRAAP Test** is a list of questions to determine if the information you have is reliable. Keep in mind that the following list is not static or complete. Different criteria will be more or less important depending on your situation or need. So, what are you waiting for? Is your Web site credible and useful, or is it a bunch of ... ?

Currency: *The timeliness of the information.*

When was the information published or posted?

Has the information been revised or updated?

Is the information current or out-of-date for your topic? Are the links functional?

Relevance: *The importance of the information for your needs.*

Does the information relate to your topic or answer your question?

Who is the intended audience?

Is the information at an appropriate level (i.e., not too elementary or advanced for your needs)?

Have you looked at a variety of sources before determining the one you'll use?

Would you be comfortable using this source for a research paper?

Authority: *The source of the information.*

Who is the author/publisher/source/sponsor?

Are the author's credentials or organizational affiliations given?

What are the author's credentials or organizational affiliations?

What are the author's qualifications to write on the topic?

Is there contact information, such as a publisher or email address?

Does the URL reveal anything about the author or source (e.g., **.com, .edu, .gov, .org, .net**)?

Accuracy: *The reliability, truthfulness, and correctness of the informational content.*

Where does the information come from?

Is the information supported by evidence?

Has the information been reviewed or refereed?

Can you verify any of the information in another source or from personal knowledge?

Does the language or tone seem biased or free of emotion?

Are there spelling, grammar, or other typographical errors?

Purpose: *The reason the information exists.*

What is the purpose of the information? to inform? teach? sell? entertain? persuade?

Do the authors/sponsors make their intentions or purpose clear?

Is the information fact? opinion? propaganda?

Does the point of view appear objective and impartial?

Are there political, ideological, cultural, religious, institutional, or personal biases?

Chapter 17

Using Sources

Since in academic writing you're constantly using other people's texts to support your case and seek answers to your questions, a large part of the art consists of smoothly weaving other people's words and thoughts into your own paragraphs. There are three ways to do that: summary, paraphrase, and quotation. Let's look at them in order of difficulty, hardest first, and in order of desirability—summarize most, paraphrase next most, and quote least.

SUMMARY AND PARAPHRASE

Professionals summarize a lot, often reducing a large article or report to a single sentence. You read David Rakoff's wonderful 3,500-word essay "Streets of Sorrow" (*Condé Nast Traveler*, November 2006), and you summarize it this way: "Although Hollywood destroys the dreams of most who come seeking fame and fortune, those dreams are still worth having." When you summarize like that, you can refer to several difference sources or articles in a single paragraph.

Paraphrasing is saying someone else's content in about the same number of your own words. It's what you do when you tell a friend what another friend told you. David Rakoff writes, "People have been coming out West with stars in their eyes for so long, and for just as long, some have returned to where they came from, their hopes dashed. But if the fulfillment of one's dreams is the only referendum on whether they are beautiful or worth dreaming, then no one would wish for anything." I might paraphrase, "According to David Rakoff, like all those who came West only to return home, their dreams destroyed, we must continue to dream, to continue to wish for things." Notes: (1) You see how my paraphrase loses the urgency, the grace, and the overall power of the original, which is why sometimes it's better to quote a passage, or parts of a passage—see below. (2) It's important that even when paraphrasing, you acknowledge the source of the original; if not, you're plagiarizing. See Quotation and Documentation, in the following pages.

Why paraphrase when it's easier to quote? For at least three reasons: (1) You don't want your paper to be simply a list of things other people have said. (2) Your audience is probably different from the original audience. You might be taking a quotation from *American Film*, a journal for serious film scholars, and using the material in an article for high school English teachers who use film in their classes. (3) Oftentimes, paraphrasing helps you understand the original. In fact, when you put a passage into your own words you internalize it in a way that you don't when you simply quote.

Considering the following quotation from *All Music Guide*:

"U2 started out as a Dublin pub band and began earning recognition after the band won a talent contest sponsored by Guinness in 1979. This led to the release of a three-track EP, U2–3, that topped the charts in Ireland and won them quite a following" (Erlewine 336).

Now you could simply change that around and put it into your own words or you could make it your *own*. I look at that, and I think, Hmm, rock band, pubs, Guinness, Ireland, contest, and so I would do something like this:

It seems only natural that a band that started out playing Dublin pubs would get it its big break by winning a talent contest, in 1979, sponsored by Guinness, makers of the Emerald Isle's famous ale. According to Iotis Erlewine, the contest led them into the studios, where they recorded U2-3, which became hugely popular despite containing only three songs (336).

Or:

It seems only natural that a band that started out playing Dublin pubs would get it its big break by winning a talent contest, in 1979, sponsored by Guinness, makers of the Emerald Isle's famous ale, after which they recorded U2-3, which became hugely popular despite containing only three songs (Erlewine 336).

My versions are longer, but I don't think they're "wordier"—still pretty tight writing, thank you very much. But they're mine now; I've brought something to them that I think makes them work as well as the original in other ways.

Remember too that when you're paraphrasing, you need to **change the original in two ways:**

- You must change the *language* of the original, or, as your teachers used to say, "Put it into your own words."
- You must change the *structure* of the original. That is, you need to change the way the original sentence or passage was structured.

Read the original below and the paraphrases that follow. Which are plagiarism, and which are acceptable?

> Original: "Good grades in English may or may not go with verbal sensitivity, that is, with the writer's gift for, and interest in, understanding how language works."
>
>   (JOHN GARDNER, ON BECOMING A NOVELIST, 3)

1. *People may or may not do well in English classes depending on how sensitive they are to language, or to their talent or interest in making sense of language (Gardner 3).*
2. *According to John Gardner, a writer's sensitivity to language, or her gift for or interest in understanding how language works, may or may not have a bearing on the grades she gets in an English class (3).*
3. *According to John Gardner, it's difficult to know why students do well in English classes. It may have to do with how sensitive they are to language—whether it's natural talent or just interest in the subject (3).*

What do you think? Plagiarism? Number 1 keeps the structure of the original and a lot of the original language as well. Verdict? Plagiarism. Number 2 changes (reverses) the structure but keeps too much of the original language. Plagiarism. Number 3? This one changes both the structure *and* the language. This one's acceptable. Note that all three document the original correctly: if there's no signal phrase ("According to John Gardner") or the source is otherwise unclear, then it must be identified in the parenthetical, by the author's name and page number (MLA format). If the source is identified or otherwise clear, all that's required is the page number. (Note: page numbers are used for books; it's different with electronic sources. See p. 307.)

QUOTATION

Why and When to Quote

Quoting is useful because it helps you back up your claims. But it's easy to quote too much. Instead of thinking and writing, you are simply transcribing the thinking and writing of others. So limit your use of quotations. A paper should never be more than one-fifth quotation by volume. Never quote a passage just to reproduce what it *says*. Rather, quote only when the *words themselves* are important. Quote only the few words you absolutely need: as a rule of thumb, *be reluctant to quote an entire sentence.*

Here's an example where the words are important and interesting, so it makes sense to want to keep more of them than you might in a less well-written passage:

> "Selling out can be defined as any action that puts money and celebrity as a priority over art and paying respect to one's loyal following.

There are shades of gray, and mitigating circumstances. I think, for instance, we can all agree on the Willie Nelson Rule: Any artist who once owed more than $10 million in back taxes and helped start Farm Aid can be forgiven for a Taco Bell commercial and a couple of Christmas albums."

(From the *San Francisco Chronicle*, "Give Me AC/DC, Tom Waits. They Didn't Sell Out," by Peter Hartlaub, December 1, 2008)

Here's one way to paraphrase that keeps a fair amount of the author's original wording—and, in so doing, some of the spirit of the original:

> According to Peter Hartlaub, any band that "puts money and celebrity over art and paying respect to one's loyal following" is guilty of selling out. Of course, Hartlaub acknowledges "mitigating circumstances," and suggests we forgive an artist who, for example, has made Taco Bell commercials and Christmas CDs if he also once owed millions in back taxes and was a founder of Farm Aid. Hartlaub calls that his "Willie Nelson Rule," of course.

How to Quote

Students like quoting entire sentences and passages because they're easy to punctuate:

> Hoffmeister captured the essence of Lang: "When the dust has settled and we can see him standing clearly before us, we see that the real Lang is not really comic, but tragic."

If you must do this, don't connect the quote to your previous text with a period or a comma:

> Wrong: *Everybody knows that some artists sell out. "Selling out can be defined as any action that puts money and celebrity as a priority over art and paying respect to one's loyal following" (Hartlaub).

> Wrong: * Everybody knows that some artists sell out, "Selling out can be defined as any action that puts money and celebrity as a priority over art and paying respect to one's loyal following" (Hartlaub).

Instead, integrate the key part of the quote into your own sentences:

> Everybody knows that some artists sell out, which Peter Hartlaub defines as "any action that puts money and celebrity as a priority over art and paying respect to one's loyal following."

Or:

> Everybody knows that some artists sell out. Peter Hartlaub agrees: "Selling out," he writes, is "any action that puts money and celebrity as a priority over art and paying respect to one's loyal following."

Remember that writing is not all that different from talking, and we do this when we talk.

You'd never *say:*

It's the best restaurant in town. Their burritos are awesome (my roommate).

You'd say:

It's the best restaurant in town. My roommate says their burritos are awesome.

You'd never *say:*

Professor Brown, who teaches Psychology 101, is the laziest professor in the department (Heather Jordan, psych major).

You'd say:

Heather Jordan, who's a psych major, says Professor Brown, who teaches Psychology 101, is the laziest professor in the department.

Same with writing: Don't hesitate to use "According to" and "She says" a lot (even if she's writing it and not saying it):

Peter Hartlaub says that selling out is "any action that puts money and celebrity as a priority over art and paying respect to one's loyal following."

If the quotation takes up four or more lines of (your) text, indent the entire quotation and leave space above and below it. And don't use quote marks.

Quoting whole sentences is wasteful, however, so try to avoid it, or at least don't do it very much, which is why you must learn to punctuate a quoted phrase within your own sentence. The trick is *to make the quotation match the grammar of its surroundings.* In other words, the passage must make logical and grammatical sense with or without the quotation marks. So make sure the quotation has the same number, tense, and person as the text around it. If the sentence is in past tense, the quotation will probably have to be in past tense. Here's a quotation that goes awry:

Wrong: *When George sees his mother, he doesn't know "how I can tell her of my pain."

To check yourself, read the sentence without the quotation marks and see if it makes sense:

Wrong: *When George sees his mother, he doesn't know how I can tell her of my pain.

You can solve the problem in two ways:

1. Use less of the quote:

When George sees his mother, he just isn't able to tell her about his "pain."

2. Rewrite the quotation slightly to make it fit. Surround the changes with square brackets (not parentheses):

When George sees his mother, he doesn't know "how [he] can tell her of [his] pain."

DOCUMENTATION

Why and When to Document

Readers care greatly about the sources of your insights and your information. The daily paper or *People* magazine almost never tells you where its facts come from, because readers are far more interested in the information than in where it came from, but in academic writing, your ideas and information are only as good as the place where you got them and your conclusions only as good as the facts they're based on. Scholars call telling the reader where you found the information *documentation, citation,* or *referencing.*

What needs to be documented? There are things that come out of your own head—personal feelings, opinions, memories. Those things don't need documentation. Nor do facts that are easily verifiable. If you write that Tierra del Fuego is at the southern tip of South America or that Louis Armstrong was born in New Orleans, you don't need documentation, because your reader can verify the fact in any atlas, encyclopedia, or Web site. But if you assert that Tierra del Fuego has tactical nuclear weapons or that Louis Armstrong was a major influence on Tupac, you'd better tell the reader where you found out. Here's a way of looking at it: if your reader is going to respond by saying, "I don't think so" or "Oh, come on, that can't be right," then you'd better document what you've said. If you write, "Lady Gaga was born in 1986," your reader is going to take you at your word— because the information is easily verifiable—and so he doesn't need documentation.

Note: Students are often told that they need to document anything that's not "common knowledge." That advice doesn't work, in part because what's common knowledge to some people isn't to others (remember, it's all about audience). The fact that Mt. Shasta, in Northern California, is 14,179 feet high is certainly not "common knowledge," but I don't need to document it because it's "easily verifiable" (and no one's going to say, "Oh, come on, that can't be right").

Document for two reasons. First, you must have accountability. If your reader doesn't know where the information came from, he can't evaluate your sources or see if you're using them well, and thus he can't trust you. Second, you must avoid plagiarism, the number one pitfall of the research paper.

Students are often shocked by how rabid their instructors are about documentation; they say, "But if I do that I'll be documenting every other sentence!" That's quite rare, actually, except perhaps in a highly technical or literary dissertation. Keep in mind that your job is to explore what others have said about your topic, to make connections among them, to synthesize them, and to draw conclusions. Think of it this way: a research paper that would need documentation for "every other sentence" is little more than a bibliography with excerpts. Instead of having someone read your paper, you might as well just refer her to your sources. What you want to do instead is "own" the citations, make them your own, as in my paraphrase above about the origins of U2's success.

How to Document

The two most common are MLA (Modern Language Association) citations, which are used by most of the humanities, and APA (American Psychological Association) citations, used by most of the sciences.

Both of these citation formats use brief information in parentheses in the text as a kind of shorthand cue to bibliography entries at the end of the paper. You write, "In fact, Earth has been invaded three times by aliens" ( ), and between those parentheses you put just enough information to point your reader to the complete publication information in the bibliography. The two systems give different cues, and consequently they format the bibliography differently as well.

MLA Citations.   The MLA has established a citation system used by scholars in literature and allied fields. It puts in parentheses the author's last name—or a keyword from a Web site, for example—and the page number. That's all—no punctuation, no "p.," *nada*.

```
In fact, Earth has been invaded three times by aliens
(Smith 12).
```

This tells the reader to look through the bibliography until he gets to a work by Smith; there he'll find out the author's full name, the work's title, the publisher, date of publication, and anything else he needs in order to find a copy of the source himself.

In any of these citation systems, the basic rule is to put in parentheses the minimal information the reader needs to find the bibliography entry. So if your text tells the reader the author's name, the parentheses don't have to:

```
Smith showed that Earth has been invaded three times by
aliens (12).
```

But if there is more than one Smith in the bibliography, you'll have to tell the reader which one you mean:

```
In fact, Earth has been invaded three times by aliens
(J. Smith 12).
```

And if Smith has more than one title in the bibliography, you'll have to tell the reader which one you mean by including an abbreviated version of the title:

```
In fact, Earth has been invaded three times by aliens
(Smith, Aliens 12).
```

It's often easier to include that sort of information in the text itself:

```
Jolene Smith, in Aliens Among Us, argues that Earth has
been invaded three times by aliens (12).
```

If you're working with plays, poems, long works divided into books, or any text where the page number isn't the most useful way of directing the reader to the spot, give her whatever is. For a play, give act, scene, and line numbers; for a poem, give line numbers; for a long poem divided into books, give book and line numbers:

```
Hamlet blames himself for his "dull revenge" (4.4.33).

The people on Keats's urn are "overwrought" (42) in more
than one way.

We're reminded by Milton that Adam and Eve don't cry for
very long when they leave the Garden of Eden (12.645).
```

Hamlet's line occurs in Act 4, scene 4, line 33, Keats's comment in line 42 of "Ode on a Grecian Urn," and Adam and Eve's tears in line 645 in Book 12 of *Paradise Lost*.

When you find yourself in a situation not quite covered by the rules, just use common sense and remember what citations are for: to get the reader to the bibliography entry. If the work has no author, you'll have to use the title as a cue:

```
In fact, Earth has been invaded three times by aliens
(Aliens Among Us 12).
```

If the title gets bulky, it's cleaner to put it in the text:

```
"Studies of UFO Sightings in North America, 1960-1980"
offers strong evidence that Earth has been invaded three
times by aliens (12).
```

Or use a short form of the title, if it's unambiguous:

```
In fact, Earth has been invaded three times by aliens
("Studies" 12).
```

Rules of Thumb for MLA Works-Cited List. In 2009 the MLA simplified its format for bibliographies. It's still called "Works Cited"; the sources are in alphabetical order (not numbered); the first line of each entry is still unindented. But writers no longer include the URLs of online sources (instructors might still ask for this; if yours does, do it). (Note: If the keywords aren't enough to point your reader to the source— that is, if he would not likely find the correct source without the URL—then you should include it.) Instead, with each entry you must indicate the medium of publication, usually as "Print" or "Web." In the entry, you include all information the reader might need to locate the source itself (*not* a particular page or passage in the source). Here's a typical entry for a book:

```
Smith, Jolene. Aliens Among Us. New York:
    Vanity, 2007. Print.
```

Here's a typical entry for a magazine article:

> Smith, Jolene. "Aliens Among Us." *UFO Today*
>   14 Jan. 2007: 10–19. Print.

The title of the article is in quotation marks; the title of the whole volume is in italics. All information about volume numbers, issue numbers, seasons (e.g., the fall issue), days, months, and years is included. The page numbers are the pages the article covers, not the pages you used or referred to in the citations.

For online sources, you need to include the author's (or editor's) name, if available; the name of the article (in quotation marks), the title of the Web site or article (in italics); any available publishing information; page numbers (if available); the medium of publication (Web); and the date you access the site. Note: If there is no author or editor given, alphabetize by the title of the article or Web page.

Here's a typical entry for an online source:

> Smith, Jolene. "Aliens Among Us." *UFO Blogopedia*.
> 14 Jan. 2007: 10–19. Web. 5 Dec. 2010.

APA Citations

The APA has a citation system that is used by many of the social sciences. Sometimes called the name/date or the author/year system, it gives the author *and the year of publication* in parentheses, and usually omits the page number:

> In fact, Earth has been invaded three times by aliens
> (Smith, 2007).

APA encourages you to put the author's name into the text, put the year in parentheses immediately following the name, and put the page number (with the "p.") at the end of the sentence if you choose to include it:

> According to Smith (2007), Earth has been invaded three
> times by aliens (p. 12).

Rules of Thumb for APA References List.   Because the APA scheme asks the reader to find sources by author and year, you must structure the entries in the bibliography (which the APA calls References instead of Works Cited) so the year of publication immediately follows the author:

For a book:

> Smith, J. (2007). *Aliens among us*. New York:
> Vanity Press.

For an article:

> Smith, J. (2007, January 14). Aliens among us.
> *UFO Today*, pp. 10–19.

APA Citations.   List the following elements in this order, when available:

1. Author
2. Date of work or date last modified
3. Title
4. Information on print publication
5. Type of source, in brackets: for instance, [Online], [Online database], [CD-ROM]
6. Name of vendor and document number, or "Retrieved from" followed by the URL

Rules of Thumb and Helpful Hints for Using Online Sources

1. See if the source itself gives you citation instructions. More and more, encyclopedias and other sources online include a header that begins with something like "Cite this article as ..." You can just copy it down.
2. Unless otherwise instructed, use the traditional citation format as a template and make the electronic citation conform to it as closely as possible. For instance, if there is no title for the piece, ask yourself, "What is the nearest thing to a title here?" and put it in the title's place. Personal email isn't titled, but it usually has a subject line (aka the "re" line) when it appears in your mail cue, and that will serve.
3. The less bibliographical information you have on a source, the less you should use it at all. Even online, a work of integrity tends to have an author with a real name, some sort of page-numbering system, a publication date, and a permanent existence in some stable archive. If your source has none of these, maybe you shouldn't be taking it seriously.
4. Print at least the first page of any electronic source you use—it will preserve the reference data across the bottom or top.
5. If you use an electronic version of a print source (like a newspaper article from a database), do not cite the print version—acknowledge in your citation that you used the electronic form (since the page numbers are different, for one reason).
6. When making a parenthetical reference to an Internet source that has no author (which is happening more and more frequently), remember the parenthetical's main purpose: simply to point your reader to your Works Cited or References page. So find a keyword that will appear on that page and use it in the parenthetical. Example: You're citing a sentence from Junior's Juke Joint (a personal favorite Web site; you'll recognize it by the bullet holes in the pages ...), which does not identify its author. Just quote the sentence, and then use a keyword from the name of the site, like this:

"If you're hanging around a Delta juke joint and you notice somebody sipping a clear liquid from a plastic milk jug, the liquid probably ain't water. Ask them for a sip; it's wonderful stuff" (Juke).

7. Perhaps the most important rule of all: never include the URL in the body of your text, even in parentheses. There's little that's more annoying, or that makes a writer look lazier or more uninformed, than a twenty-seven-character URL right in the middle of an essay or research paper.

MAKING SENSE OF IT ALL

Obviously, both MLA and APA citation formats are quite complex, what with your needing to document everything from government documents to YouTube clips to personal interviews, so it's impossible to memorize everything. Do you write the date of a magazine "December 2," "Dec. 2," "2 December," or "12/2"? Do you italicize record album titles or put them in quotation marks? If you have four authors, do you list them all or just list the first and write "et al."? Don't try to memorize answers to all such questions; instead, remember four principles:

1. Use common sense and blunt honesty. If you're entering something weird and you're not sure how to handle it, just tell the reader what it is. If it's a cartoon, write "Trudeau, Gary. 'Doonesbury.' Cartoon," then the usual newspaper information. If it's an interview, use "Interview" as your title. If it's a private conversation or a letter, write "Private conversation with author" or "Personal letter to author."

2. Err on the side of helpfulness. When in doubt about whether to include information—a government pamphlet's serial number or a TV show's network— put it in.

3. Be consistent. Once you do it one way, keep doing it that way.

4. Get a style manual or research guide, or bookmark an online guide and use it frequently and carefully. (I had to do it for working on this chapter!) My favorite is the Purdue Online Writing Lab (Web).

MODEL CITATIONS

Here are templates for common bibliography entries, in MLA and APA formats.

A book with an edition number and multiple authors:

MLA: Tremaine, Helen, and John Blank. *Over the Hill.*
         10th ed. New York: Houghton, 1946. Print.

APA: Tremaine, H., & Blank, J. (1946). *Over the hill.* (10th ed.). New York: Houghton Mifflin.

A book with an editor:

MLA: Blank, John, ed. *Over the Hill*. New York:
      Houghton, 1946. Print.

APA: Blank, J. (Ed.). (1946). *Over the hill*. New
      York: Houghton Mifflin.

A book with an author and an editor or a translator:

MLA: Blank, John. *Over the Hill*. Ed. Helen Tremaine.
      New York: Houghton, 1946. Print.

APA: Blank, J. (1946). *Over the hill* (H. Tre-
      maine, Ed.). New York: Houghton Mifflin.

MLA: Blank, John. *Over the Hill*. Trans. Helen
      Tremaine. New York: Houghton, 1946. Print.

APA: Blank, J. (1946). *Over the hill* (H. Tre-
      maine, Trans.). New York: Houghton Mifflin.
      (Original work published 1910)

A government pamphlet:

MLA: United States. Dept. of Commerce. *Highway
      Construction Costs per Mile, 1980–1990*.
      #32768. Washington: GPO, 1991. Print.

APA: U.S. Department of Commerce. (1991). *High-
      way construction costs per mile, 1980–1990*
      (DOC Publication No. 32768). Washington, DC:
      U.S. Government Printing Office.

Anonymous article in a well-known reference work:

MLA: "Alphabet." *Collier's Encyclopedia*. 1994 ed.
      Print.

APA: Alphabet. (1994). *Collier's Encyclopedia*.

Anonymous newspaper article:

MLA: "Remembering the Horror." *San Francisco
      Chronicle* 11 Sept. 2007: A1. Print.

APA: Remembering the horror. (2007,
      September 11). *San Francisco Chronicle*, p. A1.

Television show:

MLA: *Company's Coming*. ABC. KZAP, San Francisco.
      13 Oct. 2006. Television.

APA: *Company's coming.* (2006, October 13). San
           Francisco: KZAP.

Lyrics from a record album or compact disc:

MLA: The Rutles. "Company's Coming." *Live Rutles.*
           RCA, 1964. CD.

APA: The Rutles. (1964). Company's coming. On
           Live Rutles [CD]. New York: RCA.

World Wide Web journal article (these model citations have been taken verbatim from Nick Carbone's Writing Online, 3rd edition, Houghton Mifflin, Boston and New York, 2000):

MLA: Lewis, Theodore. "Research in Technology
           Education: Some Areas of Need." *Journal of
           Technology Education* 10.2 (Spring 1999):
           85–89. Web. 2 Aug. 1999.

APA: Lewis, T. (Spring 1999). Research in tech-
           nology education: Some areas of need. *Journal
           of Technology Education, 10*(2), 85–89.
           Retrieved from http://scholar.lib.vt.edu
           /ejournals/JTE/v10n2/lewis.html

Personal email:

MLA: Russell, Sue. "E180 Fall 1999." Interview with
           the author 10 June 1999. Email.

APA: The APA discourages including in the ref-
           erence list any source that can't be accessed
           by the reader. Cite personal e-mails in the
           body of the text.

Database:

MLA: U.S. Census Bureau. "Quick Table P-1A: Age and
           Sex of Total Population: 1990, Hartford-
           Middletown, CT." 1990. *U.S. Census Bureau,
           American FactFinder*. Web. 10 June 2010.

APA: U.S. Census Bureau. (1990). Quick Table
           P-1A: Age and sex of total population: 1990,
           Hartford-Middletown, CT. *U.S. Census Bureau,
           American FactFinder*. Retrieved from http://
           factfinder.census.gov

EXERCISES

1. You've written a term paper citing the following sources. Make two end-of-paper bibliographies, one in the MLA citation system and one in the APA.

    a. A book called *Mystery Train: Images of America in Rock 'n' Roll Music,* by Greil Marcus, published by Plume Press in New York City in 1997.

    b. A book called *The Best American Travel Writing,* 2005, edited by Jamaica Kincaid, published by Houghton Mifflin Company in Boston in 2005.

    c. An article titled "Google's Moon Shot," written by Jeffrey Toobin, in *The New Yorker,* February 5, 2007. The article runs from page 30 to page 35.

    d. An essay called "Dancing with Dylan," by Wendy Lesser, in a book called *The Rose and the Briar: Death, Love, and Liberty in the American Ballad,* edited by Sean Wilentz and Greil Marcus and published by W. W. Norton and Company in New York in 2005. The essay begins on page 317 and ends on page 325.

    e. An anonymous editorial called "What Was He Thinking?" in the *San Francisco Chronicle* on February 2, 2007, on page 7 of Section B.

    f. A personal email sent to you by Stan Bimee, with the subject line "Song Allusions in Stephen King Movies," sent on January 27, 2006, and received by you the same day.

    g. An anonymous article called "Redneck Pig Roast," at www. deltablues .net/roast.html. No author, no page numbers, no dates.

    h. A YouTube clip of Paul McCartney, George Harrison, and John Lennon doing the famous "Pyramus and Thisbe" scene from *A Midsummer Night's Dream* on an old British television variety show at www.youtube.com/watch?v=Y8obSjg8IXw.

2. Imagine that the following sentences each cite one of the sources in Exercise 1, sentence "a" citing source "a," sentence "b" citing source "b," and so on. Add parenthetical citations to each sentence in each of our two citation formats. For example, the first sentence with a citation in MLA format might look like this: "Marcus claims that Elvis Presley is a metaphor for the American experience and represents both the best and the worst of our society" (12). Invent page numbers as you need them.

    a. Marcus claims that Elvis Presley is a metaphor for the American experience and represents both the best and the worst of our society.

    b. In her introduction, Kincaid writes, "The Travel Writer doesn't get up one morning and throw a dart at a map of the world, a map that is just lying on the floor at her feet, and decide to journey to the place exactly where the dart lands."

    c.   Toobin writes, "Google intends to scan every book ever published, and to make the full texts searchable, in the same way that Web sites can be searched on the company's engine at google.com."

    d.   Bob Dylan's songs have more to do with traditional dance than most people realize.

    e.   San Francisco mayor Gavin Newsome is in deep trouble after news of his affair with an employee leaked to the public.

    f.   "Stephen King is both a musician and scholar of pop music, and his stories that have been made into movies make effective use of music."

    g.   "Since they have nothing to do the rest of the day but stand beside the fire and season the pig and turn it every once in a while and, since it's a cold winter morning, that's a damn good time to pass around a bottle of Old Stumphole 90 proof sour mash. At lots of pig roasts, the fellows who started the pig to roasting are sound asleep at eating time."

    h.   At a time when the Beatles were the darlings of the pop world, they could get away with anything and in fact be quite successful even as comic Shakespearean actors.

3. Write two unacceptable and one acceptable paraphrase of each of the following. Share them with your classmates, discussing the degree to which both the language and the structure of the originals were changed.

"While jazz matured in a climate of segregation, and rhythm and blues out of the inequality that fueled the civil rights movement's push for racial integration, the newer form of black expression, known as hip hop, took shape during the 1970s and 1980s as the American economy was being deindustrialized."

(RICHARD CRAWFORD, *AMERICA'S MUSICAL LIFE: A HISTORY*, P. *848*)

"Throughout the inhabited world, in all times and under every circumstance, the myths of man have flourished."

(JOSEPH CAMPBELL, *THE HERO WITH A THOUSAND FACES*, P. *3*)

Chapter 18

The Academic Research Paper

SETTING OUT

The very idea of a research paper strikes terror in the hearts of many students, or at least makes their eyes glaze over. Fear not, though: they're not that bad. You just need to rearrange your thinking a bit. First of all, keep in mind that research itself is not a bad thing, and it's not exclusively an academic thing. In fact, it's something you probably do every day. Thinking about buying a new laptop? Getting a puppy? Thinking about where to go on spring break? Whether to get a flu shot? Wondering about that exchange program to London? Trying to decide between economics and history as a major? A Honda Civic or a VW Jetta? A new snowboard?

Research, my friend, research.

That's right. You wouldn't go into any of those decisions or purchases blind, would you? So you research. You ask your classmates about their experiences with their Dell laptops and their PowerBooks. You read consumer reports about Civics and Jettas. You demo some snowboards.

Second, remember that the paper itself has a purpose, which means of course that it has a reader. You're doing the research and then putting it together for the benefit of a reader, who will make some use of it. He'll find out from reading your paper whether a flu shot is a good idea or what to look for when purchasing a snowboard.

Of course, chances are you're not going to be writing a college research paper on snowboards. More likely, your instructor will ask you to choose an "academic" topic and submit the paper at the end of the term. If you're lucky, the assignment's parameters will allow you to find a topic that you're truly interested in so that the research you do is useful to you and the paper you write is engaging to a reader. To increase the chances of that happening, here are seven things to keep in mind:

Like all good seeds, a term paper is a task to be performed. It is a question to be answered—or at least explored—or a thesis to be defended.

Your paper has an audience, a potential reader whom you can describe in detail.

Your paper is useful to the reader. She's going to go out and do something with it: quit eating bluefin tuna, set up a compost pile, select a treatment for her disease, put on a fund-raiser for Doctors Without Borders.

You'll know the moment the project has ceased to be useful to someone: when you find yourself copying down information from a source just because it's "on your topic," with no sense of how you're going to use it or why it matters. When that happens, stop and ask yourself again who's going to use your work and how they're going to use it.

The task is achieved primarily through information gathering, not by expressing your opinion.

The subject is something you know enough about to ask intelligent questions. If you write about something you're totally ignorant of, you'll be almost forced into hiding your ignorance, writing on topic instead of task, pointless information gathering, and plagiarism. The good project is one you know enough about to know what still needs knowing. Let's say you're thinking of buying a new laptop computer. Certainly you know quite a bit already, in terms of what you want to use it for: word processing, emailing, online research, burning CDs, streaming movies, taking it with you to class. There are a lot of computers that have these capabilities. How much memory do you need? Which ones offer the best tech support? Which ones offer the best warranties? Which ones are the easiest to upgrade? Which ones have the best screens for viewing movies? These, and probably others, are all questions you'd research before making your purchase.

Your project does something no other source has quite done for you. If you find a book or article that simply does your task, beautifully and finally, you're out of business. You must find a new task, or you'll have nothing to do but plagiarize the source.

Approach the problem in two ways. First, write about what's new. Study the latest advances in a field, before other writers have worked them over. Don't write about how to buy a mountain bike; write about the advantages and disadvantages of the new generation of mountain-bike air-suspension forks. Second, narrow the audience. If you write on alternatives to fossil fuels, a host of writers will have been there before you. If you're writing on the comparative virtues of different kinds of home heating for someone who's building a small cabin in Trinity County, California, considering the area's peculiar wood-fuel supply, power company rates, and local building codes, and your reader's floor plan and budget, it's unlikely that it's been done. If you write on anorexia, everything seems to have been said already; but if you write to freshmen anorexics attending college away from home and talk about the special pressures of that environment on that particular personality type, you're more likely to find new ground to break. And narrowing the audience will make it easier to remember that this work is something someone will *use*.

> The task is neither too big nor too small. "The term paper must be twenty-five to thirty pages," the instructor says, and you just know what's going to happen. Either you'll pick a topic that runs dry after eight pages and you end up padding and stretching, or to prevent that you'll pick a gargantuan topic like U.S. foreign policy and never finish the background reading. How can you find the task that is the right size?
>
> First, any *topic* is too large, because the amount of information on any topic is endless, however narrowly the topic is defined: there's an endless stream of information on Russia, but the stream on Moscow is equally endless, and so is the stream on the Kremlin. Second, any almanac-type question is too small: "How many people in this country actually avoid prison via the insanity plea?" Interesting question, but after you write down "On the average, thirty-five a year," the report is over.
>
> Beyond that, any task that fits our other criteria will prove to be the right size, once you master the skills of Chapter 8 for making a prompt expand or shrink as the need arises. You don't define a thirty-page task at the outset. Rather, you pick a task and begin; as you read and write and think you say, "This is getting to be too much—I have to cut back," or "I'm getting to answers too quickly—I've got to broaden my scope." And you shrink or expand to suit. If I'm looking into chartering a sailboat versus taking sailing lessons, and it proves to be too much, I can write about the pros and cons of chartering only; if it proves too little, I can write about all possible ways to get into sailing, including crewing for other boat owners, or discuss the cost of sailing, including insurance, maintenance, and hardware options. If I'm writing on how effectively the Food and Drug Administration monitors drug testing and marketing and that proves too large, I can write on whether the FDA dropped the ball on Nutra-Sweet; if it proves too small, I can write about whether federal regulatory agencies are effective in your county.

FRAMING YOUR QUESTION

To avoid the problems above, it's important to frame your question usefully. First of all, keep in mind that questions to which the answer is either "yes" or "no" are often useless, or at least keep you from exploring your topic fully. Not only do they oversimplify issues and lead to black-and-white thinking, but they keep you from getting as much out of your sources as they most likely have to offer you. If your research question was "Are bluefin tuna endangered?" and you had the opportunity to interview a marine biologist, all he could say is either "yes" or "no," and then you'd be stuck. So, try framing your question using a phrase such as "To what degree...?", leaving room for gray areas and discussion: "To what degree are bluefin tuna fisheries in trouble?"

Second, you want a question to which there will be a range of answers, from experts. That's why the example above ("How many people in this country actually avoid prison via the insanity plea?") doesn't work. Better: "How successful are alternatives to prison terms granted by insanity pleas?"

Third, you probably don't want a question that simply leads to a list: "What resources are available in Butte County for single moms?" A perfectly good response to that would be just a bulleted list of possible resources, with no need for transitions or discussion (or documentation). Better: "How can Butte County single moms make the best use of the resources available to them?"

GETTING THINGS ORGANIZED

Term papers are largely exercises in handling data avalanches. You need a system for handling bits. Bits are pieces of information: facts, figures, quotes, your own thoughts and ideas, titles of works to be read. You need to be able to find information in your notes, cluster and recluster information quickly, tell whether or not information already has been used in the report, and cite the information in the final draft. Here's how.

Keep track of everything and everything, even stuff you think you might not end up using. Open a separate "Favorites" or "Bookmark" folder on your computer dedicated solely to the project, and save all potential Web sites and other pages there. Write down the full names of book authors, the complete titles of the work, the publishers, and publication information. If it's a periodical, record the volume number, issue number, and date. Record the page number(s) where the things you're taking notes on appear, and absolutely everything else you might need to find it again later. Make photocopies of hard-copy sources and use highlighting pens.

Invent a cueing/categorizing system for your notes. You need a way of labeling your notes so you can tell what they're about without rereading them. Some people use keywords: when they've taken notes on an article, they head the notes with a few keywords (or phrases) identifying the article's main issues. If you're writing on alternative heating sources, you might read an article hostile to wood-burning stoves and end up with a list of keywords like "wood-burning stoves," "air pollution," "shrinking resources," and "health hazards." If three weeks later you want to deal with the health hazards of indoor open fires, you simply make a stack of all note cards bearing the "health hazards" keyword and your data is ready to go.

Build cubbyholes—physical or electronic sites to house notes according to topic or keyword. For hard-copy sources, get a lot of manila folders or even shoeboxes.

Never let the information and its bibliographical data get separated. As you move a quote or a stat from cubbyhole to cubbyhole, keep all information on where it came from attached to it.

Don't forget to brainstorm. As you strive to control the data avalanche, don't get so organized that you forget the lessons of the earlier chapters: writing and thinking are messy, recursive businesses, and you need a lot of loose time to wander and discover. Don't take too much control. Especially don't try to do one task at a time. Writing is multitasking, and you do a creative task best when you're busy doing others. For instance, don't resolve to do the background reading, then draft, because both reading and writing are ways of thinking, and each will propagate the other—read and write simultaneously and continuously throughout the term paper process.

Use Subheads

Subheads are very useful in longer papers to indicate their different parts or sections. And they're helpful to both you *and* your reader. They're helpful to you because they keep you focused, and they're helpful to your reader because she can see more clearly what each part of the paper is about, and it gives her room to come up for air now and then—note the use of subheads throughout this book—or to skip sections she's not interested in.

A couple of semesters ago, one of my students was looking into the "Gross National Happiness Index," which charts the degree to which people are happy in countries around the world. (He got interested in the topic after reading that the United States slipped to number 107 on the list in 2012.) He brought a draft to my office, and it was twelve long pages without any breaks at all—and, frankly, rather hard to get through, and he knew it. But when we simply *talked* about the material, it got more interesting; he told me that generally a people's happiness is determined by the degree to which family is important, the degree to which they believe in a "god," and the degree to which they pursue material possessions—"What if you use those as subheads," I suggested, "to divide up the paper?" He nodded. "Or I could use various countries." Perfect. Then he pointed to a part of the paper where he talked about serotonin and what actually goes on the brain when people are happy. "This doesn't really seem to fit, does it?" he said. I asked him if he might be able to make it work by simply giving it a subhead. When he turned the paper in, that section—just two or three paragraphs—was subheaded "The Chemistry of Happiness," and it worked perfectly.

FORMAT

Since a term paper is bigger than an essay, the format may be more elaborate, with several elements that shorter papers usually don't have. Be sure to read your prompt/assignment carefully so you know exactly what your instructor is expecting, and remember that both MLA and APA formats are very specific in terms of formatting. Among the elements you might be including with your paper:

A *letter of transmittal* on the front, addressed to the receiver of the report, saying in essence, "Here's the report"

A *title page,* on which you give the title, your name, the date, and usually the course name and number and instructor's name

A *table of contents*

An *abstract* before page 1, summarizing the paper for the reader who has only a minute

Section headings: "Introduction," "Conclusion," "Discussion," "History of the Problem," "Three Possible Solutions," "Recent Advances"

Graphics—pictures, tables, graphs—either in appendices or throughout the paper

A *list of illustrations* following the table of contents, if you have graphics throughout the work

Appendices, where you put the raw data the average reader won't want to read

A *bibliography* ("Works Cited" for MLA, "References" for APA) listed at the end

There are models of most of these features in the sample term papers beginning on p. 320. Use those models as templates unless your instructor has her own format.

Important: Don't fall in love with format for format's sake. Many beginning researchers make the mistake of getting too fancy with formatting (like a PowerPoint presentation that's all flash and no substance). Use formatting to make the paper easier for your reader to make sense of, not to impress him.

GRAPHICS

Graphics—tables, graphs, illustrations, photographs—can really increase your paper's effectiveness. They can put complicated data into easily understood images. They can provide concrete evidence of a point you're making (e.g., the way women were typically portrayed in 1960s television sitcoms). In addition, they simply give your reader a break from the text. And with the ease of downloading images, combined with computer programs that easily translate raw data into tables, it's not difficult to end up with a very professional-looking presentation. Some things to remember: (1) Images *are* easy to download, but that means it's also easy to plagiarize. You must acknowledge your sources. (2) Graphics are there to clarify, oftentimes to put what you've said in words into one easily graspable image—for example, a look at how well students do on reading tests based on their parents' income level. News magazines like *Time* and *Newsweek* are masters of that art, so study their graphics for lessons in effective presentation. Here are four principles to follow.

Graphics are not self-explanatory. Be sure to tell the reader exactly what she's looking at and what it means. Title the graphic informatively, label its parts clearly, and explain whatever needs explaining, in notes below the graphic or in the report's text right above or below the graphic. These often take the form of what are called graphic narratives, with the points you want emphasized in bullets directly below the illustration.

Avoid overload. A graphic's power is in its ability to dramatize and clarify a point or show the relationships between a few bits of data. If you try to make a graphic do too much, its power is lost. Better three graphics making three points clearly and forcefully than one spectacularly ornate graphic making three points at once and obscuring all of them.

Number all graphics, unless you have only one. That way you can readily refer to the graphic by saying, "as shown in Figure 4."

Express ideas as drawings. We understand pictures better than numbers, so whenever possible express your data as a drawing, not as columns of numbers—use figures instead of tables, technical writers would say.

Let's pretend you're writing about your "senioritis" at your old high school, and you're claiming that seniors don't take school—especially tests—very seriously. You'd probably make that point in your text, but you could definitely underscore it with an illustration, as shown in Figure 18-1.
Narratives:

- Test scores increased for each of the first three class levels, freshman through junior.
- Junior scores were over twenty points higher than freshman scores.
- Senior scores were five points lower than junior scores, but still higher than freshman and sophomore scores.

Note that different kinds of graphs serve different purposes. Pie charts, for example, are useful for looking at the breakdown of 100 percent of a complete group, such as ethnic groups in a school or different places your monthly income is going. Double bar graphs are good for comparing things like how

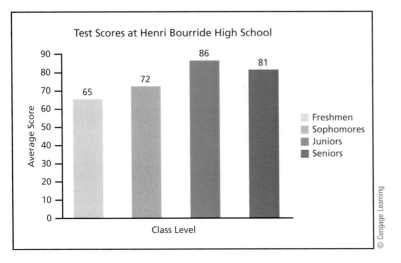

FIGURE 18-1 A bar graph such as this can provide lots of information at a glance

two specific groups—for example, genders—do on tests. A double bar graph in Figure 18-1 could have been indicated by gender as well as by class level, to show the differences between boys' and girls' scores. Line graphs—single or multiple—show growth. Economists love line graphs because they very clearly track change and growth in stock values, employment rates, consumer confidence, and other such figures.

TWO MODEL RESEARCH PAPERS

Here are examples of two quite different research papers—by former students of mine, Miles Reiter and Nicole Benbow.

Miles took a while to get the point where he was ready to write this paper. He and I had talked a lot over the course over the semester about fishing, and I knew that he would propose a final paper on that topic. But his first proposal didn't work: he wanted to write about the state of the world's oceans and the decline of the world's fisheries. "What is this?" I asked him, "a multi-volume book proposal or your life's work?"

"My topic's too big, huh?"

"Uh … yeah."

So he submitted another proposal. This time he wanted to write about the decline of the seafood industry around the world.

Still too big.

Proposal number three: the decline of seafood on the west coast. We were finally getting somewhere, but it was still too big for the "roughly ten-page" paper I had assigned and the six weeks he had to research it. "What if I wrote just about salmon on the west coast?" he said as we talked in my office. I nodded. "Why don't you see where that goes?"

The next class meeting he showed up beaming. "I've got it," he said. "I'm going to look into the decline of steelhead from California rivers." Now he had something to work with, and his paper turned out wonderfully. I think you'll agree (I especially love the descriptive opening).

Nicole was very interested in how women have been portrayed in television sitcoms, knew enough about the subject to get going, but still had lots of questions to ask and experts to consult in order to make her points convincing. Note how, while she takes her subject very seriously, she obviously had some fun writing the paper—and how that translates into wonderfully readable prose.

CAN STEELHEAD SURVIVE?

MILES REITER
STEPHEN METZGER
ENGLISH 2
DECEMBER 8 2012

A lone angler walks briskly through the moss-laden forest on a chilly, damp January morning. As the angler slips through the silent forest his heart begins to race as he recognizes the extra chill in the air and steam sitting almost stagnant in the fog just up ahead: he has arrived. The river appears a stained greenish color, due to a heavy rain that had subsided just two days prior. The angler knows that with rain come the silvery bullets that dominate his imagination: steelhead. He slowly unhooks his lure from his rod, and makes a precise cast, in the slower water just behind a fallen tree. His senses and instincts are sharp and his mind is 100% focused on getting that perfect drift that might result with a fish on the end of the line.

On his third drift, his rod doubles over and his reel begins to scream as a chrome bright, ten-pound steelhead inhales his lure and cartwheels downstream head over tail. The thing the angler lives for is happening and his heart is beating so rapidly he feels that it might pop out of his chest. The fish tries its best to entangle itself and the line in a submerged brush pile, but the angler knows the river, and is able to steer the fish away from it. After five minutes of strenuous battle, the angler gently pulls the fish into the shallow water of the bank and admires the trophy of his dreams. The fish's tail and dorsal fin are see-through clear and its body is a bright, perfect silver. Sea lice cling to the fish, indicating that it may have been swimming in the ocean only earlier that morning. When the fish regains its energy, the angler releases the wild fish back into its ancestral waters, and thanks God for allowing him to get that close to the beautiful, wild fish that define his view of perfection.

What Are Steelhead?

Steelhead are rainbow trout that are born in a river or creek, then after a certain amount of time (it varies), head out to the ocean where they grow large, eating and living at sea. After one to five years, steelhead return to the stream where they were born, lay/fertilize their eggs (spawn), then head back out to sea. A fish may complete this cycle multiple times in its life. According to the Pacific

Northwest Fisheries Program, the average size for adult steelhead is eight to eleven pounds, although anglers have recorded catches of monsters over forty pounds! They are bright silver while at sea and during their first days in the river. Once they have been in the river for a while and are reaching their time to spawn, steelhead become a dark red/purple color, similar to salmon. When a steelhead enters the river fresh from the ocean, it's one of the most beautiful fish on earth.

Disappearing Steelhead

Wild steelhead once flourished in rivers ranging from the Santo Domingo River in northern Baja (Gotshall 51), all the way up the Pacific coast to the rivers of southern Alaska, Kodiak Island, and the Kamchatka peninsula of Russia. They also inhabited all of the tributaries and headwaters of California's Sacramento and San Joaquin River systems (Gotshall 43). Steelhead were very abundant in all of these waters. Nowadays, wild steelhead are still to be found in California, although their range and numbers have reduced significantly. This reduction in population is most noticeable and drastic in southern California, where the species has gone extinct in Orange and San Diego counties (Gotshall 51), and "Most of the remaining stocks are on the verge of extinction" (Gotshall 56) elsewhere in southern California. However, such tiny populations were not always the case in southern California. Gotshall notes that there were "large and consistent runs into the Ventura and Santa Clara rivers" (55). In the Santa Ynez River, which is in Santa Barbara county and is the largest river in coastal southern California, wild steelhead returns in the early 1940s were shown to be as high as over 25,000 adults (Gotshall 54). That is an extremely strong/healthy number of wild steelhead that would be a boon year in any fishery in the Pacific Northwest, where populations are still relatively strong and stable.

Why the Decline?

With the knowledge that there once was a strong wild steelhead population in southern California, and that populations are currently dangerously low, we must look at the factors that have contributed to the decline of these once prolific native fish. Found on the Wild Steelhead Coalition website is a theory that four main groups are responsible for the demise of wild steelhead and salmon in North America. These are known as the "H's" and consist of the following: Harvest, Habitat, Hydro, and Hatcheries. From the same website: "Steelhead habitats include intact watersheds with clean, stable spawning gravels, off-channel habitats and beaver ponds for juvenile overwintering, healthy estuaries and near shore habitats and productive coastal oceans for adult feeding migrations."

In some areas, such as northern California, logging and overgrazing of cattle near streams have caused increased siltation which prevents successful spawning for steelhead, as well as warmer river temperatures due to reduced shade from riparian habitat and the widening and shallowing of the rivers themselves (Moyle, Israel, Purdy, 51). This also lends to easier predation from river otters, other fish (in the case of juvenile steelhead), etc. However, in southern California, "Water development appears to be the primary cause of localized extinctions and decline in numbers within southern steelhead populations" (Gotshall 56). Also, southern California has significantly lower rainfall than the rest of the steelhead's range, with river conditions that are generally not as good as steelhead streams to the north (Gotshall 57). Oftentimes, this low amount of rainfall will create sand-bars that block the stream's flow into the ocean, sometimes resulting in the drying up of lower stream portions (Gotshall 57).

As with many other steelhead streams on the Pacific Coast, dam construction on southern California rivers has blocked access to the more pristine spawning areas found in the headwaters. Natural events such as floods, fires, and droughts occur frequently in southern California and these can all have a severely degrading effect on southern California steelhead (Gothshall 58).

Steelhead of the Central California Coast

Now, we will look at the current state and challenges facing steelhead in the central coast area, roughly from San Luis Obispo County up through San Francisco. Almost all of these streams still contain native runs of fish, albeit usually a fraction of what they once were. Wild steelhead have a higher survival rate in these streams due to several factors. Among them: more consistent rainfall and therefore water flow, cooler water temperatures, and more pristine streams, which haven't been, affected much by humans. Several of these unaffected streams occur in the Big Sur area of southern Monterey and Northern San Luis Obispo counties. However, moving south into the more heavily populated areas of San Luis Obispo County, steelhead populations have declined severely (Gotshall 54).

I am from Santa Cruz County, and the San Lorenzo River that flows into the ocean right next to the boardwalk used to be a world-class steelhead and coho salmon stream. Well into the seventies, anglers would line up shoulder to shoulder in the lagoon area, casting to abundant wild coho salmon and steelhead. Although the river still sees significant angling pressure for winter steelhead, catch rates are a fraction of what they used to be, and the coho salmon fishery is negligible. In the mid-sixties, spawning populations of steelhead in the San Lorenzo River were around 19,000 fish (Moyle, Israel, Purdy 75). In 2005 the estimate for the San Lorenzo River steelhead population was believed to less than 15% of the population only thirty years prior (Moyle, Israel, Purdy 75).

Several factors contribute to the severe decline of wild steelhead in the San Lorenzo River. Mary Spicuzza states that the problems began after the San Lorenzo flooded Santa Cruz in 1955 and was deemed as one of the worst flood hazards in the country. In 1959, the Army Corps of Engineers completed construction of a massive levy in the lower San Lorenzo. They removed the riparian habitat along the banks, which is very critical to steelhead smolt survival. Urban development was built up along the banks, and to this day, much trash, and gasoline and oil runoff persist in the river. Also, as Spicuzza points out, the city was not able to dredge the sediment that accumulated in the lower San Lorenzo fast enough. As a result, the river grew shallower, silt covered spawning areas, and flooding still occurred. Spicuzza writes, "We've been trashing that river for 200 years ..." but with an increased awareness of the river's importance to the local salmonid population, and the dedicated individuals working with the Monterey Bay Trout and Salmon Project, the future for the San Lorenzo River and its steelhead looks positive.

Another factor affecting steelhead populations that is not often looked at is poaching. I am not proud to say it, but I know several individuals who have been involved in poaching wild steelhead in the small creeks near my house. They usually walk the creek, in low-water periods, which doesn't occur during legal steelhead season. Often times they find big, wild steelhead trapped in the few remaining deep holes, and then stick them with spears. I also know of people who set up lines underneath bridges, and catch steelhead that way. It's a sad but true current state in Santa Cruz County streams.

North Coast Steelhead

The streams north of the San Francisco Bay have larger, more established runs of steelhead than the more southerly streams. In many of the small towns along north coast rivers, steelhead and salmon fishing are very important for the economy. That being said, north coast steelhead streams have seen their share of degradation at the hands of man, and wild steelhead populations are suffering accordingly. A perfect example of this is the Russian River. The Russian River enters the ocean in Jenner, in Sonoma County, and used to be one of the top steelhead destinations in the world, with anglers travelling from all over to try to catch the abundant, trophy steelhead. Russian River wild steelhead populations in the 1960s were thought to be around 50,000 fish; in the 1990s, a mere thirty years later, population estimates ranged from as low as 1,750 fish, to as high as 7,000 fish (Moyle, Israel, Purdy 75).

In either case, this is an extremely severe decline. According to a report titled "A History of the Salmonid Decline in the Russian River," "The last 150 years of human activities have transformed the Russian River basin into a watershed heavily altered by agriculture and urban development." Problems on the Russian River are ones we are already familiar with. There are two large dams, Coyote Valley and Warm springs, as well as over 500 small dams on tributaries. Also, water from the Eel River is diverted to the Russian River, and this extra water has increased summer flows many times higher than what they used to be. These extra summer flows would seem beneficial to steelhead, but unfortunately this is not the case. Juvenile steelhead habitat has declined severely with these increased summer flows. Deep, slow moving pools which one contained cool water suitable for steelhead smolt has given way to wider, shallower areas, and the water is warmed due to hot summers and little shade due to a decrease in riparian habitat. All of these factors have created river conditions that are ideal for warm-water fish. Introduced warm-water fish such as striped bass, along with native warm-water species like the Sacramento squawfish compete with, and oftentimes prey on steelhead smolt. Agricultural runoff, sedimentation due to dams, and riparian habitat removal due to timber harvest and urbanization are central themes to declining California steelhead populations, but they are especially notable on the Russian River.

Many of the other famous coastal northern California rivers such as the Gualala, Garcia, Mattole, Mad and others have suffered similar, though less drastic, declines in wild steelhead populations. The area around these rivers contains far fewer people than other areas in California, though man has certainly affected these streams as well. The main adverse effect on these streams comes in the form of logging (Gotshall 38). Logging on unstable and steep slopes leads to massive runoff during high rain periods, causing sedimentation at a time when steelhead need to spawn. Poaching during low-water periods (summer) has also been documented (Gotshall 38). Dams are also a problem on the north coast's two largest river systems, the Eel and the Mad, the Klamath River not included (Moyle, Israel, Purdy 50).

The Smith River, located in Del Norte County in far northwestern California, is a success story in terms of wild steelhead and salmon populations and habitat, as well as wild rivers in general. This river is designated and protected by the federal government as a Wild and Scenic River (Gotshall 35). As such, there are no dams and the river remains in a pristine state, with healthy numbers of wild steelhead and salmon. Although there is no official estimate for the number of wild steelhead that enter the Smith every year, I have heard numbers around 15,000 fish. Smith River steelhead are the biggest in the state, with the largest recorded fish weighing in at 27lbs 40 oz. (*California Department of Fish and Game*)! The Smith River is also home to massive king salmon, the record weighing in at 85 pounds (Martin 36)! This is heavier than any recorded salmon in Oregon or Washington, and the Smith is the best king salmon river outside of Alaska (Martin 36).

The Klamath, Sacramento, and San Joaquin river systems are massive and require their own separate paper in order to thoroughly cover the current state, history, and problems associated with their respective wild steelhead populations. They suffer the same problems as other streams discussed earlier, with many dams blocking prime, historic spawning grounds. The Klamath system, which includes the Trinity River, its largest tributary, has the largest population of steelhead in the state (Gotshall 35). The other two rivers contain steelhead, though they aren't thought of as steelhead fishing destinations.

Maybe It's Not Too Late

Wild steelhead in California are in trouble, particularly in the southern part of the state. Steelhead these days must compete with man for use of their ancestral streams. However, as we have seen with the Smith River, wild steelhead are able to thrive in this day and age. There are many local, state, and federal organizations out there working hard to make sure these wonderful fish will forever return to their native streams. Humans are ultimately the ones who decide the steelhead's fate. It's up to us to make smart decisions that enable these fish to survive and flourish.

Works Cited

"A History of the Salmonid Decline in the Russian River" *North Coast Integrated Regional Water Management Plan.* Aug. 1996. Web. 3 Dec. 2012.

Gotshall, Daniel W. *Steelhead Restoration and Management Plan for California.* Feb., 1996. PDF file.

Martin, Andy. "Smith River Fall Kings." *Salmon Trout Steelheader.* Aug. 2011: 36–37. Print.

Moyle, Israel, Purdy. *Salmon, Steelhead, and Trout in California.* UC Davis Center for Watershed Sciences. 2008. Web. 3 Dec. 2012.

"Salmon/Steelhead." *Pacific Northwest Fisheries Program.* n.d. Web. 3 Dec. 2012.

Spicuzza, Mary. "River's Phoenix." metroactive news & issues. 15–21 Jan. 1998. Web. 3 Dec. 2012.

—Permission provided by Miles Reiter

LUCY, YOU HAVE SOME 'SPLAININ' TO DO

NICOLE BENBOW
PROFESSOR STEVE METZGER
ENGLISH 130H
8 DECEMBER 2008

Abstract

I Love Lucy revolutionized society when it hit the airwaves in 1951. Lucille Ball was the epitome of the stereotypical housewife. However, since the time when that first episode began, America's thinking has not changed much. To this day, there are subtle and elaborate hints that are constantly telling women that they do not belong in the work force, but in the kitchen cooking and cleaning. For better or worse, women are fighting a battle against the portrayals of famous television sitcoms and the ideals of what women's roles should be.

Riddle

A father and son go out fishing for the day. On their way back, they are broadsided in their car and both are in critical condition when they are wheeled into the closest hospital. The doctor, just about ready to operate, looks down and notices the patient. The doctor says, "I cannot work on this patient; this is my son!" How is this possible?

A Woman's Place?

A large heart appeared on the screen, and the familiar theme song to *I Love Lucy* began. The black and white screen cannot take away from the large redhead that filled up the screen. Without fail, a smile would form on my face and I would begin to bob my head and hum along with the theme song. My fifth grade homework, chores, and other activities soon forgotten, I sat engrossed on the couch to watch half an hour of one of my favorite shows. Time has passed since then, and I see Lucy in a new light. She is still an icon and the epitome of clean-cut humor, but things have changed. I no longer laugh when Ricky belittles Lucy for being a "crazy" woman, or smirk when Fred and Ricky think that Lucy and Ethel have it easy staying at home all day. I find myself drawn to the way women were treated in those old days, and even more transfixed that society's wayward thinking has not changed much since 1951. Classic television sitcoms tend to depict the same story over and over again. Women belong inside cooking, cleaning, sewing, etc., while men are supposed to be out working and bringing in the money.

History of the Problem

Show after show illustrates this misconception about women's roles. On the TV hit *I Dream of Jeannie*, Jeannie must always be nice so that her "master" will not send her away. In *Leave It to Beaver*, Mrs. Cleaver always had a bright phony smile on her face; it was such a phony smile it made you wonder what Mrs. Cleaver was really thinking about. Most likely, she wanted to shed her uncomfortable skirts, dresses, and pearls for a nice pair of capri slacks like Mary Tyler Moore did on the *Dick Van Dyke Show*. In fact, Mary Tyler Moore had to fight tooth and nail to be able to wear pants on screen. According to Vince Waldron, author of *The Official Dick Van Dyke Show Book*, her decision "may not seem like a particularly radical choice today, but Mary Tyler Moore's insistence on wearing her own form-fitting slacks on television was little short of revolutionary in 1961" (128).

Since television made its debut, women have been seen and cast as the care-takers. When women did step outside the house and get jobs or become interested in the business world they were usually ridiculed on many television shows. On *I Love Lucy,* Lucy was in charge of paying the bills. To determine which one she would pay she would spin them on a lazy Susan. Ricky sees her do this and just shakes his head at her absurdity. "Her acts of rebellion—taking a job, performing at the club, concocting a money-making scheme, or simply plotting to fool Ricky—are meant to expose the absurd restrictions placed on women in a male-dominated society" (Anderson). However, in episode after episode she could still be seen cooking Ricky's breakfast every morning.

Some Things Never Change

Even the hit TV shows of today do the same thing. On *Desperate Housewives,* only a handful of women have jobs. Susan writes children's books (note that her office is at her home). Lynette is the working mom, and there have been several episodes where she has taken the brunt from family, friends, and strangers for not taking enough care of her family and working too much.

Two nights ago I sat down to watch several television shows and started jot-ting down things that I noticed. From a news program, a reality television show, and a television sitcom, and all the commercials that came in between, there were several things I noted. Why was it that sports broadcasters rarely spent any time covering women's sports? Sports like NFL, NASCAR, NBA, and MLB all got the broadcasters' time and attention. However, sports dominated by females of the same sport got limited coverage. Why is it that women were always seen in com-mercials advertising items like vacuum cleaners, kitchen utensils, and cleaning products while men are seen more often next to rugged trucks and in suits? The answers are simple; these misconceptions are based on the depictions that women should stay at home and be the perfect Mrs. Cleaver.

The patriarchal society is founded on the concept that the male is the head of the household. This idea has been around for decades and will continue to be the dominating force. In today's world, women are actually the majority of the popu-lation, but are treated as the minority. There is a huge underrepresentation of women in politics, sports, and corporate executive positions. Could it be because we constantly depict media images of women not being capable of being indepen-dent over and over again?

About two weeks ago I saw a Dove commercial that rocked my mind. The commercial is called "Evolution," and whenever you get some free time, go to YouTube and watch it. The commercial is less than two minutes long, and it completely challenges the ideals of what beauty is and what we label as right. Women are constantly being showcased on television as needing to be beautiful stay-at-home moms that love every minute of driving their kids to soccer and planning elaborate dinners for their families, and Dove wanted to push the limits of what they consider the new evolution of beauty.

The joke about the college professor is something that always fascinated me too. A college professor wrote the words "woman without her man is nothing." The professor then told the students to punctuate the sentence correctly. The women in the class wrote, "Woman! Without her, man is nothing!" The men in the class punctuated the sentence to be "Woman, without her man, is nothing!" It is a simple joke that is made to bring laughter to a subject as simple as punctuation. However, the sad truth of the matter is that those classic women of the fifties really did rely completely on the men. They were helpless women who stayed at home and did as their husbands asked. It was not common for a woman to have a job, so her say in any matter was what she chooses to cook for dinner each night.

The book *Mass Media in a Changing World*, by George Rodman, discusses the golden age of television and its lasting effect on society. He wrote,

> … critics point out that the golden age wasn't golden for everyone. Lucy wasn't the only woman who was portrayed as incompetent outside of her traditional gender role. Programs such as *Father Knows Best* and *Ozzie and Harriet* portrayed women as stereotypical housewives whose husbands made all the important decisions. Even when female characters ventured out of the home, as Lois Lane did in *Superman*, they were usually subordinate to men (263).

This same book goes on to include the top ten most influential shows of the time. *I Love Lucy* landed in the top spot. *I Love Lucy* changed what people were talking about and had the entire country on the edge of their seats for the episode when Lucy gave birth to her first child.

San Diego State University communications professor Martha Lauzen conducted an annual study of television content. She found that nowadays the higher the number of female creators, actors, editors, etc., working on a show, the more likely the program will be "moved around and surrounded by programs not getting high ratings or shares" (Lauzen). Women are still not taken seriously when it comes to important topics like what is aired for the world to see and watch night after night.

In Michiko Kakutani's article "Books of the Times: A Feminist Eye Studies Portrayals of Women," she discusses the book *Where the Girls Are Growing Up Female With the Mass Media*, by Susan J. Douglas. According to Kakutani, Douglas views many Disney heroines as sweet, beautiful women who need rescuing by a prince and "the wicked stepmothers and queens are 'older, vindictive' women, who have 'way too much power for their own good, embodying the age-old truism that any power at all completely corrupted women and turned them into monsters'" (1). Every Disney movie I have ever seen goes along with this concept that when a woman gets power things go bad. Maleficent and Cruella de Vil will forever be on Santa Claus's bad list for their evil deeds.

Speaking Out

I can remember when the country band the Dixie Chicks was on top of the world. Their albums sold by the millions and their concerts were sold out. The main singer, Natalie, made a comment about how she was ashamed that President George Bush was from Texas. Whether or not you thought the comments were made in good or bad taste, these women had every right to express their opinions on the subject. However, the backlash these women experienced as a result of the statements that one of them made was phenomenal. Fans that had supported them for years were stomping on their CDs or burning them in protest. Tickets sales dropped dramatically and their latest CD fell off the top album list immediately. Emily Robinson, one of the band members, felt that much of the anger stemmed from the fact that they were an all-female band speaking their minds. In the *Playboy* (December 2005) issue she was quoted as saying, "It's way worse. A guy would have been an outlaw, the Johnny Cash or Merle Haggard of his generation…. Read the stuff on the Internet: 'Just tell that bitch to shut up.' They don't want to hear mouthy women to begin with. Forget about its going against their political grain." Oh, no, are you telling me that there are really women out there that speak their minds on hush-hush topics—how revolutionary!

Women have proven that they are equals when it comes to men. Nevertheless, women take a backseat to men. Lucille Ball, a woman who was seen as an icon, was put under great inquiry in newspapers and gossip columns when she and Desi Arnaz divorced. People could not believe that the characters on TV were not really in love in real life, and I guess they could not believe that women did not "belong" in the kitchen either.

Real women everywhere are still captivated by the idea that they need to be reliant on the man. Dr. Nick Neave, an evolutionary psychologist from Northumbria University, published the article "Sorry, but Women Are Dependent on Men." He reports:

> One might argue that it's only natural for today's women in their 30s or 40s to feel dependent on a man. After all, the vast majority were raised by mothers who by and large didn't have careers and were forced to rely financially on their husbands. Yet study after study proves that today's women in their 20s are just as insecure.

Studies have shown that photographs and movies leave a much longer and more lasting impression than just captions or words. Millions of people tuned in to watch shows that showcased the woman-stays-at-home sitcoms, like *I Love Lucy*. These images influenced people more than any speaker, newspaper, or article could. Seeing the same kind of images over and over makes people believe that they must be true. Albert Bandura created the social learning theory that states that an audience's attitudes are shaped by what they learn through others' behaviors. Another theorist invented the Gerbner's Cultivation theory that is based on the philosophy that when people see the same thing over and over again it changes their beliefs.

I will admit that the episode that has Ethel and Lucy going out and getting jobs still makes me laugh so hard my stomach aches afterward. Who knew that watching these two try to package candy would be so funny? What is unfortunate, though, is that when the ladies try to go out and get a decent job they fail miserably. Once again, the show was subtly hinting that women did not belong in the work force.

Hopes and Dreams

Lucille Ball did pave the way for many female actresses in the entertainment business, but she also created the stereotype that women need to be the perfect wives that stay home all day. Lucille Ball was even quoted once as saying, "Women's lib? Oh I am afraid it doesn't interest me one bit. I've been so liberated it hurts." No doubt Lucille Ball had no idea that her acting would change this country and shape some of the basic ideals of women today. She was a young woman who was born to act; she played a character when she became Lucy Ricardo. Her hopes and dreams for the future were not to sit at home and discover recipes and dust every spec of the house. She was a woman who was capable of great things, just like every other woman.

Answer to the Riddle:

The doctor was not a grandfather or stepfather (as many others suspect if my Principles of Sociology class is an indication), but is actually the son's mother! Women's roles are not usually seen as being strong, independent, reliable, and smart, and it makes it hard to cast a woman doctor into the scenario.

Works Cited

Anderson, Christopher. "I Love Lucy." *The Museum of Broadcast Communications*. Web. 28 Oct. 2006.

"Dove Evolution." *YouTube.com*. Dove. Web. 1 Nov. 2006.

Google Images. Google. 2 May 2003. Web. 10 Nov. 2006.

Kakutani, Michiko. "Books of the Times: A Feminist Eye Studies Portrayals of Women." *New York Times* 14 June 1994. Print.

Luzen, Martha. "Statistics on Women Directors." *Movies Directed by Women* 26 Aug. 2001. Web. 29 Oct. 2006.

"Lucille Ball Quotes." *BrainyQuote*. BrainyMedia.com. Web. 30 Oct. 2006.
Neave, Nick. "Sorry, but Women Are Dependent on Men." *Daily Mail*. Web. 11 Dec. 2006.

"The Playboy Interview: Dixie Chicks." *Playboy* Dec. 2005: 10. Print. Rodman, George. *Mass Media in a Changing World*. New York: McGraw, 2006. Print.

Waldron, Vince. *The Official Dick Van Dyke Show Book: The Definitive History and Ultimate Viewer's Guide to Television's Most Enduring Comedy*. New York: Hyperion, 1994. Print.

—Permission provided by Steve Metzger

Part Six

A Collection of Good Writing

Here are some wonderful essays, divided into five groups: personal essays, informative essays, argumentative essays, academic essays, and four pieces *about* writing, by well-known professional writers. Read them, use them as models, learn from them. Most of all, enjoy them.

PERSONAL ESSAYS

YA GOTTA GET A GIMMICK

MEGAN SPROWLS

Student Essay

"Megan, I don't see your name anywhere. Where is it?"

"It's right here, next to—oh no."

"What? Who's … Mazeppa?"

"You don't want to know, Jaime. You don't want to know."

In all reality, Mazeppa was the shield-carrying, gladiator-belt-wearing, trumpet-bumping burlesque dancer I had been cast as in Sondheim and Styne's musical *Gypsy*. She was a horror. She was crude. She was racy. She was a stripper. She was everything I feared.

She was my savior.

I've always carried around a few pounds that I didn't really need, and during my early high school years, my mind had somehow developed a sort of "funhouse mirror" complex which made me think I was a lot larger than I actually was. I decided that I would be able to hide my pudginess by draping myself in baggy jeans, extra large T-shirts, and the biggest possible sweatshirts I could find. I was keeping my true self enclosed under layers of cotton and polyester. I was wearing this exact outfit when my director held up the costume I was expected to wear. It was a black bikini embellished with puff paint and sequins, the highlights of which were two strategically placed tassels.

"Megan, are you okay? You look a little pale."

"Parker, I can't wear that. I just can't. I'll die."

"You can wear bicycle shorts."

"What about the stomach part, Parker? The audience isn't going to want to see *aaaall* of this."

"I guess you can wear a leotard if it makes you feel better."

"Yeah, it would. A lot."

Crisis one was averted. The next day, however, was our first choreography rehearsal. I walked into the theater with a knot twisting and tightening in my stomach at the prospect of having to bump and grind. The choreographer beckoned me onto the stage and I slowly trudged up the stage steps, my worn jazz shoes making a scuffing sound on the stone. Biting my lip, I stepped center stage and prepared for my dance instructions, fiddling idly with the strings on my dance pants, hoping the choreographer would somehow see how uncomfortable I was and take pity on me. She didn't. I bumped and grinded my way across the stage at least twenty times that day, my face flushed with embarrassment the entire time, mostly at the part where I was required to bend completely over and stick my head through my legs with my bottom facing the audience.

I didn't know it at the time, but playing Mazeppa and being forced to confront some of my greatest fears about my body had slowly begun to change the way I looked at myself. Gone were the sweatshirts, the baggy jeans, and the large T-shirts. In their place were cute blouses and Arizona jeans. I began to take pride in my appearance and paid more attention to my hair instead of just pulling it into a ponytail. However, there was still one problem remaining: I had no idea how the audience would react to me playing a burlesque dancer.

Opening night finally arrived and all too quickly intermission was over. I zipped up my knee-high black boots and gave myself one last look in the mirror. I didn't recognize the creature I saw staring back at me. From the three-inch-heel boots and the gladiator-style skirt to the black leotard stretched taut over the flab I had tried so desperately to conceal and the dark red lipstick to the heavily lined eyes, and the gladiator helmet overflowing with purple feathers, I was a completely new person. My transformation was complete: I was no longer the shy, unkempt looking girl I had been a year prior. I had blossomed into a beautiful butterfly after being faced with adversity and took flight as I grew into my femininity.

My breath caught in my throat, I grabbed my trumpet and slowly walked backstage to where my entrance was. Nerves I hadn't felt in years suddenly multiplied by the thousands and settled into my stomach. My hands were shaking. I couldn't do this. I couldn't do it. They would laugh at me. I would be a laughing-stock. Oh, was that my cue line? Cringing inwardly, I burst forth from the sheltering wings of the theatre and stormed on stage, expecting to be booed off. Instead, I heard a very different noise: A whistle. First one, then another. Was that a cheer? Another whistle! I was almost smiling when I opened my mouth to begin my lines. Energized by the audience's response, I performed my dance to the best of my abilities and, from what I hear, "stole the show."

A good actress learns something from every part she plays. She takes something away from being another person and the character becomes part of her, almost as if she were infused into her soul. I thought Mazeppa was a curse, but it turned out that she was the catalyst I needed. I still have my low points, as does everyone, but most of the time I feel that sassy, spunky, take-no-crap-from-anyone character living inside of me. As my song said, "Kid, ya gotta get a gimmick/If you wanna get applause." After playing Mazeppa, I finally had a gimmick: Myself. I was going to show myself to the world instead of hiding behind clothes and bushy hair. If they didn't like me, well then that was just fine, but at least I was out there. I know none of this would have happened if I hadn't sucked it up, gritted my teeth, confronted my fears, and become a stripper who bumped it with a trumpet.

—Permission provided by Steve Metzger

This is a great example of a writer having fun not only with language but with her own childhood perceptions of herself. Remember, we don't like to be preached at. We like people and writers who don't take themselves too seriously. And the language! Just listen: "She was a horror. She was crude. She was racy. She was a stripper. She was everything I feared. She was my savior." Megan leads us one way and then all of a sudden switches directions—with a one-sentence paragraph. Beautiful. And it certainly breaks rules ("Don't use lots of short sentences in a row"), doesn't it? She's even having fun with her title, with all those "g's." And that ending: "… who bumped it with a trumpet." Good stuff.

ONE HUNDRED MILES AWAY

MOLLY COBB

Student essay

On September 27th, 2010, my phone chimed with the following message: *I'm at the top of Royster Clark. If you get this, it means I'm jumping.*

There was more. I'm sure Kyle had written more. Probably something about how much he loved me—how my life, and the rest of the world, would be better off without him. But I didn't care about Kyle's rationale. Only two things mattered: my boyfriend stood on the top of a building, ready to step off, and I stood one hundred miles away in a small dorm room that seemed to be growing smaller by the second.

Maybe I realized it then. Maybe I didn't. But somewhere in the back of my mind, I knew this was the moment where everything would change.

I called his mother, rushing to explain the situation and hoping that through my jumbled words, she'd know what to do. I called my mom and tried to cling to her calming words. "Molly, there's nothing else you can do right now."

And there wasn't. Because when bits of my life seemed to crumble away in front of me, what could I do but stand and watch? Time moved fast and slow all at once. Every ring of the telephone dragged on; every second of doing nothing raced past me, wasted.

I left my room at a dead sprint, racing across campus to my friends, passing people who were completely oblivious to the turmoil I faced. Once in Lyza's dorm room, I sat down in their circle. Lydia to my left, Rose and Ella to my right, and Lyza straight across. My legs trembled from adrenaline I didn't know what to do with, and I frantically looked into their concerned eyes, wanting an answer, reassurance, something we could do. Lyza had already called the police. The waiting began.

The conversations buzzed like white noise around me as I sat through dinner, staring at my plate of a slice of meat, bread, and canned peaches. Eventually I gave up on real food and tried to follow my mom's advice of eating ice cream when feeling overwhelmed, but the mint chocolate chip seemed like tar collecting in the bottom of my stomach.

Everyone did their best to distract me from the dread that seemed to lurk in the corners of the room. Classes, movies, and inside jokes filtered their way in and out of the conversation, but I could barely contribute. It seemed impossible to act so normal. To act as if this night was just like any other.

Lydia's fingers laced through mine tightly, her cold skin refreshing. I leaned against Ella's shoulder, while across the room Lyza conversed over her laptop with our friends back home, the rapid clicking of her keyboard our only sign of contact from the world outside.

We kept waiting. Waiting for a call, a message, some sort of communication from his family, anything to answer the question: will he jump?

"There's no way he did it," Lydia said. I nodded, trying to picture him safe with two feet planted on the ground. Lyza put on a favorite TV show, trying to lighten the mood, but the humor seemed cheap and juvenile, and I couldn't muster a laugh to save my life.

My conversation with Kyle from the night before plagued my mind. We had always talked about problems he dealt with—feeling sad and not knowing why, acting different ways to get attention. But that night he told me he had lied about everything. The secrets and stories that had brought us together over the last few months were nothing but manipulations. Lies to make me act a certain way. My last words, *I can't talk to you*, said with no way of realizing I may never say anything to him again, because even in my darkest dreams and deepest worries, I never could have imagined what this would actually feel like. This terror of not knowing. It was a sharp pain to the center of my chest, a hook in my skin that wouldn't stop tugging.

I pulled out my calculus homework, because math always made sense. Math never lied, never cried out for help through irrational means. Derivatives were honest. Integrals were consistent.

After a couple hours, my phone rang. An unfamiliar number lit up the screen. His sister. She explained that the doctors wanted to take an MRI to make sure the impact had not damaged Kyle's brain irrevocably. She told me about the other tests they had to run as well, but I barely registered anything she said. My worst fears were coming true, but I had to hear the words directly.

Why? I heard myself say. My heart thudded in my ears. *Why is Kyle in the hospital?*

Silence answered my question, as if she was gathering herself together.

"He jumped."

My math binder flew across the room, the pages scattering to the floor. The words rang through my ears, over and over again. *He jumped, he jumped, he jumped.* I felt someone's arms come around me. I pushed my face into the crease of my elbow, and cried for the first time that night.

When I think about Kyle, my thoughts are not of the days we spent sitting side by side at his piano, the muted gray light streaming through the window. The melodies and harmonies of his compositions like whispered secrets between us. I don't think about how close Kyle and I became after only a summer, or the wonder I felt over all the new experiences of a first relationship. I don't think about the last time we saw each other before I left for school, when Kyle took my hand, whispering quietly and confidently, *you can do it.* I wanted to cling to those words forever as I faced the unknown of a new school, new friends, new everything.

Instead I remember the nights I didn't sleep in my own room because I didn't want to be alone. I remember the hospital visits that followed. I remember his face, swollen two sizes too big. I remember the tube down his throat, forcing him to write the question, *do you still love me*, with bruised hands. I remember the pain as I slowly, over months, began to understand that trying to be friends again wasn't healthy for me.

Every day I make new memories. I make new decisions. I form new relationships. I try to figure out the things I value most. Like drops of water, those parts of my life pool together to make who I am. But that night in September is a single drop of blood tainting the water, discoloring it with swirls of red, until I can't remember that the pure, clear liquid ever existed.

—Permission provided by Molly M Cobb

In this powerful essay, Cobb deftly handles a difficult and painful topic— a suicide attempt of all things—without getting maudlin or sentimental. Again, it's the details at work, speaking volumes about not only her relationship but allowing her to step back and put it into perspective. Read over those last two paragraphs again and note how she uses the simple word "remember" both to provide a sense of rhythm to the piece and also bring it home—after all the details she can remember, she wonders if there might be something that she can't.

BIGGER IS BETTER

MORGAN F. HEUSCHKEL

Student Essay

Like many people in this country, I drive my own car. Well, perhaps "car" is a misnomer. I actually drive a boat. A land yacht. It's a 1984 Mercury Grand Marquis—four-door, beige, and big enough to require its own zip code. Ten years ago, I would have laughed at the mere thought of driving such an oversized behemoth. But things have changed. I have changed. I'm almost embarrassed to say it, but I actually like my car. I really like my great big American car.

I certainly didn't start out that way. I had spent most of my youth being driven around in small imports, like the Nissan and Mazda owned by my parents. Both were most sensible and economical cars. Then, at age 23, I inherited my grandmother's Grand Marquis (I guess when you're a grandparent you can drive what you want). I balked, even in the face of this unconditional generosity. "Drive this ... this tank?" thought I, while my friends zipped around town in their Volkswagens and Toyotas. Never! But drive it I did.

It took some getting used to. At first I got agoraphobia sitting in the front seat, and it took half an hour to scrape off the bumper sticker that read "Retired and Loving It!" I had one or two minor "incidents" before I fully learned the Mercury's perimeters. But, please, don't tell my mother—I blamed any and all body damage on irresponsible, anonymous drivers backing into the car in the parking lot at Penney's while I was shopping for blouses. However, I can now parallel park in places like San Francisco with such grace and acumen that bystanders often burst into spontaneous applause. No, really. And soon I found myself warming to the Creature.

For one thing, the Merc had some undeniable practical virtues. It could seat six without even blinking, and was obscenely comfortable. It had a stereo like a concert hall and automatic everything—windows, seats, mirrors, brakes, steering, you name it. The suspension practically levitated over speed bumps and potholes and did ninety miles per hour like a walk in the park, albeit a very fast one. And I'm safe. Thirteen years ago safety features like anti-lock brakes and air bags weren't the relatively standard additions they've become today, so the Mercury went without them, but it more than made up for them by surrounding me with two tons of solid beige steel and at least twelve feet of breathing space between me and either the nose or the tail of the car. Garbage trucks bounce off me.

But the matter went beyond pragmatics. I began to relish the unapologetically un-P.C. nature of the car. In this age, when smoking has the same social cachet as baby seal slaughtering, the Mercury has three (yes, three) sets of lighters and ashtrays. My mother's '92 Mazda didn't even come with a lighter. And mileage? While I never did any formal number crunching on the subject, a rough estimate places the car's mileage at around eleven miles to the gallon, under the most optimal of conditions (say, the hand of God pushing you down the freeway). If you're used to driving and being driven around in smaller cars, it can take a while to get used to being behind the wheel of a car with such … presence. There is much to be said for what a big car can do for your self-image. It is not coincidence that many larger American cars are reminiscent of armored personnel carriers. While tooling down the road, imagine that you are A Most Powerful Person. What would you do to solve the budget crisis? How about that nasty little mess in the Middle East? Go on, give those kids at the bus stop a presidential wave and a flash of your famous smile. Chomp on a big see-gar. There, feels good, doesn't it? Try getting that sense of empowerment from a Hyundai.

I began to notice that smaller, more economical cars were no longer attractive to me. While eyeing the ads in magazines and newspapers, I would pass over the colorful spreads on Sentras, Accords, and Tercels, and home in on the layout for the new Oldsmobile Cutlass Sierra. On the street, El Dorados and Impalas would sing to me. And when I got to borrow a friend's 1982 Cadillac Brougham de Ville for a week while he was on vacation, I thought I'd died and gone to heaven. Azure blue, with wondrous lines and a body in pristine condition, this monster and I spent a glorious week touring the countryside. Replete with leather interior, four built-in lighters, and every button, knob, and gadget known to man, the Cadillac showed me that there were even bigger, more luxurious fish to fry than my little Grand Marquis.

Sure, people can call cars like mine "gas guzzlers," "space hogs," and "boats," but are theirs the voices of economic and ecological practicality, or the green-tinged song of jealousy? Tired and grumpy from years of bumping knees, noses, and elbows in the cramped interiors of their "practical" cars, these people turn their ire on us, the drivers of luxury liners, in an attempt to salve their pride. Might I suggest, good people, that you put aside your indignation and mistrust and consider taking a drive on the wide side? Borrow your Aunt Ethel's yellow Cadillac for a week and discover the joys of driving big. Sit behind the wheel of that cavernous expanse of leather and steel and knobs and dials, of foot wells roomy enough to make a basketball player giggle and a trunk so big you need a miner's helmet to see it all. See if your heart doesn't melt just a little.

—Permission provided by Steve Metzger

This is a personal essay that, despite the fact that it's decidedly "me-oriented," connects to a reader. It's funny, and it's fun, and you don't get the sense that Morgan is full of herself or trying to teach us anything—partly because, like Megan does, above, she acknowledges that there might be just a slight gap between her perceptions of herself and others' perceptions of her. And she's fine with that, in a lighthearted way. It's also fun because she's exaggerating, and we know it, and she knows we know it. And she's got a great eye for detail (she "shows"): four-door beige 1984 Grand Marquis, shopping at Penney's for blouses, Aunt Ethel's yellow Cadillac, the "Retired and Loving It!" bumper sticker, for example. Additionally, she brings up issues we can all relate to, like the cost of gasoline, the "nasty little mess in the Middle East," and the difficulty of parking in big cities (San Francisco).

HIDE AND SEEK

EMILY ANDERSON

Student essay

I remember my childhood in bits and pieces. I used to write it all down, but those journals have since disintegrated into ash under red-hot flames. Burning paper doesn't erase the past, but once it's gone, the permanence of the memory seems to float away with the fire's thick smoky curls. Burning journals is one form of therapy I have found most helpful in relieving myself from the little girl I used to be.

When she silently cried herself to sleep, it was because she believed that nobody loved her. She was a sad little girl with a troubled family life. Wrapped in her mind like a vine to a tree, this little girl over-analyzed most things and blamed herself for just as many. Her family fostered a black hole of dark secrets, enough to match each star in the sky. She often covered up for her parents and their dangerous habit, hoping to save at least a little face. No one could possibly comprehend the feelings that consumed her from day to day. She found solace in guidance counselors and the school nurse. Adults often excused her from her normal classes so she could be with them in peace. In middle school she found herself with few friends to confide in. It's hard to go over to a friend's house on the weekend when your parents are always too drunk to drive.

She remembers the responsibility that weighed on her shoulders, pulling her closer to the ground each day. She often prepared dinner for herself and her brother. Macaroni and cheese was the easiest. She loved the way the spoon *schloped* through the gooey noodles. After dinner it was up to her room to read or attempt homework. Help on homework was as foreign and unreachable as the Himalayas. It's easy to reach the base but impossible to get to the top. This little girl's parents were either too intoxicated to comprehend the math or too angry to offer a helping hand. She remembers cold, salty tears streaming down her face from the frustration of her life situation. What did she do to deserve this? Will it ever end? She always thought that her parents were supposed to help her. They did just the opposite.

She remembers that day mom took the rusty scooter up to the store to buy a gallon of milk. With only a swimsuit and a skirt, the hard plastic wheels *thump-thumped* across the sidewalk, skirt flowing gracefully behind her. She told her children to keep an eye on the macaroni and cheese until she returned. Four hours later, her father's work phone was ringing, and his daughter asked if he had talked to Mom lately. The mac and cheese was still sitting out on the stove, anticipating the milk.

In her head, this all seemed so bizarre. Moms are supposed to be the ones looking out for their children, not the other way around. She briskly walked five blocks to the store to ask the clerk if he had seen her mother. She asked the neighbors if they had seen her. A twelve-year-old girl should not be faced with such serious errands. After many unfulfilling responses, a discontent feeling began to settle in her stomach like water sinking through sand. She felt like she was on a scavenger hunt, almost like this was all just a game of hide-and-seek. Where was her mother hiding?

One hour and one phone call later, Dad was on his way home from work. Two hours later, Grandma was on the phone. Three hours later, we were calling around to different family friends. Four hours later, hospitals. Five hours later, the bus station. Six hours later, the credit card companies. Nothing. It was like she vanished into thin air. Why had she left and not come back? A river of questions rushed down the canyons in my mind. Twelve hours later, Mom had still not come home. Why would someone who loved their family put them through this misery? We didn't sleep a wink that night.

Alcoholics are smart when it comes to covering up their sickness. This little girl was well aware of the deceitfulness involved in keeping up a habit as consuming as alcoholism. She learned how to make excuses for herself through her parents' modeling. Two days later and this little girl's mom had still not come home. The police were informed, and an investigation began. The news they reported back to her family was revolting. Their alcoholic was smart and called into work every morning claiming to be too sick to come in. This prevented her family from being able to file a missing person report. She wasn't missing; she was just hiding. It really had turned into a game of hide-and-seek.

The little girl remembers making excuses for her mother. Making excuses for her actions. There must be a reason she left her family. She'll come home tomorrow. Or the next day. Or the next. The mac and cheese on the stove began to crust around the edges, still waiting for the milk that never came back. It wouldn't give up; it would hold out as long as it possibly could. No one in her family dared remove it from the stove. That pan was the last memory the girl had of her mom. Her family secretly clung on, hoping that soon the meal would be completed.

After many days of painstaking excuses, she realized something more powerful than all her previous excuses combined. The answers to her questions were simple. Why would someone who loved their family leave and not come back? Someone who truly loved their family *wouldn't* put them through that pain. She didn't truly love her family.

Four days later, the scooter, swimsuit, and skirt finally returned home. Although there was no gallon of milk in this mother's hands, the family was grateful for her safe return. While her mother was away, this little girl realized she had to grow up fast. She emptied the dried, spoiled macaroni into the garbage can, thinking to herself as she scraped the noodles from the sides. As she watched them fall and mix in with the rest of the garbage, she swore off her mother from her life. From that point on, she decided she didn't need to waste energy on someone who chose a liquid substance over her family. She scraped those feelings away with the macaroni. She told her mother she was done until she decided to put her family before alcohol. Years passed before that became a reality.

As time passed, she began to see her family more as roommates and less as a family. She longed for the day she turned 18 and could move out of her nauseating household. She would move far, far away and never have to deal with her parents' childish behaviors ever again. She was done with fun and games. No more hide-and-seek. She was not that little girl anymore.

—Permission provided by Emily Anderson

This is a courageous essay, one that could have easily gone awry. But Emily makes it work with a cool little technical device: she switches from first person, which is how most personal essays are written, to third. While there's never any doubt that the "she" is the same person as the "I," the switch provides some distance, which I imagine made it easier for her to write. It also makes it easier to read. I think that if she'd written the whole thing in first person, it might have come off as whiny. She avoids that and in so doing writes a very moving piece about growing up in a very difficult environment.

HOW TO TALK TO YOUR KIDS ABOUT DRUGS

ROSA LEVY

Student Essay

If you get to that day when you have kids and they grow up a little and they want to know about drugs, do you tell them? Do you tell them all of the things you did, starting at age sixteen, when you met Suzie and Jenn and started drinking and smoking cigarettes and driving around in your car all night or sitting down by the river talking about boys and sex (which you had never had then, but it wouldn't take long—your friends were always bragging that they had slept with so many and teasing you that you hadn't, and you felt small and silly even when you drank beer and drove your car fast and stopped going to school for a while)? Will you tell them how drinking made you sleep with boys who were mean to you, how you would go to anyone then, how your mother (good, smart, bewildered mother, who always taught you to make your own way, never thought you would be mean and dumb and waste your life and mind and body as if they were a worthless burden to you) waited up for you at night afraid that you had died and then screamed "I don't know what you are turning into" and you screamed back that you hated her because the last thing you would ever be able to do was admit that who you were turning into was somebody you hated too? And maybe if you told your kids this story when they were young enough that they still had that kind of perfect adoring love for their parents then later when they got mad and mean they would remember that story and not want to lose themselves or you, even if it is only for a little while.

There are other stories too, increasing in depravity (or at least intensity)—do you tell those? How at the first college you went to you met Megan and Mark and started to smoke pot and then drop acid and eat those bitter little mushrooms but it was an intellectual, spiritual experience then or so you all liked to say and so you would take acid and look at trees and talk about books and ideas and lie in the park twirling perfect flowers over your head and go to concerts in dark halls with day-glow amoebas crawling the walls and the music exploding through you and it always seemed like everyone should be hallucinating, like you had discovered the true Tao of life, but that there is a lesson here too because it ended with flunking out of college, with a dull head and sad-achy, realizing that another year or so had passed and you still didn't know how to make yourself happy by working and making stuff that lasts and that every time you fail even a little bit you remember it, so that the next time you try to do something your past reminds you how easily you gave up before? So maybe your kids will look at you and see all that wasted time, and how the drugs never did open you up so much as divide you into pieces of people and that sometimes you still have to collect the pieces off the floor and stuff them into clothes and try to walk around like you are whole, hoping nobody can see the places where you are coming apart.

Do you tell the last tale, the one that hurts the most, which you probably shouldn't tell them because most days you can barely tell it to yourself, because there are some things that can be forgiven and some that can't, some that hang around and hover at the edges of sleep, smack you awake and gasping knowing that whatever you do, you were once this person capable of these things and that knowledge never goes away? So do you tell them how you were married and somehow you didn't want to be married any more so you started to sleep with Eddie, and Eddie sold but mostly used cocaine, and somehow you started doing it with him in his bedroom in his mother's house while she slept and how for ten minutes at a time you got to be this superstar in your own life, and how the two of you moved on to amphetamines and would get high and walk all over the city, laughing and talking about life as if it were this curious, trifling thing and ordering food in restaurants and walking out without eating it and figuring you must be the smartest people in the world to have discovered something so easy and fun that hurts no one and they say isn't addictive? Or about the inevitable divorce and how you began begging money from all your friends until they ran from you and all you cared about was getting high, until finally you went to Europe to escape everything, especially yourself, who you hated for ever thinking there was a way out of living besides getting up and facing yourself every day unblinking, and drugs, which you hated for taking sweet people and smart people and good people and destroying them by telling them that horrible lie that living a life that is sometimes quiet and disappointing and ordinary isn't good enough, that you need a life where you get to be a superstar? Maybe that is the thing to tell them, the one thing, and maybe you don't even have to sacrifice yourself, maybe you can just tell them that there are ways to escape your life for a minute or two and that these ways can feel incredible for a minute or two but the loss is that you trick yourself into believing that there is a way out of the work and drudgery that sometimes is life, and that if you trick yourself too many times you may not remember how to look at life on a spring day and see the sun shining and feel all the wonder of that growing and not need anything to make you feel how beautiful and perfect that moment is.

—Permission provided by Steve Metzger

I always tell my composition students to take risks in their writing, especially in early drafts, which they can run by readers to see if those risks are paying off. If you're not sure what "taking a risk in writing" means, read this one. Talk about risks! It's a personal essay and an argument at the same time. It seems to be rambling talk, but it's a very hard kind of thing to write. Our reaction to Rosa keeps getting more and more complex, because her view of herself is so multifaceted. She describes her weaknesses with so much skill that we both accept her self-loathing and admire her for her courage. And what courage this essay has! Not only the courage to discuss the author's sins in the raw without sentiment, but also the courage to take the reader on an exhausting roller coaster. And notice that while it's utterly fresh and original, it's a redressing of two of the oldest clichés in essay writing: "Just say no to drugs" and "Don't make the mistakes I made as a youth."

THE DOS AND DON'TS OF GETTING OVER THAT SUMMER-BETWEEN-HIGH-SCHOOL-AND-COLLEGE FLING WITH A BOY WHO HAPPENS TO BE ONE OF YOUR BEST FRIENDS AND IS NOW GOING TO A DIFFERENT COLLEGE THAN YOU ARE

MEGAN SPROWLS

Student Essay

Imagine, for a moment, that in your senior year of high school you met the most gorgeous guy you've ever seen in your life and he turned out to be ... for lack of a better word: perfect. But due to your lack of luck in the love department, your newly found soul mate ends up being your best friend. Summer rolls around and on the night of your commencement from high school, you sit with your chum on the front steps of his beautiful Victorian house. The night is balmy and the first stars are beginning to appear. Chirping crickets provide a musical background as you confess your love for him and find out that (gasp!) he feels the same way. Great, right? Well, not quite.

The next day he goes to camp for the entire summer, so nothing can come of it. Yet you spend every Saturday with your cell phone glued to your hand in the off chance that he might come home and call you. Then, one night, it rings. He's home. So you gather up all your friends, grab a cake, and drive to his house. That's right. It's his surprise birthday party. Fifteen people roaming around with no chance of being alone. Yet through a stroke of luck (and some deliberate planning on your part) you end up being the last one to leave. You murmur a soft good-bye but he says nothing. Instead, he pulls you onto the couch with him and you spend the next two and a half hours with your lips locked together as you try to suck each other's face off.

After your glorious night of PG-13–rated bliss, he goes back to camp for another month and doesn't call you. Just like a man. The next time you see him, he says nothing about what happened and you don't bring it up because you're at the county fair and once again surrounded by friends who can't seem to take the hint. You drive him home at the end of the night and park your car in front of his house and immediately get out to say goodbye to him. No words come and instead you latch yourself on to him, your arms encircled around his waist in a Kung Fu death grip.

As he hugs you back and you listen to the steady beat of his heart, a nightmare suddenly flashes across your eyes: The next time you see him there could very well be a beautiful, blonde, big-breasted bimbo hanging on his arm. This could be your last chance to have him to yourself. Gathering up all your courage, you break your grip on him, stand on your tiptoes and pull him down to you for what you know will be your last kiss. He doesn't resist and instead pulls you closer to him. Eventually you both settle on standing with your foreheads pressed against each other's in complete silence—you trying to memorize everything about this moment and him thinking God-only-knows-what. Soon, it is time to go. You have one final embrace. This time your head is positioned directly over his heart. It's racing now. He breaks away, turns, and goes into his house leaving you alone in the dark with an empty car and an even emptier heart.

Five minutes later, you lie on your bed, numbly staring up at the darkened ceiling. In five hours, you will get in your car and drive a hundred miles north and he will drive a hundred miles west. You roll over and hug your pillow. As tears slip out of your eyes, you think to yourself, "Oh crap. Now what?"

- **DO** cry. It's a perfectly healthy emotion and even though it makes your nose run like a fountain and your eyes look like you've been smoking something, you'll feel better after you're done. Well, maybe you should cry a little more just to be sure.

- **DO NOT** keep licking your lips to see if they still taste like his. They don't, and now you have to buy Chapstick because you've managed to make them raw and chafed.

- **DO NOT** scream out his name in the middle of campus while you're moving in because you see a guy who looks a little bit like him. All you will get is very strange looks from people.

- **DO NOT** go up to the look-alike after he doesn't respond to your call and confront him about how he could be so rude. All you will get is a restraining order.

- **DO** keep in touch with him. After all, he is your best friend and just because you're at college doesn't mean you can't talk, right?

- **DO NOT** scream obscenities at your cell phone when it doesn't connect to his on the first try.

- **DO** try calling him back.

- **DO NOT** let your paranoia take over and start to think that in the 48 hours he's been at that hippie school he's turned into the biggest man whore in the planet and is now sleeping with anything that moves and has boobs when he doesn't pick up the phone.

- **DO** leave him a message.

- **DO NOT** joke about him suddenly turning into the biggest man whore on the planet and sleeping with anything that moves and has boobs while you're leaving him a message.

- **DO** realize what an ass you just made of yourself.

- **DO NOT** call him back and leave him another message telling him that.

- **DO** tell your roommate the story. That way when you're sobbing in the middle of the night she won't think you're a psycho.

- **DO NOT** gather the rest of the girls from your floor and tell them the story because you think that they should be "informed."

- **DO NOT** use senior pictures given to you to help illustrate the story as you tell it to the girls on your floor.

- **DO** leave him messages on MySpace or Facebook to let him know you still care … but not in a creepy, stalker-type way.

- **DO NOT** make lists while looking at Facebook of all the new female friends he is adding from his hippie college and plot ways to eliminate them should they get between him and you.

- **DO** listen to your other friend when she tells you that, for your own good, you should take his name out of your cell phone, off your instant messenger list, off your MySpace, and take down all pictures of him in order to cleanse yourself from him.

- **DO NOT** add him back to your cell phone, put him back on your instant message list, put him back in his #2 spot on MySpace, and put back up all the pictures of him the very next day because you miss the sight of his adorable face.

- DO NOT be disappointed when he doesn't come home to go see a football game the exact same weekend you do. Even though you may not think so, calculus midterms *are* important in the grand scheme of things.
- DO NOT, however, run around the football stand screaming and jumping up and down when he calls you at half time to tell you he's on his way home and he'll meet you at Denny's after the game.
- DO feel free to run and leap into his arms when you see him in the Denny's parking lot. This is the first time you've seen him since you've gone to college, after all.
- DO NOT forget to check and make sure you don't lock your keys in your car in your excitement to see him. When your dad has to drive to Denny's at 12:30 in the morning to give you the spare key, he won't find it half as amusing as you do.
- DO NOT break down into tears as you're driving home from Denny's because you miss him already.
- DO decide that you're sick of crying and that you're going to stop.
- DO stop.
- DO realize that maybe … maybe you just had a breakthrough. Could you possibly be getting over him?
- DO NOT try to then convince yourself that maybe you don't *want* to get over him. You know you have to.
- DO continue the healing process of getting over him. Keep in touch: instant message him, call him every once in awhile, and see him if you are home at the same time. You may not ever be a couple, but at least you will always be friends. You will always …
- DO look at the cute boy who just passed you in the hallway and interrupted your internal monologue. Boy, does he have a nice—

Imagine, for a moment, that in your senior year of high school you met the most amazing guy you've ever met in your entire life and he turned out to be … for lack of a better word: perfect. The perfect best friend. He spends hours with you in his hot tub talking about college, his hopes, his dreams, and his future. You both plan Denny's trips with the rest of your friends and spend the entire time doing things that could probably get you kicked out if you hadn't made friends with the manager and all the wait-staff. He talks to you when you call him in tears at one in the morning and gently talks you down by getting in a fight with you about whether or not there are penguins in Hawaii and almost convinces you that he can, in fact, speak Eskimo. You tell him that you think he should learn to speak Polar Bear. You both laugh and then realize that you need to go to bed. He says goodbye and is about to hang up when you say his name. He waits and, biting your lip, you whisper, "I love you" into the phone. There is a pause, and then he whispers, "I love you too." Immediately you hang up the phone and spend the next twenty minutes dancing around your room. Because it's true: you do love him. It's a deep love felt between really good friends that can't really be explained.

However, just because you love him in this way doesn't mean you can't occasionally have the urge to pin him up against a wall and do naughty things to him.

- DO NOT actually do that …
  … unless you have a really good excuse.

—Permission provided by Steve Metzger

This is a good piece of writing to get us to start thinking about the transition from personal essays to informative essays, because it's a little bit of both, isn't it? What Megan's done here is turned a lesson that she has learned from personal experience into a sort of tongue-in-cheek instructional manual—you don't have to read too deeply to see that the "you" to whom she refers is really the "I" of her own experience. And I think she succeeds marvelously, even though those instructions really only amount to a list of things that went wrong for her. So how is it an "informative" essay? I think it is in the bigger picture. She's not really saying "leap into his arms when you see him in the Denny's parking lot"; she's asking readers to think in larger terms about their long-distance relationships.

IN SEARCH OF THE SOUL OF AMERICA

STEPHEN METZGER

Let us be lovers, we'll marry our fortunes together
I've got some real estate here in my bag
So we bought a pack of cigarettes and Mrs. Wagner pies
And walked off to look for America

—Paul Simon, "America"

Our plan was modest at first, a little road trip to celebrate our 30th wedding anniversary. Maybe head up to Boise to visit relatives, then drop down through Colorado and New Mexico. Back along Route 66, then up the east side of the Sierra. A week? Ten days?

Then Betsy upped the ante: "How 'bout 30 days? For 30 years. We can drive across the country."

A bluff? I saw her 30 years and raised her: "And 30 states."

"Really?"

"We're going to Graceland," I sang. "Graceland, in Memphis, Tennessee."

We packed light, planning to stay mostly in motels, although we threw light camping gear into our Outback just in case. We also brought along a small plastic bag of ashes—my mother had died 10 months before, and she always loved family road trips in our old station wagons. We'd take her back to her favorite places, as well as to places she still had wanted to see.

Later, we would joke that we both hoped we'd be returning together in the same car—30 days is a long time to spend with *anyone*.

We left Chico one morning in late June and spent the first night in Wells, Nev., and early the next morning got coffee to go at Bella's Café. We didn't realize the significance of the "I Got Off in Wells" T-shirts that they were selling until we stepped outside and noticed the "other" Bella's, next door behind a Cyclone fence: "Bella's Hacienda Ranch and Brothel."

That night we stayed in a lodge outside Grand Teton National Park, where as a child I had camped with my parents. I had elk sliders as we sat at the bar chatting with the young couple who ran the place—from South Carolina, he loved hillbilly hand-fishing.

In the morning, we sprinkled some ashes along the shore of Jenny Lake, the Tetons reflected across its surface. Then we headed up into Yellowstone, where we spotted a lone white wolf slinking in and out of the firs along the far bank of the Yellowstone River. Small herds of bison, among the 15,000 left in North America—50 million having been killed in the 19th century by settlers, railroaders and the U.S. Army—grazed in distant meadows.

In the afternoon we drove across snowfields and granite ridges far above the timberline, crossing into Montana near 10,947-foot Beartooth Pass, then dropped down into Red Cloud and found a room at the Bavarian-style Yodler Motel ski lodge, whose marquee advertised "Groovy and Corporate-Free since 1968."

The next few days would take us from the prairie lands of the Little Big Horn Battlefield National Monument in western Montana, into the Black Hills of South Dakota—Deadwood and Mt. Rushmore—and then on to southern Minnesota and into Wisconsin. We drove through seemingly endless rolling fields of corn and soybeans, punctuated by bright red barns right out of central casting.

One evening in a motel room in Mitchell, South Dakota, I asked my Facebook "friends," "Who would be a good fifth bust for Mount Rushmore?" Among the answers: Ronald Reagan, Bob Dylan, Rosa Parks, Susan B. Anthony, Martin Luther King, Jr., Bob Hope, Stephen Colbert and Tina Fey. I was thinking maybe Johnny Cash or Frederick Douglass.

On a narrow country road outside Blair, Wis., we drove by the abandoned two-story farmhouse where Betsy's dad had lived as a child in the 1920s, its weathered siding warped, the long front porch sloping into the overgrown yard. Then we spent an afternoon on the farm with her cousins and for lunch had sausages made from last year's county fair entries.

In Milwaukee, we had brats and craft beer at a Brewers game, then drove through brutally impoverished neighborhoods to the downtown area, vital, upscale, and largely white, where we'd been told we'd find great music and delicious ethnic food at the city's Summerfest.

We spent about 10 minutes watching groups of drunk, flirting teenagers, then tossed most of our "Scotch eggs" (hardboiled eggs encased in sausage) into a trash can and headed uptown on foot in search of The Office, a bar that *Esquire* magazine's annual list of best bars in America had described as a "businessmen's dive."

We sat down at the bar, only one other couple in the whole place, and when we told Bob the bartender we'd driven 2,000 miles to get there, he offered to buy the first round, then apologized when Betsy ordered chardonnay. "I'm sorry, we don't serve wine." She had a vodka tonic.

For 12 years I taught Introduction to American Studies at Chico State. One of the required texts was Jacob Needleman's *American Soul: Rediscovering the Wisdom of the Founders*. In the book Needleman claims that the soul of America lies in the country's contradictions—the individual and the group; states' rights and central government; city and country; the very rich and the very poor.

One of the most powerful parts of the book is the chapter on Frederick Douglass, which includes most of his famous July 5, 1852, speech, "The Meaning of the Fourth of July for the Negro," in which Douglass, speaking to a white audience, said, "This Fourth of July is yours, not mine. You may rejoice, I must mourn."

Needleman also discusses what he says is one of the most profound symbols of the American character, when Douglass stood up to his brutal slaver,

Edward Covey, and in a violent fight took back control of his own soul—Needleman likens the struggle to the colonists standing up to the crown.

The final assignment each semester, then, asked the students, in small groups, to make cases for where they thought the "soul of America" could be found.

The projects were fascinating and wide-ranging. The soul of America, various students claimed, could be found in muscle cars, in Jackie Robinson, at the Continental Divide, taco trucks, the Civil War, NASCAR, in the Suffragette Movement, a Fourth of July barbecue, the KKK (some took a rather cynical view...), at Ellis Island, in a Friday-night high-school football game, the Emancipation Proclamation.

On the morning of the Fourth of July, passing through several small Midwestern towns, main streets lined with American flags and families in lawn chairs awaiting parades, we were surprised to tune to an NPR interview with Needleman himself, and were both struck by something he said: Most Americans are very aware of their rights but very few understand the responsibilities that go with them. "Remember," he said, "from good thought must come action."

Outside Green Bay we stopped at a little roadside market ("Stop here! Local Wine and Cheese Moccasins!") and checked out the moccasins, made in the Dominican Republic. In the corner was an Aaron Rodgers shrine, with green No. 12 jerseys, pennants, bobbleheads, posters, cheesehead "hats," and "You're in Mr. Rodgers' Neighborhood" T-shirts.

That night, we sat on the lawn in front of our hotel in touristy Mackinaw City and sipped Wisconsin wine from plastic cups as we watched a stunning fireworks display over Lake Michigan. We were planning to take the ferry over to Mackinac Island—one of my mother's favorite places—the next morning and then cross the border into Canada. We woke to a heavy downpour, though, and a note in the tour book about needing passports to get into Canada as of 2009 (oops...).

Instead we walked down to the lake, sprinkled some ashes across the water and headed south through the poplars and white pines of central Michigan. "Philadelphia?" Betsy said, reading the map as I drove.

Outside Cleveland, exhausted at the end of a long day, we turned off the Ohio Turnpike in Elyria and checked into a motel, then headed out for dinner—but kept getting turned back by cop-car roadblocks. Even the off-ramp was blocked off. Back at the motel, the clerk—who had stepped out into the parking lot to watch the action—pointed to the turnpike and said, "Obama's coming through." We waved as the motorcade went by 50 feet away.

At Kent State, we stood silently for several minutes at each of the spots where the four students—Allison Krause, Jeffrey Miller, Bill Schroeder, and Sandy Scheuer—were killed on May 4, 1970, when the Ohio National Guard fired 67 rounds in 13 seconds into a crowd protesting the Vietnam War. In the spring, the memorial is surrounded by a field of 58,175 blooming daffodils—one for each American killed in the war.

Later, the afternoon sun casting long shadows across the green hills of eastern Pennsylvania, we wound along a narrow road toward the spot where United Flight 93 slammed into a sloping hillside, the ground completely swallowing the plane. Neither of us spoke.

We parked and walked over to a series of displays with the crews' and passengers' photographs and short bios, then followed the marble wall out toward the crash site. A docent, who lived "just over that hill there," described hearing the crash and seeing the fireball, then pointed, moving his arm in a wide arc, as he indicated the flight path.

On the way back to the car, we stopped at a kiosk with a bulletin board and table with index cards and pens—the board covered with notes, mostly thanking those who had attempted to take back control of the plane.

We pulled into Philadelphia on the afternoon of July 7, navigating the narrow, 200-year-old streets to our downtown hotel, then walked over to the City Tavern Restaurant—built in 1773, reconstructed in 1948—the unofficial meeting place of the first Continental Congress. The menu includes venison, rabbit, and West Indies pepperpot soup.

I had two pints of ale, one made from Jefferson's recipe, one from Washington's. Perfect for my constitution.

The next day, in line to view the Liberty Bell, we passed tables with protesters handing out literature condemning the Chinese government's persecution of Falun Gong followers. After the obligatory photo op beside the bell, we headed back onto the street, surprised to hear bells and shouting ringing out across Independence Square.

We followed the noise and the crowd to the steps of the State House, where an actor in breeches, powdered wig, and tri-corner hat was recreating—as is done just once a year—the first public reading of the Declaration of Independence, July 8, 1776. Hip, hip, huzzah.

In the morning we headed across the Walt Whitman Memorial Bridge and down the New Jersey shore to Cape May and caught the ferry, dolphins racing alongside, over to Delaware, then drove across the tip of Maryland and into Virginia.

We followed a series of back roads and miles-long bridges just yards above endless tidal marshes to Chincoteague Island, the area home to a large herd of wild ponies, according to legend descendants of horses that swam ashore after a Spanish galleon sank in a storm in 1750. For dinner we had local flounder as we sat looking out over the harbor.

We rose early and drove down the eastern Virginia peninsula, over the 20-mile bridge across the mouth of Chesapeake Bay, then headed for the Outer Banks, a 200-mile long strip of narrow barrier islands off the coast of North Carolina. We found a room in a hotel on the beach in Nag's Head, had shrimp and grits and blackened crab cakes in Kill Devil Hills as a storm rolled in, and in the morning braved torrential rains to visit the Wright Brothers National Memorial, where you can walk the paths, down sand dunes and across grassy fields, of their first four flights.

Mostly deserted—and reachable only by ferry or private plane or boat—Ocracoke Island is 12 miles long by a quarter-mile wide, a small fishing village (year-round population 950) on its southwestern shore, where tourists ride around in golf carts and locals drive pickups with fishing-pole racks mounted to their front bumpers. In the early 18th century, the Ocracoke harbor was a favorite hangout of Blackbeard, who was killed offshore in 1718 in a swordfight, his head hung from the bowsprit of the HMS Pearl.

At the Jolly Roger Pub and Marina, the bartendress told us that she'd recently returned from a college on the mainland where she earned her credential to teach high school English. I asked her if she'd be teaching on the island. She smiled and shook her head. "No, my boyfriend has that job." We also met Crazy Keith, a leathered sailor, his 36-foot sailboat, aboard which he spent most of the year alone exploring the eastern seaboard, anchored in the harbor.

The morning we left, our huge ferry passed a small boat a couple of hundred yards to our portside, its sails furled, outboard throttle barely open. I waved back to the captain waving from the cockpit before realizing, as the boat slipped into our wake, that it was Crazy Keith.

Two hours later we drove off the ferry onto Cedar Island and followed a narrow marsh-side road through tiny backwater towns, Spanish moss hanging from trees, fresh shrimp for sale out of the backs of roadside pick-up trucks. In Cape Carteret, we passed a pet-grooming shop called Doggie Styles. Then we crossed over into South Carolina and through a series of beach towns full of high-rise hotels, miniature golf courses, Hooters diners—and a bar advertising "free martinis for girls in bikinis."

Pulling into downtown Charleston that afternoon, we were struck once again by the chasm between the haves and have-nots, in this case separated by little more than one street, one side blighted and boarded up and African American, the other side upscale hotels and gigantic stone mansions belonging to white families of Old South means and money.

On our way to visit friends in Atlanta, we were startled by a sign west of Augusta: "Laurel and Hardy Museum next exit." We turned off the highway and headed 10 miles south along the narrow empty country road through the pines, finally pulling into Harlem, Ga. (pop. 2,000), the birthplace of Oliver Hardy, where a little brick museum is packed floor to ceiling with costumes from films, scripts, dolls and knickknacks sent from fans all over the world. We sat in folding chairs, laughing at the short 1932 film *County Hospital*.

That evening our friends took us to a Crosby, Stills and Nash concert in Alpharetta, outside Atlanta, and the next day out into the countryside, where multimillion-dollar mansions crest sprawling hillside horse ranches and farmers sell produce—watermelon, peaches, tomatoes—on tree-shaded roadside tables.

We stopped near a circle of some 20 shacks right out of a Dorothea Lange photo, cold-water sinks on crumbling porches, screen doors hanging from broken hinges—the Holbrook "campground," where the same Methodist and Southern Baptist families have been coming for 175 years for their annual revival.

We walked over to the large tent and joined the congregation, the preacher talking about having found Jesus after a losing season as a high-school football coach, and then imploring anyone who hadn't found Him to come on down to get healed.

The following evening, in Asheville, we listened to the Stillwater Hoboes—in plaid pants and suspenders, with banjo, guitars, Irish bouzouki, and fiddle—busking on the sidewalk in front of Woolworth's.

Later, we bought them drinks on the outdoor patio across the street and learned that they were English majors from the University of Dallas in town to play music for the summer. An hour out of Asheville the next morning, we realized that we should have scattered some ashes there, too, knowing that my mother would have loved the joke.

We'd hoped to see Charlie Daniels and the Oak Ridge Boys at the Grand Ole Opry, but the show was sold out, and I wasn't interested in Death Cab for Cutie at the Ryman Auditorium. (The Ryman, the "mother church of country music," was home to the Grand Ole Opry from 1943 to 1974, when it moved out by the interstate). So, after checking into our hotel we walked down to Honky Tonk Row. Kitty Wells had died the day before, and every band in every honky tonk we visited—we made it to only five or six—was playing tributes.

We ended up at Robert's Western World, originally a Western-wear store (you can still buy cowboy boots), where we met a local construction worker who ordered a shot of moonshine for Betsy. "Welcome to Tennessee, darlin'," he said, then added, "I can't believe you can buy this stuff legally here and my cousins are still getting arrested for making it."

In the morning, we sprinkled some ashes on the empty sidewalk of Honky Tonk Row, my mother having wanted to see Nashville before she died.

Graceland the next day was a disappointment: schlocky, 10 bucks to park alongside motor homes and tour buses, tickets for tours $32-$70. Instead, we headed down to Beale Street and had delicious dry-rubbed smoked ribs at Pig on Beale, then walked around the corner to the Gibson guitar factory, where kids sat on stools in the showroom test-driving Hummingbirds and Les Pauls.

By now it was Day 23. We'd driven 6,400 miles and seen 21 states, if some only briefly. We'd settled into a very comfortable rhythm and were loving every minute of the trip. At the same time, we were tired, and we missed Chico and our friends. So what if we didn't make 30 days and 30 states. We'd made 30 years. We headed west across I-40, the old Route 66, instead of dipping down to Austin as planned.

In Oklahoma City, we walked by the reflecting pool where the Alfred P. Murrah Federal Building once stood and looked at the chairs representing those killed in the bombing on the morning of April 19, 1995. We took the elevator to the third floor of the three-story museum next door, where a docent ushered us into a small room, empty except for a tape recorder sitting on a desk.

It turned out that a water-rights meeting was being held across the street the day of the bombing and had been recorded. We listened, through speakers in the ceiling, to the clerk calling the meeting to order. Two minutes later, the explosion, and the room went black. When the lights came back on, they were trained on the wall, now covered with photos of all 168 victims. Nineteen were children.

The rest of the tour took us through the rescue—one woman's life was saved when an off-duty doctor amputated her leg with a Swiss Army knife, although her two young children were both killed—and the aftermath.

In one room, the twisted axel from McVeigh's rented Ryder truck sits behind glass, while several rooms are dedicated to the victims, with short notes about them by their photos. One man pointed to a photo and said to someone who looked to be his teenage son, "That's your aunt. She would have been 47 today."

In the late 1980s and early '90s we'd spent long summers exploring every corner of New Mexico researching guidebooks that I wrote for Chico's Moon Publications, so I was excited to see it again. But I was saddened by what the economy had done to the little towns, which even during better times struggled to hang on. Now, from Tucumcari to Gallup, streets were emptier, more storefronts boarded up. Ghosts of gas stations sat at intersections, paint-peeled and crumbling.

We pulled into Flagstaff on the 25th day and spent the afternoon with some friends who'd moved out from Oakland 20 years ago. Two days earlier they had received notice that their house wasn't being foreclosed after all—Rick, a carpenter, having been unemployed for two years, had found work. We left around 5, heading through junipers and pines—and a pounding monsoon-season rainstorm—crossing the Colorado River into California and pulling into Needles shortly after 9. It was 108 degrees.

The next morning we flew over Tehachapi Pass then dropped down into the valley, cutting over to I-5 just north of Buck Owens Boulevard in Bakersfield.

By mid-afternoon, Sacramento was in our rear-view mirror. We high-fived as we passed the Chico Welcomes You sign around 4.

The soul of America? Needleman's contradictions? Slaveowners crafting a document proclaiming that all men are created equal. The Stillwater Hoboes joining together to make something bigger than the sum of their parts, and Crazy Keith, alone on his boat at sea. Turnpikes and dusty back roads. Old-money mansions and sharecropper shacks and honky tonks, even the schlock of Graceland.

Recently, we were talking about the Flight 93 Memorial with our good friend Francesca, who has lived in France, Senegal, the Philippines and Japan. The attempts to retake control of the plane, she said, seemed like a "very American thing." Tomo, her Japanese friend, had agreed—at the time telling her he couldn't imagine Japanese attempting such a thing.

From good thought comes action—perhaps the most heroic interpretation of what Needleman called the responsibilities that go along with our rights.

The night we got home we sat in Adirondack chairs on our front lawn in Chico drinking California wine. We toasted 8,463 miles, 26 days and 26 states. And 30 years. And agreed that, despite the occasional storm, it's been a beautiful journey.

—Permission provided by Steve Metzger

I hope it doesn't seem arrogant of me to include one of my own essays in "A Collection of Good Writing," but I wanted to use it to point out a couple of things: (1) Note how useful outside sources can be in a personal essay. I think the reference to Jacob Needleman—his book and radio discussion—really flesh out the piece. (2) Note how the conclusion works. While it doesn't sum everything up in a prescribed manner, it does bring elements from earlier in the essay back around: Flight 93, Needleman, occasional storms, Crazy Keith, the Stillwater Hobos, and wine, though from California, not Wisconsin. Nothing fancy, just a brief reminder of where we've/you've been.

THANKSGIVING

LAURA KATE JAMES

Student Essay

I sit next to her on the cold concrete steps of our front porch—our exhale hangs in the frigid air, mine of vapor, hers of smoke—we watch the scarce late-night traffic pass. "I forgot how little happens here," she scoffs, as if the idea of a small town should have been ixnayed at the first draft of civilization. It's November already and three months have elapsed since I've seen her. Even the jeans she's wearing are foreign to me, ones I've never borrowed. Her fingernails are painted black. Black like her hair, colored with cheap dye that cost her little more than eight dollars at Fred Meyer. Black like her hooded sweatshirt advertising Lewis and Clark College in white Old English style lettering. She brings the butt of her cigarette to her lips and inhales quietly. I watch her do this and she knows it. She flicks her thumb and bits of ash fall on her shoes. Smoke issues from her mouth.

I rest my chin on my knees and survey our street. A solitary lamp. A few parked cars. Our cousins' house, two doors down. The mailbox at the end of our driveway with the flag shaped like a hummingbird. The grass she and I used to run across in our swimming suits with the sprinklers on. The walkway leading up to where we sit now. Her weekend baggage waiting patiently to be brought inside.

"There's enough to keep me entertained," I answer, though it's nothing near the truth and she knows. She's lived there too.

She laughs. "It's just so weird to be back here again, you know?" No. I don't know. This is my home. I don't have anywhere else to be like she does. I wrap the yellow scarf higher around my nose and mouth and pull my green jacket sleeves over my knuckles. It's cold sitting next to her there. And quiet. Already we have exhausted the subjects of Portland and school on the drive home from the airport and I have little else to say.

She takes another drag and throws the remains of her Marlboro onto the damp and browning lawn, littered with leaves. "How are things with the parental unit? Is it annoying? Being their center of attention and all?" I shrug. She lights another. "You don't *have* to sit out here," she says, noting my apathy. "You're gonna smell like smoke." I shrug again, and look at my shoes. Too many days have inserted themselves between us, and the familiar companionship I knew in our childhood has dissipated like the smoke in the mist that hangs in the glow of the street-light. She offers me a drag; I fill my lungs with smoke.

—Permission provided by Steve Metzger

This is an even better piece of writing to get us thinking about the link between personal writing and informative writing—or, perhaps more accurately, the blurry line between the two and the problems with labeling any kind of writing. Note that the very next essay in The Writer's Way is an "informative" version of this very same essay. Laura Kate emailed me one day several years after she was in my honors composition class at Chico State. She was getting ready to graduate from Lewis and Clark College in Portland, Oregon, and was writing to say hello. I asked her if she had any more writing she'd like me to consider for the book. "How 'bout this one?" she wrote in a follow-up email, to which "How to Be Younger" (below) was attached.

INFORMATIVE ESSAYS

HOW TO BE YOUNGER

LAURA KATE JAMES

Student Essay

Begin at the age of seventeen when your sister offers you a cigarette—a Marlboro Red.

You are sitting together on the cold concrete steps of your parents' front stoop. The orange glow of the streetlamp shifts uneasily in the night's slowly settling fog. You pull your green jacket sleeves over your knuckles and wrap your scarf higher around your neck.

Say something about the cold.

Say: Goddamn.

She is sitting next to you, the black hood of her black sweatshirt (Lewis & Clark College printed in white letters across the chest) pulled over her black hair (which she had just dyed two weeks ago, apparently, with a coloring kit that cost her nine bucks at Fred Meyer). It is late November: three months have passed since she moved away to college, three months since you'd seen her last. Even the jeans she's wearing are foreign to you—ones you've never borrowed.

(Other moments on the steps:

– 1993: Also foggy. Also cold. You are five and she is six and the two of you build a fort out of blankets hung across the railing, pretending to be spies.

– 1997: First day of the Fourth and Fifth Grade—you will both be at the middle school this year. You sit with your arms around each other's shoulders, matching monogrammed L.L. Bean backpacks at your feet, smiling for your mother's camera.

– 1999: Competition to See Who Can Jump the Farthest From the Top Step: you bust your chin open and have to get three stitches—automatic forfeit.

– 2002: She kisses Brandon Tyler. You witness from inside, through the front room window.

– 2003: In your pajamas, you watch as she drives down the street. It's Christmas morning and your grandpa has just given her his old, beat-up, Ford Taurus. She will name the car Phoebe but you won't call it anything because, you argue, cars don't have names.

Remember all of this, but not so neatly.)

When this happens, when she sets the pack of cigarettes down between the two of you and lights one for herself: be quietly shocked. Quietly because you are above any "Holier Than Thou" kind of attitude—although, you are made of such a strong moral fiber and have such a clear sense of what is Good and what is Bad. Shocked because the only other person you know who smokes is Cameo Reister, and she skips Spanish almost every day and cheats on all the vocabulary tests to keep her grade just above passing. Your sister was Salutatorian when she graduated. She cried when you got caught cheating on your pre-calculus final. Your freshman year, the first (and last) season you ran for the track team, your sister was the one who showed you how to come out of the starting blocks and how to tie your cleats right. She was the one who said, Hurtles, you should run the hurtles. You ran the hurtles. She set the California North State record for the JV one hundred yard dash that year. You had bruises on your shins all spring. She has been better than you at everything always. Everything.

Take out one of the cigarettes and light it.

Tell her thanks—though for what, you aren't exactly sure.

Do not cough.

You breathe in and hope you're doing it right. As you sit there waiting for your head to spin, she tells you about a guy named Drew Kelly, about how they sometimes sit on the bench outside their dorm hall chain-smoking all night long, talking about "everything." She tells you about his pierced lip and his eyeliner, about his college radio show, his sensitiveness or sensitivity, and a band called

The Dandy Warhols. You somehow (perhaps wrongly) come to blame him for whatever it is you are doing now.

And for her hair dye. And this strange sense of loss.

When she brings the butt of her cigarette to her lips and inhales: watch her.

When she flicks her thumb and lets bits of ash fall onto her shoes: do the same.

You wonder vaguely what your parents might say if they walked out the front door to see the two of you sitting there beneath the cloud of smoke. They have always given you all the freedom in the world to become your own persons, as your mother says. But they'd be angry, wouldn't they? Surely they would. And who would they be mad at? (At whom would they be mad, you correct yourself.) Her, of course. You have a talent for talking your way into innocence and she has a terrible time with lying. Anyway, these aren't your cigarettes. Years later this moment will become a tidy, rarely-revisited memory—2005: You smoke your first cigarette with your sister on the front steps of your parents' house. You will forget how much it felt like the first time she was setting a less-than-perfect example. You will forget the pleasure you felt in following, in taking her lead, not because of the cigarette but because her failure seemed to double when you did the same. Try hard not to be too conscious of your cigarette. Try to hold it like the people in movies and in parking lots hold their cigarettes. Loosely maybe? Between your index and middle fingers? Try to make it look natural, like the cigarette is a part of you, like the cigarette isn't even there. You want to seem to her unfazed by anything. This is always what you've wanted. The twin ribbons of smoke rising in curls above you unwind as she gets up from the steps and walks down—away from you—across the lawn, still wet from the evening rain—down to the sidewalk—the smoldering tip of her cigarette, a lighthouse on some distant shore—down—where she crosses her arms and smokes the last inch of her Marlboro. You do not follow, though you want to. Looking upward, she tells you that this is what Portland is like all the time, cloudy like this, but colder. And all the city lights make the sky glow orange. You'd love it, she says.

Nod your head, but say nothing because you have nothing to say.

She rubs the butt of her cigarette out on the sidewalk and stashes the remains in the tailpipe of your father's pickup parked out in the street. You make a careful note of this and look down at your own cigarette, nervously gauging how much longer it will last. Will she smoke another? Will you? She makes her way back across the lawn and climbs back up the steps. Gathering up the lighter and the pack of cigarettes, she puts them in the pocket of her sweatshirt and sits back down next to you in their place. Are you feeling okay? She asks you if you're dizzy, or have the shakes. You answer honestly: you don't know. Dizzy, a little bit, maybe.

When she asks you what it's like without her around: shrug.

Say: Fine.
Say it twice.

—Permission provided by Steve Metzger

"Informative" writing? Well, sort of. Laura Kate uses second person ("you"), which is characteristic of informative (how-to) writing, and

even the title is classic "how-to," but it's really a little bit of a whole lot of stuff, isn't it: personal essay, instructions, argument. Also, it's a classic example of an essay that defies labeling and is evidence of what I discussed in Chapter 2: the difficulty of listing, describing, or quantifying all the ingredients of an effective piece of writing, "for the same reasons that it's impossible to list, describe, or quantify all the ingredients of a Beethoven concerto, a great Beatles song, or even a well-played soccer game: the finished products equal more than the sum of their parts."

SCRATCH THAT ITCH

BENNETT LINDSEY

Student Essay

You feel that burning, untamable desire again. You know you shouldn't do it. It will only make it worse. You try to think about something else. You rock back and forth in your chair. Finally you give in and scratch that mosquito bite. For a brief moment, you experience pleasure akin to orgasm—then you realize you've only made the problem worse. Now the bite hurts twice as much and in a few minutes it will be swollen and infected. Luckily, there is no need to ever go through this misery again. There are several simple preventatives that will encourage those vile bloodsuckers to keep their distance or minimize the damage if the preventatives fail.

Everyone's favorite bug repellent is a spray can of chemicals, like Off! Unfortunately, these products are sticky and gooey and stink and are generally carcinogenic. The better they work, the worse they are for you. The most effective, and therefore the most lethal, is DEET (diethyl toluamide). You can buy bug repellent that is 100% DEET, or any smaller percentage—just read the ingredients label. It's wise to carry DEET on trips into serious mosquito country, just for those emergencies when nothing else works and your back is to the wall.

But there are less toxic, less repulsive products. Any bug spray that is citronella-based is safe to use, feels OK on the skin, and is effective enough to keep off all but the most voracious bugs. There are two schools of thought on the smell. Some consider it aromatic; others hate it. Wear it to an outdoor concert and you'll find out which group your neighbors are in. Citronella in any form works, so you can use citronella candles on your picnic table. Other plant products that produce smells that mosquitoes don't like are tea tree oil, eucalyptus oil, and any citrus juice.

You can protect yourself over the long term by altering your diet. Mosquitoes bite you because they like the way your sweat smells, and that is largely a product of what you eat. To take yourself off the mosquito menu, avoid refined sugar and alcohol and consume foods rich in thiamin (vitamin B1): brewer's yeast, molasses, and wheat germ, all of which are good for you in other ways. Or simply take a vitamin B pill. The old wives' tale that garlic keeps vampires away turns out to have a grain of truth in it—ingesting garlic or rubbing it on your skin turns mosquitoes off. You can add it to almost anything you eat, and it will only cost you your social life. Mexicans, who have learned to cope with mosquito swarms of Biblical proportions, swear by the tequila diet—after a couple of Tequila Sunrises your problems will be gone, or at least you won't be conscious of them anymore. Anything that smells good—perfume, hair spray—is to be avoided.

You can bathe in chlorine—mosquitoes don't like the smell any more than people do. A dip in a heavily chlorinated pool should do the trick. Or you can smoke. It's horrible for you, so if you don't want the cancer you might consider hiking with a friend who has the habit and just standing downwind. A campfire will have the same effect at night without the health hazards.

If none of this seems appetizing, wear clothing. Modern outdoor clothing is so light and breathable that you can wear it on even hot summer days. You can even buy mosquito-net hats from outdoor catalog companies, if you don't mind the fashion statement. But determined mosquitoes will bite right through thin cloth, so you may end up bug-spraying your shirts and pants. Or you can hang your clothes in that evening camp-fire. And choose dull-colored clothing—mosquitoes like bright colors.

If the barricades fall and you do get bitten, there are several things you can do to minimize the damage. As with all bites, begin by washing the area. Then apply one or more of the following lotions or poultices: baking soda, goldenseal, tea tree oil, walnut oil, Vitamin E oil, charcoal, a slice of onion, or good old calamine lotion. Take lots of Vitamin C. And don't scratch! Your mother told you the truth: if you pick at it, it will never get well.

—Permission provided by Steve Metzger

This is a straightforward informative piece of writing. Its usefulness is obvious and low-key. Bennett wisely doesn't try to make more of it than it is; he just organizes the information well and adds a lightly amusing, pleasant tone. And he's framed the essay core with a funny opener and a good punch line.

THE SPROUT ROUTE

WINSTON BELL

Student Essay

You take nutritional supplements. You exercise and eat well-balanced meals. You've even started doing more of your grocery shopping at the health food store. What's missing from your program? Home-grown sprouts. Sprouts are the richest source of whole-food nutrition on the planet, and by far the easiest to grow on your own.

Sprouts are nutritious because they're alive when you eat them. Living foods supply something you can't get anywhere else: enzymes, living organisms that break down food so the nutrients can be absorbed. When you eat living foods, the enzymes needed for digestion are included in the food, but with cooked, aged, or processed foods, your body has to add enzymes from its own limited supply. As enzymes are depleted, your body loses vitality and numerous health problems arise. Living foods are also a rich source of essential nutrients—proteins, vitamins, minerals, sugars, and oils.

The easiest and most practical way to get living foods onto your plate is by growing your own sprouts. You don't need to be a scientist or even a gardener.

Sprouts demand very little care, so they're perfect for the person with limited time or space—in other words, all of us. It's simple: soak the seeds, rinse them, and watch them sprout. It takes a few minutes a day, and you don't have to wait long to enjoy the fruits of your labor—a seed will germinate into a mature sprout in one to seven days. And sprouts reduce your time in the kitchen, because you don't cook them.

Sprouts are cheap. You can buy seeds for a couple of dollars per pound. That pound will grow into many, many pounds of wonderfully healthy food. And the materials for your sprout farm are cheap and never have to be replaced.

Cooking with sprouts is easy. Just throw them into almost anything you're making, as little or as much as you like. You can start in the traditional way, by adding them to sandwiches and salads, but soon you'll want to think outside the box. Sprouts can be used in juices, yogurts, cheeses, dressings, breads, and desserts. Eventually you can base your entire diet on sprouts, since living foods can provide your body with everything it needs.

Sprouts have many advantages over those other healthy staples, raw fruits and vegetables. If you buy your fruits and veggies at the store, they are already days old and most of their enzymes and nutrients are gone, since foods retain their life force for only three days after harvest. And if you try to grow them yourself, the commitment of time, money, energy, and space is enormous—vegetable gardening isn't a sidelight, it's a career. Sprouting takes almost no space, and since it takes place indoors, you have no problems with weather, irrigation, pest management, soil conditioning, or disease control.

You can buy sprouts in the store, but you want to grow your own, for lots of reasons. First, the sprouts you buy in the grocery store are old, so a lot of their enzymes and nutrients are history. Second, growing your own means you can experiment with different varieties and combinations, which will give your body a wider range of nutrients—your local store probably only stocks one or two kinds of sprouts. Third, seeds are much cheaper than sprouts. And fourth, sprouting is fun.

So what do you need? First, seeds. Buy organic seeds in bulk at the health food store. For a well-balanced diet, grow more than one kind of sprout. You can sprout almost any kind of seed, but start with the seven traditionals: almond, mung bean, sesame, sunflower, alfalfa, and wheat. Next, buy some wide-mouth canning jars and non-toxic screening material at the homeware store. Cut the material into circles, put water and seeds into the jars, put the rings from the lids over the jar mouths (throw away the flat part), and screw the rings down tight over the mesh. Now all you need to do is rinse the seeds two to four times a day and harvest your sprouts when they are a few inches long. You'll probably want to buy Ann Wigmore's *The Sprouting Book*, which will give you more detailed instructions, lots of nutritional information, and delicious recipes.

—Permission provided by Steve Metzger

Part argument, part informative essay, "The Sprout Route" succeeds in many ways. The writer is confident and passionate but not preachy, just taking us through the process step-by-step. He's very aware of his readers and what they know and want, and he's likable as a writer—so easy to agree with. Finally, he has the courage to avoid a traditional/conventional conclusion, letting the piece simply end where it wants to.

WHY FALLING IN LOVE FEELS SO GOOD

JUDY KRAUSE

Student Essay

After a few years of marriage, I realized I had married the wrong person. We had nothing in common. All the magic was gone. So I got divorced, and have deeply regretted the time I wasted in the marriage and the pain the divorce caused my kids and family.

Why did I make the mistake in the first place? How could I have been so blind? I was a typical young American adult when I married. My parents had been married thirty years to each other. I wanted to be married. And I was in love. Surely that was the sign. If I was in love, that must mean he was the man for me.

I was making the same mistake that thousands of Americans make every year. Perhaps if I'd known just a little more about the physiology of love, I'd have done a better job picking a partner, and my children wouldn't have had to live in two homes. If we teach our children more about love, perhaps the astronomical divorce rate in this country will come down a little.

The simple truth is, Nature programs us chemically to select the wrong partner, or at least the first partner. I discovered this while reading a wonderful book about women's physiology and psychology, *A Woman's Book of Life,* by Joan Borysenko, Ph.D., where I learned about the relationship between the infatuation stage and one's ability to pick a mate. Here's what happens. When a human meets a member of the opposite sex, her old reptilian brain makes a few quick checks to see if he would be a suitable mate: Is he strong, is he healthy, does he smell right? If the old brain is satisfied, it orders her limbic system to kick in, where a neurotransmitter called phenylethylamine, or PEA, is released. She doesn't realize what is going on, but she's in mating mode, and with one look of interest from the lucky guy, her infatuation mechanism takes over.

PEA gives you those wonderful "in love" feelings—the wild euphoria, the skyrocketing libido, and the self-esteem you've always craved. Suddenly the world is wonderful, you're wonderful, the other person is wonderful. Suddenly you can stay up making love until the wee hours with your boyfriend and go to work the next day looking fresh. Suddenly you are understanding, generous, tolerant, and loving toward everyone. PEA makes you unable to reason, you know it, and you like it—what did reason ever do for you? And then PEA gives you the big lie: It says to you, All these wonderful feelings are proof that your new partner is the one. You feel this good because he is so right for you. And you'll always feel this way.

It's all a lie, because PEA remains in your system for about six months after meeting Mr. or Ms. Momentarily Right—then it leaves, and you return to earth, and you see your partner for the first time without the benefit of chemicals. Who is that person? And did you really promise to spend the only lifetime you have with ... that?

This system worked well when we lived in caves, people needed to mate constantly to provide fresh population reserves, humans lived until they were thirty, couples stayed together long enough to raise the children, and smell was a fairly good indicator of partner potential. But times have changed, and Mother Nature hasn't caught on. With divorce rates at about 50% in this country, wouldn't it be great if we told each other, and especially our kids, what's really going on? If we published the knowledge that it's a chemical we're in love with, not a person, that the chemical's sole purpose is to mislead us into a committed relationship we'll regret, and that it doesn't last, we could be on our guard.

How do we spread this information? The perfect vehicle already exists—sex education classes in high school. Let teens know about the infatuation stage and PEA. Tell them their feelings are marvelous and to be celebrated and enjoyed, but they are unique to a 3–6 month period and are in no way something to base life-long decisions on. They will learn that choosing a life partner should be done after the infatuation stage has passed, or at least calmed down. If young people hear this, maybe the next generation of children won't consider living between two homes a normal lifestyle.

—Permission provided by Steve Metzger

This essay has a great sense of what Chapter 12 calls the "argumentative edge"—it's saying loudly, "I think you need this information—it will save your life." It reminds us that informing is not a boring recitation of facts; it's tossing the reader a life preserver. Its sense of "should" is so strong that a case could be made for putting it in the argumentative essay group.

ARGUMENTATIVE ESSAYS

WHY I NEVER CARED FOR THE CIVIL WAR

SHAWNI ALLRED

Student Essay

I got mostly A's and a few B's all through high school and have managed, for the most part, to do the same in college. I'm sure that most people, when they hear that, are thinking, "That means she's really smart." Well, I'm not stupid, but I don't know near as much as people think I know. I just learned how to pass tests. I got an A in history, but I couldn't tell you where the first battle of the Civil War was fought. I got an A in geometry, but I couldn't in a million years tell you the area of a circle. There are many things I "learned" that have vanished from my memory, thanks to some flaws in the teaching system.

The setup is always the same. The teacher lectures, and the students take notes. I'm thinking of one class in particular, a history class. We went from the Pilgrims to Harry S. Truman in twelve weeks. I was bored out of my mind. I tried so hard to care about the soldiers in the Civil War, but with the teacher outlining the lecture on the board and citing facts as though he were reading from a cookbook, my passion for them was lost. As a result, I remembered what I needed to remember to pass the test, but then it was gone.

The tests reinforce the problem. Comprehensive, timed tests encourage short-term memory. The students, knowing all along their grades will rest heavily on tests, study for the sake of passing the test, not for the sake of learning. They stay up late the night before, cramming as much information into their minds as they can. And it works. They pass the exams and get rewarded. Unfortunately, that A or B is often only a measure of the student's ability to cram.

Is this what we want education to accomplish? To teach students how to cram? Or to teach them to remember the Civil War like it was a recipe? I hope not. I hope the aim is to teach students information they will remember, that means something to them, information they can teach others and use themselves for the rest of their lives. The first step to improving the quality of education is for educators to agree that these are their primary objectives. From there, the solutions to achieving these goals are exciting and endless.

Controlled discussions could be used in place of lectures. For example, if my history class could have had us sit around in a circle and bounce ideas off one another, I might have gotten to the heart of what the Civil War was all about. We could have asked each other questions like, Why did we allow slavery? How do you think the slaves felt? What would you have done if you were one of them?

Even more creative is the idea of using experience as the basis for learning. A friend once had a class where the students acted out the Salem witch trials. Some were judges, some townspeople, some witches. He says he'll never forget that part of history. Another friend had a philosophy class where students walked into strange classrooms and stood inside the doorway until they felt the stares of the other students, in order to understand what Sartre meant by "the Look."

Finally, we could grade, not on timed tests, but on class involvement, homework, and maybe take-home exams. Students would feel they were being rewarded for getting involved in their education, not for becoming experts in test taking.

The question remains whether teachers are willing to step out of old ways of teaching. Some already have. It's because of one teacher I had in the fifth grade that I remember the names of the micro-organisms that live in a drop of pond water. We went to the far end of the playground and scooped up the muddy green water all by ourselves and took it back to the classroom to look at it under a microscope. There were paramecia, volvoxes, and amoebas. I remember.

—Permission provided by Steve Metzger

This is a wonderful example of how you can effectively use narrative and personal experience in argument papers. Note again how the details work—in this case in her conclusion, especially, which just makes her point even more emphatic. She remembers.

WISHING FOR THE END

JOSH INDAR

I never thought I'd live to see 20. I know that sounds dramatic, but I was a fatalistic kid. By the age of ten, I was absolutely convinced that I would die as a child in a worldwide nuclear holocaust. There wasn't any special reason for it. I was convinced because I wanted to be convinced. I was a normal(ish) kid growing up in the '70s and '80s in California, and from as far back as I can remember, people talked about nuclear war.

The news on TV was always MX Missiles, B-1 bombers, Soviet aggression, mutual destruction. When Jimmy Carter told us to wear sweaters, it got confused in my mind with preparing for nuclear winter. Cold war kitsch was popular with the art school crowd my folks ran with, and they'd drag me to this old, smoky theater to see movies like *Doctor Strangelove* and *Atomic Café*. It seems to me now that every film I saw in that theater ended with a mushroom cloud. I guess I just figured I'd end that way, too.

I should have gotten over it, like a person gets over any random childhood fear, but I let it get away from me. I was afraid of it for so many years I perversely began to long for it. At night, I'd close my eyes and see those bright, beautiful mushroom clouds—the sudden, white burst of Trinity, or the Enawetak test at sea, filmed from the air in saturated blue Kodachrome—and I'd feel myself vaporizing, fading into nonexistence. I looked in library books at photos from Hiroshima, of the charcoal shadows on walls where people once stood, and I froze myself in their shapes and wondered what they were thinking when the flash came.

My stepdad told me if a war really did break out, he hoped we would be close to the blast. Better to die quick and get it over with, he said, then have your skin fall off and start shitting out your kidneys. He made a good case for incineration.

But at some point, I allowed myself to imagine surviving. Huddled under my blankets with a flashlight, I aged five or ten years, grew some manly stubble and became the teenage general of a gang of paramilitary youth, scavenging the wreckage of post-nuclear Los Angeles. It was, in a word, rad—a much more fulfilling fantasy than my stepdad's, and one I clung to for way too long. We moved around a lot when I was a kid, and because of that I already felt disconnected from everyone else. As I bounced from school to school, trying and usually failing to make friends, I decided I preferred my own morbid fantasy over the boring and frustrating real world.

It's not like I was the only one obsessed with nuclear war back then, either. The Reagan years produced a treasure trove of late-period cold war culture—the *Road Warrior* movies, *On the Beach*, *The Day After*, *Night of the Comet*, *War Games*, *Missile Command*, *Threads*, *A Boy and His Dog*, *Red Dawn*, not to mention a hundred classic hardcore songs—and they all added new images to my nuclear fantasy highlight reel.

I remember walking to school one morning in about fifth grade, looking up to see the contrail of a passing jet. I stopped on the sidewalk and stared, wondering if this was THE bomber, the one sent by the USSR to finally deliver my Technicolor deathwish. I knew exactly what to do. I would run home, gather supplies, bring them under the house, fill the bathtub with water... I had a whole checklist.

But the world failed to end. My eyes followed that jet on its landing path to LAX, and you might think I'd have felt some relief. Maybe I did feel some. But mostly I was disappointed, because my extensive preparations and vast knowledge of post-nuclear survival were all for nothing, and on top of that, I still had to go to school that day.

Isn't this kind of where America's at, culturally, right now? Looking up with a sigh, wishing it would all just end already?

I mean, if the insanity and paranoia currently polluting our culture was just garden variety milleniallism, it should have peaked with the Y2K scare. Yet we've dragged out our once-every-100-years millennial freakout for an extra 13 years, and now that even the bloodthirsty Mayans have failed to bring about the end, there's been a weird, pensive mood over America.

Our bestsellers are almost all dystopias in some way, we've got zombies eating our brains on every screen, survivalists have rebranded themselves into "preppers," gun sales are booming and millions of us are switching to "paleo" diets in anticipation of some future primitive where we hunt our meat with clubs and eat it raw.

The signs are all there. Civilization is on a serious death trip. We have worried ourselves into a place where we are so fearful that the end is near, we've crossed the line and begun to wish for it.

Scientific American magazine will back me up on this. They published a story on 18 December called, "Do we all secretly want the world to end?" which quotes a gaggle of neuroscientists saying that doomsday predictions activate primal areas of the human brain which cause us to react with fatalistic responses. Our evolutionary predilections bid us to prepare for the worst, and when we do, we reinforce the fear, which re-triggers the behavior, which reinforces the fear, and so on. When people invest time and energy into this cycle, they begin to see it as part of their identity, and they form communities of like-minded people who again reinforce those beliefs. Thus, we have average citizens in peacetime hoarding military-grade weapons, stocking their basements full of dehydrated food, suspicious of their neighbors, skeptical of facts, seceding into their own little fiefdoms.

Psychologically, hoping for the end of the world is soothing in an odd and perhaps counterintuitive way. But think about it. How many times does the average person dream of getting away, to a tropical island maybe, or any place without a lot of people? What's the difference between that and simply daydreaming that all the faceless people in our crowded cities are gone? No more long lines, mean bosses, bad drivers, politicians, telemarketers—who hasn't fantasized about getting rid of everyone they hate all at once? How many of us have wished in times of doubt that morality and social expectations could be condensed into simple problems, the kind that can always be solved with foreknowledge and firepower?

For all our technology, humans are still essentially apes. But we live in a messy, complicated, 24-hour world, where our roles are unclear and success at anything is a moving target. In the same way people find comfort in complex conspiracy theories about space lizards running the U.N. and the president being from Kenya, a lot of people are enthralled by the idea of making a clean break from history and society. They want to say goodbye to all that and get back to our roots, stripped of the confusing and burdensome requirements of civilization.

I can tell you from personal experience, though, it's not a great way to run your life. Like I said, I clung to my fantasies of global annihilation way longer than I should have. It was a nice crutch, thinking the end of the world was always around the corner. It made me feel superior to all the saps who knocked themselves out trying for a better future, because I knew that future wasn't coming. I didn't see the need to get an education or try for a better job, because the nukes would turn it all to ashes anyway. And wouldn't all those overachievers feel stupid then?

I spent ten nonproductive and unhappy adult years on that track and still have the occasional relapse. But see, I have kids now, and it makes all the difference. It's one thing to wish for your own destruction. But once your kids start to show up in that post-nuclear highlight reel, the whole apocalypse thing starts to look like a downright drag.

The worst thing about all this doomlust is that we really are facing an existential threat in the form of anthropogenic climate change, and like idiots we refuse to do anything about it. We've had 30 years to come up with a plan and we've squandered those years by distracting ourselves with fake doomsdays in order to avoid dealing with the real, albeit slower-moving one. It's like dropping out of school on the first day because you're afraid you won't pass finals in four months. Stupid, sad and avoidable.

I love my dystopias and zombie flicks as much as the next guy. And yeah, I've got a survivalist streak. But we have to see these things as the myths they really are. We have to stop believing that the end is preordained. Because if there's any day worse than doomsday, it's the one when you wake up and realize you've spent your whole life preparing for things to get worse, when all along, you could have been working to make them better.

Josh Indar is a recovering journalist who currently writes novels and short stories. He lives in a little college town in Northern California, where he tutors homeless and foster youth and plays in a band called Severance Package. He holds an MFA in creative nonfiction from Antioch University, Los Angeles.

—Permission provided by Josh Indar

Josh, a former student of mine, originally wrote this piece for his regular column at popmatters.com, and I read it, and loved it immediately, when he posted it on his Facebook page. One of the things that makes it work especially well is that it's self-effacing: it's largely about mistakes that he's made in his life. And while there's a "lesson" here, it's not at all preachy.

CRAZY IN LOVE

STEPHANIE BETHELL

Student Essay

Note to self: I know he smells like musky pine trees. He's tall and alluring like an Abercrombie model with that perfectly chiseled orthodontic smile. He talks to you enough to keep you interested but not enough for you to know *he's* interested. Stop. Wait.

Why am I focusing on this?! Because it feels good to know he might care. Vomit. That sounds so mushy and desperate. Young women should strive for self-definition in their own success instead of in their love life because self-exploration for a young woman is power in the long run. Who am I kidding, though? College boys are subjects I am very much interested in.

What is it I find so unattractive about relationships? I worry that I would choose someone like me: young, insecure, judgmental, and unsure. As college students, we're all young and a little insecure. Throw hormonal into the mix and you end up with your heart run over by a bulldozer.

Don't get me wrong! I'm a sucker for love. I love slinging on my pajamas, making brownies and popping *The Notebook* in my DVD player. Or, soaking in a bubble bath, surrounded by candles, hearing how Trey Songz got his heart broken. I've been in love—and believe me, I miss being in a relationship. Spending all the waking hours of the day thinking about him. Cuddling up in blankets and watching *21 Jump Street*. The late-night phone calls just to hear how my day went. Feeling like I had a partner for whatever the future would bring, it made me feel unstoppable! But that ex is a cheating, lying jerk. "And remember, ladies, it's true what they say: 'Cheaters never prosper.'" So excuse me if I seem a little bitter on the subject. For me—an awkward, overemotional, overanalyzing eighteen year old-- there's too much to lose in love in a world where there's so much to gain. Plus, I would rather have a degree and a couple bills in my pocket so when I fall on my ass after he dumps me it won't be too catastrophic. But there's that one cute guy in my psych class...

Let's face it; boys are psychos at this age. Hell, we're all psychos at this age. Boys are classless, jobless, heartless drug-abusing pigs. If you find yourself wanting to be with one of these cretins picture it like wanting to go pet the lion at the Sacramento Zoo. Yeah, the thought alone is cool, but nine times out of ten you're going to get your heart mauled right out of that chest of yours. Being independent is a great thing to be in college. You don't need a man. Tyra Banks doesn't need one. Ellen Degeneres *really* doesn't need one. You really wanna stick yourself with some loser in the prime of your life? Dr. Laura Schlessinger puts it well, "Ariel, the little mermaid, aspires to 'greater things' and ends up with a stupid prince. For this, Ariel gives up her world, her family, and her fins." (But there are *so* many cute guys everywhere! Trust me, I know.)

Girls are discouraged by media at a young age from being independent and autonomous. Young girls have to deal with not only the craving to be desired but to feel beautiful enough as well. So much so, we grow up with low self-esteem and dependency issues. It's not surprising girls toss their dreams like a forgotten childhood doll when a man makes her feel loved. This generation of young women is overly tolerant, easy and with low self esteem to boot. As I preach Dr. Laura, "Hormones and heart are not necessarily our best leaders."

Now here's my thought: instead of lying on your bed for hours waiting for that stale, one-word text from him, channel that energy. Write that English paper that's due tomorrow. It doesn't seem like you were born too long ago, does it? Childhood went by like a blink of an eye. I looked at my junior high school yearbook the other day. One classmate of mine is dead; two have kids now, and most are away at college. Everywhere I look life has drastically changed. I don't have time to waste on someone who doesn't care about me when I have the ability to invest in myself.

I want to be young. I want to be free. I want to be able to not care. I don't want to be mangled with emotion for some guy. Granted, love is beautiful, but when you lose yourself in someone, you miss out on everything else. Bewitched by the way he moves or the sound of his voice, when you're in love, everything ever so slightly falls to the wayside. Relationships with once-close friends, grades, that road trip to Vegas you were supposed to take all slowly fade. Girls love the feeling of love. Their presence is appreciated and cherished. (Hopefully! If not, you're with the wrong person!) They crave that feeling and the person that comes with it. It's a beautifully vicious cycle.

For me, a part-time job, a full schedule of classes with all my buds and coming home to my own tiny yet precious apartment sounds likes heaven. I want to be able to throw my sweats on, tie my hair up, make noodles and shamelessly watch hours of *The Bachelor* after a long day of school. My heart is too naïve and vulnerable; I care too much too fast—and I figure if I know that about myself, it's time for a much needed break. Boys are cool, but at the end of the day, making money and getting an education gives you options in life. Lying around with nothing better to do forces you to settle and accept less than what you want and deserve.

—Permission provided by Stephanie Bethell

This is a good example of a writer's taking a not-so-serious tone to talk about something pretty darn serious: how young women can let relationships keep them from being happy and successful. Again, like Josh's, there's a lesson here, but Stephanie doesn't preach. Instead, she uses her own mistakes and misjudgments to walk us through her thesis and support. It's also a great example of how useful outside sources can be in a personal essay (in fact, I originally considered including this in the Personal Essays section above, but realized that the argument she's making is really what we're left with.).

SCIENCE BILLS LIKELY TO CONFUSE STUDENTS

CAITLIN GREY

As a high school senior and an ardent environmentalist, I have mixed feelings about new legislation in various states that would change science curricula to include "other views" on climate change, much like the way some school districts have tried to open up the theory of evolution for debate.

I know the goal of such legislation—to downplay the severity of climate change and to cast doubt on its man-made causes—is against everything I stand for as an advocate for all things green. And yet, there's something pretty convincing about how lawmakers have framed these bills: as catalysts for "open discussion" and "intellectual freedom." I mean, who's against that? Indeed, often the most memorable parts of my classes are the fiery debates about contentious topics. It's when I learn the most. Like when my environmental science teacher led my class in a discussion about the pros and cons of nuclear energy. I've never been a proponent of nuclear power, which got me into ideological tiffs with some classmates. But being forced to use facts and data that I had read in my textbook to hold my own is probably the only reason I remember so much about something I was once so opposed to.

The wording of the latest of these bills, Kentucky's "Science Education and Intellectual Freedom Act," seems to be a perfect setup for such in-class intellectual throwdowns: "Teachers, principals, and other school administrators are encouraged to create and foster an environment within public elementary and secondary schools that promotes critical thinking skills, logical analysis, and open and objective discussion of the advantages and disadvantages of scientific theories being studied."

But how would this mandate to discuss the "disadvantages" of climate change play out in a real classroom? Would teachers hand out articles about NASA scientist James Hansen's hacked e-mails? Would students learn about the "hockey stick controversy" alongside the Kyoto Protocol? Would the objections of a few wayward scientists play down the consensus scientists have built over the past 15 years? At my school, teachers grade classroom debates by giving one point to students who voice an opinion and two points to students who back up their arguments with facts. It's a good system—the winners are usually the students who have studied up the most. If students could support their arguments against anthropogenic climate change with just as much evidence as the arguments for it, then: hear, hear! But I would guess, given the dearth of credible data that goes against the scientific consensus on global warming, student climate deniers wouldn't get the best grades.

Underneath a mask of seemingly benevolent requests for more discussion and viewpoints lie political, religious and corporate agendas that ultimately will hurt our nation's next generation, my generation. All it takes is one teacher to gloss over textbook science and overemphasize controversy, and more students will leave the classroom feeling confused about why polar ice caps are melting. These bills would let teachers get away with that. "Open discussion" might sound like unicorns and rainbows, but underestimating the effects of climate change is going to bite our country in the butt—if not in time for today's lawmakers to notice, definitely by the time today's students are in charge of the country.

—By Caitlin Grey, Youth Radio. Reprinted with permission.

Caitlin Grey is a reporter with Youth Radio *in Oakland, California.*

This is a very well-written essay—and by a high school senior! It's thoughtful, specific, acknowledges the complexity of the issue, and while it considers both sides—recognizing the logic of her opposition ("I mean, who's against that?")—in the end it takes a firm stand. She also has no qualms about using phrases such as "bite our country in the butt," whose informal nature is more than offset by her obviously well-informed and sophisticated command of the issues. Note how helpful quoting the language from the Kentucky bill is.

Now read the next essay, which responds to Caitlin's.

GLOBAL WARMING—LET'S TALK ABOUT IT

ANDREW DAVID KING

After reading Caitlin Grey's piece in the March 28 Sunday *Insight* warning about legislation aimed at introducing multiple theories of climate change, I felt something familiar in the pit of my stomach—much like when classmates pressure you to stay silent in class. The conversation about global warming is an important one, but more and more I feel like keeping my hand glued to my desk might be easier than dealing with the slew of insults leveled at skeptics.

Welcome to the modern discourse about global warming and the Orwellian divide it has spawned. Believe in climate change, even if you don't know anything about it? Congratulations—you're intellectual. Have a question, or, even worse, a doubt? You must be a Bible-thumping hillbilly with a smaller-than-average-size brain.

Except, I'm neither of those. I'm of a rare breed, one the advocates of environmental groupthink haven't yet learned how to address. I support same-sex marriage, edit my high school's literary magazine, and think evolution is the reason humans and chimps share 96 percent of their DNA. Still, I'm not convinced that the topic of global warming is as indisputably simple and one-sided as it is so frequently construed.

What I am convinced of, however, is that the most dangerous attitude students can encounter in their schooling is that voicing, or even considering, an idea is academic suicide. Whether they intend to or not, this is the mantra Grey and her fellow activists are repeating when they equate questioning something with denying it.

Since when did the two become identical? For the past few years, I've watched as environmental-moralist crusaders have attacked even the most intellectual inquiries into the validity of the global-warming movement, branding those brave enough to articulate their doubts with unsavory labels.

If the science behind global warming is as rock solid as so many charge, then it should stand up to public debate.

Schools should teach students how to think, not what to think, and Grey's well-intentioned but naïve article, on a whole, insinuates that young people can't be trusted to differentiate worthwhile information from detritus. As a high school senior myself, I find this, and the pressure put on skeptics to partake in self-censorship, to be far more disconcerting than any doubts I might have about global warming.

There's nothing sinister about the questions I have to ask. But as long as intelligent people with skepticism in their minds are shunned as Luddites and villains, I'm afraid there will be no public conversation about the issue that will supposedly define my generation—just a single voice preaching.

—Permission provided by Andrew David King

This is a sophisticated and effective response to Grey's piece on the politics of global warming (above)—by another high school senior. Note how King establishes his credentials and defines his positions on several other issues, lest we think he's in some kind of "camp." Then he takes off the gloves and comes out swinging. These two essays together provide evidence to what we talked about in Chapters 14 and 15: that there will be an intelligent counterargument to any good thesis.

Andrew David King is a student writer and reporter from Hayward and was recently the California representative at the Al Neuharth Journalism Conference for young reporters, sponsored by USA Today.

A MORAL VICTORY?

ANGELA COOP

Student Essay

In 1984, a group of white male police officers brought suit against the city of San Francisco, alleging that they were the victims of reverse discrimination. They maintained that they had been passed over for promotion in favor of less qualified women and minority officers because of the city's affirmative action policy. The U.S. Supreme Court has recently refused to hear their case.

This action is seen by some as a victory for women and minorities, but, if the allegations are true, isn't it really a loss for us all? The law prohibiting discrimination is intended to ensure equal opportunity for everybody. No group is exempted. It doesn't mean equal opportunity for everybody except white males.

I'm not a white male, but I've been married to one for fifteen years, and I've seen a lot through his eyes. My husband is a mechanical engineer. He's a professor now, but he worked in industry for seven years, and he had a consulting business for six years while he taught, so he has a good understanding of his place in the professional world. Unfortunately, reverse discrimination is nothing new to him. It's a fact of life. Employers are forced by federal equal-opportunity quotas to give preference to Hispanics, blacks, and women.

My sister is also an engineering professor. Although she teaches in the same system with my husband, her experience has been vastly different. Basically, what she wants she gets. It's that simple. It has to be that way, because the quota system makes her a sought-after commodity, and her employer can't afford to lose her.

It took my sister a long time to appreciate the injustice of this. For years, she felt like she deserved everything she got, even though other professors actually quit working in her department because she was treated so favorably. Somehow she felt like she was rectifying the problem of sexism in the workplace, a goal so virtuous as to be worth any cost.

When I talked to my sister last week, she was excited because her department was interviewing the wife of one of my husband's friends. The department doesn't actually have an open position, but the University has funding for a certain number of faculty who meet "specific criteria." As luck would have it, this woman, who normally wouldn't be considered because of her lack of experience, is black. She's irresistible!

We feel an awful sense of collective guilt in this country for what we've done to women and minorities, and we should. We've behaved inexcusably. Affirmative Action policies were developed in an attempt to make up for those past injustices. But do we really think we can right past wrongs by creating new ones? It's said that those who forget history are condemned to repeat it. I would never propose that we do that. But I think it's time to forgive ourselves and move on.

—Permission provided by Steve Metzger

Note how this essay moves through its material with complete sureness but no sense of thesis plop or wooden outline. It's an anti-cliché essay, or was when it was written, and it sets the reader up for the surprise thesis nicely in the first paragraph by inviting the clichéd response. The conclusion is a lovely lesson in how to end without summary restatement.

THE GOOD MOTHER

KAREN ARRINGTON

Student Essay

If you're raising a child and it's going beautifully, you can pat yourself on the back for doing a great job. But it's possible there's another explanation. And if you find yourself sitting in judgment of mothers who appear to be doing the less-than-perfect job, don't convict too quickly. You may find in a few years that you've been condemning yourself. It happened to me.

I had my first child when I was twenty-three. I sailed through my first initiation into motherhood with flying colors, approving nods from elders in grocery stores, and rave reviews at family reunions. My son was bright, sweet, mature, and well-behaved. He was creative, clean, not spoiled, and nicely dressed. He was a testament to my superior mothering skills—what else could it be?—and

I was quite proud of a job well done. I was set apart from those stressed mothers in supermarkets barking short-tempered commands at their out-of-control offspring and receiving cool glances from the other moms.

I couldn't understand how mothers could be reduced to tears by small children, or how they could have trouble asserting their parental authority. Spanking, of course, was out of the question, and any civilized and competent parent would refrain from this medieval atrocity. It was obvious to any onlooker that my majoring in Child Development and working in the mental health field had paid off. I was the one other mothers asked for advice. And after twelve years of motherhood, I could walk the talk. Or so I thought.

I had my second child when I was thirty-six. The tempo of my life was very different. The nightly feedings weren't as easy to accommodate to, and I had to return to work after only six weeks. Determined to offer this child the same amenities as I had my first, I dutifully split my lunch break in half so I could tear home to nurse him. My sitter shook her head in amusement, or amazement, and said that I had brought new meaning to the term fast food.

Ryan was born May 5, and he grew curls that flipped up over his ears resembling horns. I had joked that he was my little Taurus, my bull, and indeed when pressed or angry he would drop his head and lower his eyebrows, stopping just short of pawing the ground. But he was a beautiful, happy, and very sociable baby, and I was still giving my arm a work-out patting myself on the back.

Then he turned two. At this point, his crying took on a new velocity and pitch that would after a time leave his brother and me grimacing with our hands to our heads. However cute at first, his stubbornness was relentless and began to pose major problems. When opposed, he would become inconsolable, his crying escalating.

I was, however, resolved to be the capable, intelligent mother equipped to shape this young one's psyche. When the going gets tough, the tough moms get going. I consulted psychologists and counselors. I read more books on parenting the strong-willed child. And I attended parent meetings where parents and authorities shared experience and advice.

While I was seeking out better methods to form Ryan's personality, I didn't realize how much he was reshaping mine. I found myself resorting to yelling, snapping, and even—unbelievable—spanking. I had become the recipient of the chilly and disapproving glances in the grocery store aisles.

Ryan changed every concept that I held about myself as a mother and a person. He changed my views about parenthood, children, and personality. He showed me that children are not simply empty slates awaiting impression; they are active participants in their environment, making their own imprints on the world, evoking response from their caregivers. I have had to redefine my goals as a parent, and recognize that infants are born with distinct personalities intact. My job is to guide what is there by nature, not create the perfect person with my superior nurturing skills. I have less power than I thought. And all those simple absolutes about who I am—I'm not a spanker, for instance—now seem open to debate and dependent on context.

Now that I am pursuing a teaching career, these discoveries have gained a new relevance. As a teacher, I expect to put my best foot forward and bring students along in their learning in every way available to me. But, as with Ryan, I can't determine what my students will walk away with, what mark they will leave, or who they will be. Their own personalities will make those choices. I can do a good job and the results might not show it. That is important to know, because to bank on your own image as Super Mom or Super Teacher is to set yourself up for a devastating reality check.

My enlightenment has also changed my relationship to my peers. I listen to students in my University classes loudly voicing their ohso-sure opinions on all subjects and passing judgment on others, including parents, from their unassailable position of ignorance. At family gatherings, my outspoken in-laws and cousins do the same. I once might have joined them, but now I look and listen longer before I speak. I sit back more quietly, and, if not more wisely, then surely more humbly.

And now when I meet disheveled mothers in the supermarket vocalizing shrill, ignored refrains to their progeny, I don't automatically react with silent pity for the kids, as I once did. I'm slower to assign blame, and I ask if my condolence for those unlucky children couldn't be better replaced with compassion for mothers who may find themselves struggling to understand and cope with the complex little people who have graced their lives.

—Permission provided by Steve Metzger

This essay earns our deep respect. Karen speaks to us from a deep and gutsy place. She's saying, "I had my own simplistic, idealized view of myself handed to me in pieces, and I'm going to relive the pain of that in public so you can share in the wisdom I gained." Sometimes writing is good because the writer is good—honest, daring, generous. We should appreciate the gift.

VIOLENT MEDIA IS POISONING THE NATION'S SOUL

MICK LASALLE

We enter 2013 with the sickening, dispiriting events in Newtown, Conn., still fresh in mind and yet without much conviction that anything can be done to prevent such future horrors. Obviously, the overriding issue is that we have a gun problem in the United States and a political climate that has been, at least until now, too timid to do anything about it.

But we also have a culture problem, and we know this. We know, because though Newtown shocked us and stopped us in our tracks and continues to haunt our imaginations, it did not surprise us. If the Newtown killings were an act of terrorism, the whole country would be mobilized to protect itself from the Other. But this felt like something from within, not just from within our borders, but from within the soul of the nation. And in talking about matters of the soul, our cultural gatekeepers have been just as timid as our politicians.

Fourteen years ago, Lt. Col. Dave Grossman and Gloria DeGaetano, in *Stop Teaching Our Kids to Kill*, were warning us about the effects of violent video games and movies on young and impressionable minds. They compared the games that kids play with the conditioning that soldiers get in order to desensitize them to killing. They pointed out that by the time children reach adulthood they have witnessed hundreds of thousands of simulated violent deaths and have come to associate witnessing death and mayhem with pleasure.

That same book contained an introduction by then-President Clinton, pleading with filmmakers and game makers to self-censor in the interest of children. That plea went unheeded, if it was noticed at all.

The interaction between real-life and movies is complicated. Some will claim that movies influence behavior, even as producers will invariably insist that movies only reflect society, as though movies were some unobtrusive aspect of culture, unnoticed by the world. The truth is that movies and society influence each other in ways that overlap and are therefore arguable. But clearly something seems to be going on, and something is in need of changing.

My own epiphany came about six months ago and was occasioned by the film *The Dark Knight Rises*. When I saw it at an advance screening, I regarded it as a wallow in nonstop cruelty and destruction, a film that was anti-life. But when I wrote the review I said none of those things, which I considered to be too subjective and personal, and instead concentrated on objective aspects of the movie that I deemed deficient, and I gave it a middling-to-negative review.

Then came the events in that movie theater in Aurora, Colo., and suddenly my own writing about this film seemed to me limp and inadequate—no, flat-out pathetic. It's not that *The Dark Knight Rises* directly caused a maniac to start killing people in a movie theater; obviously, it didn't. But it did seem to me that the soul-crushing chaos of the film—ultimately reflected in what happened in Aurora—warranted a response that it never got.

Survivors of the Aurora tragedy mentioned that, at first, they thought the gunman was part of the movie's promotion. That says something about the nature of our cinema, and it also invites us to consider what if that were true. Imagine Aurora never happened, but instead a summer movie contained a scene of a gunman going into a movie theater and slaughtering people. What would be the public and the critical response to that?

I think we know. Audiences would walk out saying that the theater-slaughter scene was the coolest thing in the movie, and critics, appalled, would nonetheless talk themselves into a neutral response by the time they wrote their reviews. For critics, the thought process would go something like this: *Yes, it's sick, but isn't that a moral judgment? And is it my place to comment on morality and decency? I don't want to be like that old dinosaur Bosley Crowther in The New York Times, slamming* Bonnie and Clyde *in 1967. Maybe this is something new that I'm not grasping. Maybe the very fact that I hated it so much means that it's good.*

And so the critic would end up writing something like this: "The movie contains a disturbing yet highly effective scene of violence transpiring at a movie theater." Forget any mention of the insidiousness of inserting such poison into the national mind, of the morality or decency of feeding audiences crack. It would be a review as written by one of Mr. Spock's dim-witted cousins, on vacation from Vulcan. Well, fellow critics, it's time to take off the big ears.

The central confusion that embarrasses critics, and progressives in general, is the notion that this is a free speech issue. Yes, it's absolutely true that strong images are needed to tell strong truths. You can't attack the old regime and talk about the violence of government, of sexism, and of racism without depicting that violence. Some of the best filmmakers of the 1960s and '70s, coming off of decades of suffocating censorship, knew this.

But let's not fail to recognize that today violent media *is* the new regime. The industry, in cinema and gaming, which is monstrously profitable, is a mechanical, repetitive neural training ground for action. And like the Taliban, it targets disenfranchised young men and boys who are unformed and weak in personality.

So what do we do? What can we do? Forget censorship. It's socially immoral. It doesn't work, and it makes for awful movies. In terms of specific action, critics must, first of all, identify the messages that movies are communicating.

If movies are cruel and nihilistic, say so. Say it explicitly. Don't run from that observation. It may be wrong and certainly pointless to review films as good or bad depending on how well they comport with our own individual morality. But that does not obviate the clear obligation to report on the philosophical content of movies. Widespread disapproval will impact box office.

Likewise, critics need to let the public know, repeatedly and unrelentingly, each time the Motion Picture Association of America gives a PG-13 rating to celebrations of violence, such as *The Dark Knight Rises* and *Jack Reacher*.

The public has a bigger role, and that's to insist that any movie with any violence at all—any shooting, stabbing, bombing or rape—gets an R rating. If enforced, this would reduce the violence in PG-13 movies and prevent some violent films from getting made. Quentin Tarantino and Martin Scorsese will still be able to make their R-rated movies for an adult audience.

If raising violent films to an R-rating has no effect, and it might not, try NC-17.

Just as there is profit in violence, there is enormous profit in pornography, and yet our films don't routinely depict graphic sex acts for two reasons: 1) The public wouldn't stand for it; and 2) Critics would feel on solid ground deploring it.

It's time to stop behaving as if we were paralyzed. It's time to lose our squeamishness about confronting screen violence—and the monolith of profit behind it—and to start acting like a community.

—Permission provided by San Francisco Chronicle

Mick LaSalle is *The San Francisco Chronicle*'s movie critic.

Wow! Talk about a gutsy essay, LaSalle not only takes on the industry that he claims has contributed to this culture of violence, but he also takes on his peers—fellow film critics—who are in positions to act but are being cowardly. And again, one of the things that make this so powerful is the author's acknowledgment of his past mistakes, and his sharing his epiphany about that with us.

RESCUE DOGS: THE BEST OPTION

DANIELLE SMITH

Student Essay

Coming home to a dog is one of the best feelings in the world. Dogs wait all day for you to return home, just to run up for the chance to worship the ground you walk on. When it comes to loyalty and absolute selfless friendship, dogs are the best by far. However, just like there are many options as to which pet to get, there are many options as to where to get the pets. If you are looking to buy a dog, getting one at a shelter is better than purchasing a pedigreed dog. When you get your dog from an animal shelter, you spend less money, you have the assurance that the shelter dedicates time to the friendliness and health of the animal, and you do something for your dog in return for the love they bestow upon you: you save their life.

For various reasons, dogs purchased from an animal shelter cost less. Statistically, these dogs are not purebred dogs; the dog is not the offspring of certain expensive breeds, and they do not come with "papers." For these reasons alone, purchasing a dog from a shelter costs hundreds of dollars less. Jacque Lynn Schultz, Companion Animal Programs Adviser, lists the costs of a shelter dog in her article "Counting on You," which total a little over $300, including spaying or neutering, initial vaccination, a wellness exam, items for the dog, and training. When I got my Australian-shepherd mixed dog, Gypsy, she cost only $75, and though we put a deposit down on her surgery, we got it back once she had been spayed. Good shelters provide this service free as an investment in order to prevent future strays; plus, "fixing" extends the life of the pet.

Another article from a site owned by Best Friends Pet Care, Inc., "Purebred vs. Mutt—the Pros & Cons," confirms that "purebreds can be very costly, running anywhere from several hundred dollars to over a thousand dollars." Additionally, there is the possibility of future costs; the owner could end up paying much more money in hospital bills due to the genetic conditions inherent in purebreds. Best Friends Pet Care, Inc., goes on to state that "[purebreds] are more prone to health problems, many of which are often due to overbreeding. These can include immune system diseases, skin diseases, bone and joint disorders, sudden heart disease, eye diseases, epilepsy or seizures, cancers and tumors, neurological diseases, and bleeding disorders." Any one of those problems can run up veterinarian bills in a way only six-figure incomes can heal. Plus, the fact that purebreds are more delicate adds to the worry of the owner concerning the health of the dog. Mixed-breed dogs don't have these problems as a whole and with good care of the dogs, their health problems run few and far between. I have had my dog for over five years now, and she has not had to be taken to the vet due to illness once.

Along with rescue dogs being cheaper in the short term and long run, people running the shelters also have a tendency to provide more care and attention to a dog before it goes to a new home. Shelters make sure that their animals are socialized and can happily live with people. No such guarantee on the pedigreed. Pedigreed dogs and dogs from a pet store might come from bad breeders who breed their dogs in "puppy mills." Norma Woolf's article "Just What Is a Puppy Mill?" defines them as places that mass-produce purebred dogs, and may mistreat their dogs, as the owners have too many to properly care for. A licensed breeder of dogs would provide them with better care, but again, that would cost much more. Shelters rely on volunteers to socialize and provide care to the animals, and those sorts of animal lovers are readily available. The San Francisco SPCA website states that volunteers give the dogs "love, companionship, attention, exercise and training," along with aiding events such as "dog play groups" and "field trips." Quite possibly the best example of pre-care to the animals is the fact that volunteers will "teach basic skills that will help dogs find a home more quickly and stand them in good stead throughout their life" and "assist at public dog training classes offered at the SF/SPCA."

Even with all this extra attention, some people are skeptical about getting a dog at a pet shelter because although a lot of dogs were strays picked up on the streets, there are still quite a few of the animals that had been given to the rescue shelter by their former home. These people think that the dogs given up have something wrong with them. However, from my experience of going to the pet shelters and reading the reasons (they have the reasons the animal was put up into the shelter printed on a profile of the animal outside their kennel), most people put up the dogs for minor reasons. The most common reason I found was that the animals had simple-to-fix problems, like they barked a lot, or weren't properly toilet trained, or maybe were too hyper. I know from experience that these problems are usually easily fixed through simple training or proven prevention methods. Some people just couldn't financially support the animal, or had children that they were afraid to have the dog around. Another reason is that the people were moving, and couldn't take the animal with them. There are some incredibly bad reasons people put animals in shelters, too: I have heard cases of some people giving up their dog because they were going on vacation, and it was simply cheaper to get a new dog upon their return than pay for the kennel costs. The above reasons are valid things to consider when getting any dog: whether or not these things would bother you, because they are problems even with pedigreed dogs.

Another problem people see with getting a kennel dog is that most of the dogs at an animal shelter are adult dogs. Most people simply want puppies because they are adorable, but a lot of other people think in terms of money, and getting the most value in years out of a dog. However, there are many advantages to getting an older dog. It's very likely that older dogs have training to some extent, or at least it is more likely over puppies. Puppy behavior like teething or urinating due to excitement is also not a problem with older dogs. Additionally, older dogs are usually more mellow than your average puppy, much less excitable, and therefore also better around children. The saying "You can't teach an old dog new tricks" is also not necessarily true. It gets harder for older dogs to learn, just like an older person, but it is not impossible. I didn't get my dog as a puppy, but we trained her after getting her, and even later into her life I taught her new tricks like balancing a treat on her nose until I say "go."

However, above money and above the sort of care an animal receives, the best reason to rescue a dog from an animal shelter is that you save the lives of animals. Animal shelters can only hold animals for so long before they have to euthanize the pets to make room for more; if the animal is there for a long period of time, they are considered by the shelter to be "unrescueable." A lot of people know that animals are euthanized in pet shelters, but they fail to realize that even if they only rescue one pet, they save multiple lives. In the article "Pet Adoption Is the Loving Option!" Pia Salk writes: "Adoption saves more than just the life of the pet you adopt.... If you adopt from an animal shelter, you're making room for another dog or cat, or you're allowing other dogs or cats at the shelter to be kept for a longer period of time." Breeders who manufacture good purebred dogs in a healthy environment usually have no problem in selling their puppies, and would probably not euthanize unsold dogs if the issue ever arose. Therefore, acquiring your dog at the animal shelter is the right thing to do. Plus, you still receive the best companionship money can buy.

The choices you make regarding acquiring a pet are totally your own, and there are many more facets to the issue to be considered. If you breed animals or want to participate in a pet show, a purebred dog is surely the way to go. If you want the extreme temperament of a pure-bred guard dog, or the specific abilities of a bred hunting dog, these qualities could be found in a mixed breed. My mixed dog is an excellent guard dog that easily recognizes friends and family but is very protective against strangers, even though she is not even a fraction of the "traditional" guard dogs, like pit bulls. If you need to be certain, you could still get a purebred. However, for the same doggy loyalty and companionship at a fraction of the price and twice the "feel-good" quality from saving a life, the best option by far is to acquire a rescue dog.

Works Cited

"Purebred vs. Mutt—the Pros & Cons." Best Friends Pet Care, Inc. Web. 10 Oct. 2006.

Salk, Pia. "Pet Adoption Is the Loving Option!" Humane America Animal Foundation. Web. 10 Oct. 2006.

Schultz, Jacque L. "Counting on You." Petfinder. Web. 10 Oct. 2006. "Volunteer Opportunities at the SF/SPCA." San Francisco SPCA. Web. 10 Oct. 2006.

Woolf, Norma B. "Just What Is a Puppy Mill?" Canis Major Publications. Web. 10 Oct. 2006.

—Permission provided by Steve Metzger

This essay showcases two of the requirements of the successful argument paper. First, it's a very small, and manageable, topic. It's not about abortion or euthanasia or the legalization of marijuana. It's about rescuing dogs from a shelter. Simple. Second, it's got a very small audience, whose concerns and counterarguments the writer can address fully. This isn't for everyone. It's not even for animal lovers. It's for people who are looking to buy a dog. Remember, the narrower your audiences, the better you can know them.

ACADEMIC ESSAYS

"WELCOME TO MY WORLD, BITCH!"

HEIDI MALLORY

Student Essay

As Tremell* walks into a maximum security prison the smug and arrogant look on his face steadily fades into a frown as he feels his superior self-confidence melt away. Being patted down and treated like a hardened criminal, ordered to walk in a single-file line through the halls is enough to make anyone feel uneasy. The guards treat him with zero respect, but it's not like he deserves any better given the disrespect he's shown to society through vandalism, robbery and assault. Steel bars repeatedly close behind him as he walks, a sound so loud that he can feel it rattle his bones as if the brisk air in the halls wasn't already enough to make him tremble. The smell of urine and other human waste in the

---

*This fictionalized passage is based on the writer's many experiences visiting both operating and historical prisons as well as researching the behavior of inmates and the programs themselves.

air is so strong that he can practically taste it, making his stomach retch. Walking past the prisoners in the cell block he feels violated beyond belief; to them he is just another piece of fresh meat to play with and annihilate when given the chance. Tremell, along with over a dozen other adolescents like him, is brought into a room with just as many prisoners who have been charged with violent crimes including armed robbery and murder. Just imagine being in a room with these guys; some of them are already in prison for life. Who's to say that they won't hurt someone just for fun? Being inside, behind bars, feels unlike anything in the outside world. For those who are sentenced to be behind bars for life, to be given the chance to go back out into the real world again would be a fate just too good to be true.

Youth and Crime—The Sad Truth

Sadly, juveniles have played a major role in serious crimes in the United States of America. The crime rates of adolescents are rising twice as fast each year as those of adults, and roughly half of all major law offenses are carried out by adolescents aged ten to seventeen (Feinstein 40). In order to help combat these statistics, "scared straight" programs have been put into effect for a wide range of ages and reasons. Some adolescents are even brought into programs as early as eight years old, others as old as eighteen for any number of crimes, including shoplifting, armed robbery, grand theft auto, drinking, drugs, assault and even prostitution.

There is even a program created especially for prospective NFL players who need help to realize that there is much more to football than playing well, that attitude and behavior go a long way. For some, a short stay in jail following an infraction is necessary to feed the realization that they need to clean up and get back on track or suffer the consequences. This was true for former NFL player Byron "Bam" Morris, who spent ninety days in Rockwell County Detention Center near Dallas, Texas. After that stay at Rockwell, Morris wanted to stay on the right track, to do anything but end up "back in that cell smelling the urine from the leaky toilet" (Silver 55).

To live life as an American, free to do as you please within the legal parameters set forth by our government, is really a privilege. When incarcerated, individuals find their own free will to be violated. To be "told what to wear, what to eat, when to get up and go to sleep, where to work, and when to see family… living in an 8'X10' cell, with one double bunk bed, and two shelves shared with a stranger" (Feinstein 42) is humiliating.

Why would anyone want to give up their freedom to live life happily? To see family whenever they damn well please? To eat what they want and when they want? To wear anything they want rather than an embarrassing orange jumpsuit? To sleep in their own bed in the privacy of their own room? Having your own free will is essential to quality of life; without it, you may as well be a minion.

Programs in Action-Confrontational to Counseling to Early Intervention

"Scared straight" programs are implemented for the sole purpose of preventing individuals from continuing down the wrong path in life and are aimed mainly at helping at-risk youth. Despite the existence of countless confrontational programs, many prisons claim to have "gotten out of the business of trying to scare kids straight" (Finckenauer 123). That said, we will now discuss some of the various types of programs both currently in existence as well as in the past.

As a result of the award-winning film, *Scared Straight!*, the most widely known program in the United States has been the Juvenile Awareness Program (JAP) in New Jersey. The Juvenile Awareness Program, run by the Lifers group at East Jersey State Prison in Rahway, New Jersey (formerly known as Rahway State Prison), has been successful thanks to the facility's small group of hardened prisoners who have been allowed to utilize some of their time in prison to try and help kids who could end up like them someday. These convicts, though the kids may not see it this way while in the program, are here to help, to show these kids that continuing down the path of crime they have chosen is not wise for their future. In this type of setting, there is a definite "tough love" feel to how the prisoners interact with the kids. These convicts say that when they look at the kids they see younger versions of themselves. In this film, one of the prisoners even comes out and says, "If somebody did this to me when I was younger, I wouldn't be here today!"

The original program that inspired this elemental approach is the San Quentin Utilization of Inmate Resources, Experience and Studies Program (SQUIRES Program) in California which has been in existence since 1963 (Finckenauer 130). Though the SQUIRES program did help mold the JAP in Rahway, they claim that the main factor of their success does not stem from "scaring" the adolescents, but from counseling them "on matters such as drug use, AIDS, family relations, education, and violence, through open communication between inmates and [youth]— and not by the use of intimidation" (Finckenauer 131). The SQUIRES pride themselves on giving youth a real look into life at San Quentin through personal discussion and storytelling and they also encourage follow-up visits to the program.

Judge Glenda Hatchett is Chief Presiding Judge in one of this country's largest juvenile court systems (Fulton County, Georgia). Her television show, "Judge Hatchett," is focused on helping kids reach their dreams, despite the challenging paths they must cross. Hatchett is a single mother and child advocate. Kandice Morgan was brought onto the show by her mother, LeShon, as Kandice had become a runaway and started to toy with prostitution in order to survive on the streets of South Central Los Angeles. "Upon meeting Kandice, Hatchett said she 'needed someone to get in her face.'" Shake her up. Give her a reality check about where her choices might lead. So I took the one tough-love approach I believed could save her: I sent Kandice to spend some time with two former prostitutes" (Burford 146). These meetings with former prostitutes, Pommie and Brenda, who had both nearly died on the streets of New York City, really scared Kandice. Their stories made Kandice ask herself, "Where would I end up? Maybe strung out. Maybe homeless. Maybe even dead. I knew I wanted something better for myself" (Burford 148). After her "Judge Hatchett" experience, Kandice completely turned herself around and decided to work toward becoming a juvenile advocate.

What seems to have proven to be the most effective was a program which was only in effect for six years. Located in a rural area in the South (Lawrence County, Tennessee), the program focused on early intervention for children ages eight through twelve. The children had committed petty crimes like vandalism, theft, and juvenile extortion; they were referred to the program through parents, social workers and judges. Accompanied by parents, the kids were brought to the county jail along with a counselor and the deputy chose a prisoner to speak with each child. "[The prisoners] adopted a gentle, 'big brother' style when talking to [the children, and] would usually state that they began their careers with similar small offenses and that they hoped the child would not end up the same way they had" (Moore 115).

After the experience, the counselors would meet with the children from one to three times to debrief them on their understanding; this helped to enforce and clarify expectations, making sure the kids shared the proper principles. Being run for only six years and having nineteen children put through it, for the duration of the Lawrence County program's existence, the children were neither convicted of committing another crime nor brought to the attention of the judicial system again. This result should show support that programs are helpful with early intervention before the teenage years. Those who ran this program feel that "[f]irsthand understanding of possible consequences is superior to threats and lectures, and the opportunity for the children to debrief their experience [one-to-one] in the jail is most important" (Moore 116).

Do the Programs Work Well Enough?

It has proven extremely difficult to measure the effectiveness of any juvenile delinquency program as their crime rates do associate with problems in our society like those of under education and poverty. The intricate web that we must try to navigate through to find a resolution to our problems with juvenile crimes is endless. "Programs like Scared Straight may not stop crime, but they may deter it for a period of time" (Feinstein 44).

Though many feel that these programs are helpful in deterring future encounters with our judicial system, experts "Lundman and Scarpitti (1978) wrote that there was no program that prevents delinquency. To expect a two-hour program to combat a condition that involves inner city schools, poverty, and dysfunctional families was unrealistic" (Feinstein 41).

We all know that there have always been good kids and bad kids. The good kids tend to stay on task, out of trouble, and succeed in life more often than not; this is often due to an intact family and for economic reasons which allow for a better childhood. Bad kids are often known as the trouble makers and law breakers, but it isn't necessarily always their fault. Many of these adolescents come from poor, broken homes and they do not have an adult to look up to. Most often they have no one to believe in their abilities or future; this can lead to loss of spirit, even to a spiraling downfall into criminal behavior. Although these kids make the wrong decisions, we cannot solely blame them as there are many factors which can come into play when things go badly.

Thanks to "scared straight" programs, there have at least been some adolescents who have realized the consequences of their own actions and decided to change for the better. Although the effectiveness is not one-hundred percent, there are many individuals who have gone through the programs and admitted that without the help of people like those of the Lifers group, they may not have changed for the better. Sadly, for most programs aimed at the Scared Straight approach "tracking the long-term effects of any program with adjudicated youth is difficult, if not impossible" (Feinstein 43). However, if you can save one child from a life of crime, there is no reason to stop trying; to save one from a life of crime is better than none at all.

It is unreasonable to believe that a juvenile intervention program is an unqualified failure simply because it has a less than a one-hundred percent success rate. Judges, probation officers and counselors continue to send at-risk youth to these programs. They would not do so if these programs were not producing results. The shock aspect of these programs is a great first step in helping these at-risk youth realize that there are serious consequences to the choices they make in life.

Regardless of how high the success rate, there is deep-seated shock experienced when having to smell that crowded cell with the combination of urine and bodies which have not showered in days. There is also the inherent fear of the violence among inmates which is still prevalent today despite many legislative reforms, including the Prison Rape Elimination Act, as well as many improvements in security measures. To be in the mere presence of some of these prisoners with their histories is enough to make your skin crawl, let alone to be living among them due to ill decisions.

While these intervention programs do need to help combat broken homes, the negative effect of peer groups, and dilapidating inner-city education systems, they are at the very least a step in the right direction.

Works Cited

Burford, Michelle, Judge Glenda Hatchett, and Kandice Morgan. "Scared Straight." *Essence* Dec. 2002: 144–148. Print.

Feinstein, Sheryl. "Another Look at Scared Straight." *The Journal of Correctional Education* Mar. 2005: 40–44. Print.

Finckenauer, James O., and Patricia W. Gavin. "Scared Straight and with a Twist." *Scared Straight: The Panacea Phenomenon Revisited*. Prospect Heights: Waveland Press, Inc., 1999. 123–141. Print.

Moore, Helen B., and Jack H. Presbury. "Taking the 10-Year-Old Offender to Jail: An Alternative to 'Scared Straight.'" *The Personnel and Guidance Journal* 62.2 (1983): 114–116. Print.

Scared Straight!. Dir. Arnold Shapiro. Perf. Peter Falk, Danny Glover. Docurama, 2003. DVD. Silver, Michael. "Scared Straight." *Sports Illustrated* 4 May 1998: 54–60. Print.

—Permission provided by Heidi Mallory

I was a little nervous about including this in the Academic Essays section, especially with a title like that. But I think it's a wonderful example of a well-researched, compelling, and convincing piece of writing appropriate for college work, despite, or perhaps because of, the fact that the subject matter might make some instructors and students squeamish (some instructors might suggest at least on a title change...). And the fact that the paper's a little rough around the edges, not as slick as some college writing, makes it all the more effective—again, given its subject.

SOME ALTERNATIVES TO BURNING RICE STRAW

JAIME RAYNOR

Student Essay

In California a controversy has raged for years over whether or not to allow rice farmers to burn the straw left over after harvest. The California Air Resources Board and most California citizens don't want the farmers to burn, because burning pollutes the air and makes many residents of agricultural areas suffer from allergies. The farmers argue that they must burn because burning is cheap and gets rid of molds and diseases that wreak havoc on the rice crop.

The State Government is currently trying to find a solution to the problem. At present their only solution is to compromise and let the farmers burn a fraction of their straw but not all. This is only a temporary solution. If farmers are allowed to burn only 20% or 25% of their fields, they are still polluting the air and people are still getting sick. A satisfactory, long-term solution is still being sought. Senate Bill 318, which regulates the amount of rice straw that can be burned, mandated a committee to explore the different ways to put rice straw to use or get rid of it in ways that don't involve burning.

At first glance, burning can appear both necessary and justifiable. Rice crops are highly susceptible to diseases, and even large amounts of pesticides have been found ineffective in controlling them ("Why"). And rice burning is hardly the only culprit in California's pollution problem. When interviewed, rice farmer Lyle Job argued, "I don't understand why the government wants to restrict us when all the agricultural burning—wheat, corn, oats, and others, not just rice—is only 2% of all the pollution in the air. Cars pollute the air more than agriculture does, and the government doesn't tell drivers they can only drive their car 10,000 miles a year."

Despite these arguments, there are presently several methods in place which provide workable alternatives to rice burning. Many of these methods have been used by enlightened rice farmers for years with success, while others are very new.

Lundberg Family Farms in Richvale, California, has been growing organic rice using non-polluting technology for years. Most simply, Wendell Lundberg explained in a personal interview, when a rice field gets diseased Lundberg's simply lets the field go unplanted for a year. Another alternative is to rotate crops. That way when a field becomes infected, a crop can be grown that isn't susceptible to the disease for a year.

Rice stubble can also be worked back into the soil instead of burned. The Lundbergs crush the stubble with huge rubber rollers, then work the stubble into the soil with a chisel ("Straw"). All these procedures cost more than conventional burning, and many farmers are therefore resistant to them, but they work and the gains to our health and air are worth the cost.

Ecologically friendly ways of handling rice stubble have other benefits. The Lundbergs flood their fields after working the straw into the ground. This gives migrating birds such as geese, ducks, and swans a place to rest in mid-migration. It also benefits hunters in the area, because the time when the fields are flooded is around the same time when hunters are getting ready for duck and pheasant season. The flocks of birds actually help decompose the straw by trampling it

("Soil"), while their excrement provides "natural fertilization" for the crops, which the Lundbergs call "vital to the soil building program" ("Soil").

Traditional farmers who embrace these new methods are going to have to adopt a larger view of the agricultural cycle. The Lundbergs explain, "Most farmers consider the soil to be merely an anchor for the plant's roots, and treat it as a sterile medium in which they attempt to control growth, weeds, insects, and diseases with chemicals and burning" ("Soil"). The Lundbergs view the soil as a living organism. For instance, they plant nitrogen-fixing legumes as a cover crop during the winter after the rice season is over. The nitrogen from the legumes helps grow better rice without the Lundbergs having to resort to polluting chemical additives.

If farmers don't want to go to the expense of plowing rice straw into the ground or letting fields lie fallow for a year, there are other ways to avoid burning. First, straw can be bailed like hay and used as a construction material. Second-generation rice farmer Rick Green is using baled rice straw to build houses (Sirard). Green explains his methods in this way:

> The straw is set upon a concrete base, placing it out of contact with the ground and moisture, its worst enemy. Once the straw is stacked two bales high, a metal plate is placed across the top to cinch down the bales. At eight feet, stucco is poured over the project, making it look like an adobe wall.

The resulting walls are fifteen inches thick and have an astounding insulation rating of R-53, according to Green: "When it's 105 degrees outside, the inside of the house is about 70 degrees," he says (Sirard).

Building houses out of rice bales is currently still more expensive than using lumber, but only because we pretty much give the lumber companies our forests for free. Since rice straw is almost limitless in supply, a waste product, and annually renewable, doesn't it make more sense to use it and save the trees we have left?

Another way to market rice stubble is to bury people in it. Hard as it may be to believe, Will Maetens has begun selling rice straw coffins (Gabrukiewicz). A six-foot, eight-inch coffin of compressed rice straw costs only $375, compared to conventional coffins, which run anywhere from $2,000 up. This is a great idea for those who are not so well off, who want to be buried in a more natural way, or who like the idea of becoming one with the earth.

A third way of marketing rice stubble is to turn it into fuel. The city of Gridley in Northern California recently secured a letter of intent from BC International of Boston to construct a plant in their town, at a cost of $60 million, for the conversion of rice straw to ethanol (Gonzales). This may prove to be the best solution to the burning problem so far. If it works, it will not only solve the problems associated with rice burning, but will also help solve our energy problem and create needed jobs in economically depressed rural areas.

With all these alternatives to burning, and more on the way, it seems that burning is unnecessary. The alternatives may cost a little more now, but as industries like rice home building and ethanol become established, that should change. And even if it doesn't, the benefits of these alternatives are so many and so great, for the farmers and the community, that I feel the time has come for rice farmers to give up their old ways and turn away from burning.

Works Cited

Gabrukiewicz, Thom. "Businessman's Rice Straw Coffins Designed for Ecolog-
    ically Correct." *Sacramento Bee* 8 Dec. 1997: B3. Print. Gonzales, Anne.
    "Pesky Rice Straw Could Fuel New Business for Grid-ley." *Sacramento Bee*
    28 Sept. 1997: E1. Print.
Job, Lyle. Personal interview. 1 Nov. 1998.
Lundberg, Wendell. Personal interview. 31 Oct. 1998.
Sirard, Jack. "Rice Farmer Constructs Walls of Waste." *Sacramento Bee* 22 June
    1998: IB3. Print.
"Soil Enrichment." *Lundberg Family Partnership with Nature.* Web. 1 Dec. 1998.
"Straw Incorporation." *Lundberg Family Partnership with Nature.* Web. 19 Oct.
    1998
"Why Burn Rice Straw?" Rice Disease: How an Old Flame Burns Them *Out and
    Protects Our Crop.* Web. 17 Oct. 1998.

---

*This essay has a fine sense of its own importance. Jaime is saying, "I'm
not writing this just to fulfill an assignment. Hey, people are choking to
death out there on that smoke, and there are lots of things we can do
about it!" It's also about an issue close to home—Jaime and his readers
are actually breathing that stuff.*

JACK KEROUAC: ON THE ROAD AND OTHERWISE

LAURA KATE JAMES

Student Essay

> *And before me was the great raw bulge and bulk of my American continent;
> somewhere far across, gloomy, crazy New York was throwing up its cloud of
> dust and brown steam. There is something brown and holy about the East;
> and California is white like the wash lines and emptyheaded—at least that's
> what I thought then. (Kerouac 89)*

Jack Kerouac was born in 1922 in Massachusetts. Mother, father, sister—
brother died young. Grew up, went to school. To Columbia, Columbia to play
football, they paid him too. A year or so of college, went mad, dropped out,
joined the Merchant Marine then the Navy. Then back to New York to write
for a spell. And then to the road, the holy open road, and our story begins.

Da Beats: According to Jack Kerouac

> *The only people for me are the mad ones, the ones who are mad to live, mad
> to talk, mad to be saved, desirous of everything at the same time, the ones
> who never yawn or say a commonplace thing, but burn, burn, burn like fab-
> ulous yellow roman candles.... (Kerouac 8)*

Such were the Beats, these "mad ones," writing and speaking and singing, taking
root in the foreign soil of the American-post-war continent. After the bomb was

dropped, the US dove into a period of paranoid conformity, influenced by McCarthy and the like. Quiet submission and support of their government was demanded of the American people, along with a Cleaver-esque lifestyle and attitude; toe the line for God and Country, they were told. Feared were the free thinkers, the creative ones, speaking out and doing what they pleased. This counterculture, this bohemia that never yawned, sprouted and grew up like weeds among the roses of American ideals (Martinez 68). And they called it a Beat Generation.

Kerouac, a "key figure" in planting these seeds, coined the phrase "Beat," meaning "beaten-down" and "beatific," both miserable and holy (Zott 63). This new genre, mindset and breed were manifested in Kerouac, Ginsberg, Burroughs, Huncke, and Homes—poet saints—and a few other madmen who sought freedom from conformity and mainstream literary molds through their spontaneous and chaotic prose (Sterritt 7). With each turn of the pen they moved further and further away from the demands of the 1950s society and led thousands into the new lands they were discovering. Their writings and interactions were water to the sleeping seeds and called the weary ones to life.

Men and the Music

I got sick and tired of the conventional English sentence which seemed to me to be so ironbound in its rules, so inadmissible with reference to the actual format of my mind as I learned to probe it in the modern spirit of Freud and Jung, that I couldn't express myself through that form any more....
—*Jack Kerouac (Weinreich 2)*

Jack Kerouac lived a full rich narrative that was punctuated by three things: two friends and a trumpet—each having significant pulls on the direction of his writing. Sticking close to Allen Ginsberg and Neal Cassady and living on a steady diet of bop jazz and booze, Kerouac channeled his surroundings through his pen and out of it filtered his own unique style and beat. His muses:

Allen Ginsberg

Ginsberg, a pillar of Beat Literature, served Jack as Loyal Friend, Critic, and Fellow Beat, one who helped first give shape to the genre that Kerouac fit into. In 1956 Ginsberg published his "revolutionary" poem *Howl,* a highly controversial political and social statement that was brought under intense legal fire soon after publishing (Munger). It was the solitary rain cloud in the scorching political/social climate that gave shade and water to Kerouac's work, allowing it to dig down its roots and grow up into the defining oak that it was destined to become (Zott 64). Together, Jack and Allen's symbiotic writings created a niche in the literary environment, goading each other on, refining their talents and styles in a tireless game of bigger and better.

Neal Cassady

Cassady served as Divine Inspiration and Hero (Dean Moriarty) of Kerouac's novel *On The Road.* A madman who published hardly a thing—famous for personality rather than talent (though he was talented) —Neal Cassady was Kerouac's golden god, a "street cowboy" that Jack was bent to emulate and capture in words, a friend he chased across the map (Sher). Kerouac says of their meeting, "with the coming of Dean Moriarty began the part of my life you could call my life on the road"

(Kerouac 3). Their correspondences put Kerouac on the path toward his spontaneous narrative prose, inspired and encouraged by Cassady to venture from his Thomas Wolfe influences and blaze his own trail across the English plains (Weinreich 18). Without Neal Cassady the history of the world would be dramatically altered: (a) Dean Moriarty wouldn't exist, (b) Kerouac's novel wouldn't exist, (c) the road itself might disappear,(d) Jack would still be a slave to proper verb usage and such grammar things, and (e) "Further" would be left without a driver in 1964.

Jazz

> *[He] hopped and monkeydanced with his magic horn and blew two hundred choruses of blues, each one more frantic than the other, and no signs of failing energy or willingness to call anything a day. The whole room shivered. (Kerouac 202)*

In the '40s, Kerouac and his posse witnessed and worshiped a new wave of jazz—musicians like Miles Davis, Charlie Parker, Dizzy Gillepsie and Slim Giallard shook the genre with their quivering horns and unpredictable beats—the birth of bebop; they went mad for it (Sterritt 51). Mused by the improvised harmonies and extempore of bop music, Kerouac developed his own style that reflected its creative spontaneity. His goal was to reproduce in words the tenor man's blow of a sax, exhaling sentences until he said what he wanted and emptied his lungs, period (inhale), then blow again—he called it "breath separations of the mind" (Swartz 10). The most illustrative *On the Road* passages are those that recount Sal and Dean's endless nights in jazz joints, dancing and digging the tenor man blowing on the bandstand, "shaking and swaying," lungs pulling from the bottom of his feet, vibrating the low notes "Mu-u-u-u-sic pla-a-a-ay!" into the microphone so all the glasses jumped and bounced in the booths, ice rattling (Kerouac 198–199). Bop became a drug to Kerouac, it affected and hypnotized him. Each yawp of those magic horns pulled and tugged at the spirit of his writing.

On The Road

> *"You boys going to get somewhere, or just going?" We didn't understand his question, and it was a damned good question. (Kerouac 22)*

Jack Kerouac wrote his legendary *On the Road* in three weeks, or so he told Steve Allen. He was determined to keep his novel true, sure that his spontaneous writing would produce the purest upheaval of his soul, so was his habit of writing in one sitting on long rolls of teletype paper his thoughts uninterrupted by the ending of a page ("Kerouac," *The Steve Allen Show*).

Sur la Route or *On the Road*, as essential as it was, had mixed reviews to say the least. A novel published in 1957 about a nomadic young man abandoning traditional American life for the road, chasing after madmen, engaging in all sorts of drunken squalor and tea-smoking good times, was rejected by middle-class Stepford America, seen as "objectionable." People held up the book, pointed to the cover and said, "Here is proof that today's youth is going straight to hell" (Zott 64). It was embraced by others as a "major" work of the times, by the generation that named Kerouac its "avatar." *They* held up the book, pointed to the cover and said, "Here is the holy word, here is *it*, this is what I live by" (Millstein).

On the Road gave voice to the weary masses, the social deviants, Kafka's cockroaches; it—in its 310 pages—captured the creed of a million American madmen. Of this, Kerouac said to the *New York Journal,* "It is not my fault that certain so-called bohemian elements have found in my writings something to hang their peculiar beatnik theories on" ("32479"). The purpose of *On the Road* was to record Jack's glorious life on the road, his quest for meaning and all those who were a part of it. But it grew far beyond its original goals into the social statement of the decade, it was a damn good hook to hang those hippie hats on.

Kerouac died young in an alcoholic pit of squalor. At the end of his life he left over twenty books recounting his holy quests, but no evidence that he ever really found what he was looking for.

Works Cited

"32479. Kerouac, Jack." *Columbia World of Quotations.* New York: Columbia University Press, 1996. Web. 9 Nov. 2006.

"Kerouac." *The Steve Allen Show 1959.* YouTube.com. Web. 11 Nov. 2006.

Kerouac, Jack. *On the Road.* Cutchogue, N.Y.: Buccaneer Books, 1975. Print.

Martinez, Manuel Luis. *Countering the Counter Culture: Rereading Postwar American Dissent from Jack Kerouac to Tómas Rivera.* Madison: University of Wisconsin Press, 2003. Print.

Millstein, Gilbert. "Books of the Times." *New York Times* 5 Sept. 1957. Web. Nov. 2007.

Munger, Kel. "The Beat Goes On." *Chico News and Review.*: Chico, Calif.: Chico Community Publishing, 2006. 16 Nov. 2006. Web.

Sher, Levi A. "Jack Kerouac." *LitKicks: Jack Kerouac.* 19 Sept. 2002. Web. 3 Nov. 2006

Sterritt, David. *Mad to Be Saved: The Beats, the 50's, and Film.* Carbondale: Southern Illinois University Press, 1989. Print.

Swartz, Omar. *A View from On the Road: The Rhetorical Vision of Jack Kerouac.* Carbondale: Southern Illinois University Press, 1999. Print.

Weinreich, Regina. *The Spontaneous Poetic of Jack Kerouac: A Study of the Fiction.* Carbondale: Southern Illinois University Press, 1987. Print.

Zott, Lynn M., ed. *The Beat Generation: A Gale Critical Companion.* Detroit: Gale, 2003. Print.

Suggested Reading

Amran, David. *Offbeat: Collaborating with Kerouac.* New York: Thunder's Mouth Press, 2002. Print.

Foster, Edward Halsey. *Understanding the Beats.* Columbia: University of South Carolina Press, 1992. Print.

Holton, Robert. On the Road: *Kerouac's Ragged American Journey.* New York: Twayne Publishers, 1999.

"Kerouac's *On the Road.*" *NPR: Present at the Creation.* National Public Radio. Web.

Theado, Matt. *Understanding Jack Kerouac.* Columbia University of South Carolina Press, 2000. Print.

Watson, Steve. *The Birth of the Beat Generation: Visionaries, Rebels, and Hipsters, 1944–1960.* New York Pantheon Books/Random House, 1995. Print.

—Permission provided by Steve Metzger

What I really like about this piece is how it's written in the spirit of her subject. That is, it's about writers who broke rules, forged new ways of using the English language. Lived their lives that way. So Laura Kate breaks rules herself—look at those sentence fragments—and in so doing underscores the points she's making. The result is a kind of nonacademic academic essay. A very successful one.

WRITERS, ON WRITING

TIME LOST AND FOUND

ANNE LAMOTT

I sometimes teach classes on writing, during which I tell my students every single thing I know about the craft and habit. This takes approximately 45 minutes. I begin with my core belief—and the foundation of almost all wisdom traditions—that there is nothing you can buy, achieve, own, or rent that can fill up that hunger inside for a sense of fulfillment and wonder. But the good news is that creative expression, whether that means writing, dancing, bird-watching, or cooking, can give a person almost everything that he or she has been searching for: enlivenment, peace, meaning, and the incalculable wealth of time spent quietly in beauty.

Then I bring up the bad news: You have to make time to do this.

This means you have to grasp that your manic forms of connectivity—cell phone, email, text, Twitter—steal most chances of lasting connection or amazement. That multitasking can argue a wasted life. That a close friendship is worth more than material success.

Needless to say, this is very distressing for my writing students. They start to explain that they have two kids at home, or five, a stable of horses or a hive of bees, and 40-hour workweeks. Or, on the other hand, sometimes they are climbing the walls with boredom, own nearly nothing, and are looking for work full-time, which is why they can't make time now to pursue their hearts' desires. They often add that as soon as they retire, or their last child moves out, or they move to the country, or to the city, or sell the horses, they will. They are absolutely sincere, and they are delusional.

I often remember the story from India of a beggar who sat outside a temple, begging for just enough every day to keep body and soul alive, until the temple elders convinced him to move across the street and sit under a tree. Years of begging and bare subsistence followed until he died. The temple elders decided to bury him beneath his cherished tree, where, after shoveling away a couple of feet of earth, they found a stash of gold coins that he had unknowingly sat on, all those hand-to-mouth years.

You already have the gold coins beneath you, of presence, creativity, intimacy, time for wonder, and nature, and life. Oh, yeah, you say? And where would those rascally coins be?

This is what I say: First of all, no one needs to watch the news every night, unless one is married to the anchor. Otherwise, you are mostly going to learn more than you need to know about where the local fires are, and how rainy it has been: so rainy! That is half an hour, a few days a week, I tell my students. You could commit to writing one page a night, which, over a year, is most of a book.

If they have to get up early for work and can't stay up late, I ask them if they are willing NOT to do one thing every day, that otherwise they were going to try and cram into their schedule.

They may explain that they have to go to the gym four days a week or they get crazy, to which I reply that that's fine—no one else really cares if anyone else finally starts to write or volunteers with marine mammals. But how can they not care and let life slip away? Can't they give up the gym once a week and buy two hours' worth of fresh, delectable moments? (Here they glance at my butt.)

Can they commit to meeting one close friend for two hours every week, in bookstores, to compare notes? Or at an Audubon sanctuary? Or a winery?

They look at me bitterly now—they don't think I understand. But I do—I know how addictive busyness and mania are. But I ask them whether, if their children grow up to become adults who spend this one precious life in a spin of multitasking, stress, and achievement, and then work out four times a week, will they be pleased that their kids also pursued this kind of whirlwind life?

If not, if they want much more for their kids, lives well spent in hard work and savoring all that is lovely, why are they living this manic way?

I ask them, is there a eucalyptus grove at the end of their street, or a new exhibit at the art museum? An upcoming minus tide at the beach where the agates and tidepools are, or a great poet coming to the library soon? A pond where you can see so many turtles? A journal to fill?

If so, what manic or compulsive hours will they give up in trade for the equivalent time to write, or meander? Time is not free—that's why it's so precious and worth fighting for.

Will they give me one hour of housecleaning in exchange for the poetry reading? Or wash the car just one time a month, for the turtles? No? I understand. But at 80, will they be proud that they spent their lives keeping their houses cleaner than anyone else in the family did, except for mad Aunt Beth, who had the vapors? Or that they kept their car polished to a high sheen that made the neighbors quiver with jealousy? Or worked their fingers to the bone providing a high quality of life, but maybe accidentally forgot to be deeply and truly present for their kids, and now their grandchildren?

I think it's going to hurt. What fills us is real, sweet, dopey, funny life.

I've heard it said that every day you need half an hour of quiet time for yourself, or your Self, unless you're incredibly busy and stressed, in which case you need an hour. I promise you, it is there. Fight tooth and nail to find time, to make it. It is our true wealth, this moment, this hour, this day.

THE WRITING LIFE

DAVE EGGERS

I've been avoiding writing about "The Writing Life" ever since I first heard those words about 10 years ago. When I hear them, I hear the voices of high school and college friends, of my uncles and my cousin Mark, who would have rolled their eyes and maybe punched me, gently, in the face, for even trying to weigh in on the subject.

They would say the phrase seems pretentious; it's pretentious to ponder the writing life, even more pretentious to write about it in a newspaper such as this one, with its history of doing the serious work of preserving our democracy.

By comparison, the writing life, at least as it concerns me, is not so interesting. I just re-watched *All the President's Men*, which I do every year or so, and, every time, I marvel at how interesting Woodward and Bernstein's lives were at *The Post*, and how well the film explains the reporting process, its doggedness and randomness, and how great an excuse it is to get out in the world and ask every seemingly obvious question you can think of (What books did the man check out?), because you never know, you might bring down a government that has it coming.

When I watch that movie, I also think about how mundane my own "writing life" can be. For example, I'm putting together this essay, not in a bustling metropolitan newsroom, but in a shed in my backyard. I have a sheet draped over the shed's window because without it the morning sun would blast through and blind me. So I'm looking at a gray sheet, which is nailed to the wall in two places and sags in the middle like a big, gray smile. And the sheet is filthy. And the shed is filthy. If I left this place unoccupied for a week, it would become home to woodland animals. They probably would clean it up first.

And here is where I spend seven or eight hours at a stretch. Seven or eight hours each time I try to write. Most of that time is spent stalling, which means that for every seven or eight hours I spend pretending to write—sitting in the writing position, looking at a screen—I get, on average, one hour of actual work done. It's a terrible, unconscionable ratio.

This kind of life is at odds with the romantic notions I once had, and most people have, of the writing life. We imagine more movement, somehow. We imagine it on horseback. Camelback? We imagine convertibles, windswept cliffs, lighthouses. We don't imagine—or I didn't imagine—quite so much sitting. I know it makes me sound pretty naive, that I would expect to be writing while, say, skiing. But still. The utterly sedentary nature of this task gets to me every day. It's getting to me right now.

And so I have to get out of the shed sometimes.

One thing I do to get out is teach a class on Tuesday nights. Back in 2002, I co-founded a place in San Francisco called 826 Valencia, which does everything from after-school tutoring to field trips, publishing projects and advanced writing classes for kids from age 6 to 18. For the last eight years I've taught a class, made up of about 20 high school students from all over the Bay Area, and together we read stories, essays and journalism from contemporary periodicals—from the *Kenyon Review* to *Bidoun* to *Wired*. From all this reading we choose our favorite stuff, and that becomes a yearly anthology called *The Best American Nonrequired Reading*.

Sometimes we read things that are okay. Sometimes we read things that we find important in some way—that we learn from, but that don't particularly get us all riled up. And sometimes we read something that just astounds and grabs and makes its way into the bones of everyone in the class. A couple Tuesdays ago someone on the teaching committee picked up a journal called Gulf Coast, published out of the University of Houston, and he found a story called "Pleiades," by Anjali Sachdeva.

None of us had read this author before, so we read her story without any expectations. But one page into it, I thought, Man, this is a great writer. This is something different. This shows great command, wonderful pacing. The story—about septuplet sisters conceived via genetic manipulation—could have been told in a thousand terrible ways, but she's managing to make it sing. In the story, after the initial triumph of conception, the sisters begin to die, one by one, leaving Del, the narrator, alone and forced to choose between awaiting her fate or taking control of her destiny. The story seemed to me some kind of small masterpiece, and I hoped the class felt the same. But I knew to temper my hopes; often I love something and the kids think I'm nuts. This time, though, I didn't have to wait long to know I wasn't alone.

Gabby, who takes an hour-long subway ride from East Oakland every week to come to this class, was leaning forward, waiting to speak, practically holding her copy to her heart. Describing what she loved about it, she made an impassioned speech about connectivity, about the limits of science, about Del's search for a more human, even humble, path, and what this means to her, to us all.

Nick, who had brought his own little sister to class, was floored by the ending—how, in the final act, the protagonist reclaimed a life both made possible and doomed by science. At the end of the class, when we voted Yes, No or Maybe, all the hands said Yes and I went home feeling electric about the possibility of the written word. I don't need to be reminded of it all that often—I'd just read Philip Roth's "The Humbling," and holy hell, that guy, even at 76, can still write something so ferocious, kinky, horribly depressing and yet full of the manic mess of life! —but truthfully, any reminder helps. When you spend eight hours in a shed to get a few hundred words down, you need every bit of inspiration you can get. And the best place to find inspiration, for me at least, is to see the effect of great writing on the young. Their reactions can be hard to predict, and they're always brutally honest, but when they love something, their enthusiasm is completely without guile, utterly without cynicism.

And I thought, okay, the writing life—damn that phrase—it doesn't have to be romantic. It can be workmanlike, it can be a grind, and it can take years to make anything of any value. But if, at the end of it all, there's a Gabby who holds the words to her heart and rides the subway through the night, back to Oakland, thinking of what those words on a page did to her, then the work is worth doing.

WRITE TILL YOU DROP

ANNIE DILLARD

People love pretty much the same things best. A writer looking for subjects inquires not after what he loves best, but after what he alone loves at all. Strange seizures beset us. Frank Conroy loves his yo-yo tricks, Emily Dickinson her slant of light; Richard Selzer loves the glistening peritoneum, Faulkner the muddy bottom of a little girl's drawers visible when she's up a pear tree. "Each student of the ferns," I once read, "will have his own list of plants that for some reason or another stir his emotions."

Why do you never find anything written about that idiosyncratic thought you advert to, about your fascination with something no one else understands? Because it is up to you. There is something you find interesting, for a reason hard to explain. It is hard to explain because you have never read it on any page; there you begin. You were made and set here to give voice to this, your own astonishment.

Write as if you were dying. At the same time, assume you write for an audience consisting solely of terminal patients. That is, after all, the case. What would you begin writing if you knew you would die soon? What could you say to a dying person that would not enrage by its triviality?

Write about winter in the summer. Describe Norway as Ibsen did, from a desk in Italy; describe Dublin as James Joyce did, from a desk in Paris. Willa Cather wrote her prairie novels in New York City; Mark Twain wrote "Huckleberry Finn" in Hartford. Recently scholars learned that Walt Whitman rarely left his room.

The writer studies literature, not the world. She lives in the world; she cannot miss it. If she has ever bought a hamburger, or taken a commercial airplane flight, she spares her readers a report of her experience. She is careful of what she reads, for that is what she will write. She is careful of what she learns, because that is what she will know.

The writer knows her field—what has been done, what could be done, the limits—the way a tennis player knows the court. And like that expert, she, too, plays the edges. That is where the exhilaration is. She hits up the line. In writing, she can push the edges. Beyond this limit, here, the reader must recoil. Reason balks, poetry snaps; some madness enters, or strain. Now gingerly, can she enlarge it, can she nudge the bounds? And enclose what wild power?

A well-known writer got collared by a university student who asked, "Do you think I could be a writer?"

"Well," the writer said, "I don't know.... Do you like sentences?"

The writer could see the student's amazement. Sentences? Do I like sentences? I am 20 years old and do I like sentences? If he had liked sentences, of course, he could begin, like a joyful painter I knew. I asked him how he came to be a painter. He said, "I liked the smell of the paint."

Hemingway studied, as models, the novels of Knut Hamsun and Ivan Turgenev. Isaac Bashevis Singer, as it happened, also chose Hamsun and Turgenev as models. Ralph Ellison studied Hemingway and Gertrude Stein. Thoreau loved Homer; Eudora Welty loved Chekhov. Faulkner described his debt to Sherwood Anderson and Joyce; E. M. Forster, his debt to Jane Austen and Proust. By contrast, if you ask a 21-year-old poet whose poetry he likes, he might say, unblushing, "Nobody's." He has not yet understood that poets like poetry, and novelists like novels; he himself likes only the role, the thought of himself in a hat. Rembrandt and Shakespeare, Bohr and Gauguin, possessed powerful hearts, not powerful wills. They loved the range of materials they used. The work's possibilities excited them; the field's complexities fired their imaginations. The caring suggested the tasks; the tasks suggested the schedules. They learned their fields and then loved them. They worked, respectfully, out of their love and knowledge, and they produced complex bodies of work that endure. Then, and only then, the world harassed them with some sort of wretched hat, which, if they were still living, they knocked away as well as they could, to keep at their tasks.

It makes more sense to write one big book—a novel or nonfiction narrative—than to write many stories or essays. Into a long, ambitious project you can fit or pour all you possess and learn. A project that takes five years will accumulate those years' inventions and richnesses. Much of those years' reading will feed the work. Further, writing sentences is difficult whatever their subject. It is no less difficult to write sentences in a recipe than sentences in "Moby-Dick." So you might as well write "Moby-Dick." Similarly, since every original work requires a unique form, it is more prudent to struggle with the outcome of only one form—that of a long work—than to struggle with the many forms of a collection.

Every book has an intrinsic impossibility, which its writer discovers as soon as his first excitement dwindles. The problem is structural; it is insoluble; it is why no one can ever write this book. Complex stories, essays and poems have this problem, too—the prohibitive structural defect the writer wishes he had never noticed. He writes it in spite of that. He finds ways to minimize the difficulty; he strengthens other virtues; he cantilevers the whole narrative out into thin air and it holds.

Why are we reading, if not in hope of beauty laid bare, life heightened and its deepest mystery probed? Can the writer isolate and vivify all in experience that most deeply engages our intellects and our hearts? Can the writer renew our hopes for literary forms?

Why are we reading, if not in hope that the writer will magnify and dramatize our days, will illuminate and inspire us with wisdom, courage and the hope of meaningfulness, and press upon our minds the deepest mysteries, so we may feel again their majesty and power? What do we ever know that is higher than that power which, from time to time, seizes our lives, and which reveals us startlingly to ourselves as creatures set down here bewildered? Why does death so catch us by surprise, and why love? We still and always want waking. If we are reading for these things, why would anyone read books with advertising slogans and brand names in them? Why would anyone write such books? We should mass half-dressed in long lines like tribesmen and shake gourds at each other, to wake up; instead we watch television and miss the show.

No manipulation is possible in a work of art, but every miracle is. Those artists who dabble in eternity, or who aim never to manipulate but only to lay out hard truths, grow accustomed to miracles. Their sureness is hard won. "Given a large canvas," said Veronese, "I enriched it as I saw fit."

The sensation of writing a book is the sensation of spinning, blinded by love and daring. It is the sensation of a stunt pilot's turning barrel rolls, or an inchworm's blind rearing from a stem in search of a route. At its worst, it feels like alligator wrestling, at the level of the sentence.

At its best, the sensation of writing is that of any unmerited grace. It is handed to you, but only if you look for it. You search, you break your fists, your back, your brain, and then—and only then—it is handed to you. From the corner of your eye you see motion. Something is moving through the air and headed your way. It is a parcel bound in ribbons and bows; it has two white wings. It flies directly at you; you can read your name on it. If it were a baseball, you would hit it out of the park. It is that one pitch in a thousand you see in slow motion; its wings beat slowly as a hawk's.

One line of a poem, the poet said—only one line, but thank God for that one line—drops from the ceiling. Thornton Wilder cited this unnamed writer of sonnets: one line of a sonnet falls from the ceiling, and you tap in the others around it with a jeweler's hammer. Nobody whispers it in your ear. It is like something you memorized once and forgot. Now it comes back and rips away your breath. You find and finger a phrase at a time; you lay it down as if with tongs, restraining your strength, and wait suspended and fierce until the next one finds you: yes, this; and yes, praise be, then this.

Einstein likened the generation of a new idea to a chicken's laying an egg: "Kieks—auf einmal ist es da." Cheep—and all at once there it is. Of course, Einstein was not above playing to the crowd.

Push it. Examine all things intensely and relentlessly. Probe and search each object in a piece of art; do not leave it, do not course over it, as if it were understood, but instead follow it down until you see it in the mystery of its own specificity and strength. Giacometti's drawings and paintings show his bewilderment and persistence. If he had not acknowledged his bewilderment, he would not have persisted. A master of drawing, Rico Lebrun, discovered that "the draftsman must aggress; only by persistent assault will the live image capitulate and give up its secret to an unrelenting line." Who but an artist fierce to know—not fierce to seem to know—would suppose that a live image possessed a secret? The artist is willing to give all his or her strength and life to probing with blunt instruments those same secrets no one can describe any way but with the instruments' faint tracks.

Admire the world for never ending on you as you would admire an opponent, without taking your eyes off him, or walking away.

One of the few things I know about writing is this: spend it all, shoot it, play it, lose it, all, right away, every time. Do not hoard what seems good for a later place in the book, or for another book; give it, give it all, give it now. The impulse to save something good for a better place later is the signal to spend it now. Something more will arise for later, something better. These things fill from behind, from beneath, like well water. Similarly, the impulse to keep to yourself what you have learned is not only shameful, it is destructive. Anything you do not give freely and abundantly becomes lost to you. You open your safe and find ashes.

After Michelangelo died, someone found in his studio a piece of paper on which he had written a note to his apprentice, in the handwriting of his old age: "Draw, Antonio, draw, Antonio, draw and do not waste time."

POLITICS AND THE ENGLISH LANGUAGE

GEORGE ORWELL

(This classic essay was originally published in 1946.)

Most people who bother with the matter at all would admit that the English language is in a bad way, but it is generally assumed that we cannot by conscious action do anything about it. Our civilization is decadent and our language—so the argument runs—must inevitably share in the general collapse. It follows that any struggle against the abuse of language is a sentimental archaism, like preferring candles to electric light or hansom cabs to aeroplanes. Underneath this lies the half-conscious belief that language is a natural growth and not an instrument which we shape for our own purposes.

Now, it is clear that the decline of a language must ultimately have political and economic causes: it is not due simply to the bad influence of this or that individual writer. But an effect can become a cause, reinforcing the original cause and producing the same effect in an intensified form, and so on indefinitely. A man may take to drink because he feels himself to be a failure, and then fail all the more completely because he drinks. It is rather the same thing that is happening to the English language. It becomes ugly and inaccurate because our thoughts are foolish, but the slovenliness of our language makes it easier for us to have foolish thoughts. The point is that the process is reversible. Modern English, especially written English, is full of bad habits which spread by imitation and which can be avoided if one is willing to take the necessary trouble. If one gets rid of these habits one can think more clearly, and to think clearly is a necessary first step toward political regeneration: so that the fight against bad English is not frivolous and is not the exclusive concern of professional writers. I will come back to this presently, and I hope that by that time the meaning of what I have said here will have become clearer. Meanwhile, here are five specimens of the English language as it is now habitually written.

> *These five passages have not been picked out because they are especially bad—I could have quoted far worse if I had chosen—but because they illustrate various of the mental vices from which we now suffer. They are a little below the average, but are fairly representative examples. I number them so that I can refer back to them when necessary:*

1. I am not, indeed, sure whether it is not true to say that the Milton who once seemed not unlike a seventeenth-century Shelley had not become, out of an experience ever more bitter in each year, more alien [*sic*] to the founder of that Jesuit sect which nothing could induce him to tolerate.
    Professor Harold Laski (*Essay in Freedom of Expression*)
2. Above all, we cannot play ducks and drakes with a native battery of idioms which prescribes egregious collocations of vocables as the Basic *put up with* for *tolerate*, or *put at a loss* for *bewilder*.
    Professor Lancelot Hogben (*Interglossa*)
3. On the one side we have the free personality: by definition it is not neurotic, for it has neither conflict nor dream. Its desires, such as they are, are transparent, for they are just what institutional approval keeps in the forefront of consciousness; another institutional pattern would alter their number and intensity; there is little in them that is natural, irreducible, or culturally dangerous. But *on the other side*, the social bond itself is nothing but the mutual reflection of these self-secure integrities. Recall the definition of love. Is not this the very picture of a small academic? Where is there a place in this hall of mirrors for either personality or fraternity?
    Essay on psychology in *Politics* (New York)
4. All the "best people" from the gentlemen's clubs, and all the frantic fascist captains, united in common hatred of Socialism and bestial horror at the rising tide of the mass revolutionary movement, have turned to acts of provocation, to foul incendiarism, to medieval legends of poisoned wells, to legalize their own destruction of proletarian organizations, and rouse the agitated petty-bourgeoise to chauvinistic fervor on behalf of the fight against the revolutionary way out of the crisis.

Communist pamphlet

5. If a new spirit is to be infused into this old country, there is one thorny and contentious reform which must be tackled, and that is the humanization and galvanization of the B.B.C. Timidity here will bespeak canker and atrophy of the soul. The heart of Britain may be sound and of strong beat, for instance, but the British lion's roar at present is like that of Bottom in Shakespeare's *Midsummer Night's Dream*—as gentle as any sucking dove. A virile new Britain cannot continue indefinitely to be traduced in the eyes or rather ears, of the world by the effete languors of Langham Place, brazenly masquerading as "standard English." When the Voice of Britain is heard at nine o'clock, better far and infinitely less ludicrous to hear aitches honestly dropped than the present priggish, inflated, inhibited, school-ma'amish arch braying of blameless bashful mewing maidens!

Letter in *Tribune*

Each of these passages has faults of its own, but, quite apart from avoidable ugliness, two qualities are common to all of them. The first is staleness of imagery; the other is lack of precision. The writer either has a meaning and cannot express it, or he inadvertently says something else, or he is almost indifferent as to whether his words mean anything or not. This mixture of vagueness and sheer incompetence is the most marked characteristic of modern English prose, and especially of any kind of political writing. As soon as certain topics are raised, the concrete melts into the abstract and no one seems able to think of turns of speech that are not hackneyed: prose consists less and less of *words* chosen for the sake of their meaning, and more and more of *phrases* tacked together like the sections of a prefabricated henhouse. I list below, with notes and examples, various of the tricks by means of which the work of prose construction is habitually dodged:

Dying metaphors. A newly invented metaphor assists thought by evoking a visual image, while on the other hand a metaphor which is technically "dead" (e.g. *iron resolution*) has in effect reverted to being an ordinary word and can generally be used without loss of vividness. But in between these two classes there is a huge dump of worn-out metaphors which have lost all evocative power and are merely used because they save people the trouble of inventing phrases for themselves. Examples are: *Ring the changes on, take up the cudgel for, toe the line, ride roughshod over, stand shoulder to shoulder with, play into the hands of, no axe to grind, grist to the mill, fishing in troubled waters, on the order of the day, Achilles' heel, swan song, hotbed.* Many of these are used without knowledge of their meaning (what is a "rift," for instance?), and incompatible metaphors are frequently mixed, a sure sign that the writer is not interested in what he is saying. Some metaphors now current have been twisted out of their original meaning without those who use them even being aware of the fact. For example, *toe the line* is sometimes written as *tow the line.* Another example is *the hammer and the anvil*, now always used with the implication that the anvil gets the worst of it. In real life it is always the anvil that breaks the hammer, never the other way about: a writer who stopped to think what he was saying would avoid perverting the original phrase.

Operators or verbal false limbs. These save the trouble of picking out appropriate verbs and nouns, and at the same time pad each sentence with extra syllables which give it an appearance of symmetry. Characteristic phrases are *render inoperative, militate against, make contact with, be subjected to, give rise to, give grounds for, have the effect of, play a leading part (role) in, make itself felt, take effect, exhibit a tendency to, serve the purpose of,* etc., etc. The keynote is the elimination of simple verbs. Instead of being a single word, such as *break, stop, spoil, mend, kill,* a verb becomes a *phrase,* made up of a noun or adjective tacked on to some general-purpose verb such as *prove, serve, form, play, render.* In addition, the passive voice is wherever possible used in preference to the active, and noun constructions are used instead of gerunds (*by examination of* instead of *by examining*). The range of verbs is further cut down by means of the *-ize* and *de-* formations, and the banal statements are given an appearance of profundity by means of the *not un-* formation. Simple conjunctions and prepositions are replaced by such phrases as *with respect to, having regard to, the fact that, by dint of, in view of, in the interests of, on the hypothesis that;* and the ends of sentences are saved by anticlimax by such resounding commonplaces as *greatly to be desired, cannot be left out of account, a development to be expected in the near future, deserving of serious consideration, brought to a satisfactory conclusion,* and so on and so forth.

Pretentious diction. Words like *phenomenon, element, individual* (as noun), *objective, categorical, effective, virtual, basic, primary, promote, constitute, exhibit, exploit, utilize, eliminate, liquidate,* are used to dress up a simple statement and give an air of scientific impartiality to biased judgements. Adjectives like *epoch-making, epic, historic, unforgettable, triumphant, age-old, inevitable, inexorable, veritable,* are used to dignify the sordid process of international politics, while writing that aims at glorifying war usually takes on an archaic color, its characteristic words being: *realm, throne, chariot, mailed fist, trident, sword, shield, buckler, banner, jackboot, clarion.* Foreign words and expressions such as *cul de sac, ancien regime, deus ex machina, mutatis mutandis, status quo, gleichschaltung, weltanschauung,* are used to give an air of culture and elegance. Except for the useful abbreviations *i.e., e.g.,* and *etc.,* there is no real need for any of the hundreds of foreign phrases now current in the English language. Bad writers, and especially scientific, political, and sociological writers, are nearly always haunted by the notion that Latin or Greek words are grander than Saxon ones, and unnecessary words like *expedite, ameliorate, predict, extraneous, deracinated, clandestine, subaqueous,* and hundreds of others constantly gain ground from their Anglo-Saxon numbers.* The jargon peculiar to Marxist writing (*hyena, hangman, cannibal, petty bourgeois, these gentry, lackey, flunkey, mad dog, White Guard,* etc.) consists largely of words translated from Russian, German, or French; but the normal way of coining a new word is to use Latin or Greek root with the appropriate affix and, where necessary, the size formation. It is often easier to make up words of this kind (*deregionalize, impermissible, extramarital, non-fragmentary* and so forth) than to think up the English words that will cover one's meaning. The result, in general, is an increase in slovenliness and vagueness.

---

*An interesting illustration of this is the way in which English flower names which were in use till very recently are being ousted by Greek ones, *Snapdragon* becoming *antirrhinum, forget-me-not* becoming *myosotis,* etc. It is hard to see any practical reason for this change of fashion: it is probably due to an instinctive turning away from the more homely word and a vague feeling that the Greek word is scientific.

Meaningless words. In certain kinds of writing, particularly in art criticism and literary criticism, it is normal to come across long passages which are almost completely lacking in meaning.[†] Words like *romantic, plastic, values, human, dead, sentimental, natural, vitality,* as used in art criticism, are strictly meaningless, in the sense that they not only do not point to any discoverable object, but are hardly ever expected to do so by the reader. When one critic writes, "The outstanding feature of Mr. X's work is its living quality," while another writes, "The immediately striking thing about Mr. X's work is its peculiar deadness," the reader accepts this as a simple difference of opinion. If words like *black* and *white* were involved, instead of the jargon words *dead* and *living*, he would see at once that language was being used in an improper way. Many political words are similarly abused. The word *Fascism* has now no meaning except in so far as it signifies "something not desirable." The words *democracy, socialism, freedom, patriotic, realistic, justice* have each of them several different meanings which cannot be reconciled with one another. In the case of a word like *democracy*, not only is there no agreed definition, but the attempt to make one is resisted from all sides. It is almost universally felt that when we call a country democratic we are praising it: consequently the defenders of every kind of regime claim that it is a democracy, and fear that they might have to stop using that word if it were tied down to any one meaning. Words of this kind are often used in a consciously dishonest way. That is, the person who uses them has his own private definition, but allows his hearer to think he means something quite different. Statements like *Marshal Pétain was a true patriot, The Soviet press is the freest in the world, The Catholic Church is opposed to persecution,* are almost always made with intent to deceive. Other words used in variable meanings, in most cases more or less dishonestly, are: *class, totalitarian, science, progressive, reactionary, bourgeois, equality.*

Now that I have made this catalogue of swindles and perversions, let me give another example of the kind of writing that they lead to. This time it must of its nature be an imaginary one. I am going to translate a passage of good English into modern English of the worst sort. Here is a well-known verse from *Ecclesiastes:*

> *I returned and saw under the sun, that the race is not to the swift, nor the battle to the strong, neither yet bread to the wise, nor yet riches to men of understanding, nor yet favour to men of skill; but time and chance happeneth to them all.*

Here it is in modern English:

> *Objective considerations of contemporary phenomena compel the conclusion that success or failure in competitive activities exhibits no tendency to be commensurate with innate capacity, but that a considerable element of the unpredictable must invariably be taken into account.*

[†]Example: Comfort's catholicity of perception and image, strangely Whitmanesque in range, almost the exact opposite in aesthetic compulsion, continues to evoke that trembling atmospheric accumulative hinting at a cruel, an inexorably serene timelessness ... Wrey Gardiner scores by aiming at simple bull's-eyes with precision. Only they are not so simple, and through this contented sadness runs more than the surface bittersweet of resignation." (*Poetry Quarterly*)

This is a parody, but not a very gross one. Exhibit (3) above, for instance, contains several patches of the same kind of English. It will be seen that I have not made a full translation. The beginning and ending of the sentence follow the original meaning fairly closely, but in the middle the concrete illustrations—race, battle, bread—dissolve into the vague phrases "success or failure in competitive activities." This had to be so, because no modern writer of the kind I am discussing—no one capable of using phrases like "objective considerations of contemporary phenomena"—would ever tabulate his thoughts in that precise and detailed way. The whole tendency of modern prose is away from concreteness. Now analyze these two sentences a little more closely. The first contains forty-nine words but only sixty syllables, and all its words are those of everyday life. The second contains thirty-eight words of ninety syllables: eighteen of those words are from Latin roots, and one from Greek. The first sentence contains six vivid images, and only one phrase ("time and chance") that could be called vague. The second contains not a single fresh, arresting phrase, and in spite of its ninety syllables it gives only a shortened version of the meaning contained in the first. Yet without a doubt it is the second kind of sentence that is gaining ground in modern English. I do not want to exaggerate. This kind of writing is not yet universal, and outcrops of simplicity will occur here and there in the worst-written page. Still, if you or I were told to write a few lines on the uncertainty of human fortunes, we should probably come much nearer to my imaginary sentence than to the one from *Ecclesiastes*.

As I have tried to show, modern writing at its worst does not consist in picking out words for the sake of their meaning and inventing images in order to make the meaning clearer. It consists in gumming together long strips of words which have already been set in order by someone else, and making the results presentable by sheer humbug. The attraction of this way of writing is that it is easy. It is easier—even quicker, once you have the habit—to say *In my opinion it is not an unjustifiable assumption that* than to say *I think*. If you use ready-made phrases, you not only don't have to hunt about for the words; you also don't have to bother with the rhythms of your sentences since these phrases are generally so arranged as to be more or less euphonious.

When you are composing in a hurry—when you are dictating to a stenographer, for instance, or making a public speech—it is natural to fall into a pretentious, Latinized style. Tags like *a consideration which we should do well to bear in mind* or *a conclusion to which all of us would readily assent* will save many a sentence from coming down with a bump. By using stale metaphors, similes, and idioms, you save much mental effort, at the cost of leaving your meaning vague, not only for your reader but for yourself. This is the significance of mixed metaphors. The sole aim of a metaphor is to call up a visual image. When these images clash—as in *The Fascist octopus has sung its swan song, the jackboot is thrown into the melting pot*—it can be taken as certain that the writer is not seeing a mental image of the objects he is naming; in other words he is not really thinking. Look again at the examples I gave at the beginning of this essay. Professor Laski (1) uses five negatives in fifty three words. One of these is superfluous, making nonsense of the whole passage, and in addition there is the slip—alien for akin—making further nonsense, and several avoidable pieces of clumsiness which increase the general vagueness. Professor Hogben (2) plays ducks and drakes with a battery which is able to write prescriptions, and, while disapproving of the everyday phrase *put up with*, is unwilling to look *egregious* up in the dictionary and see what it means; (3), if one takes an uncharitable attitude towards it, is simply meaningless: probably one could work out its intended meaning by reading the whole of the article in which it occurs. In (4), the writer knows more or less what he wants to say, but an accumulation of stale phrases chokes him like tea leaves blocking a sink. In (5), words and meaning have almost parted company. People who write in this manner usually have a general emotional meaning—they dislike one thing and want to express solidarity with another—but they are not interested in the detail of what they are saying. A scrupulous writer, in every sentence that he writes, will ask himself at least four questions, thus: 1. What am I trying to say? 2. What words will express it? 3. What image or idiom will make it clearer? 4. Is this image fresh enough to have an effect? And he will probably ask himself two more: 1. Could I put it more shortly? 2. Have I said anything that is avoidably ugly? But you are not obliged to go to all this trouble. You can shirk it by simply throwing your mind open and letting the ready-made phrases come crowding in. They will construct your sentences for you—even think your thoughts for you, to a certain extent—and at need they will perform the important service of partially concealing your meaning even from yourself. It is at this point that the special connection between politics and the debasement of language becomes clear.

In our time it is broadly true that political writing is bad writing. Where it is not true, it will generally be found that the writer is some kind of rebel, expressing his private opinions and not a "party line." Orthodoxy, of whatever color, seems to demand a lifeless, imitative style. The political dialects to be found in pamphlets, leading articles, manifestoes, White papers and the speeches of undersecretaries do, of course, vary from party to party, but they are all alike in that one almost never finds in them a fresh, vivid, homemade turn of speech. When one watches some tired hack on the platform mechanically repeating the familiar phrases—*bestial atrocities, iron heel, bloodstained tyranny, free peoples of the world, stand shoulder to shoulder*—one often has a curious feeling that one is not watching a live human being but some kind of dummy: a feeling which suddenly becomes stronger at moments when the light catches the speaker's spectacles and turns them into blank discs which seem to have no eyes behind them. And this is not altogether fanciful. A speaker who uses that kind of phraseology has gone some distance toward turning himself into a machine. The appropriate noises are coming out of his larynx, but his brain is not involved as it would be if he were choosing his words for himself. If the speech he is making is one that he is accustomed to make over and over again, he may be almost unconscious of what he is saying, as one is when one utters the responses in church. And this reduced state of consciousness, if not indispensable, is at any rate favorable to political conformity.

In our time, political speech and writing are largely the defense of the indefensible. Things like the continuance of British rule in India, the Russian purges and deportations, the dropping of the atom bombs on Japan, can indeed be defended, but only by arguments which are too brutal for most people to face, and which do not square with the professed aims of the political parties. Thus political language has to consist largely of euphemism, question-begging and sheer cloudy vagueness. Defenseless villages are bombarded from the air, the inhabitants driven out into the countryside, the cattle machine-gunned, the huts set on fire with incendiary bullets: this is called *pacification*. Millions of peasants are robbed of their farms and sent trudging along the roads with no more than they can carry: this is called *transfer of population* or *rectification of frontiers*. People are imprisoned for years without trial, or shot in the back of the neck or sent to die of scurvy in Arctic lumber camps: this is called *elimination of unreliable elements*. Such phraseology is needed if one wants to name things without calling up mental pictures of them. Consider for instance some comfortable English professor defending Russian totalitarianism. He cannot say outright, "I believe in killing off your opponents when you can get good results by doing so." Probably, therefore, he will say something like this: "While freely conceding that the Soviet regime exhibits certain features which the humanitarian may be inclined to deplore, we must, I think, agree that a certain curtailment of the right to political opposition is an unavoidable concomitant of transitional periods, and that the rigors which the Russian people have been called upon to undergo have been amply justified in the sphere of concrete achievement."

The inflated style itself is a kind of euphemism. A mass of Latin words falls upon the facts like soft snow, blurring the outline and covering up all the details. The great enemy of clear language is insincerity. When there is a gap between one's real and one's declared aims, one turns as it were instinctively to long words and exhausted idioms, like a cuttlefish spurting out ink. In our age there is no such thing as "keeping out of politics." All issues are political issues, and politics itself is a mass of lies, evasions, folly, hatred, and schizophrenia. When the general atmosphere is bad, language must suffer. I should expect to find—this is a guess which I have not sufficient knowledge to verify—that the German, Russian and Italian languages have all deteriorated in the last ten or fifteen years, as a result of dictatorship.

But if thought corrupts language, language can also corrupt thought. A bad usage can spread by tradition and imitation even among people who should and do know better. The debased language that I have been discussing is in some ways very convenient. Phrases like *a not unjustifiable assumption, leaves much to be desired, would serve no good purpose, a consideration which we should do well to bear in mind*, are a continuous temptation, a packet of aspirins always at one's elbow. Look back through this essay, and for certain you will find that I have again and again committed the very faults I am protesting against. By this morning's post I have received a pamphlet dealing with conditions in Germany. The author tells me that he "felt impelled" to write it. I open it at random, and here is almost the first sentence I see: "[The Allies] have an opportunity not only of achieving a radical transformation of Germany's social and political structure in such a way as to avoid a nationalistic reaction in Germany itself, but at the same time of laying the foundations of a co-operative and unified Europe." You see, he "feels impelled" to write—feels, presumably, that he has something new to say—and yet his words, like cavalry horses answering the bugle, group themselves automatically into the familiar dreary pattern. This invasion of one's mind by ready-made phrases (*lay the foundations, achieve a radical transformation*) can only be prevented if one is constantly on guard against them, and every such phrase anaesthetizes a portion of one's brain.

I said earlier that the decadence of our language is probably curable. Those who deny this would argue, if they produced an argument at all, that language merely reflects existing social conditions, and that we cannot influence its development by any direct tinkering with words and constructions. So far as the general tone or spirit of a language goes, this may be true, but it is not true in detail. Silly words and expressions have often disappeared, not through any evolutionary process but owing to the conscious action of a minority. Two recent examples were *explore every avenue* and *leave no stone unturned*, which were killed by the jeers of a few journalists. There is a long list of flyblown metaphors which could similarly be got rid of if enough people would interest themselves in the job; and it should also be possible to laugh the *not un-* formation out of existence*, to reduce the amount of Latin and Greek in the average sentence, to drive out foreign phrases and strayed scientific words, and, in general, to make pretentiousness unfashionable. But all these are minor points. The defense of the English language implies more than this, and perhaps it is best to start by saying what it does *not* imply.

To begin with it has nothing to do with archaism, with the salvaging of obsolete words and turns of speech, or with the setting up of a "standard English" which must never be departed from. On the contrary, it is especially concerned with the scrapping of every word or idiom which has outworn its usefulness. It has nothing to do with correct grammar and syntax, which are of no importance so long as one makes one's meaning clear, or with the avoidance of Americanisms, or with having what is called a "good prose style." On the other hand, it is not concerned with fake simplicity and the attempt to make written English colloquial. Nor does it even imply in every case preferring the Saxon word to the Latin one, though it does imply using the fewest and shortest words that will cover one's meaning. What is above all needed is to let the meaning choose the word, and not the other way around. In prose, the worst thing one can do with words is surrender to them. When you think of a concrete object, you think wordlessly, and then, if you want to describe the thing you have been visualizing you probably hunt about until you find the exact words that seem to fit it. When you think of something abstract you are more inclined to use words from the start, and unless you make a conscious effort to prevent it, the existing dialect will come rushing in and do the job for you, at the expense of blurring or even changing your meaning. Probably it is better to put off using words as long as possible and get one's meaning as clear as one can through pictures and sensations.

Afterward one can choose—not simply *accept*—the phrases that will best cover the meaning, and then switch round and decide what impressions one's words are likely to make on another person. This last effort of the mind cuts out all stale or mixed images, all prefabricated phrases, needless repetitions, and humbug and vagueness generally. But one can often be in doubt about the effect of a word or a phrase, and one needs rules that one can rely on when instinct fails. I think the following rules will cover most cases:

(i)   Never use a metaphor, simile, or other figure of speech which you are used to seeing in print.

(ii)   Never use a long word where a short one will do.

(iii)   If it is possible to cut a word out, always cut it out.

(iv)   Never use the passive where you can use the active.

(v)   Never use a foreign phrase, a scientific word, or a jargon word if you can think of an everyday English equivalent.

(vi)   Break any of these rules sooner than say anything outright barbarous.

---

*One can cure oneself of the *not un-* formation by memorizing this sentence: *A not unblack dog was chasing a not unsmall rabbit across a not ungreen field.*

These rules sound elementary, and so they are, but they demand a deep change of attitude in anyone who has grown used to writing in the style now fashionable. One could keep all of them and still write bad English, but one could not write the kind of stuff that I quoted in those five specimens at the beginning of this article.

I have not here been considering the literary use of language, but merely language as an instrument for expressing and not for concealing or preventing thought. Stuart Chase and others have come near to claiming that all abstract words are meaningless, and have used this as a pretext for advocating a kind of political quietism. Since you don't know what Fascism is, how can you struggle against Fascism? One need not swallow such absurdities as this, but one ought to recognize that the present political chaos is connected with the decay of language, and that one can probably bring about some improvement by starting at the verbal end. If you simplify your English, you are freed from the worst follies of orthodoxy. You cannot speak any of the necessary dialects, and when you make a stupid remark its stupidity will be obvious, even to yourself.

Political language—and with variations this is true of all political parties, from Conservatives to Anarchists—is designed to make lies sound truthful and murder respectable, and to give an appearance of solidity to pure wind. One cannot change this all in a moment, but one can at least change one's own habits, and from time to time one can even, if one jeers loudly enough, send some worn-out and useless phrase—some *jackboot, Achilles' heel, hotbed, melting pot, acid test, veritable inferno*, or other lump of verbal refuse—into the dustbin, where it belongs.

Author Index

Title Index

Subject Index

peer editing in groups, 166
pronoun agreement, 181–182
pronoun reference, 182–183
rules of logic, 179
subject-verb agreement, 181
tense changes, parallelism and, 180
unparallel lists, 180–182
graphics in research papers, 318–320
graphs, 243
groups, peer editing in, 165–174
assigning specific jobs to readers, 167
mechanics and grammar, 166
peer editing session, 167–174
writer's role, 166

H

hasty generalization, 262
Head Principle, 55–56
Hemingway, Ernest, 58, 64
hooks, 151
however comma splice, 188
"how I came to write this essay" opener, 151
humanity, displaying in argument, 271–272
hyperlinks, 292
hyphens, 191–192, 195

I

ideas for writing
connecting, 54–56
content prompts from reading, 51
from first thoughts to drafts, 58–59
models from writing of others, 52
moving from small things to large ones, 54
reacting to prompts, 50
responding to visuals, 53–54
seeds for essays, 49
sources of, 45–49
thinking all the time about, 49
writing from rage, 57–58
from your life, 46–49
illustrations
in informative writing, 242, 243
in research papers, 318
imperatives, in informative writing, 242
in-class writing, 40–41
indexes, searching, 294
indignant tone, 99
informative writing, 206, 222–246
challenges of, 233–234
COIK problem, 239–240
examples of, 225–229, 352–359
making it interesting, 239
not feeling knowledgeable enough, 233–234
profiles of, 223–224
strategies for, 244–246
teaching tips, 240–243
visuals in, 243
warming up with mock-informative essay, 234–239

in medias res, 151
intentions, getting ideas from, 49
Intermediate Choke Rod, 240
Internet. *See also* online research
plagiarism and, 36–37
interviews, documenting, 308
introductions, 148, 149–154
evaluating, 153
examples of good openers, 149
stock openers, 150
tasks performed by openers, 152–153
writer's block, on overcoming, 149–150
introductory commas, 184–185
investigative essays, 125
ironic distance, quotation marks for, 194
issues, specific and larger, 144
italics, titles in, 194
it is/are, sentences beginning with, 197–198

J

jargon, 35
journals
citations for online journal articles, 310
in libraries, 294
personal, 67–68

K

Keillor, Garrison, 56–57

L

lab reports, 125
language
ambiguity of, 253–255
clichés, 254–255
eliminating language problems in thesis, 251
loaded, 254
natural love of, 9
neutral, 254
process of learning, 5–7
using language of the course, 35
writing in speaking language, 11, 61
Latinate diction, 91–92
length, revising for
lengthening the draft, 141–147
shortening the draft, 139–144
letters, documenting, 308
letter writing, 69
Lewis, C. S., 153
Lewis, Thomas, 63
libraries, using for research, 292–295
books, 292–293
government documents, 294
newspapers, 293–294
periodicals, 294
reference sections of, 293
search tools, 294–295
Library of Congress Subject Headings, 293